The
International Turnaround Management Standard™
Version 1.5

January 2014

by

Dr. Christoph Lymbersky

It is highly recommended that you take an online class which explains the use of the ITMS in detail.

For more Information please visit:

www.Turnaround-Society.com
&
www.Turnaround-Standard.com

Turnaround Management Society

International Turnaround Management Standard

Author: Dr. Christoph Lymbersky

Exclusive rights by the Management Laboratory and Dr. Christoph Lymbersky

Published by the MLP Management Laboratory Press UG, a business unit of the Management Laboratory, Luetkensallee 41, 22041 Hamburg. Copyright © 2010 by the Management Laboratory.
All rights reserved.

No part of this publication may be reproduced or distributed in any form or by any means, or stored in a database or retrieval system, without the prior written consent of the Management Laboratory, including but not limited to, in any network or other electronic storage or transmission, or broadcast for distance learning.

Case material in this book is made possible by the cooperation of business firms and other organizations which may wish to remain anonymous by having names, quantities and other identifying details disguised while maintaining basic relationships. Cases are prepared as the basis for class discussion rather than to illustrate either effective or ineffective handling of an administrative situation.

Registered with:

ISBN-Agentur für die Bundesrepublik Deutschland in der MVB Marketing- und Verlagsservice des Buchhandels GmbH
Bibliografische Information der Deutschen Nationalbibliothek
Die Deutsche Nationalbibliothek verzeichnet diese Publikation in der Deutschen Nationalbibliografie; detaillierte bibliografische Daten sind im Internet über http://dnb.d-nb.de abrufbar.

Interior Design: © MLP Management Laboratory Press UG

Exterior Design: © MLP Management Laboratory Press UG

First Publication: 1st , June 2011: pre-version
  10th , August 2013: version 1.1 (pre-version)
  15th , October 2013 version 1.2 (pre-version)
  1st , January 2014 version 1.5

When ordering this title, use ISBN: 978-1491084939

www.Management-Laboratory.com
www.Turnaround-Society.com

To my parents.

About the Author

About the Author

Dr. Christoph Lymbersky, MAcc, MBA, PRINCE2 Practitioner, CFMP, CITM – Level B has lived, worked and done research in Germany, France, Australia and the United States. He holds a Master of Accounting as well as a MBA from Bond University in Australia and received a PhD in Strategy & Turnaround Management.

He has worked for international companies such as IBM and Wal-Mart, has founded and co-founded different companies like COMODEX Internet, the IT – Management Group and B2B Network.

Christoph Lymbersky has written and published a variety of books in International Management and Finance. Currently, Dr. Lymbersky serves as the director of the Turnaround Management Society and is a top management consultant at DETECON International advising senior management of multinational corporations on restructuring and transformation programs.

Dr. Lymbersky has been a lecturer, examiner and speaker at conferences at various universities worldwide.

About the Author

Participants

The following list of participants is an excerpt of people who have significantly contributed to the development of this standard by reviewing it, giving feedback and contributing parts themselves.

Prof. Dr. Christophe Bredillet

Christophe N. Bredillet, PhD in Project Management, MBA, D.Sc., MSc Eng, ESC Lille, Certificated Program Director IPMA Level A, PRINCE2™, CCE, has 30 years of experience with industries (banking, IT, International Development). Christophe Bredillet is director of the Project Management Academy at the Queensland University of Technology in Australia and a Senior Expert at the World Bank. He has been Executive Editor of the Project Management Journal (Wiley) since May 2004, member of International Academic Editorial Board, International Journal of Managing Projects in Business (Emerald) since 2007. He was Professor, Chair of Project Management & Economics at University of Technology Sydney from 2000 to 2001. He has been an External Examiner for Henley Management College (2005-2009).

Prof. Dr. Rodney J. Turner

Professor J. Rodney Turner, MA, MSc, DPhil (Oxon), BE (Auck), CEng, FIMechE, FAPM, MInstD, is Professor of Project Management at the SKEMA Business School, in Lille, France, where he is Academic Director of the Executive PhD in Project and Programme Management. He is Adjunct Professor at the University of Technology Sydney, the Kemmy Business School, Limerick, and Visiting Professor at Kingston University and the Technical University of Berlin.

Prof. Dr. Frank T. Anbari

Frank T. Anbari (Ph.D., Project Management and Quality Enhancement; MBA; MS Engineering; PMP; PE; and ASQ Certified Six Sigma Black Belt) is a Clinical Professor in the Project Management Program, Multidisciplinary and Emerging Programs, School of Technology and Professional Studies at the Goodwin College of Professional Studies of Drexel University in Philadelphia, Pennsylvania. He serves as a member of the editorial boards of the Project Management Journal (PMI/Wiley), the International Journal of Project Management (Elsevier), and the International Journal of Managing Projects in Business (Emerald) as well as a Co-Author of PMI's Project Management Book of Knowledge.

Alan Harpham

Alan is the chairman of the APM Group. Originally a civil engineer, he later worked on major North Sea and petrochemical construction projects. He was an early director of Cranfield University's MSc in Project Management, then MD of a leading consultancy in programme and project management - Nichols Associates. He is chairman of Cranfield University's Science and Engineering Research Ethics Committee and SPD's Medical Ethics committee.

He also chairs Ecumenical Partnership Initiatives Limited which runs Workplace Ministry in Hertfordshire and Bedfordshire and is a volunteer chaplain to the East of England Ambulance Service. He was a director of the International Center for Spirit at Work; a board member of the Cranfield Management Association and is a Certified Management Consultant and Fellow of the Institute of Business Consultants.

Richard Pharro

Richard Pharro is the CEO of The APM Group Limited. He trained as a Civil Engineer and worked on projects in the UK and the Middle East and was part of the Programme Management Team responsible for the re-development of London Docklands in the 1980s. In the past Richard has been a member of the IPMA Board, a previous Vice Chairman of APM and with colleagues has built APM Group into an international organization with offices on each continent specializing in accreditation and certification. He is a joint author of one book - The Relationship Manager - and is a frequent speaker at conferences.

Dr. Donald D. Bibeault

Dr. Donald B. Bibeault is Managing Partner at Verto Partners, LLC. and is one of the founding directors of the Turnaround Management Association. In 1979 Dr. Bibeault's pioneering Ph.D. Dissertation, which is based on more than 15 years of research, first enunciated the strategic and tactical frameworks for turnaround management. In 1981 McGraw-Hill published Don's book "Corporate Turnaround: How Managers Turn Losers Into Winners" Over the last 45 years that Don has worked in the turnaround industry he has become a main contributor to the advancement of the industry and has been the leader of over 35 turnaround situations; nine as CEO. In 2005 the Association of Certified Turnaround Professionals awarded Don its first ever Lifetime Achievement Award. He is one of the most respected and popular turnaround experts worldwide... His advice in many conversations has had a great influence on this book.

John M. Collard

John M. Collard is inducted into the Turnaround Management, Restructuring, and Distressed Investing Industry Hall Of Fame, Past Chairman of the Turnaround Management Association (TMA), and Chairman of the Association of Interim Executives (AIE). John is a Certified Turnaround Professional (CTP), and a Certified International Turnaround Manager (CITM), who brings 35 years senior operating leadership, $85M asset and investment recovery, 43+ transactions worth $780M+, and $80M fund management expertise to run troubled companies, serve on boards, advise company boards, litigators, institutional and private equity investors, and raise capital. John is Chairman of Strategic Management Partners, Inc. (410-263-9100) in Annapolis, Maryland.

Eugene Rembor

Eugene Rembor, MBA, has held Managing Director and CEO positions within Top Fortune 500 and FTSE 100 corporations. Since the beginning of his career Eugene specialized in turnaround, change and transformation and his 32 years of turnaround experience make him one of the longest serving professionals in this industry. Eugene is an expert in rapid bottom line improvement and turnaround management. He has published three books and writes business columns for various magazines and newspapers. He regularly accepts international speaking engagements. Part of the UKTI envoy, he spoke in Abu Dhabi and Qatar, at NEOCON in Chicago, Hong Kong, Oslo and London. He is a lecturer at the National Enterprise Academy, lectures at various Chambers of Commerce and Embassies on international business and is a member of the Institute of Directors in London, the Turnaround management Association and the Turnaround Management Society.

The Turnaround Management Society

The Turnaround Management Society is an industry specific organization for Turnaround Management. Its members are turnaround professionals, distressed dept investors and academics.

It is the objective of the Turnaround Management Society to bring together the knowledge of Turnaround Management academics and the experience of Turnaround Management professionals. The TMS provides a link between academics who are engaged in research and the professional community that seeks research outcomes and provides academics with professional insight, guidance and feedback. The community of turnaround professionals of the TMS has contributed hugely to this project by participating in questionnaires, feedback rounds, turnaround data and cases as well as interviews. Developing a standard would not be possible without the input from turnaround professionals, working in crisis situations every day.

Participants

Prof. Dr. Ralf Müller

Ralf is an international lecturer, researcher, author, and business consultant. He is Professor at BI Norwegian Business School, Norway, where he lectures and researches in project, program and portfolio management, in project governance, as well as in research methodologies. Furthermore he is the Associate Dean for the joint BI-Fudan MBA programs in China.

Table of Contents

About the Author 5
Participants 7
Table of Contents 11

Introduction 23

Definitions 29

Turnaround *29*
Distressed Turnaround *31*
Turnaround Situation *32*
Turnaround Management *34*
Disambiguation of Crisis Management *34*
Turnaround Success *34*
Chapter 7 .... *35*
Chapter 11 .... *36*
The Debtor *36*
Debtor in Possession *36*
Creditor's Committee *37*
Judge of the Bankruptcy Court *37*
The Bankruptcy Trustee *37*
Decline *37*
Retrenchment *38*
Relevant Definitions in Strategy *39*
Goals *39*
Objectives *40*
Mission *40*
Business Model *40*
Strategy *41*
Policies *41*
Corporate Strategy *41*
Business Unit Strategy *41*
Strategic Business Unit *42*

Strategic Capability *42*
Strategic Turnaround Capability *42*
Generic Strategy *42*

What is a Crisis? 45
What are the Reasons for a Crisis? 47
The Crisis Process 51

The Strategy Crisis *51*
The Success Crisis *52*
The Liquidity Crisis *53*
Insolvency *53*
The Stakeholder Crisis *54*
Crisis Impact *55*
Reduced Support by Stakeholders *56*
Loss of Efficiency and Decreased Competitiveness *57*
Change in Decision-Making Processes *57*
What a Crisis is Good for *57*

Why Companies Fail 59
Success of Turnaround Strategies 61
What is the ITMS? 63

IT Issues *64*
Legal Issues *65*

The Structure of the ITMS 67

Seven Components *67*
Ten Support Components *67*
Four Stages *68*
Four Processes *68*
Justification *69*
Differences from PRINCE2™ and Other Project Management Methods *72*

Benefits of Using the ITMS 75

Advantages for the Troubled Firm *76*

Advantages for Turnaround Leaders..76

Advantages for Stakeholders 77

The Seven Components 79

The Diagnostic Review Component (DR)...79

Emergency Procedures (EP) 83

Financial Restructuring (FR) 84

Strategic Restructuring (SR) 86

Operating Strategies (OS) 92

Process Improvement (PI) 99

Marketing and Sales (MS)...103

The Ten Support Components 107

The Pre-Turnaround Component (PC)..107

Starting the Turnaround Process (ST) 107

The Crisis Stabilization Stage (CS) 107

The Turnaround Stage (TS)...107

Communication Procedures (CP)..107

Directing the Turnaround (DT) 108

Risk Management (RM) 108

Planning the Turnaround (PT) 109

Change Management (CM)...109

Communication Procedures (CP)..110

Closing the Turnaround Process (CT) 111

The Four Stages 115

Pre-Turnaround Stage (PS)..115

Diagnostic Review Stage (DR) 115

Crisis Stabilization Stage (CS) 116

Turnaround Stage (TS) 118

The Four Processes 119

Change Control/Out-of-Tolerance Management..119

Quality Management, Risk Management, Change Management 120

The Components 121

Pre-Turnaround Stage Component (PS) 121

PS 1 – Creating the Turnaround Mandate *121*
PS 2 – Preparing Basic Information *124*
PS 3 – The Search for a Turnaround Leader *131*
PS 4 – Analysis of Required Turnaround Management Team Skills *137*

Starting the Turnaround Process (SP) 139

SP 1 – Assembling a Turnaround Advisory Board (TAB) *141*
SP 2 – Appointing a Turnaround Leader *144*
SP 3 – Assembling the Diagnostic Review Team *147*
SP 4 – Setting Up Turnaround Files *149*
SP 5 – Setting Up Turnaround Controls *155*
SP 6 – Preparing the Turnaround Brief *157*
SP 7 – Centralizing Power *159*
SP 8 – Planning the Diagnostic Review *162*
SP 9 – Proposing Emergency Procedures *164*

Diagnostic Review Component (DR) 167

Diagnostic Review: Analysis Phase (DR AP) 167

DR AP 1 – Committing Resources *169*
DR AP 2 – Conducting a Viability Analysis *170*
DR AP 3 – Financial Analysis *177*
DR AP 4 – Company Analysis *188*
DR AP 5 – Product Analysis *195*
DR AP 6 – Industry Analysis *202*
DR AP 7 – Competitor Analysis *206*
DR AP 8 – Prepare Bridge Financing *208*
DR AP 9 – Survey Employees *210*
DR AP 10 – Management Analysis *212*
DR AP 11 – Profitability Analysis *221*
DR AP 12 – Customer Analysis *223*
DR AP 13 – Identify Special Dealings *226*

DR AP 14 – Stakeholder Analysis 228
DR AP 15 – Designing the Turnaround Management Team 233
DR AP 16 – Starting Emergency Procedures 235
DR AP 17 – Creating the Diagnostic Review Folder 236

Diagnostic Review: Evaluation Phase (DR EP) 239

DR EP 1 – Creating an Executive Decision Matrix 241
DR EP 2 – Classifying the Situation 243
DR EP 3 – Assessing Options 248
DR EP 4 – Operative Decisions 250
DR EP 5 – Business Divestment Decisions 252
DR EP 6 – Planning Assurance 257
DR EP – 7 Updating the Turnaround Business Case, Risks, Controls, and Communications 259
DR EP 8 – Identifications and Estimations 262
DR EP 9 – Preparing the Turnaround Initiation Document (TID) 265
DR EP 10 – Appointing the Turnaround Management Team (TMT) 1 269
DR EP 11 – Initiating the Turnaround Process 271

Emergency Procedures (EP) 273

EP 1 – Planning Emergency Procedures 275
EP 2 – Authorizing Emergency Procedures 277
EP 3 – Stem Major Costs 278
EP 4 – Stop Marketing Activities 280
EP 5 – Divestment of a Business Unit in Emergency Procedures 282
EP 6 – Assessing Progress in Emergency Procedures 284
EP 7 – Escalating Issues in Emergency Procedures 285

Planning the Turnaround (PT) 287

PT 1 – Producing a Rolling Cash Forecast 289
PT 3 – Setting Turnaround Goals 291
PT 4 – Identifying, Defining, and Analyzing Activities 293
PT 5 – Estimating 296
PT 6 – Scheduling 298
PT 7 – Incorporating Risks 300

- PT 8 – Creating a Stage Plan 302
- PT 9 – Setting Stage Targets 305
- PT 10 – Stage End Meetings 307
- PT 11 – Defining Exceptions 309
- PT 12 – Setting Key Performance Indicators 310
- PT 13 – Redesigning the Organization 312
- PT 14 – Building a Transition Map 314
- PT 15 – Producing the Financial Plan 316
- PT 16 – Producing Operational and Strategic Plans 320
- PT 17 – Producing the Turnaround Plan 323
- PT 18 – Completion of the Turnaround Plan 329
- PT 19 – Creating a Turnaround Plan Summary 331
- PT 20 – Updating the Turnaround Plan and Turnaround Business Case 333
- PT 21 – Updating Logs 335
- PT 22 – Updating the Stage Plan 337
- PT 23 – Producing an Exemption Plan 339
- PT 24 – Updates to the Turnaround Plan 341

Directing the Turnaround (DT) 343

- DT 1 – Approval to Proceed 345
- DT 2 – Signing Off on PS 346
- DT 3 – Confirming the Turnaround Leader 347
- DT 4 – Approving the Turnaround Brief 348
- DT 5 – Approving the Diagnostic Review Plan 349
- DT 6 – Approving Emergency Procedures 350
- DT 7 – Evaluating the TID 351
- DT 8 – Approving the Turnaround Plan 352
- DT 9 – Assessing Status 353
- DT 10 – Approving Plans 354
- DT 11 – Direction on Issues 355
- DT 12 – Approving Reorganization 356
- DT 13 – Approving an Exemption Plan 357
- DT 14 – Reviewing Process Improvements 358
- DT 15 – Reviewing Financial Restructuring Strategies 359

- DT 16 – Reviewing Operational Plans *361*
- DT 17 – Reviewing Strategic Restructuring (SR) Strategies *363*
- DT 18 – Assessing Stage Ends *365*
- DP 19 – Closing the Turnaround *366*

Crisis Stabilization Stage (CS) 369

- CS 1 – Appointing the Turnaround Management Team (TMT) 2 .... *371*
- CS 2 – Authorizing Crisis Stabilization Procedures *376*
- CS 3 – Hiring and Laying Off Staff *378*
- CS 4 – Improve HR Management *380*
- CS 5 – Assessing Progress in the Crisis Stabilization Stage *382*
- CS 6 – Implementing Short-Term Controls *385*
- CS 7 – Rebuilding Stakeholder Trust *392*
- CS 8 – Capturing and Assessing Issues in the Crisis Stabilization Stage *394*
- CS 9 – Taking Corrective Action in the Crisis Stabilization Stage *397*
- CS 10 – Authorizing Work Packages in the Crisis Stabilization Stage *399*
- CS 11 – Escalating Issues in the Crisis Stabilization Stage *400*
- CS 12 – Reporting Highlights in the Crisis Stabilization Stage *402*
- CS 13 – Building an Incentives Scheme *403*
- CS 14 – Introducing Management by Objectives (MBO) *406*
- CS 15 – Completing the Crisis Stabilization Stage *408*

Turnaround Stage (TS) 411

- TS 1 – Authorizing the Turnaround Stage *413*
- TS 2 – Assessing Progress in the Turnaround Stage *415*
- TS 3 – Further Workforce Reductions *418*
- TS 4 – Capturing and Assessing Issues in the Turnaround Stage *420*
- TS 5 – Authorizing Work Packages in the Turnaround Stage *423*
- TS 6 – HR Management *424*
- TS 7 – Decentralizing Power in the Turnaround Stage *426*
- TS 8 – Compensation Programs *427*
- TS 9 – Taking Corrective Action in the Turnaround Stage *429*
- TS 11 – Escalating Issues in the Turnaround Stage *431*
- TS 12 – Reporting Highlights in the Turnaround Stage *433*
- TS 12 – Completing the Turnaround Stage *434*

Table of Contents

Financial Restructuring (FR) 437
Financial Restructuring During the Crisis Stabilization Stage (FR CS) 439

- *FR CS 1 – Creating Short-Term Cash Forecasts 441*
- *FR CS 2 – Injecting Equity 446*
- *FR CS 3 – External Financing 448*
- *FR CS 4 – First-Step Cost Reductions 452*
- *FR CS 5 – Debt Restructuring..454*
- *FR CS 6 – Improving Working Capital...456*
- *FR CS 7 – Purchasing Improvements in the Financial Restructuring Component 458*
- *FR CS 8 – Improving Overhead Costs..460*
- *FR CS 9 – Implementing Emergency Cash Management Controls 462*
- *FR CS 10 – Cash-Generating Strategies..467*
- *FR CS 11 – First-Stage Survival Financing..476*
- *FR CS 12 – Long-Term Financial Restructuring..481*
- *FR CS 13 – Amendments to the Financial Restructuring Plan 484*
- *FR CS 14 – Working Capital Reductions 486*

Financial Restructuring During the Turnaround Stage (FR TS).........................489

- *FR TS 1 – Financial Schemes...491*
- *FR TS 2 Financial Guidelines...493*
- *FR TS 3 – Forecast and Track Expenses 495*
- *FR TS 4 – Financial Modeling 498*
- *FR TS 5 – Introduce Activity-Based Costing..500*
- *FR TS 6 – Balance Sheet Improvements 502*
- *FR TS 7 – Managerial Accounting Improvements 503*

Strategic Restructuring (SR) 507
Strategic Restructuring During the Crisis Stabilization Stage (SR CS) 509

- *SR CS 1 – Creating a Mission Statement 511*
- *SR CS 2 – Creating a Corporate Strategy...513*
- *SR CS 3 – Divestment of a Business Unit in Strategic Restructuring 515*
- *SR CS 4 – Licensing Products 518*
- *SR CS 5 – Outsourcing 520*

SR CS 6 – Discontinuing Products 523
SR CS 7 – Product Shift 525
SR CS 8 – Exploiting Existing Products... 527
SR CS 9 – Downsizing.. 529
SR CS 10 – Building Competitive Advantages... 532
SR CS 11 – Apologizing to Customers 533

Strategic Restructuring During the Turnaround Stage (SR TS) 535

SR TS 1 – Revise the Mission Statement... 537
SR TS 2 – Growth via Acquisition.. 538
SR TS 3 – Refocusing... 542
SR TS 4 – Product-Market Refocusing 547
SR TS 5 – Strategic Alliances.. 553
SR TS 6 – Mergers.. 555
SR TS 7 – Introducing New Products 557
SR TS 8 – Re-evaluating the Organizational Structure 559
SR TS 9 – Corporate Name Change 561
SR TS 10 – Renewing Products 563
SR TS 11 – Building up a New Business 565

Operational Strategies 567

Operational Restructuring During the Crisis Stabilization Stage (OR CS) 569

OR CS 1 – not relevant in this version 570
OR CS 2 – Reduction of the Workforce... 571
OR CS 3 – Restaffing... 575
OR CS 4 – Reduction of Inventory.. 577
OR CS 5 – Optimization of Inventory... 578
OR CS 6 – Asset Redeployment in the Crisis Stabilization Stage 580
OR CS 7 – Reducing Salaries 582
OR CS 8 – Reducing Suppliers and Partnerships.. 584

Operational Strategy During the Turnaround Stage (OR TS) 586

OR TS 1 – Regular Effective Profit Improvements 588
OR TS 2 – Manufacturing Efficiencies 590
OR TS 3 – Maintenance Improvements... 592

    OR TS 4 – Transportation Improvements *594*
    OR TS 5 – Inventory Management *596*
    OR TS 6 – Value Analysis *598*
    OR TS 7 – Asset Redeployment in the Turnaround Stage *600*
    OR TS 8 – Development Projects *601*

Process improvements (PI) 605

Process Improvements During the Crisis Stabilization Stage (PI CS) 607

    PI CS 1 – Cost Improvements During the Crisis Stabilization Stage *609*
    PI CS 2 – Quality Improvements in the Crisis Stabilization Stage *611*
    PI CS 3 – Termination of Products *613*
    PI CS 4 – Improving Management Information and Performance Systems *614*
    PI CS 5 – Purchasing Improvements in the PI Component *618*
    PI CS 6 – Inspecting Deliveries *622*
    PI CS 7 – Inspecting Deliverables *624*
    PI CS 8 – Collaboration of Executives *625*

Process Improvements During the Turnaround Stage (PI TS) 627

    PI TS 1 – Cost Improvements in the Turnaround Stage *629*
    PI TS 2 – Quality Improvements in the Turnaround Stage *630*
    PI TS 3 – Improving Operations *632*
    PI TS 4 – Improve Scheduling Functions *637*
    PI TS 5 – Establish Service Levels, Stock Levels, and Lead Times *639*
    PI TS 6 – Supply Chain Improvements *641*
    PI TS 7 – Process Value Analysis *644*
    PT TS 8 – Customer Service Improvements *646*
    *PI TS 9 – Undertake Value Engineering *649*

Marketing and Sales (MS) 651

Marketing and Sales During the Crisis Stabilization Stage (MS CS) 653

    MS CS 1 – Implement Sales Forecasting *655*
    MS CS 2 – Evaluating Salespeople in the Crisis Stabilization Stage *659*
    MS CS 3 – Sales Process Improvements *662*
    MS CS 4 – Focusing the Sales Effort *664*
    MS CS 5 – Introducing Key Account Management *667*

- MS CS 6 – Sales Force Motivation *671*
- MS CS 7 – Monitoring the Performance of the Sales Force *674*
- MS CS 8 – Promotional Costs *676*
- MS CS 9 – Price Changes *678*

Marketing and Sales During the Turnaround Stage (MS TS) 685

- MS TS 1 – Overall Marketing Strategy *687*
- MS TS 2 – Understanding the Customers *689*
- MS TS 3 – Improving the Cost-Effectiveness of Marketing *691*
- MS TS 4 – Product Line Refocusing *694*
- MS TS 5 – Evaluating Salespeople in the Turnaround Stage *697*
- MS TS 6 – Placeholder for the Introduction of Yield Management *699*
- MS TS 7 – Reviewing the Price Structure *700*
- MS TS 8 – New Corporate Design *701*
- MS TS 9 – Famous Customers *703*

Change Management 705

- CM 1 – Fresh Start *707*
- CM 2 – Corporate Culture *709*
- CM 3 – Managing Resistance *711*
- CM 4 – Implementing a New Corporate Culture *714*

Risk Management (RM) 717

- RM 1 – Laying Off Employees *719*
- RM 2 – Establishing and Monitoring Control Systems *721*
- RM 3 – Managing Conflict *722*
- RM 4 – Updating the Risk Log *724*

Communication Procedures (CP) 725

- CP 1 – Communication Guidelines *727*
- CP 2 – Confidentiality Assurance *729*
- CP 3 – Assigning a Communications Manager *731*
- CP 3 – Communicating with Lenders *733*
- CP 4 – Establish Communications for the Diagnostic Review Stage .. *735*
- CP 5 – Communicating Emergency Procedures *736*

CP 6 – Creating the Communications Plan *738*
CP 7 – Review Communications Plan *743*
CP 8 – Workforce Kick-Off Meeting *744*
CP 9 – Communicating Draft Plans *748*
CP 10 – Communicating Plans *749*
CP 11 – Reporting Updates *750*
CP 12 – Communicating Lay-Offs *752*
CP 13 – Restrictive Communication on Issues *754*
CP 14 – Communicating with the Sales Force *755*
CP 15 – Motivating the Workforce *757*
CP 16 – Communicating Standards and Culture *759*
CP 17 – Keep Up Open Communication *761*
CP 18 – Communicating the Closure of the Turnaround Process *762*

Closing the Turnaround Process (CT) 765

CT 1 – Starting Closure Procedures *767*
CT 2 – Future Recommendations *769*
CT 3 – Preparation for Growth Strategies *771*
CT 4 – Refocusing the Business on its Long-Term Strategy *773*
CT 5 – Re-evaluate Cost-Cutting Activities *774*
CT 6 – Appointing a Permanent Crisis-Monitoring Agent *776*
CT 7 – Re-evaluation of the Product-Market Mix *778*
CT 8 – Realign Compensation *780*
CT 9 – Decentralizing Power in Closing the Turnaround *782*
CT 10 – Evaluating the Turnaround *783*
CT 11 – Post-Turnaround Review *786*
CT 12 – Handing Over *788*
CT 13 – Closing the Turnaround Process *789*

Qualifications 791

Qualification Levels *791*
Maintaining the Qualification *792*

References 797

Introduction

This work is a guided system through a corporate turnaround based on over 1,000 references, countless interviews and more than 150 turnaround cases. It is applicable to virtually any situation and industry, and targets the most common reasons why turnarounds fail while utilizing the factors and strategies that have led to successful turnarounds over the past 30 years.

When I started studying corporate turnarounds I found that very little was known about them and their strategies. In fact, seven years ago I was not able to find a single book that properly described how a turnaround should be carried out or what influences one. Most books were either extended case studies or focused primarily on financial turnarounds, operative turnarounds, or the strategic side. Academic articles focused mainly on crisis factors, symptoms, and very specific aspects of turnaround situations. In the past five years, as a result of the economic crisis and an increased awareness that distressed investing and turnarounds can be a very lucrative business for consulting companies, more books have been published on this very complex and difficult area.

Most of the reasons behind crisis situations are not simple; the more time passes, the more areas of the business are affected, and a quick fix is seldom the solution to the problems that have developed. In the past, many turnarounds were carried out by lawyers, accountants, and financial experts who restructured the business from their point of view. However, a business is highly complex: what is done in one area of the business affects the others, and there is rarely an action that has only a single effect. A team of area-specific experts is not sufficient to treat a corporate crisis that has many different symptoms and causes. Problems will be overlooked because of lack of knowledge and understanding of the complexities behind the business. In the end, this is why most turnaround efforts fail.

Therefore a question remains: how can the failure of corporate turnarounds due to lack of knowledge and understanding be prevented? I found a solution in part by thinking about what the ideal Turnaround Leader should bring with them when taking on an assignment.

For one, they should have a wide range of soft skills. They will need to be able to lead and motivate people who are frustrated, scared, and often without hope, a dangerous mix for any company and a situation that can either explode—as in the case of Enron—or implode when people leave the company—these are companies that die quietly. While there is no way to upload soft skills into a Turnaround Leader's personality, you can offer a set of guidelines. I found many answers to people's problems in change management and crisis communication.

A Turnaround Leader also needs to have significant experience in finance, strategy, process optimization, marketing, sales, business valuation, debt restructuring, stakeholder management, and so on, along with specific knowledge of turnaround management, including familiarity with at least a few hundred turnaround cases and the lessons learned from them.

Few people have all these skills, which is why most turnarounds should be done by a team of people with a variety of skills and areas of knowledge. The team must also work well together and have specific responsibilities and workflows that can help them deal with unforeseen changes and accommodate the urgency of such situations.

A detailed analysis of the company is required to avoid overlooking problems that might be hidden in plain sight. This analysis uses a structured checklist approach adapted to address crises and their causes while not leaving out unknown problem areas.

A further problem often encountered in turnarounds is a lack of stakeholder support. Banks send their own investigative accountants into the company, the court might assign a warden, and suppliers and customers can resign their support for the company's turnaround efforts if they are not properly informed and involved.

The next question is: how can all these requirements be combined to handle a turnaround situation properly? I found the answer in project management, which provides an overall framework for this standard for turnaround management, serves as a structured guide to keep the turnaround process within a controlled environment, and provides the right information at the right time to the Turnaround Management Team (TMT). Picture 1 shows the structure of the International Turnaround Management Standard (ITMS) grouped into processes and stages.

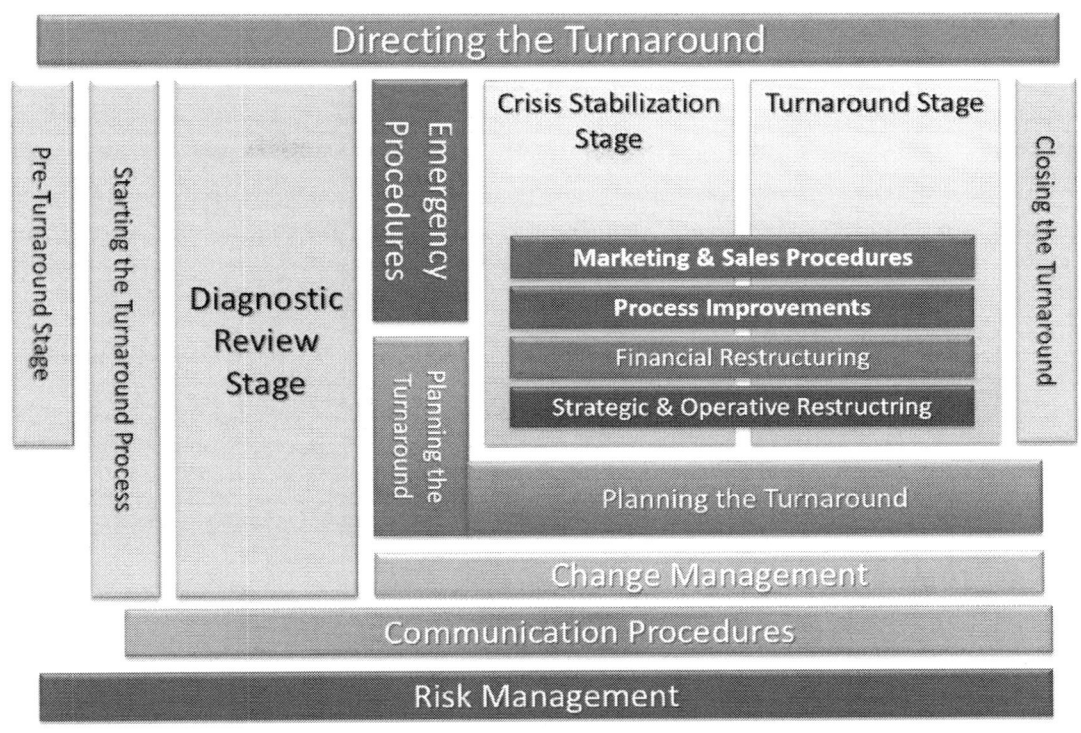

Picture 1 The stages and processes of the International Turnaround Management Standard

According to this standard, the turnaround process starts with a corporate analysis, which leads to a detailed report about the company's situation. This report provides the TMT with a set of possible strategies and ways out of the situation.

The standard combines all aspects of the business that are important in turnaround situations and links them in a unique way. Each step taken throughout a turnaround process has an effect on other areas of the business, so this standard links the effects, makes the user aware of them, and provides guidance on how to control them.

The ITMS divides the turnaround process into 250 components and subcomponents that are all interrelated in some way. Since every subcomponent represents an action, each one has an effect on other actions in the turnaround process. The connections between subcomponents are outlined under the heading "Context" for each one. The overarching idea behind the ITMS is that by following this standard the user will be guided through a turnaround process using proven strategies without overlooking important elements (subcomponents) that have led to failures of turnarounds in the past.

For the purpose of this work, a database of around 150 case studies was created and used to build the standard. I make reference to some cases where noteworthy strategies were employed in order to outline some of the creative approaches I came across in my research. This focus also led to some subcomponents being explained in more detail than others. They all need to be included for the system to work and to be comprehensive, but some subcomponents are so well known that not every topic, such as SWOT analysis, needs to be explained in detail. In those cases I have referred to existing work for more detailed explanations.

This work combines all the relevant literature on corporate turnarounds that I could find; the strategies and methods were extracted from over 150 successful turnaround cases, and the feedback from many professionals in the area of corporate restructuring. Using literature from the fields of strategy, finance, communications management, change management, project management, process optimization, and marketing and sales this book provides proven strategies and methods in a structured, step-by-step guide through a turnaround process. In doing so, it provides TMTs with knowledge and lessons learned from professional experience that is not otherwise available from a single source.

Picture 2 shows the links between the actions that can be taken throughout a turnaround process and the implications they have for others. The picture shown is unreadable and is only supposed to illustrate the complexity of the standard. While writing the ITMS I had to keep every subcomponent in mind and think through its implications for the more than 300 other subcomponents.

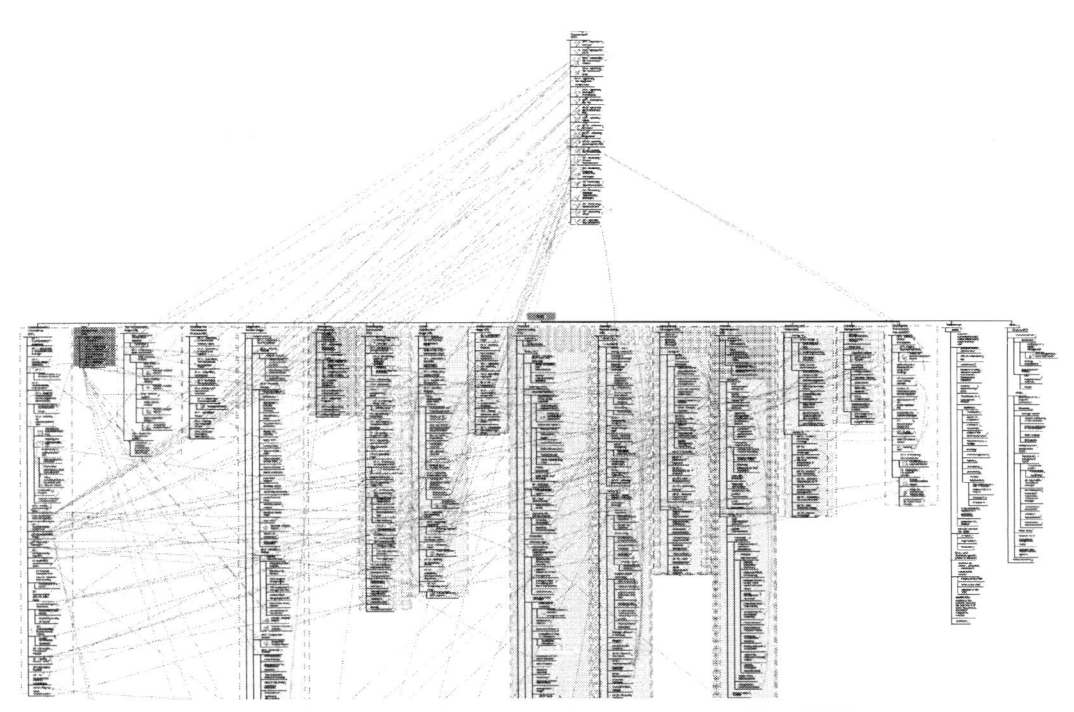

Picture 2 Connections between subcomponents of the ITMS

In order to highlight the dependencies in text form, each of the standard's subcomponents contains a heading, "Context", which shows the dependencies and links to other subcomponents.

Even though this standard is not by any means exhaustive and needs to be extended through additional analysis, its usability and contribution to the body of knowledge is clear.

Table of Contents

Definitions

Turnaround

A corporate turnaround is the set of actions and strategies applied in order to reverse a company's trajectory from free fall back to profitability and growth.[1] Turnarounds are reserved for companies in need of decisive, immediate action to ensure survival for the following 12 months.[2] While I agree with this definition for the most part, it is necessary to clarify that sustainable turnarounds are undertaken to ensure the survival of a firm in the long term, not just for 12 months. However, there are occasions when turnarounds are carried out to ensure short-term survival, such as the proposed sale of a business.

Barker and Duhaime found in their 1997 study that a turnaround occurs when a company has fully recovered to normal operations and sustained profitability after a threat to its survival.[3]

Turnaround studies have variously defined decline and turnaround.[4] Both can be linked to a firm's profitability relative to historical company levels.[5] Decline and turnaround in profitability can also be linked to an objective financial benchmark, such as ten percent return on investment.[6] A firm with more than ten percent return on investment would be considered to have been turned around, and one with less than ten percent profitability would be considered in decline. Decline and turnaround can also be based on a company's proximity to bankruptcy.[7] A firm that faces a decreased risk of bankruptcy is in turnaround,[8] and a company that faces an increased risk of bankruptcy is in decline.[9]

---

[1] (Roman, 2010, p. 5)
[2] (Roman, 2010, p. 5)
[3] (Barker & Duhaime, 1997)
[4] (Lohrke, Bedeian, & Palmer, 2004), (Hambrick & D'Aveni, 1992), (Melin, 1985), (Pearce & Robbins, 1993), (Zimmermann F.), (O'Neill H., 1986)
[5] (Chakravarthy, 1986), (Venkatraman & Ramanujam, 1986)
[6] (Shepherd, 1970), (Hansen & Wernerfelt, 1989), (Barker & Duhaime, 1997), (Ramanujam, 1984), (Graham & Richards, 1978), (Hambrick & Schecter, 1983), (Robbins & Pearce, 1992)
[7] (Altman E., 1983)
[8] (Barker & Duhaime, 1997), (Robbins & Pearce, 1992), (Stanwick, 1992)
[9] (Ferrier, Fhionnlaoich, Smith, & Grimm, 2002), (Hambrick & D'Aveni, 1988)

Definitions

At the same time, decline[10] and turnaround[11] can be based on a company's level of financial resources[12] or be defined from the stakeholder perspective.[13]

The lack of a general definition makes it difficult to compare successful past turnarounds. Turnarounds are often measured in unique, case-by-case ways, and success depends on the definition of performance.[14] Performance can be defined in terms of the company's stock price and its own historical record,[15] in terms of its survival,[16] the normalized net income to reflect industry trends,[17] or a wider standard.[18] Measures can be inflation corrected[19] or historical.[20]

The literature has little to say about the time span of a turnaround and varies between three to eight years[21] [22] including a base year, as a reasonable time span for turnarounds in the banking industry.

There are five different types of turnaround: management-component turnaround; economic turnaround; government-related turnaround; product-breakthrough turnaround; and competitive-environment turnaround.[23]

Management turnarounds are used in 68 percent of successful turnarounds.[24]

Even now, there is no generally accepted definition of the term "turnaround" in the business literature. Some use the term to describe the necessary measures and processes used to increase a company's profitability or to give it a new strategic position,[25] while others use it to signal that a crisis has been successfully mastered and the company has been turned around. A

---

[10] (Hambrick & D'Aveni, 1988)
[11] (Lohrke & Bedeian, 1996)
[12] (Bourgeois L., 1981), (Singh, 1986), (Cyert & March, 1963)
[13] (Chen, Farh, & MacMillan, 1993), (Sousa deVasconcellos e Sa & Hambrick, 1989)
[14] compare (O'Neill H. M., 1986)
[15] (Bibeault, Corporate Turnaround: How Managers Turn Losers into Winners, 1981)
[16] (Altman E., 1968)
[17] (Schendel, Patton, & Riggs, 1976)
[18] (Schendel & Patton, 1976)
[19] (Schendel & Patton, 1976)
[20] (Hofer, 1980)
[21] (Hambrick & Schecter, 1983)
[22] (O'Neill H. M., 1986, p. 177)
[23] (Bibeault, Corporate Turnaround: How Managers Turn Losers into Winners, 1981)
[24] (O'Neill H. M., 1986)
[25] (Bibeault, 1981)

corporate turnaround can be described as a substantial and sustained positive change in the performance of a business,[26] therefore the following Turnaround Management Society definition is proposed for use throughout the book:

> *A turnaround transforms a company that has a general lack of resources and/or strategic disposition and/or is in an abnormal period to be profitable enough to support its own operations and to have a strategic chance to survive in its environment on a stable platform for renewed growth*[27]

Schendel, Patton, and Rigges define a turnaround as a decline and recovery in performance.[28] However, this definition does not make clear at what point in the development of the crisis the turnaround begins. Following the TMS definition, the turnaround can start as soon as a strategic disposition is recognized, which does not mean that there must also be financial distress.

Distressed Turnaround

To clarify the various definitions of a turnaround, I will introduce another version that happens in a clearly distressed environment:

> *A distressed turnaround, with the help of professional turnaround management skills, transforms a company that has a general lack of resources, lack of strategic disposition, or current or foreseeable financial distress and is in an abnormal period, to be profitable enough to support its own operations and to have a strategic chance to survive in its environment on a stable platform for renewed growth.*[29]

The definition of a distressed turnaround helps to distinguish between more severe situations that affect all aspects of the business and less severe turnarounds that affect only parts of the business, since in turnarounds there may be an imminent danger to survival.[30]

---

[26] (Bibeault, 1981, p. 81)
[27] (Lymbersky C. , 2011)
[28] (Schendel, Patton, & Riggs, 1976, p. 3)
[29] (Lymbersky C. , 2011)
[30] (Hofer, 1980)

Therefore, the distressed turnaround occurs later on in the decline cycle of a company than the more general turnaround. It is important to understand that a company does not need to have financial problems to conduct a turnaround in its strategic direction to correct a shortage of resources, and it is not necessary that a company has a lack of resources to be in financial distress. The term "distressed turnaround" applies later in the company's decline cycle, when all preconditions for a distressed turnaround are met or will be met in the near future.

Turnaround Situation

A turnaround situation is usually referred to as an existence-threatening situation in which crucial company goals cannot be met anymore and in which a turnaround needs to be undertaken in order to ensure the future growth and survival of the company—that is, when a company's financial performance shows that the firm is very likely to fail in the foreseeable future if near-term corrective action is not taken.[31] The return on capital employed in such a situation is often lower than it is for comparable companies in the same industry.

The Turnaround Management Society's definition of a turnaround situation includes companies that are not in a current cash crisis, although if there is a cash crisis the company is certainly in a severe crisis. My definition is extended to firms that don't have liquidity problems yet but have recognized that they need a turnaround to stay competitive and/or profitable in the future. For example, this could be the case if the company is in the stage of a strategy crisis. Therefore profitability alone is not a clear indicator for a turnaround situation. For example, if a company sees a loss in one year because of heavy acquisitions, a change of accounting rules, or write-offs the company may still be well positioned for the future and may not need a turnaround. However, a firm that is growth-orientated and that has grown too fast may continue to be profitable but also be in a severe cash flow crisis.[32] Such was the case with the German solar company Conergy, which grew its turnover from 530.17 million in 2005 to 705.53 million euro in 2007, but also had serious cash flow problems and was clearly in a turnaround situation.

---

[31] (Slater & Lovett, 1999)
[32] (Slater & Lovett, 1999)

Definitions

Year:	2005	2006	2007
Turnover	530,17	682,33	705,53
Cash Flow	20,54	-238,07	-188,62

Table 1 Conergy turnover and cash flow development from 2005 to 2007

However, the profit picture of the typical turnaround situation is several years of successively lower profits culminating in a loss situation and a cash flow crisis.[33] This pattern is usually found in mature industries and family-controlled businesses where managers become satisfied with the status quo. Because the business is not dramatically decreasing, just stagnating, their assets are underutilized and the management is not sufficiently motivated (or perhaps they are incapable or incompetent). Once a crisis situation becomes obvious it may already be too late to rely on minor adjustments, and the management alone is usually unable to master the turnaround by itself. If a turnaround situation is recognized before the financial signals become dire, the turnaround can happen more quickly and with fewer negative effects. Picture 3 Crisis development by stages) shows several points in time and profitability where a turnaround situation persists, following the definition used in this paper.

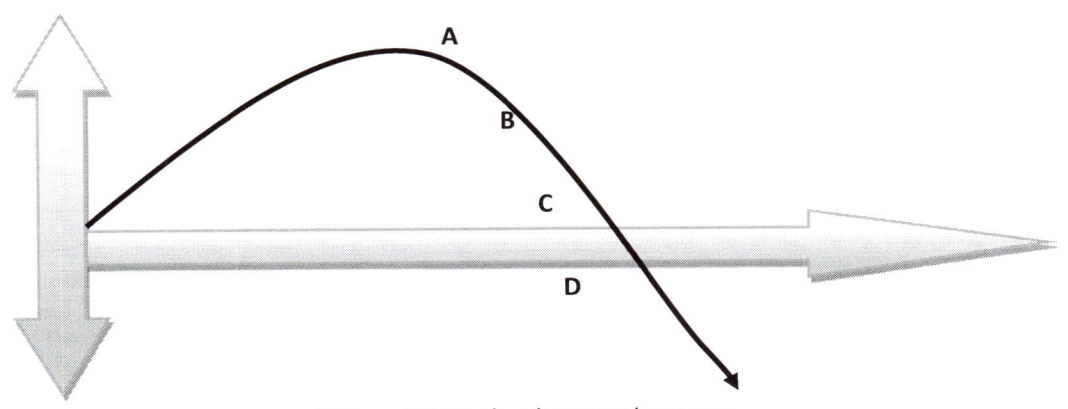

Picture 3 Crisis development by stages

---

[33] (Slater & Lovett, 1999, p. 2)

Turnaround Management

The term "turnaround management" is different from "Turnaround Management Team", which will be explained later on. Turnaround management consists of all activities undertaken by a company in an existence-threatening situation in order to return to sustainable profitability.[34] However, for the purposes of this paper I have extended the definition to include the management of situations in companies that are not yet in an existence-threatening situation but might face such a crisis, and to the management of situations in companies that are not yet in the stage of a liquidity crisis but are showing the first signs of a strategy or success crisis. Turnaround management consists of measures, including strategic, organizational, and financial, to avoid increasing the severity of a crisis and to get back to sustainable profitability.

Disambiguation of Crisis Management

The term "crisis management" is broader than "turnaround management" in that it includes the early recognition of a crisis as well as crisis prevention. Therefore crisis management starts before turnaround management. It can be divided into active/anticipative crisis management and reactive/repulsive crisis management.[35]

Active (or anticipative) crisis management describes all activities undertaken in pursuit of crisis prevention and its early recognition. Reactive (or repulsive) crisis management describes the activities undertaken to handle a crisis once it has occurred.[36] Crisis prevention is not part of this work, so it is mentioned here only to differentiate it from crisis management and to outline pre-emptive measures to avoid a crisis. The following pages focus on the reactive element of crisis management.

Turnaround Success

A successful turnaround is difficult to measure, but it generally depends on the goals agreed on in the turnaround concept. In general, a successful turnaround is reached once a substantial and enduring positive change in the company's results is reached. A turnaround is considered

---

[34] (Buschmann, 2006, S. 25)
[35] (Krystek, 1987, p. 90)
[36] (Buschmann, 2006, S. 29-30)

to be successful if "a firm undergoes a survival threatening decline over a period of years but is able to reverse the performance decline, end the threat to firm survival, and achieve sustained profitability".[37] The term "sustainable" is also used in definitions,[38] for example, a "sustainable recovery" is what distinguishes a successful turnaround from those that "survive only in the short term and then become insolvent, and those which achieve what [they] call sustainable recovery".[39]

A sustainable recovery is accomplished if the company achieves:[40]

- A viable, defensible business strategy
- An adequate organization and control structure

and if it is:[41]

- Making "good" profits
- Unlikely to face another crisis in the foreseeable future

Additionally, a company can be called successful after a turnaround if the "upturn recovery stage [is] normally four years or longer".[42]

Clearly the terms of a successful turnaround need to be explicitly described in the turnaround concept devised for each company. A successful turnaround cannot be limited to a specific definition since, in practice, the goals of one company's turnaround may vary significantly from the goals of another.

Chapter 7

In the United States of America, Chapter 7 refers to the proceedings that provide for liquidation of a business. Even though describing the proceedings of liquidation is not the primary goal of

---

[37] (Barker & Duhaime, 1997, S. 18)
[38] (Pandit, 2000, p. 32)
[39] (Slatter & Lovett, Corporate Turnaround: Managing Companies in Distress, 1999, p. 3)
[40] (Slatter & Lovett, 2004)
[41] (Slatter & Lovett, 2004, p. 3)
[42] (Bibeault, 1981, p. 83)

this work, liquidation is always an option that needs to be considered, especially during the Diagnostic Review Stage.

When a company decides to pursue the Chapter 7 option, its assets are placed in the hands of an appointed bankruptcy trustee. This trustee liquidates the assets for the best price available and distributes them to the creditors.[43] In comparison, Chapter 11 proceedings have the goal of reviving the business, often through reorganization.

Chapter 11

Many US companies in a turnaround situation consider using Chapter 11 protection for their reorganization efforts. The 11 United States Code (11 USC) is part of the 1978 Bankruptcy Code, which replaced the Bankruptcy Act of 1898. The 11 USC consists of several chapters, but the chapters directly relevant to this work are Chapter 7, which regulates the proceedings in case of liquidation, and Chapter 11, which regulates reorganizations.

The Debtor

Should a bankrupt company be taken to court, that company is called the debtor. As part of the US Bankruptcy Reform Act that took effect in 1979, the phrase "the Bankrupt" to refer to the debtor was expunged from the statute because of its negative connotations.[44]

Debtor in Possession

A debtor in possession is an entity that is still in possession of the firm's assets, as is usually the case until a trustee is appointed. "The debtor in possession has certain fiduciary duties akin to those of a trustee that require it to operate its business in a manner that is fair, equitable and in the best interest of the creditors."[45]

---

[43] (Branch & Hugh, 1992, p. 3)
[44] (Branch & Hugh, 1992)
[45] (Branch & Hugh, 1992, p. 5)

Creditor's Committee

In Chapter 11 cases, the creditor's committee is made up of representatives of the creditors who "are appointed by the US trustee or the bankruptcy judge to oversee the debtor in possession and assist in the formulation and confirmation of a plan".[46]

Judge of the Bankruptcy Court

"In the United States of America the judge who presides over the court that hears the bankruptcy case is called the judge of the bankruptcy court. He or she is referred the case by the relevant US District Court and is a judicial officer operating under that referred authority."[47]

The Bankruptcy Trustee

The bankruptcy trustee, often called the trustee of the estate, is often a private citizen with a law degree. "The trustee may be elected by the creditors and must be a qualified disinterested person."[48] "Not every Chapter 11 case has also a bankruptcy trustee appointed to it. The trustee is charged with liquidating the assets of the debtor and overseeing their equitable distribution."[49]

The trustee "performs the duties that a debtor would have performed had the estate remained outside of bankruptcy".[50]

Decline

"A firm may be said to be in decline when it experiences a resource loss sufficient to compromise its viability."[51] A company's decline can be defined relative to its peer group in the banking sector as having exhibited a continued period of decline relative to its strategic group,

---

[46] (Branch & Hugh, 1992, p. 5)
[47] (Branch & Hugh, 1992, p. 5)
[48] (Branch & Hugh, 1992, p. 3)
[49] (Branch & Hugh, 1992, p. 5)
[50] The trustee is customarily awarded a fee of 1 to 3 percent of the estate for their services. For more information please see (Branch & Hugh, 1992, p. 3).
[51] (Cameron, Kim, & Whetton, 1987)

while a turnaround bank has gained ground in comparison to its strategic group after a period of continued loss of ground.[52] Studies suggest that decline is more likely in highly competitive markets than in non-competitive ones.[53]

Retrenchment

There is no clear definition of retrenchment in connection with a turnaround process. Retrenchment can be defined as "a term that denotes a strong emphasis on cost and asset reductions as means to mitigate the condition responsible for financial downturn",[54] and Barker III and Mone "accepted their definition and added 'asset and cost reduction' in their case study about stages of the IBM turnaround process in the UK".[55] In this standard, we define retrenchment as "asset divestment and cost reduction, often by downsizing".[56]

From this definition, it follows that retrenchment must have the objective of survival and a positive cash flow. Retrenchment is a first important step towards a successful turnaround regardless of the reason for the corporate crisis.[57] "They appear to regard retrenchment as a short-run tactical response, as opposed to a broad long-term strategy."[58] Others who have followed this definition have included definitions for small firms,[59] the case of IBM in the UK,[60] or the case study of the Russian technology company Micron in 1997.[61] However, some did not focus significantly on strategic actions,[62] and others added that cutting costs and retrenchment are part of a successful turnaround, and that retrenchment combined with strategic actions can also lead to a successful turnaround.[63] Others again have supported the argument that retrenchment is part of successful turnarounds.[64]

---

[52] (O'Neill H. M., 1986)
[53] (Hofer, 1980), (Hambrick & Schecter, 1983), (O'Neill H. M., 1986, p. 175)
[54] (Robbins & Pearce II, 1992)
[55] (Barker III & Mone, 1994), (Balgobin & Pandit, 2001)
[56] (Fischer, Lee, & Johns, 2004, p. 155)
[57] (Robbins & Pearce II, 1992)
[58] (Fischer, Lee, & Johns, 2004, p. 155)
[59] (Chowdhury & Lang, 1996)
[60] (Balgobin & Pandit, 2001)
[61] (Bruton & Rubanik, 1997)
[62] (Chowdhury & Lang, 1996)
[63] (Bruton & Rubanik, 1997)
[64] (Umbriet, 1996), (Vaz, 1996)

In this study, retrenchment is a part of cost-cutting and cash control—a way to increase efficiency in the short term—therefore it takes place in the Crisis Stabilization Stage. Prior to 1992, much of the research conducted in turnaround management focused on strategy rather than financial measures such as retrenchment.[65] However, after 1992, some researchers concluded that retrenchment is not essential for a turnaround.[66] In 2000, a study of 46 US companies that had been taken over in a crisis situation was published and found "no significant relationship between the retrenchment and the companies' performance".[67] In contrast, a further 2003 study of Chinese and East Asian firms found that retrenchment improved performance for companies that were in a period of declining performance.[68] Clearly, more research is necessary to determine whether retrenchment is essential to successful turnarounds.

Relevant Definitions in Strategy

It is important to clarify the terms used by distinguishing and defining them. One of the reasons that it is sometimes difficult for organizations to formulate clear and comprehensive strategies may be that they confuse strategies with policies, goals with objectives, programs with plans, and strategic decisions with tactical decisions.[69]

Goals

"A goal is a general statement of aim or purpose."[70] Major goals are those that affect the company's overall direction—that is, the broad value principles toward which it is striving. "The overall organizational objectives which establish the intended nature of the enterprise are called strategic goals."[71] A goal may well be quantitative in nature[72]—for example, a typical goal is to gain financial freedom or to enter a foreign market—but a company's goals are often not

---

[65] (Castrogiovanni & Bruton, 2000), (Harker, 1996)
[66] (Barker III & Mone, 1994)
[67] (Castrogiovanni & Bruton, 2000)
[68] (Bruton, Ahlstrom, & Wan, 2003)
[69] (Slatter & Lovett, 2004, p. 215)
[70] (Johnson, Scholes, & Whittington, 2005, p. 13)
[71] (Slatter & Lovett, 2004, p. 216), (Quinn)
[72] (Johnson, Scholes, & Whittington, 2005, p. 13)

as well defined as its objectives. Goals are "sometimes referred to in terms of the apparently simple but challenging question: 'What business are we in?'".[73]

Objectives

An objective is a qualification (if possible) or a more precise declaration of the goal.[74] They "state what is to be achieved and when results are to be accomplished, but they do not state how the results are to be achieved".[75]

A typical objective is to gain financial freedom by March 2013, or to enter the foreign market in China in 2011 to sell cars to the lower middle classes. Hence, an objective is better defined than a goal.

Mission

"A mission is an overriding purpose [that is] in line with the values or expectations of stakeholders", therefore a mission is a general expression of the overall purpose of the organization that is concerned with its scope and boundaries.[76]

Business Model

"A business model describes the structure of products, services, and information flows and the role of the participating parties."[77] Every company should have an outlined business model that is communicated to the workforce. If employees don't understand the structure of the products, services, or information flows they will not be able to sell or work on them in a way that is beneficial for the organization as a whole. They will lack creativity in evolving in the desired direction of the company.

---

[73] (Johnson, Scholes, & Whittington, 2005, p. 13)
[74] (Johnson, Scholes, & Whittington, 2005, p. 13)
[75] (Slatter & Lovett, 2004, p. 216)
[76] (Johnson, Scholes, & Whittington, 2005, p. 13)
[77] (Johnson, Scholes, & Whittington, 2005, p. 13)

Strategy

A strategy is a pattern or plan that integrates an organization's major goals, policies, and action plans into a cohesive whole.[78] "A well-formulated strategy helps to marshal and allocate an organization's resources into a unique and viable posture based on its relative internal competencies and shortcomings, anticipated changes in the environment, and contingent moves by intelligent opponents."[79]

Strategy is the direction and scope of an organization over the long term. Strategy helps the organization achieve advantage in a changing environment through its configuration of resources and competencies with the aim of fulfilling stakeholder expectations.[80]

Policies

I regard policies as "rules or guidelines that express the limits within which action should occur".[81]

Corporate Strategy

Corporate strategy addresses the issue of which businesses a company operates in or should be in, and how its portfolio of products and services should be managed. It "is concerned with the overall scope of an organization and how value will be added to the different parts (business units) of the organization".[82]

Business Unit Strategy

"The business unit strategy addresses the question of which product-market segments to compete in and how to create competitive advantage in each of them."[83] The business unit

---

[78] (Quinn)
[79] (Slatter & Lovett, 2004, p. 216)
[80] (Corporate Strategy, 7th edition, p. 9).
[81] (Slatter & Lovett, 2004, p. 216)
[82] (Johnson, Scholes, & Whittington, 2005, p. 11)
[83] (Slatter & Lovett, 2004, p. 215)

strategy is about how to compete successfully in particular markets or how to provide the best value public services.[84]

Strategic Business Unit

"A strategic business unit is a part of an organization for which there is a distinct external market for goods or services that is different from other SBUs."[85]

Strategic Capability

"Unique resources and core competencies are the bases upon which an organization achieves strategic advantage and distinguishes itself from competitors."[86] Strategic capability is concerned with how well a company can use its competencies and resources in order to provide the best possible outcome for its clients.

Strategic Turnaround Capability

Strategic turnaround capability is concerned with the resources and competencies that an organization can use to provide value to the turnaround process in order to achieve superior value for its stakeholders.

Generic Strategy

There are six generic strategies,[87] or three types.[88] "Generic strategies are distinct types of strategies that can be applied in certain situations."[89] Each strategy type can serve as a guideline for choosing goals or deploying resources within the firm.[90] The grand strategy is used to identify the correct balance that should exist among functional allocations in the firm.[91] The

---

[84] (Johnson, Scholes, & Whittington, 2005, p. 11)
[85] (Johnson, Scholes, & Whittington, 2005, p. 11)
[86] (Johnson, Scholes, & Whittington, 2005, p. 11)
[87] (Hofer & Schendel, 1978)
[88] (Porter M. E., 1979)
[89] (O'Neill H. M., 1986)
[90] (O'Neill H. M., 1986)
[91] (Bourgeois L. J., 1980), (Hitt, Ireland, & Palia, 1982)

matrix of resource allocation may be the most common model of the relationship between generic strategy and resource deployment.[92]

The use of generic or grand strategies increases effectiveness and helps to prevent the subordination of corporate goals to functional goals.[93] Generic strategies can also be used as characteristics of incentive systems and managers.[94] However, others were not able to identify turnarounds as a generic situation.[95]

---

[92] (Fox, 1973)
[93] (Hatten, Schendel, & Cooper, 1978), (O'Neill H. M., 1986), (Rumelt, 1974)
[94] (Gluck, Kaufman, & Walleck, 1982)
[95] (Hambrick & Schecter, 1983), (Hofer, 1980), (Schendel & Patton, 1976), (Schendel, Patton, & Riggs, 1976), (Slatter & Lovett, 2004)

What is a Crisis?

Knowing the possible reasons for a crisis and knowing how a crisis develops make it easier for management to see that a crisis is forming in a company and to identify available turnaround strategies. Such knowledge may also help management to avoid being drawn into a crisis in the first place. Only one who knows their own weaknesses can minimize or avoid them, thereby creating the potential for success in the future.[96] The following paragraphs provide an overview of the empirical research that has identified what a crisis is and its potential causes.

A crisis situation can be distinguished[97] when:

- The existence of the entity as a whole is threatened.
- The time that is allowed to decide on actions to overcome the crisis is limited. If the source of the crisis is undetermined, the crisis is likely to be company-wide.

It is possible to classify the time[98] available to decide on possible actions to overcome a crisis into different stages, distinguishing between a latent crisis and an apparent crisis. The apparent crisis is already known to the company's environment and its stakeholders, while the latent crisis is not known to the company's environment and is often not known even to its stakeholders or management. Therefore, only the apparent crisis always presents a "going concern"[99] since only in this case does the management have enough time to analyze the problem and put measures in place to overcome it. However, some critics argue that this model lacks exact classifications in its substance.[100]

---

[96] (Doelling, 2003)
[97] (Witte, 1981)
[98] (Hauschildt, 1983)
[99] (Doelling, 2003)
[100] (Crone & Werner, 2007, p. 14)

What are the Reasons for a Crisis?

The reasons for a crisis need to be distinguished from its symptoms, which signal the beginning of a crisis but are not the cause of its development.[101] Knowledge of what exactly leads to a crisis and an analysis of these factors are essential in order to recognize a crisis at an early stage and serve as a foundation for handling it.

The extant research on what leads to crises in companies can be divided into qualitative crisis causation research and quantitative crisis causation research. The quantitative research tries to identify the causes of crises by analyzing statistical data such as company size, age, industry, and legal form. Some critics[102] claim that crisis symptoms and the causes of a crisis are not clearly distinguished. The symptoms are a lot less meaningful than the causes and may even distort the outcome of the research in this area.

According to a study of approximately 1,300 insolvency files that tried to to identify companies' internal reasons, "in-between" reasons, and corporate reasons for failure that led to insolvency,[103] the lack of sufficient equity and bad leadership are the most common reasons for failure. However, "bad leadership" is not a very sophisticated or specific reason for a company failing. We need more information about what exactly is meant by bad leadership and about which leadership characteristics were common in failing companies. In addition, a lack of equity can also be a symptom rather than a cause on its own, and it is important to identify the factors that contributed to the lack of equity. One might infer that raising a company's equity will turn the company around, but most of the time this is not the case. It is not enough to blame insufficient funds for a company's crisis; a company-wide crisis is usually the outcome of several coexisting factors that come about in multiple steps in a cause-and-effect relationship.[104]

Risk management companies such as Creditreform and credit management companies such as Schimmelpfeng regularly publish lists of crisis indicators. However, these lists simply outline

---

[101] (Böckenförde, 1996, pp. 22,27)
[102] (Gless, 1996, p. 22)
[103] (Krystek, 1987, p. 68)
[104] (Schendel, Patton, & Riggs, 1976, p. 7), (Krystek, 1987, p. 67)

reasons, while the underlying reasons for a crisis are much more complex than they suggest. The causes of crises can be classified in several ways:[105]

- The cause of a crisis is exogenous if the factors that lead to the crisis are external to the company, and the cause is endogenous if the crisis results from internal factors.
- Depending on how long and how often the factor affects the company, the reasons for a crisis may be chronic, acute, continuous, or periodic.[106]
- Some causes are open and some are lingering.
- Some causes are regular and some are irregular.
- Depending on how strong the factors are, the causes of a crisis can be differentiated as weak or strong.
- Some crises have a single cause and some have more than one cause. If there is more than one cause, the causes can be consecutive or simultaneous.
- Depending on whether the whole company is affected by the crisis factor or just a department or segment of the business, causes can be differentiated as total or partial.
- Crisis factors can be differentiated as general or particular.[107]
- The cause of a crisis can be differentiated as temporary or permanent unprofitability.[108]
- Others distinguish between factors that lead to a crisis that a company cannot survive and factors that can be treated.[109]

Kliege and Doelling use deductive systematization to group crisis factors.[110] They assume that there is a chain of causes that contribute to a crisis and introduce the concept of primary causes, secondary causes, and tertiary causes. Furthermore, there are multiple causal factors, coordinate factors, and complex causes.[111] The following model shows the different levels of factors that can cause a crisis. More than one individual cause can be found on each level, and the individual causes can also influence and depend on other factors on other levels.

---

[105] (Fleege-Althoff, 1930)
[106] (Le Coutre, 1926)
[107] (Hertlein & Meisner, 1956), (Hertlein, 1956), (Leist, 1905)
[108] (Fleischer, 1928)
[109] (Moral, 1924)
[110] (Kliege, 1962), (Doelling, 2003)
[111] (Keiser, 1966)

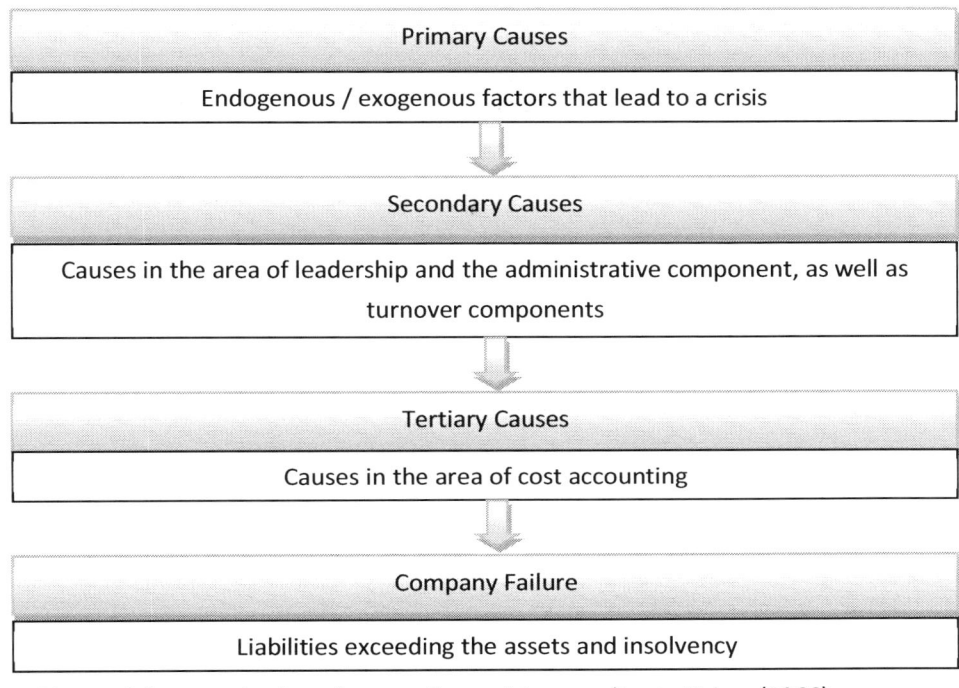

```
┌─────────────────────────────────────────────────────────────┐
│                      Primary Causes                          │
├─────────────────────────────────────────────────────────────┤
│       Endogenous / exogenous factors that lead to a crisis   │
└─────────────────────────────────────────────────────────────┘
                              ⬇
┌─────────────────────────────────────────────────────────────┐
│                     Secondary Causes                         │
├─────────────────────────────────────────────────────────────┤
│  Causes in the area of leadership and the administrative     │
│          component, as well as turnover components           │
└─────────────────────────────────────────────────────────────┘
                              ⬇
┌─────────────────────────────────────────────────────────────┐
│                      Tertiary Causes                         │
├─────────────────────────────────────────────────────────────┤
│             Causes in the area of cost accounting            │
└─────────────────────────────────────────────────────────────┘
                              ⬇
┌─────────────────────────────────────────────────────────────┐
│                      Company Failure                         │
├─────────────────────────────────────────────────────────────┤
│          Liabilities exceeding the assets and insolvency     │
└─────────────────────────────────────────────────────────────┘
```

Picture 4 Systematization of causes for a crisis according to Keiser (1966)

Examples of endogenous primary causes include insufficient employee capability and the lack of entrepreneurial idiosyncrasy[112] as well as mismanagement, misjudgment, and internally caused mistakes made by employees. Examples of exogenous primary factors are force majeure, economic downturns, and increased competition.[113]

Some secondary causes[114] resulting from other causes are miscalculations, the lack of distinct structure(s) within the business, and poor administrative processes such as bad buying terms, bad storage management, "mismanagement in production",[115] and poor decisions in research and development.

---

[112] (Keiser, 1966), for more information on entrepreneurial idiosyncrasy please see (Fuller & Telma, 2007)
[113] (Keiser, 1966)
[114] (Doelling, 2003)
[115] (Hauschildt & Leker, 2000)

Tertiary causes are causes that result from other causes that result from other causes—they are the last step before a company fails so they tend to have the characteristics of symptoms. Keiser mentions some examples such as low income, high expenses, and poor structure in financial statements, for example, a lack of equity capital.[116]

Hauschildt[117] analyzed 72 mismanagement articles from the German *Manager Magazin* between 1971 and 1982, from which he developed a systematic outline of mismanagement segments and identified four types of crisis causes.

> Type 1: The entity on breakable pillars
> Type 2: The technologically endangered entity
> Type 3: The entity that is expanding unprepared
> Type 4: The conservative, obstinate, uninformed patriarch

Each failure segment—such as production, sales, and leadership—has a different relevance within these groups, but only the sales area has a constant significant importance.[118]

Picture 5 shows Hauschildt's differentiated mismanagement causes that lead to a crisis.

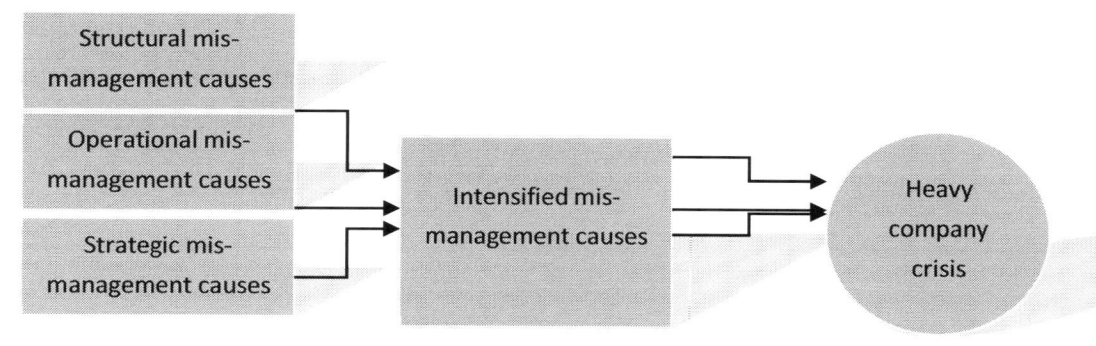

Picture 5 Reasons for mismanagement. Based on Hauschildt, Krisendiagnose durch Bilanzanalyse, (1998)

---

[116] (Keiser, 1966)
[117] (Hauschildt, 1983)
[118] (Buschmann, 2006)

The Crisis Process

The time between a company being healthy and its existence being threatened can be divided into four stages[119]—stakeholder crisis, strategy crisis, success crisis, and liquidity crisis—the last of which leads to insolvency if turnaround management is not implemented. The order may be different; for example, a crisis may start with a liquidity crisis in the case of embezzlement or bad debt losses. It is also possible that a company slides into a success crisis and then into a strategy crisis if its liquidity planning has been insufficient.[120] It is important to know which stage the company under observation is in in order to identify the correct actions.

The Strategy Crisis

The strategy crisis starts when the success potential of a company is seriously endangered. Either the factors that allow the company to grow and be successful have been used up or the company has created no new future success factors, such as a brand name, profitable products, qualified and motivated employees, competitive advantages, or loyal clients.

Symptoms[121] of a strategy crisis are:

- The company has no clear direction.
- The company's products are in a mature state of their lifecycle.
- There are no new products being developed.
- There is a drop in sales or orders and shrinking market share.

The reason for a strategy crisis is often found in companies that make profits at the beginning. Such companies often take their success for granted and don't really ask themselves how the money is made or what contributes to the success they are experiencing. If, as a result, the company stops innovating, misses a technological advancement or a competitor's product launch, or its marketing fails to address the right market then it is only a matter of time until the strategy crisis becomes obvious and turns into a success crisis. In some cases, an over-aged

---

[119] (Müller, 1986)
[120] (Seefelder, 2003, p. 57)
[121] compare (ISU Institut für die Standartisierung von Unternehmenssanierungen, 2008, p. 514)

workforce and the wrong location for production facilities can be the reason for a strategy crisis.[122] The reason may also be an insufficient control system, or self-satisfaction with the current market position or the capabilities of the company.[123] There is also the danger that measures to increase short-term earnings or to lower costs will compromise success in the long term.[124]

BMW, for example, had a growth in turnover of 46 percent between 2002 and 2007 and was basking in its success. However, the once sleek company was growing fat and the return on capital employed reduced by about 25 percent at the same time. Meanwhile, BMW stopped critical innovations, such as the Gran Tourismo CS, and hired more and more people. A McKinsey study showed that about 20 percent of BMW's workforce was dispensable.[125]

The Success Crisis

If no counteractive measures—or the wrong measures—are taken during a strategy crisis, a success crisis follows. In a success crisis, a company sees losses that slowly eat up its equity as a result of declining sales, cost increases, a drop in prices, and so on. It is also a success crisis if a company fails to reach its contribution margin. If the situation persists for a long time, overextension occurs.[126] The reasons for a success crisis are often related to the company's success potential not being optimally used, or to it having insufficient efficiency in its operative business.[127] Further symptoms of a success crisis are:

- Worsening balance sheets
- A reduction in profitability that leads to higher inventory
- Shrinking sales revenue that reduces cash flow and sometimes renders it negative[128]
- Increasing debt financing that leads to rising interest expenditures, stressing the liquidity situation even more[129]
- Increased difficulty covering losses with extraordinary earnings

---

[122] (Harz, Hub, & Schlarb, 2006, p. 6)
[123] (Slatter & Lovett, 2004, p. 61 ff.)
[124] (Brühl & Göpfert, 2004, p. 18)
[125] (Freitag, 2008)
[126] (Harz, Hub, & Schlarb, 2006, p. 7)
[127] (Keller, 1999)
[128] (Crone & Werner, 2007, p. 6)
[129] (Keller, 1999, S. 9)

The Liquidity Crisis

If there is an acute danger that the company will go bankrupt, the company finds itself in a liquidity crisis.[130] During a liquidity crisis, banks often terminate their loans, making it difficult for the company to survive the crisis. In this case, the risk of insolvency increases, and insolvency may even become inevitable. In a liquidity crisis, the success factors of the company often disappear or are not effective anymore.[131] A further reason for a liquidity crisis can be if the management does not know much about finance, which sometimes happens when former start-ups grow quickly or when a major partner, client, or associate goes bankrupt. Sometimes miscalculations or fraud can lead to a liquidity crisis as well.

The solar technology company Conergy was led by management who spent too much money on unprofitable investments and simply lost control of its spending. When the company experienced a serious liquidity crisis in November 2007, the founder, Hans-Martin Rüter, was replaced by an experienced internal management team,[132] but this move did not keep the stock price from dropping from over 65 euros in October 2007 to 11 euros four months later. The equity-to-assets ratio dropped from 43.7 percent in 2005 to eight percent in 2008.[133] The banks gave Conergy until the end of December 2008 to repay their current debt, so by the end of 2008 Conergy was in a serious liquidity crisis.

Insolvency

If no turnaround management is instigated, or if the countermeasures fail to bring the company back on track, then the company will go into insolvency. The point at which insolvency is reached depends a lot on the local laws. In Germany, insolvency is reached once the matters of fact outlined in §17 to §19 InsO are fulfilled. In the USA, the respective regulations can be found in Chapter 11. Since this book is an international work and focuses on the management of a turnaround, I will touch on the law only when it is relevant from a management perspective. In

---

[130] (Harz, Hub, & Schlarb, 2006, p. 20)
[131] (Crone & Werner, 2007, p. 4)
[132] (wal, 2007)
[133] (Coral Consors, 2008)

almost all insolvencies, the management did not act according to the crisis situation or did not recognize it.[134]

The Stakeholder Crisis

The stakeholder crisis can be the starting point for a crisis in a company. A stakeholder crisis is often not recognized by people either inside or outside the company, and usually starts with a change in leadership style that leads to increasing neglectfulness.[135] Often the development and evolution of a crisis is recognized too late.[136] The reasons for such a change are varied, and include conflict amongst senior management, a failed corporate descent, or the long-term sickness of a key manager. In a case such as this the motivation of the workforce drops and the corporate culture suffers.

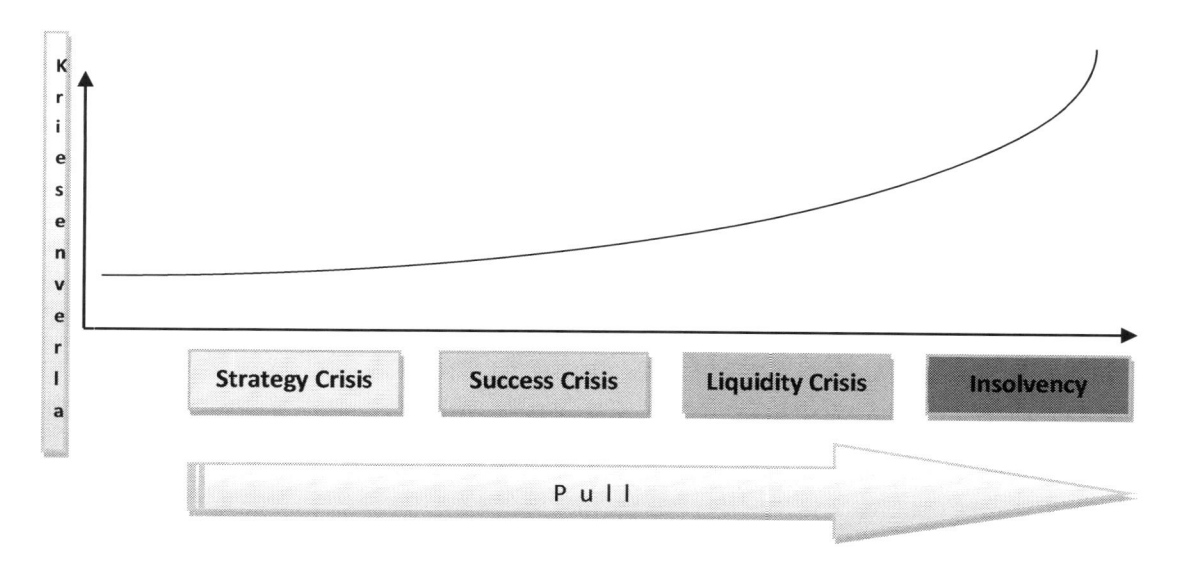

Picture 6 Crisis process according to Müller

A company often gets into a strategy or success crisis when "crisis denial" occurs—the management does not want to believe a problem exists or is blinded by current success, then, as soon as the first signs of a crisis become obvious, tries to explain them by extraordinary factors, such as the cost of introducing a new product, or temporary external forces such as

---

[134] compare (Concentro Management AG, 2009, p. 5)
[135] (Crone & Werner, 2007, p. 3)
[136] (Gless, 1996, p. 16).

cyclical fluctuations.[137] As a result, the management ignores these signs and hopes for improvement in the future. This is then called a "hidden crisis".[138]

Once the management realizes the company is heading into a crisis and puts in place the first countermeasures, it often continues to underestimate the causes and effects of the crisis, as well as its dimensions. In this case, the countermeasures simply slow down the crisis and the organization heads straight into the third stage—organizational collapse. In this stage, the management's failure becomes obvious, stakeholders and shareholders lose trust and commitment in the management, important employees leave the company, and it loses its competitiveness. "Further inefficiency finally leads to the company's crashing."[139]

Stages	Typical organizational behavior
Crisis denial	Complacency: signals completely overlooked
Hidden crisis	Crisis explained away: belief that it will disappear; no need for action
Disintegration of organization begins	Some action taken but need for action underestimated
Organizational collapse	Inability to take action

Picture 7 Crisis process according to Slatter and Lovett (Buschmann, 2006)

Crisis Impact

Crisis impacts have been highlighted in the extant practitioner literature. Very extensive research is necessary to determine the exact impact of a crisis. So far the crisis impact can be classified in three different ways, each of which can enhance the other if they are combined:[140]

a) Reduced support by shareholders

---

[137] (Buschmann, 2006)
[138] (Slatter & Lovett, 2004, p. 61ff.)
[139] (Buschmann, 2006)
[140] (Arogyaswamy, Barker, & Yasai-Ardekani, 1995)

b) Loss of efficiency and decreased competitiveness
c) Change in decision-making processes

Reduced Support by Stakeholders

A stakeholder is any party with an interest (financial or otherwise) in a business and hence an interest in or an ability to influence the outcome of a turnaround.[141]

The efficiency of an organization depends on the continued maintenance of the relationships between its transaction partners. When a crisis becomes obvious, some stakeholders will turn away from the company at the same time that the company's resources are used up, which can create a vicious circle and draw the company deeper into the crisis. This process is called "stakeholder erosion"[142] and leads to:

- Higher costs
- Reduced turnover
- Less room to maneuver

These effects can lead increasing numbers of stakeholders to reduce their support for the company.[143]

Reduced support from stakeholders can take several forms depending on the sort of interest that the stakeholder has in the company. Examples are:

- Clients who look for new sources of supply
- Banks that curtail credit
- Suppliers who want their goods paid in advance

---

[141] (Slatter & Lovett, 2004, p. 179)
[142] (Buschmann, 2006)
[143] (Arogyaswamy, Barker, & Yasai-Ardekani, 1995, p. 500)

This reduced support may be accompanied by bad press,[144] loss of image, and loss of trust in the management,[145] any of which can make things even worse for the company.

Loss of Efficiency and Decreased Competitiveness

A loss of efficiency can be the result of a crisis, but it can also cause a crisis. For example, a change in the economic environment or a new competitor can lead to shrinking turnover, which can lead to underemployed production facilities and to a loss of efficiency and increased costs per unit, which can in turn lead to a loss of competitiveness. A competitor may take advantage of this situation and lower its sales prices below the variable costs of the company in crisis to hurt it even more. A shrinking margin may reduce the money available for investment. In a time when the financial situation is compromised, this can lead to an existence-threatening situation for the company.

Change in Decision-Making Processes

In a crisis, many of a company's processes change. For example, management tends to restrict communication[146] and to implement a centralized decision authority[147] in order to make decisions quickly. These steps may result in management not listening to critical voices that have important ideas or issues to contribute, leading to increased potential for conflict[148] and reduced adaptability to a changing environment,[149] as well as reducing the potential for innovation.

What a Crisis is Good for

I will not go into detail about the positive effects of a crisis, but it can have them. Reduced company performance can have a motivating effect on its employees. Sometimes crucial changes can only be made in a high-pressure situation since internal resistance can block more risky decisions, or some decisions may be delayed because they are not perceived as sufficiently

---

[144] (Hardy, 1987)
[145] (Callahan, 1987)
[146] (Staw, Sandelands, & Dutton, 1982) (Barker III & Mone, 1998)
[147] (Cameron, Whetten, & Kim, 1987), (Staw, Sandelands, & Dutton, 1982), (Barker III & Mone, 1998)
[148] (Cameron, Kim, & Whetton, 1987)
[149] (Buschmann, 2006, S. 21).

important when a company seems to be performing well. The higher pressure of a crisis may lead to quicker decisions.[150]

---

[150] (Zimmermann F. M., 1989)

Why Companies Fail

There are many reasons for corporate crises that lead to corporate failures, but many of the reasons are similar. Most lenders and managers haven't learned to recognize the symptoms of oncoming "illness" in their business.[151] In some cases, managers simply ignore even obvious signs, instead hoping that things will improve. In other cases, managers don't know how to deal with the crisis and don't want to admit that they are the wrong people to handle it. Some companies that get into a crisis don't have a detailed enough understanding of how cash is generated,[152] leading to them not knowing which products or services are the most profitable and what to focus on if cash is scarce. In other cases, guilt can be a factor as managers worry that had they been better at their jobs they wouldn't be facing failure.[153]

Firms may experience a decline in performance due to both external and internal factors.[154] Research suggests that industry-based or environmental causes often affect all firms within an industry,[155] but how severely a company experiences the effects depends on how the management responds.[156] Corporate culture is often to blame for a downturn, at least in part, so the corporate culture must be one that embraces change.[157]

Sometimes, when a company's founder is still on board, they believe that they are the only one who can run the company and rescue it from collapse. However, a founder who runs a start-up is not always the right person to manage a corporation, and a corporation in crisis is another matter altogether. There are management skills to handle all kind of scenarios, but a specialist with experience in similar situations is the best choice in a crisis. Not all managers are born to manage and make the difficult decisions necessary in a crisis; companies often get into trouble because management procrastinates when it comes to making decisions.[158]

---

[151] (Collard, 2002, p. 28)
[152] (O'Callaghan, 2010, p. 126)
[153] (Collard, 2002, p. 25)
[154] (Lohrke, Bedeian, & Palmer, 2004)
[155] (Melin, 1985); (Ramanujam, 1984); (Pearce & Robbins, 1993)
[156] compare (Slatter & Lovett, 2004); (Haveman, 1992); (Hedburg, Nystrom, & Starbuck, 1976)
[157] (Roman, 2010, p. 35)
[158] (Collard, 2002, p. 26)

Within owner-managed companies, chronic failure to achieve stated business goals suggests a problem far more serious than lack of performance. Often it implies a lack of clarity regarding the owner's goals, and it usually indicates a failure to secure management team buy-in.[159]

There is evidence that problem firms utilize leasing to a greater extent than non-problem firms.[160] Some firms that have gone bankrupt expanded rapidly before they failed, and their expansion was financed by increased debt and preferred stock rather than common stock and retained earnings.[161] It is likely that this expansion was financed with off-balance-sheet leases.[162] The closer a company gets to bankruptcy, the higher the lease and debt costs are, often leading companies to have higher financing costs than profitability rates.

---

[159] (Collard, 2002, p. 29)
[160] (Altman E. I., 1976, p. 409)
[161] (Deakin, 1972)
[162] (Altman E. I., 1976, p. 409)

Success of Turnaround Strategies

A turnaround involves a number of negative forces, a general lack of resources, and exceptional time pressures. It is an "abnormal period" that "requires unique management approaches".[163] In discussing the feasibility and success of these turnaround strategies, Hofer compares the actions taken by management and the performance results produced by these actions with the strategic recommendations for 12 companies in ten different industries over 30 years.[164] The results show that performance improved in six cases where the management applied the recommended strategies mentioned above. In the other six cases the management did not apply the recommended strategies, and all six had weakening performance. Two further observations[165] were that the management responded in 83 percent that operating strategies were applied in the other 17 percent, the company was liquidated. It seems as though Hofer's sample were open to applying operating strategies to turnaround situations, but his sample is very small and may not be representative of turnarounds in general. Hofer also observed that, in four of six cases, the applied turnaround strategy failed. The problem may have been that an operating turnaround was conducted when there should have been a strategic turnaround. (In fact, management of companies in the sample seldom adopted strategic turnaround strategies at all.) There are several possible reasons for management's preference for operating turnarounds:

- A strategic turnaround is often possible only in certain "strategic windows", while operating turnarounds are possible at any time and are not directly dependent on the market. These windows could open with an emerging segment of the market, a competitor that fails to see an opportunity, or the recognition of some strategic advantages that the company did not see before.
- Strategic turnarounds often take longer to pay off, while an operating turnaround usually pays off quickly if it is implemented correctly.

---

[163] (Bibeault, Corporate Turnaround: How Managers Turn Losers into Winners, 1981)
[164] (Hofer, 1980)
[165] (Hofer, Turnaround strategies, 1980)

In the other two cases where the turnaround failed, it appears that the companies were utilizing the wrong operating strategies to turn themselves around and that that the management systematically overlooked or discounted the benefits of strategic turnaround.[166]

---

[166] (Hofer, 1980)

What is the ITMS?

The International Turnaround Management Standard™ (ITMS) is a management environment created to establish a controlled and structured way for a company and its stakeholders to achieve a successful turnaround.

The ITMS is a guided method to achieve a sustainable turnaround that includes all possible business areas that need to be analyzed and considered when restructuring a company:

- Financial strategies
- Operational strategies
- HR
- Communications management
- Project management techniques and methods
- Change management
- Controlling
- Risk management
- Marketing
- Quality control
- Process improvement
- And more

The goal of the ITMS is to divide the situations in which troubled companies find themselves into different stages, components, and subcomponents so a CEO/Turnaround Manager can identify the situation and find strategies to successfully turn the company around. For example, if a company is producing products that don't sell well, it operates in a competitive environment with a few global players that practically own the market, and it is in financial difficulties, the Turnaround Manager or CEO will find the situation in the ITMS, which will then provide them with proven strategies and ways out of that situation (if there is a way out). The ITMS is backed up by approximately 150 analyzed case studies of successful turnarounds in the available literature from which as many strategies as possible have been created.

The ITMS serves as a guide to what the Turnaround Leader needs to do, at what time to do it, how to do it, to whom they need to provide information, and more. The ITMS targets all the major problems and aspects of why companies fail in turnarounds: insufficient support by shareholders and lenders; bad management; wrong product-market mix; non-comprehensive turnarounds (where things are simply overseen or not regarded as important); targeting of symptoms rather than issues; unstructured approaches; and so on. All of these issues are targeted by the ITMS.

The ITMS is designed so that people who have not worked together before can start to collaborate quickly on a turnaround to produce an advantageous outcome.

An ITMS turnaround process has the following characteristics:

- There is a defined end to the turnaround process.
- The outcome is defined and measurable.
- The activities are related in order to achieve results.
- The resources are clearly defined and organized.
- Responsibilities are defined.
- The management of the turnaround process is structured and controlled.

A turnaround process is temporary in nature and is created to achieve specific results, objectives, or benefits for its stakeholders. The turnaround process covers strategic, financial, operational, and change management tactics and strategies in order to achieve these results.

IT Issues

The IT department is a support and consulting department during the turnaround unless the company has key IT-related problems. However, the Turnaround Leader needs to be aware that the people working in the IT department are usually technology-orientated people who want to upgrade to the newest and fastest technology. They are very useful because they can make processes more efficient from an IT point of view and can provide insight into ways to achieve substantial savings. Ideally, the Turnaround Leader should establish a process to inform the IT department of all changes and obtain a dedicated resource to become a part of the team, watching for possible systems implications of actions taken.[167]

---

[167] (Roman, 2010, p. 55)

Legal Issues

Legal issues are usually excluded from this standard because they are individual to each country. However, the legal department of the company is a key partner of the TMT and should advise on risk and help make things happen in a legally compliant way.[168] Local adaptions of the ITMS for specific countries are a suggested area for future research.

---

[168] (Roman, 2010, p. 54)

What is the ITMS?

The Structure of the ITMS

The ITMS consists of "components", "support components", "stages", and "processes".

Seven Components

The professional work within the company is done in the components. The components include strategies, and each subcomponent triggers different work packages. Specifics about these packages are not part of the overall structure of this standard since they go into considerable detail.

The components are:

- The Diagnostic Review Component (DR)
- The Emergency Procedures Component (EP)
- The Process Improvements Component (PI)
- The Financial Restructuring Component (FR)
- The Strategic Restructuring Component (SR)
- The Operative Restructuring Component (OR)
- The Marketing and Sales Improvements Component (MS)

Each component includes various subcomponents (e.g. EP consists of EP 1, EP 2, EP 3, and so on). The Diagnostic Review Component is divided into an analysis phase and an evaluation phase.

Ten Support Components

Support components, which are structured along the seven components, keep the turnaround process structured, organized, and controlled. The support components consist of:

- The Pre-Turnaround Component (PC)
- The Starting the Turnaround Process Component (SP)
- The Directing the Turnaround Component (DT)
- The Crisis Stabilization Component (CS)

- The Turnaround Component (TS)
- The Planning the Turnaround Process Component (PT)
- The Communication Procedures Component (CP)
- The Risk Management Component (RM)
- The Change Management Component (CM)
- The Closing the Turnaround Component (CT)

Four Stages

The four stages, which are bound by their definitions, divide certain activities.

- The *Pre-Turnaround Stage* includes PC, SP, and parts of CP. The Pre-Turnaround Stage includes all activities that are carried out before a formal and in-depth review of the organization can begin, from the recognition that a turnaround is needed to planning the diagnostic review.
- The *Diagnostic Review Stage* includes DR, and parts of CP, RM, PT, and DT. The diagnostic review includes all activities involved in analyzing the company, its environment, and its strengths and weaknesses. Toward the end of the Diagnostic Review Stage, the TMT formulates strategies and plans the turnaround process.
- The *Crisis Stabilization Stage* includes PI, FR, SR, OR, CP, RM, CM, and DT. During the Crisis Stabilization Stage the focus is on generating cash flow, stopping the loss of resources, and stabilizing the firm.
- The *Turnaround Stage* includes PI, FR, SR, OR, CP, RM, CM, DT, and CT. In the Turnaround Stage the focus is on improving operations, developing competitive advantages, and putting the company back on a stable footing.

Four Processes

Change Control / Out-of-Tolerance Management

Change control ensures that, if something does not go as planned or goes beyond the pre-set tolerance levels, the matter is handled in a structured and controlled way, involving all required stakeholders in that process. Change control ensures the proper flow of information within the company and between the company and outside stakeholders.

Quality Review

The quality review process ensures that the turnaround is performed according to the business case and the Turnaround Plan is undertaken in accordance with the needs of major stakeholders.

Risk Management

Risk management ensures that risks are properly recorded, classified, and monitored throughout the turnaround process. If a risk becomes serious, automatic risk control steps in with the creation of a preliminary exemption plan, which then develops into an exemption plan if the risk becomes immanent.

Change Management

Change management ensures the maximum possible support from outside stakeholders and employees by communicating the proper information at the right time to the right people, and by motivating employees with compensation programs, involvement in the turnaround process, open-door policies, and a three-step change of the corporate environment. Change management also involves changing the corporate culture if necessary.

Justification

Several studies have addressed the relevance of turnaround management. In Germany alone, the number of insolvencies grew from 22,344 companies in 1995 to 36,843 in 2005.[169] These

---

[169] (Statistisches Bundesamt, 2008, p. 489)

insolvencies cost Germany 168,000 jobs and about 22.8 billion euros in outstanding debt.[170] The trend decreased slightly in 2007 to 29,160 insolvencies,[171] but increased again in 2008 and 2009 because of the declining economy. The following picture shows how the number of insolvencies grew in Germany from 2000 to 2007.

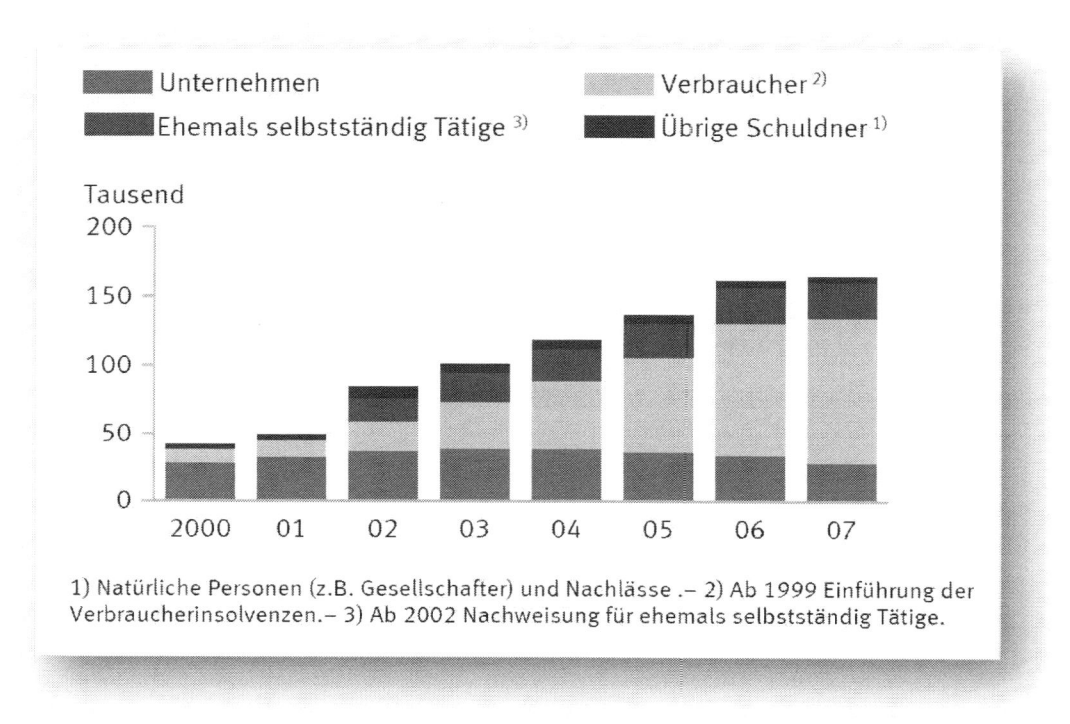

Picture 8 Development of insolvencies in Germany from 2000 to 2007[172]

The first and best justification for the ITMS is that there is nothing else like it; there was no structured, controlled way to restructure a company until the ITMS was created. Although there has been much academic research into the causes and consequences of corporate restructuring—for example, documenting how restructuring affects companies' stock prices—much less is known about the practice of restructuring.[173] The ITMS is essentially based on every book and article available on turnaround management.

---

[170] (Crone & Werner, 2007, p. 2)
[171] (Statistisches Bundesamt, 2008, p. 489)
[172] Statistisches Bundesamt, Statistisches Jahrbuch 2008 p. 489
[173] (Gilson, 2010, p. 3)

Only 38 percent of all companies that find themselves in a turnaround situation actually make the turnaround, and only 22 percent achieve sustainable returns.[174] The ITMS is intended to help increase this number by offering a structured and standardized turnaround process in addition to an analysis of which strategies and measures have actually led to successful turnarounds.

Until the introduction of the ITMS, few books were published that included real research into the strategies behind successful turnarounds, so most of what happened inside these companies was still a closed book.[175] The ITMS is based on over 150 case studies of successful turnarounds and will be extended further in the future. Many companies recognize the need to restructure too late, by which time fewer options remain and saving the company may be more difficult.[176] Leading a company out of a crisis is probably the most difficult challenge for a corporate captain—a management challenge of the highest order.[177] Not even the most successful and experienced Turnaround Leaders can retain the strategies employed in 150 successful cases and most available literature in their heads when taking on the difficult and often seemingly impossible challenge of leading a sick company back to health.

Although there has been much academic research into the causes and consequences of corporate restructuring—for example, documenting how restructuring affects companies stock prices—much less is known about the practice of restructuring.[178] The ITMS defines the practice of restructuring in a way that provides the Turnaround Leader with the necessary information at the time they need it, without them having to research the best possible strategies. If the Turnaround Leader follows the ITMS, they will minimize the risk of overlooking or forgetting a crucial activity, such as controlling a risk or informing a stakeholder. The standard will tell the Turnaround Leader whom to inform at what time. This type of decision-making process will greatly contribute to the long-term success and stability of any turnaround activity.[179]

Most extant turnaround studies have been conducted on manufacturing industries. A few studies have drawn on a sample that presents an in-depth view of a particular industry or type of industry (other than the concentrated industry often found at mature industrial stages),[180]

---

[174] (Buschmann, 2006, p. 30)
[175] (Gilson, 2010, p. 3)
[176] (Gilson, 2010, p. 3)
[177] (Bibeault, Corporate Turnaround: How Managers Turn Losers into Winners, 1981, p. 361)
[178] (Simonsen & Cassady, 2007)
[179] (Roman, 2010, p. 176)
[180] (O'Neill H. M., 1986)

but there are also major variations in the methods used to study the theory. The Turnaround Management Society (TMS) study that this standard is based on includes over 150 cases from all industries. A comparison of failed companies and companies that did not fail shows the differing factors between the two groups.[181] The conclusion shows that managing the factors that make a firm successful can reverse a decline. For example, successful companies are less resistant to change than unsuccessful companies, they avoid big projects that can become albatrosses, and they plan more.[182]

Existing research suggests that voluntary or pre-emptive restructuring can generate more value than restructuring carried out under the imminent threat of bankruptcy or a hostile takeover.[183] However, not all companies implement restructuring before a crisis hits.

Still, further research is needed to determine whether monitoring mechanisms, "e.g. executing compensation in the form of stock options linked to turnaround success, the use of external board members [as proposed in this standard], and the influence of large blocks of institutional shareholders actually curtail such managerial opportunism" (such as poison pills that serve only the short-term interest of top management), and whether they support or obstruct recovery through turnarounds.[184]

Differences from PRINCE2™ and Other Project Management Methods

Turnaround Leaders or project managers with PRINCE2 experience are likely to understand the ITMS quickly and to find familiar structures. PRINCE2 has influenced this standard, but the ITMS is not nearly as complex or specific. The primary differences between PRINCE2 and the ITMS are as follows:

- ITMS is more logical in its flow.
- ITMS's flow of activities is orientated on a timescale. Companies that use it can see at any point what activities need to be done at what stage and time throughout the turnaround process.

---

[181] (Altman E. , 1968), (Ross & Kami, 1973), (Argenti, 1976)
[182] (Argenti, 1976)
[183] (Gordon, 1994)
[184] (Lohrke, Bedeian, & Palmer, 2004)

- ITMS provides a checklist of activities derived from other turnarounds, restructurings, case studies, experiences, and collected reports of lessons learned so that nothing will be forgotten or overlooked and pitfalls will be avoided during the analysis of the company and the turnaround process, leading to a sustainable result.
- A company that uses ITMS can quickly identify the stage at which the company is operating, the situation they are facing, and the proven strategies they need to implement to successfully complete the turnaround process. In this way, the processes are speeded up and become more sustainable.
- Even CEOs who don't have much turnaround experience can easily employ the ITMS, identify their situation, and work toward turning their companies around using proven techniques, outlined checklists throughout all of the components, and guided procedures.
- ITMS manages the flow of information and distributes the right information at the right time to the right parties. It counters the need for banks to employ investigating accountants who may damage the management's reputation, and helps to maintain the support of investors and stakeholders by openly but thoughtfully communicating on the important issues at crucial times.
- Controlling is done within the stages at regular intervals.
- Effective turnaround plans have to include doing things better (process improvements) as well as doing better things (redirecting strategies).[185] The ITMS includes process improvements as core components of the standard.

---

[185] (Slatter & Lovett, 2004, p. 260)

What is the ITMS?

Benefits of Using the ITMS

The ITMS has advantages for the company in trouble, the Turnaround Leader, the turnaround project itself, and other parties involved in the turnaround process, such as stakeholders. Some of the benefits that a single structured method for turnaround projects can bring are as follows:

- The turnaround is carried out in a structured way.
- The turnaround management method can be repeated.
- The turnaround management method can be taught.
- The turnaround management builds on experience.
- Problems are indicated early throughout the turnaround process.
- Every person involved in key functions has a clearly defined role and knows what to expect, what to do, and how, when, and where to do it.
- Problems, issues and tasks that run out of tolerance are dealt with in a specially designed way.
- Communication is structured.
- Using a systemic approach, the remedies are aimed to redesign the operational structure rather than to apply a quick patch that will not last long.[186]
- The turnaround process has a controlled and organized beginning, middle, and end.
- Components are regularly reviewed against the Turnaround Plan and the Turnaround Business Case.
- Decision points are flexible.
- If components are out of tolerance or deviations occur, automatic management controls are triggered.
- It ensures the involvement of stakeholders at the right time throughout the turnaround management component.
- It provides clear and proven communication channels between the TMT and the rest of the company.
- It provides agreement on the required outcomes at the beginning and continuously monitors the actual situation against the requirements.

---

[186] (Roman, 2010, p. 11)

Advantages for the Troubled Firm

Firms that apply the ITMS can gain the following advantages:

- A controlled way of handling change in terms of investments and the return on investments
- A controlled environment for turnaround management situations
- Active involvement of users and stakeholders throughout the process to ensure that the outcome will provide the greatest possible benefits and returns for the stakeholders and the company
- An approach that distinguishes the TMT from the company board so that the approach is the same regardless of the industry in which the troubled company operates
- Benefits provided to the board and stakeholders of a company through a controllable way of using resources that manages the risks connected to a turnaround situation effectively
- A common language for all parties involved in the turnaround process
- Clear communication between subcomponents and task owners
- In most cases, interconnected key action items in the Turnaround Plan so "no department can operate in complete isolation from the rest of the business"[187]
- Formally recognized ITMS responsibilities within the turnaround process with a focus on what needs to be delivered, when, by whom, why, and how it needs to be done
- Easier and quicker access to private equity investors' money, since the analysis and due diligence of the troubled company is done independently by the TMT

Advantages for Turnaround Leaders

Turnaround Leaders using the ITMS can:

- Provide brief and regular management reports
- Establish terms of reference as a prerequisite to the start of the turnaround process
- Perform communication, authority, and delegation in a defined structure
- Divide the turnaround process into manageable stages in order to plan accurately

---

[187] (Roman, 2010, p. 27)

- Ensure the commitment of required resources and funding before every stage by obtaining and ensuring approval
- Keep meetings between the TMT and the stakeholders at a minimum but ensure that they take place at vital points throughout the turnaround process
- Keep their hands free to focus on what is important and what they do best

Advantages for Stakeholders

The ITMS provides stakeholders with several advantages as they can:

- Participate in quality checks during the turnaround management component
- Ensure that their requirements are met or in other ways satisfied
- Be informed right away if something goes wrong without being directly involved in the turnaround process because ITMS uses "management by exception", so the turnaround management has certain tolerances in which it can operate freely and outside of which notifications are triggered
- Be informed about the progress of the turnaround process at regular intervals
- Participate in the turnaround process on the advisory board

The Seven Components

The Diagnostic Review Component (DR)

There is seldom only one reason for business troubles.[188] The Diagnostic Review (or evaluation) Stage of a turnaround involves conducting a viability analysis of the firm and preparing a plan with specific actions in order to solve the problems of the business in the short term.[189] The diagnostic review should be carried out by experienced Turnaround Leaders as they know what to look for and can evaluate the situation realistically and quickly. The diagnostic review is essential to ensure that the business is capable of being turned around and that it can survive whilst a detailed business plan is developed and implemented.[190] Often Turnaround Leaders want to undertake the review themselves as they are the ones who are responsible for a successful turnaround, and also because it is a good way to get to know the staff and the processes in the company, and to get a first impression of the necessary support from stakeholders. The Turnaround Leader may be supported by accountants or external business consultants.

The seven primary objectives of the diagnostic review are:

1. To evaluate whether the company can survive in the short term, with or without external funding, in order to have enough time to conduct a viable business plan
2. To evaluate whether the company can survive in the medium and long term
3. To consider four options for outcomes—insolvency, immediate disposal, turnaround, or workout—in order to find the best possible option for the shareholders
4. To conduct the first high-level diagnosis of the most important problems, whether they are operational or strategic in nature (or both), as there is no time at this stage for in-depth analysis
5. To produce a first broad outline of available strategies and actions that are necessary to survive in the short term once these key problems are identified
6. To identify where the stakeholders stand, the level of support from each of them for a possible turnaround, and their bargaining power

---

[188] (Collard, 2002, p. 31)
[189] (Bibeault, 1981, p. 203)
[190] (Slatter & Lovett, 2004, p. 104)

7. To perform an initial evaluation of the company's management in terms of who would support a turnaround, who would need to leave, what are the key positions in the company, whether some members of the management caused the crisis, and how willing the management is to accept orders from the TMT

The turnaround consultant starts the initial diagnosis by identifying the root causes of the failure.[191] For that, the consultant needs to take a holistic view of the entire operation: people, processes, and culture. The analysis may take anything from a few days for a small company to several weeks or months for a large firm, but typically there will be pressure to report back to the board of stakeholders quickly with findings, conclusions, and recommendations.[192] Generally, it is better to get 80 percent of the answer within a month than to spend six months getting 100 percent.[193]

Getting to the real issues is the first step to change and recovery.[194] Analysis of sales and profit centers and asset utilization should indicate where the real problems—not the symptoms—are located.[195] In the Diagnostic Review Stage, it is important to focus on the seven key objectives. The analysis will be broad in scope, covering the business's strategy, competitive position, core operations, and current financial position; it is unlikely to include extensive analysis in any of these areas[196] so the Turnaround Leader should not get caught up in details that are not essential for determining the need for a turnaround process.

The diagnostic review should emphasize business units that are not performing well. In large companies it will not be possible to evaluate all business units at this stage, although doing so is important before any detailed strategic analysis is undertaken in order to categorize operating companies roughly into "winners", "losers", and "satisfactory but unexciting".[197] The Turnaround Leader should meet with the management responsible for each operating unit and evaluate the available financial data in order to determine which units are running well and which are not.

---

[191] (Roman, 2010, p. 57)
[192] (Slatter & Lovett, 2004, p. 105)
[193] (Slatter & Lovett, 2004, p. 232)
[194] (Collard, 2002, p. 31)
[195] (Collard, 2002, p. 27)
[196] (Slatter & Lovett, 2004, p. 105)
[197] (Slatter & Lovett, 2004, p. 106)

Diagnostic Review: Analysis Phase (DR AP)

Before conducting a turnaround, the company should determine whether the turnaround is feasible in the first place by examining the market, the industry, and the competitive environment. The wrong turnaround strategy may not cause the company to fail immediately, but it can drain the company's resources to the point at which a proper turnaround is no longer possible.[198]

The diagnostic review is an intense version of due diligence. The DR AP is important because precise goals cannot be set and initiatives begun without understanding the current situation.[199] Restructuring is more likely to be successful when managers understand the fundamental business/strategic problem or opportunity that their company faces.[200]

In the Diagnostic Analysis Stage, attention should first be focused on a viability analysis, then a financial analysis, a competitive analysis, and finally an analysis of the people. Financial resources are important in the short term and might need to be available quickly so decisions based on the financial analysis of the company should be made as early as possible.

A schema exists based on four generally accepted principles for a successful program to raise the performance of a company:[201]

1. Costs and prices tend to decline.
2. A company's options depend on its competitive position.
3. The customer requirements and the earnings potential change continuously.
4. Simplicity leads to good results.

There are questions and analysis tools for each of these principles that can help to evaluate a company's position and options for action.[202] Their schema is not comprehensive enough for a

---

[198] (Hofer, 1980)
[199] compare (N.A., 2009, p. 7)
[200] (Simonsen & Cassady, 2007, p. 6)
[201] (Gottfredson, Schaubert, & Saenz, 2008), compare (N.A., 2009, p. 8)
[202] (Gottfredson, Schaubert, & Saenz, 2008)

company-wide analysis, but it is integrated into the Diagnostic Review Stage and referenced throughout.

To date, there has only been limited empirical research into Top Management Teams TMT scanning behaviors in turnaround situations.[203] In order to choose a turnaround process, it is necessary to know the internal and external environment. In deciding on the best turnaround strategy, turnaround consultants tend to focus on gathering internal information.[204] Given the need for strategic realignment following stabilization, however, it is likely that a TMT would need to scan both a firm's internal and external environments to decide whether to implement an operating or strategic recovery strategy.[205] Scanning is necessary throughout the whole turnaround process, which is why turnaround files such as the Issue Log and Risk Log need to be created.

The signs that a company is in trouble are often symptoms rather than the causes of the trouble,[206] and signs and causes need to be treated differently. For example, losing money is a symptom, but the cause is something else. Failing to identify and fix the root causes that led to failure in the first place will result in a highly unstable turnaround action.[207]

The timeframe for a thorough analysis of a troubled company can vary significantly depending on the size of the company, the structure, the business model, and the reporting and controlling information already available within the company.

- If the company is small and in serious trouble, the evaluation should take from two days to two weeks.[208] At the beginning, such an analysis can be daunting because there are so many starting points.
- If the company is of medium size and is not in imminent danger of collapse, thirty to ninety days are usually sufficient.[209]

---

[203] (Lohrke, Bedeian, & Palmer, 2004)
[204] (Fredenberger, Lipp, & Watson, 1997)
[205] (Lohrke, Bedeian, & Palmer, 2004)
[206] compare (Collard, 2002, p. 25)
[207] (Roman, 2010, p. 57)
[208] (Bibeault, 1981, p. 204)
[209] (Bibeault, 1981, p. 204)

- If the company is large and in severe trouble, anywhere from three to 12 months may be needed.

Diagnostic Review: Evaluation Stage (DR ES)

The diagnostic review in the Evaluation Stage addresses the outcome of the company analysis, classified and structured in a way that the executive team can make decisions about the chances of the company's survival.

The TMT will base possible turnaround strategies on the corporate analysis and its environment outline, which will be presented to the board in the Turnaround Initiation Document (TID) along with the complete analysis and proposed strategies.

Emergency Procedures (EP)

Emergency Procedures are activities that must be started right away because the company is running out of time or money. These procedures are undertaken parallel to the planning.

EP is a set of techniques to handle the most pressing problems of the company as quickly as possible so the issues that are leaking the most cash will be put on hold or stopped completely. EP can be used throughout the turnaround process if a new problem becomes obvious in order to adapt quickly to changing conditions.

The question of when Emergency Procedures should be started is explained by Bibeault: "The real deciding factor about how fast or slow and in what fashion to move is the state of your cash flow. If you've got plenty of cash and your pile is not being depleted at an alarming rate, then take out your planning book, get your analysts and study. If you are bleeding, pull out your scalpel; if you are in danger of not surviving, get out your ax."[210]

The question of how long after the Turnaround Leader comes on board EP should be implemented depends on the Turnaround Leader. Some might take immediate action to stop the most severe bleeding, while others might wait until the Diagnostic Review Stage is

---

[210] (Bibeault, 1981, pp. 227-228)

completed. What is important is to take action when it is needed and to have quick and good intuition about what situation the company is in, and this is why the basic company analysis is so important. The Turnaround Leader should have the most important information as soon as they start, or even before, in order to take a quick overview of how serious the situation is.

The EP stage generally involves shrinking back to those segments of business that have achieved or can achieve good gross margins and can compete effectively in the marketplace.[211] In particular, assets may need to be reduced and converted into cash, and expenses cut.

Financial Restructuring (FR)

Poor financial performance is usually caused by poor management.[212] The Financial Restructuring (FR) component described here is mainly written for independent companies, holdings, and parent companies. Companies that are subsidiaries of parent companies usually have other sources of financing that are not described in detail in the FR component.

The overall objective of FR is to achieve a debt and equity structure that enables the company to implement its turnaround plans, to meet all its ongoing liabilities as they fall due (i.e. to be solvent), and to fund its strategic redirection where appropriate.[213] In normal operations, it is management's responsibility to create value for the company's shareholders, but in a turnaround situation it is management's priority to achieve stability, after which the first priority becomes restoring value. This change in focus can create concern among the funding stakeholders, but when their money is invested in an unstable environment it is unlikely they will achieve above average returns on their investments so they should be interested in restabilizing the company.

It is critical that any restructuring proposal recognizes the best option available to the stakeholders and clearly shows them that it is in their best interest to support the business plan and the proposed financial structure.[214]

---

[211] (Bibeault, 1981, p. 264)
[212] (Slatter & Lovett, 2004, p. 121)
[213] (Slatter & Lovett, 2004, p. 308)
[214] (Slatter & Lovett, 2004, p. 309)

The FR component can be split into two stages. Not all companies will need the first stage, which is designed to support short-term survival, if they started the turnaround early. The second stage is concerned with the capital structure and its financial reorganization.

The FR subcomponents are organized along a timeline; some subcomponents can or should begin during the Crisis Stabilization Stage and others can or should begin during the Turnaround Stage.

Some research suggests that a company can encourage its managers to restructure early, before a significant crisis evolves, by increasing its debt load.[215] However, equity incentives are not very widespread.[216] Other research suggests that FR is usually avoided until a crisis becomes obvious, a takeover is likely, or bankruptcy is possible in the near future.[217]

Financial Restructuring During the Crisis Stabilization Stage (FR CS)

In the Crisis Stabilization Stage (FR CS) the focus is on improving the cash flow with the goal of achieving a positive cash flow to keep the company alive, pay its dues, and if possible have cash left over to invest during the Turnaround Stage.

It is important for companies in this situation to manage their cash tightly from an operational standpoint by finding ways to minimize float: changing banking and lockbox configurations, utilizing international cash flow effectively, selectively extending payables; aggressively reducing inventories and receivables; making judicious use of leasing in place of direct capital investment; and exploiting a number of other devices to maximize the use of working capital.[218]

---

[215] compare (Wruck, 1994)
[216] (Dial & Murphey, 1995)
[217] (Denis, Denis, & Sarin, 1997)
[218] (Bibeault, 1981, p. 303)

Financial Restructuring During the Turnaround Stage (FR TS)

Prior to 1992 much of the research conducted into turnaround management focused on strategy[219] while less was focused on financial measures such as retrenchment. Liquidity improvements in the Turnaround Stage have less to do with the sale of assets than with management practice. The focus is on improving profitability rather than gaining a positive cash flow, as is the focus in the Crisis Stabilization Stage.

Strategic Restructuring (SR)

The Strategic Restructuring (SR) subcomponents are organized along a timeline with an emphasis on strategy changes, so some subcomponents can or should begin during the Crisis Stabilization Stage and others can or should begin during the Turnaround Stage. Transforming a company usually involves overhead reductions, downsizing, process optimization, and workforce reductions.[220] The SR component is mainly concerned with the strategic implications of these actions, but also of others.

Performance is a derivative of the strategy change, and strategies can be divided into those that involve a change in the organization's strategy for competing in the same business and those that call for entering a new business or businesses.[221] Most strategic turnarounds are built around key skills in marketing, production, and/or engineering.[222] [223]

One of the first attempts to identify combinations of strategies for corporate restructuring was based on 54 US-based companies that achieved a sustainable turnaround between 1952 and 1971.[224] They demand a new strategic focus for companies that have strategic problems while operative problems demand business performance-related actions.[225] Some studies analyze strategic prescriptions associated with the generic turnaround strategy in the commercial

---

[219] compare (Castrogiovanni & Bruton, 2000) (Harker, 1996)
[220] (Hamel & Prahalad, 1996, p. 6)
[221] (Hofer, 1980)
[222] (Hofer, 1980)
[223] Hofer focused only on saving the business and distinguished among turnarounds that seek no change in market share, those that seek one-level shifts in share (changes of about 100%), and those that seek two-level shifts in share (of about 200%).
[224] compare (Schendel, Patton, & Riggs, 1976, p. 3ff)
[225] (Schendel, Patton, & Riggs, 1976, p. 11)

banking industry[226] while others assert that formal strategic planning in banking has advantages (i.e. increases profitability), at least when formal planners are compared to non-planners.[227] However, "the studies that have been done are not consistent in their findings".[228] For example, it appears that strategic planning does not improve performance in service industries,[229] while firms that face a severe decline require a strategic response.[230]

Strategic turnarounds are attempts to enter new businesses or to gain a substantial position in a firm's current business. Refocusing product-market is an example of a strategic turnaround choice.[231] The turnaround prescriptions developed in the durable goods industries are found to be valid predictors in the commercial banking industry.[232]

Existing research[233] attempts to identify the content of successful strategies in the banking industry and the resource allocation required to promote a turnaround under the circumstance of relative decline, but most turnaround studies have been done in the manufacturing industries.

Few studies are drawn from a sample that represents an in-depth view of a particular industry or type of industry (other than the concentrated industry often found at mature industrial stages).[234]
Some research has been done by comparing companies that have continuously declined with companies that have reached a turnaround.[235] Others attempt to identify factors that accompany the turnaround effort.[236]

---

[226] (Hofer & Schendel, 1978), (Porter M. E., 1979)
[227] Wood and LaForge
[228] (O'Neill H. M., 1986)
[229] (Fulmer & Rue, 1973)
[230] (Stanwick, 1992)
[231] (Hambrick & Schecter, 1983)
[232] (O'Neill H. M., 1986)
[233] (O'Neill H. M., 1986)
[234] (O'Neill H. M., 1986)
[235] compare (Hofer, 1980) (Schendel, Patton, & Riggs, 1976) (Schendel & Patton, 1976)
[236] (Bibeault, 1981)

Designing Strategic Turnarounds

Before beginning a strategic turnaround, a Turnaround Leader must examine the industry, the competition, and the stages of evolution of the company's products. A strategic turnaround is appropriate when the business has a non-crisis current operating position but has lost its strategic position,[237] but I want to extend strategic turnarounds to situations that are in accordance with my definition of a turnaround situation. Most strategic turnarounds occur when a company faces a heavy decline in profits, sales, and market share so the primary method of distinguishing between different strategic turnaround strategies is based on a loss of market share and a drop in sales. There are four possible options for responses to such situations:

1. The business can focus on increasing sales or market share for one or more products or in one or more market segments. In terms of asset utilization measures, such as earnings per share (EPS) and return on investment (ROI), a segmentation/niche strategy will be more profitable if the firm is not competing in the shakeout or development stage of its product. The downside is that, unless the niche market or segment is growing considerably, there is only a small chance of gaining a leadership position in the industry in which the company operates.
2. The business can move up one level in its share position, such as from the position of a dropout in the market to a follower, or from the position of a follower in the market to a competitor, or from a competitor to a market leader. However, these moves require both financial and non-financial resources that have not been exploited. This strategy usually provides higher dollar sales and net income totals than the segmentation/niche strategy.[238]
3. The business can move up two levels in its share position, such as from a dropout in the market to a competitor or from a follower to a market leader. However, a two-level increase often requires non-monetary strategic resources and financial resources that are 150 to 200 percent more than the company usually generates.
4. A fourth but only rarely achievable possibility is for the business to design the target market in such a way as to increase sales and market share while also protecting the

---
[237] (Hofer, 1980)
[238] (Hofer, 1980)

market from competition. In most cases, however, this strategy is not possible unless there are new segments in the market. If that is the case, the firm would need to develop products that are better than its competitors' products, and it would need superior functional areas that provide services to that market in order to differentiate itself from its competitors. This task is difficult, particularly since competitors who may not be in similar financial difficulties might be able to rise to the challenge.

The second and third opportunities require significant financial resources to invest. A parent company could provide these funds if the troubled firm is part of a group. Shifts of such magnitude are possible when the current leader slips, when there is a major change in the stage of product/market evolution, or when the turnaround firm is a former leader that has recently fallen from that position.[239] In these cases a strategic turnaround has a good chance of success, but at other times it is almost impossible to make major shifts in competitive position with the resources available.[240] In most cases, companies try to achieve a turnaround to increase their sales by applying a one-level shift strategy. However, Hofer argues that there is too much attention given to strategic turnarounds today involving one-level increases in share position and not enough to those that involve segmentation and niche hunting.

Strategic Turnaround Strategies

Some turnarounds fail because the management employs an operating turnaround where a strategic turnaround is needed. Strategic actions take longer to pay off, which is why management inexperienced in turnarounds may prefer to employ an operating strategy.[241] Strategic turnarounds tend to be successful in companies that are not in a weak position overall. While there are exceptions, significant resources are needed for a strategic turnaround that a weak company might not be able to supply. In some cases, a strategic turnaround cannot be started right away; for some strategies, the time needs to be right. For example, a competitor may need to make a certain move or the market may need to evolve to a certain level before a strategic move makes sense or a strategic window opens. Shifts in relative competitive positions

---

[239] (Hofer, 1980)
[240] (Hofer, 1980)
[241] compare (Bibeault, 1981, p. 228)

occur only during times of rapid change in the industry,[242] and in some industries these windows open only once every couple of years. Therefore a strong operating position is useful.

A strategic turnaround builds on the careful analysis of the market, the competition, and the company itself that was conducted during the Diagnostic Review Stage. "In the literature, strategic turnarounds center on offloading business that, from an operational viewpoint, cannot be saved or whose divestments are needed to finance the turnaround of viable units."[243] However, my analysis of over 150 case studies has shown that these are not the only strategic turnaround strategies available for a troubled company.

The following sections address different strategies and strategic moves from the literature and case studies of turnaround management. Strategic moves usually require financial and non-financial resources.[244] However, firms that are in trouble typically cannot produce these resources on their own. In some cases, a parent company or wealthy owner finances the turnaround but, if this is not the case, a combination of operating strategies to free up cash and good relationships with banks and investors is required.

A company's strategic position can be classified as being either a leader in a market, a follower of a leader, or, in the worst case, a dropout. Enormous resources are usually needed to move from one strategic class up to another so strategic turnarounds center on either one-level increases in share position or on segmentation/niche strategies, both of which utilize the strong product position areas at the expense of or by eliminating weak products.[245] To shift a company one level up or to increase market share as a turnaround strategy is financially more promising than a strategy that focuses on creating a new niche as the sales in a new niche will be lower than in an established market. What's more, the change made by gaining leadership in the overall industry is quite small by utilizing a niche strategy as the niche is usually not very big.

To decide what type of turnaround strategy should be chosen, three questions need to be answered:

1. Is the business worth saving or is liquidation a better choice?

---

[242] (Bibeault, 1981, p. 228)
[243] (Bibeault, 1981, p. 227)
[244] (Bibeault, 1981, pp. 227-228)
[245] (Bibeault, 1981, p. 228)

2. Assuming that the business is worth saving, what is the status of its operations?
3. What is the business's strategic health?

To answer the first question it is necessary to determine whether the business can be profitable over the long term, and particularly whether it can earn a good return on the assets invested in it.[246] Before considering a turnaround, the management should ensure that the value of the company as a going concern is greater than its liquidation value.[247]

A close look at the company's operations, the competitive environment, and the industry is necessary in order to answer the second and third questions.

The choice of the right turnaround strategy depends on the company's current operating health as well as its current strategic health. A weak strategic position indicates the need for a strategic turnaround, while if the company is in good strategic health an operating turnaround is the logical choice.

- If the strategic health and the operating health are low, a niche, segmentation, or asset-reduction strategy may be right if the business can use these strategies; otherwise liquidation may be necessary. However, to produce a turnaround from this strategic and operating position strict operating controls are necessary. Alternatively, a combination, revenue-increasing, or asset-reducing operating turnaround might be attempted in the short term followed immediately by a strategic rebuilding effort.[248] Which strategy is best depends on the specific situation.
- If the strategic position is moderate or strong and the operating position is weak, an operating turnaround strategy is usually the best option. In some cases, the sale of the company may be beneficial to the shareholders.
- A strategic turnaround would follow if the strategic position is weak or average and the operating position is average. However, many firms don't recognize the need for a turnaround in this situation even though it is often appropriate.
- If the company is in average operating health and has a strong strategic position, a turnaround is usually not needed. However, some firms in this position undertake

---

[246] (Hofer, 1980)
[247] (Hofer, 1980)
[248] (Hofer, 1980)

plans to increase their operating efficiencies, but this would not be considered a turnaround under the definition used for the purposes of this book.
- A strong operating position but weak strategic positions indicate the need for a strategic turnaround.

Once it is clear what type of broad turnaround strategy is needed based on the company's strategic and operating health, it is time to choose specific strategic actions. These will depend on the industry, strengths, weaknesses, and competitors.

Operating Strategies (OS)

Operating turnarounds are those which are based on actions to increase revenues, actions to decrease assets, actions to decrease costs, or some combination thereof.[249] Asset reduction, cost-cutting and revenue-increasing/-generating strategies, and product-market refocusing are operating strategies.[250] The operating characteristics of the business include such factors as the relative level of direct labor costs and the distance of the firm from its break-even point.[251]

Most successful turnarounds are operating turnarounds and operating turnarounds should emphasize performance targets: increasing revenues; decreasing costs; decreasing assets; or a combination.[252] Therefore any option that improves performance is to be considered whether it makes long-term strategic sense or not. In practice the difference is blurred, but the distinction is necessary because of the different priorities and trade-offs with short-term versus long-term actions.[253]

An operating turnaround can take between six and 12 months—or more—depending on the size of the operation and the root causes of the failure.[254] Some operating improvements will also be found in the Process Improvements (PI) component; they are sorted under Process Improvement because, even though they are operational in nature, they should be seen as an improvement of a special process so they are linked to certain subcomponents of Process Improvement.

---

[249] (O'Neill H. M., 1986)
[250] (Hofer & Schendel, 1978), (Hambrick & Schecter, 1983)
[251] (O'Neill H. M., 1986)
[252] (Hofer, 1980)
[253] (Hofer, 1980)
[254] (Roman, 2010, p. 13)

The selection of the operating strategies that are most useful for a company is based on the company evaluation, but they often involve cost cutting. For those who dare to be creative, who have the guts to cut hard and deep, who have the courage to challenge conventional wisdom, and who possess the drive and leadership to see that improvements happen, the results are there for the taking.[255]

Operating turnarounds differ from strategic turnarounds in important ways. In the short term both may produce similar results, but an operating turnaround is focused on short-term results while a strategic turnaround has the long-term strategic direction in mind. Therefore a strategic turnaround may not compromise long-term goals for short-term gains if those gains are not in line with the strategic direction.

Because of the primary focus on short-term operating actions, the first step in any operating turnaround should be to identify the resources and skills that the business will need in order to implement its long-term strategy so these can be protected during the short-term action program that will follow.[256] Once the resources necessary for implementation of the long-term strategy have been identified, the turnaround strategy can be chosen based on how close the company is to its break-even point.

Firms whose declines are not particularly severe tend to employ operating turnaround strategies that aim for increased efficiency.[257]

There are four principal operating strategies to overcome a corporate crisis:[258]

- Grow sales
- Lower costs
- Sell assets
- Employ combination strategies

---

[255] (Bibeault, 1981, p. 284)
[256] (Hofer, 1980)
[257] (Zimmermann F., 1989)
[258] (Hofer, 1980, S. 19ff)

However, the proposed directions are not sufficiently exact to offer specific actions.[259] The dichotomization of strategic and operating strategies is critical because economic performance measures often have a strategic and operating character.[260] There are several actions to reduce costs that are part strategic and part operational in nature.[261] A study by Hambrick and Schecter analyzed 260 companies in crisis and identified 12 typical variable strategic moves.[262] They used a cluster analysis of 53 successful turnaround cases and identified three combination strategies for successful turnarounds. However, they were not able to identify a specific profile for over half of the successful turnaround cases, indicating that the most common strategic moves are company-specific. They suggest that a company's strategic moves depend on its situation when the turnaround is started, so there is no generally accepted combination of measures that lead to a sustainable turnaround.[263] This book adopts their findings in terms of the diagnostic review and suggests actions based on individual corporate situations.

Operational Restructuring During the Crisis Stabilization Stage (OR CS)

Cost reductions are usually one-shot programs aimed at expendable activities.[264] The literature offers four types of operating turnaround strategies:

1. Cost-cutting strategies
2. Asset-reducing strategies
3. Revenue-generating strategies
4. Combination-effort strategies.

Cost-Cutting Strategies:

If the company has limited financial resources, high fixed costs, or high labor costs, and if it is close to its break-even position, a cost-cutting strategy might be the right choice. The break-even point depends on the industry, but a general rule is that sales are about 60 to 90 percent

---

[259] (Lafrenz, 2004, p. 151)
[260] (Lafrenz, 2004, p. 151)
[261] (Hambrick & Schecter, 1983), (Gless, 1996), compare (Coyle, 2000)
[262] (Hambrick & Schecter, 1983, p. 241ff)
[263] compare (Lafrenz, 2004, p. 153)
[264] (Bibeault, 1981, p. 313)

of break-even.[265] Medium to large cost-cutting actions are often possible in the short term and they show quicker results than asset-reducing or revenue-generating strategies.

Asset-Reducing Strategies:

If the company is at less than 30 percent of its break-even point and if it has limited financial resources, an asset-reducing strategy may be the only feasible option. In this case, there is usually no way to cut costs enough to reach a new break-even point. However, which assets to sell is an important question that depends primarily on which assets are saleable in the first place and on whether the assets will be crucial to the business within the next one to two years. The rest of the assets should be sold off, although a precipitous sale might reduce the price that the company can achieve. Whether a pure asset-reducing strategy should be utilized depends on the future sales potential of the company's products; if future demand is substantially lower than current demand then all non-critical assets should be sold.

The choice between revenue-generating and asset-reducing strategies in such situations depends primarily on the long-term potential of the business after the turnaround is completed and on the firm's financial situation.[266] A revenue-generating strategy is more suitable if the company still has enough financial resources to invest in efforts to increase sales and if demand is high enough to last throughout the turnaround process.

If demand is expected to remain high enough for the next one or two years but financial resources are running low then a combination of asset-reducing and revenue-generating strategies may be indicated. In this case, the company should sell off assets that are not critical and that will give it enough money to fund its revenue-generating efforts for the next six months.

Revenue-Generating Strategies

In an operating turnaround designed to increase a firm's current revenues, almost total attention would be focused on a variety of short-term, revenue-generating actions.[267] In a strategic turnaround, on the other hand, there would be very few actions that were not in line

---

[265] (Hofer, 1980)
[266] (Hofer, 1980)
[267] (Hofer, 1980)

with the company's long-term direction. In a revenue-generating strategy, the company focuses on its current products. If past products can be reintroduced quickly the company might use them to supplement its existing products, and if products that were originally planned to be introduced in the future are ready to be produced the company might bring forward their production in order to optimize its facilities. At the same time, HR in all divisions other than sales will be at low levels and advertising, reduction of sales prices, and promotional campaigns will be undertaken.

Combination-Effort Strategies

A combination-effort strategy may use a combination of asset-reducing, revenue-generating, and cost-reducing efforts. A well-balanced combination of these strategies is usually most effective when the firm's sales are 50-80 percent of its break-even. The cash flow produced by a balanced effort will be sufficiently higher than would be produced by a more narrowly focused strategy that the greater complexities of a balanced effort are more than adequately compensated for.[268] Even so, the costs and benefits of such a strategy should be calculated as the managerial effort required to coordinate a combination strategy turnaround is substantially higher than that needed for a single focus turnaround. Combination strategies are particularly vulnerable when individuals pursue tasks that are relatively unproductive and engage in activities that are not focused because of this multi-focus strategy. Because time is often short, management should pay special attention to all actions that have a significant impact on the cash flow in the short term. Therefore if there is no clear advantage to using a combined strategy, a single focus strategy is preferable.

Which strategies fit the situation best depends on the financial situation of the company, the cash flow projections, and the proximity of the company's sales to the break-even point. The proximity to the break-even point also indicates how severe the strategies need to be.

It is also important that the TMT focuses on the real problems identified in the diagnostic review. Rather than having multiple projects aimed at improving policy and processes, the

---

[268] (Hofer, 1980)

turnaround consultant will remove the "patching the patch" strategy encountered in many failing operational environments.[270]

Sales 60 to 80 Percent of Break-Even

If a firm is relatively close to its break-even point—that is, its sales are 60 to 80 percent of break-even—and it has visible overhead fat, high direct labor costs, high fixed expenses, and limited financial resources then cost-cutting strategies are usually selected.[271] This is a fast way to save money as cost-cutting activities produce results more quickly than revenue-generating or asset-reducing strategies.[272]

Strategies that generate revenue are the best choice when the company has low fixed indirect labor costs. Furthermore, balanced strategies are preferable since they are more complex and may not be handled successfully by a weak organization.[273]

Sales 30 to 60 Percent of Break-Even

When sales are 30 to 60 percent of break-even, it will be all but impossible to reach the break-even point by cost-cutting alone. In this case, the most appropriate turnaround strategies are normally revenue-generating and asset-reducing strategies.[274] The extent of asset reductions necessary varies with the financial situation of the company.

Sales Less Than 30 Percent of Break-Even

If the company's sales are less than 30 percent of the break-even point and if financial resources are very low, asset-reducing strategies will probably be the only option. However, the TMT should not sell assets that are essential to the company's survival within the next two years, and the sale of the remaining assets should be done in a deliberate fashion to avoid write-downs below book value.[275]

---

[270] (Roman, 2010, p. 11)
[271] (Bibeault, 1981, p. 227)
[272] (Bibeault, 1981, p. 227)
[273] (Bibeault, 1981, p. 227)
[274] (Bibeault, 1981, p. 227)
[275] (Bibeault, 1981, p. 227)

Strong Financial Position

Some companies are in the fortunate position to have access to sound financial resources. If the firm is in a strong financial position, it can undertake revenue-generating strategies that utilize its resources in the medium term.[276]

Weak Financial Position

A weak financial position is, however, more likely during a crisis situation. The situation the company is in also depends on what triggered the crisis and what stage the crisis is in. If finances are critical and capacity is already utilized, then the firm will probably have to consider a combination of revue-generating tactics financed by an asset-reducing strategy.[277]

Operating Strategies During the Turnaround Stage (OS TS)

Operating strategies in the Turnaround Stage are different from those in the Crisis Stabilization Stage because they are more focused on profit improvements than on limiting losses and downsizing. The operating strategies employed at this stage will be important for the company to run in the long term and will directly affect its competitive advantage and its ability to survive long after the turnaround process has been completed. Profit improvement is achieved by systematic programs rather than by one-shot cost reductions: remaining plants are made more efficient rather than being shut down on a wholesale basis; manufacturing efficiencies are achieved by brainpower rather than by surgery; inventory management is intensified; and overheads are evaluated on a cost/benefit basis rather than simply lopped off.[278]

Operational subcomponents in the Turnaround Stage can also be connected to costs that could further destabilize a company as long as it is in the Crisis Stabilization Stage.

---

[276] (Bibeault, 1981, p. 227)
[277] (Bibeault, 1981, p. 227)
[278] (Bibeault, 1981, p. 312)

Process Improvement (PI)

A process may be defined as a continuous and systematic series of actions performed in a definite manner directed to some end.[279]

The aim of PI can be categorized into: demand generation, which focuses on improving sales and marketing in order to improve targeting of customers' needs; demand fulfillment, which focuses on improving supply chain efficiency through cost reductions, improving the quality of the products or services sold, and improving customer responsiveness; and key support of infrastructure, which focuses on improvement of cost management and management information systems. While this is a useful categorization into activities, I organize the activities on the first level along a timeline, so PI is organized on the first level into subcomponents that can or should be done during the Crisis Stabilization Stage and subcomponents that can or should be run during the Turnaround Stage.

On their path from small to medium to large, most companies use patches to fix problems rather than rethinking the whole from the ground up.[280] The result is too many processes that are not integrated well into other components or that are inefficient.

The following sections focus on a few critical processes where change can be implemented quickly and can have a significant impact in cutting costs, improving quality, or improving responsiveness to customer requirements.[281]

Business process improvement, like process innovation, maintains an enterprise-wide scope, establishes improvement objectives based on business goals, and provides mechanisms for linking multiple improvement initiatives.[282] It may not be sufficient for a Turnaround Leader to simply know how the business should be run and to implement the changes and processes that a well-run business would feature. Because a feature of a turnaround is considerable turbulence at all levels of the organization, it is not uncommon to find that the support required

---

[279] (Woodburn & McDonald, 2011, p. 237)
[280] (Roman, 2010, p. 180)
[281] (Slatter & Lovett, 2004, p. 261)
[282] (Davenport, 1997, p. 145)

to render these improvements effective has been wasting away while the crisis has developed.[283]

PI can be linked to quality improvement.[284] This systematic approach to streamlining processes and establishing a culture of continuous improvement is robust and comprehensive, but certain fundamental characteristics make it unlikely to achieve breakthrough results.[285] It is, however, a useful way to achieve PI on a company-wide scale.

General Process Improvements

The delivery of superior customer value is as much about a company's processes as it is about the core product or service, yet implantation gets nothing like as much attention as it needs.[286]

There are three groups of processes:

1. Strategic processes involve senior management and are concerned with the long-term direction of the company.
2. Strategy realization processes add value to the supplier and customer through realizing the agreed strategy with which the key account managers spend most of their time.[287]
3. Operational/transactional processes contribute to the delivery of what has been promised.

PI is structured along three dimensions: cost improvements, quality improvements, and time improvements.[288] I also add monetary improvements and service improvements to these dimensions.

---

[283] (Slatter & Lovett, 2004, p. 261)
[284] (Harrington, Conner, & Horney, 2000)
[285] (Davenport, 1997, p. 145)
[286] (Woodburn & McDonald, 2011, p. 237)
[287] (Woodburn & McDonald, 2011, p. 237)
[288] compare (Slatter & Lovett, 2004, pp. 263-264)

The Turnaround Leader should not be too quick in communicating everything they would like to improve because doing so could create skepticism about their ability to live up to those plans during the turnaround process.

Cost Improvements

Cost improvements generally result from taking steps out of processes in order to reduce the direct costs of carrying out a particular activity, but they can also result from improving the efficiency of technology or the speed of systems or production facilities, both of which can be done in the Turnaround Stage since they involve a detailed analysis of processes and may require investment.[289] If steps need to be taken out of the production chain, the focus will primarily be on steps that do not add value to the business system. These actions can be carried out in the Crisis Stabilization Stage.

Cost-cutting is not the only way to save money.[290] Sometimes the solutions will be in the process improvement opportunities rather than in cost-cutting initiatives.

Time Improvements

Typically, time improvements increase the organization's responsiveness to the marketplace by reducing the time required to offer new products on the market or by decreasing manufacturing lead times. Changes of this nature also tend to reduce the number of steps in a process, which can reduce the indirect costs of managing or supervising it and reduce its inventory, which can significantly reduce funding requirements.[291] A production-planning function can often improve the situation but may require additional capital investment so it may be better suited to the Turnaround Stage. However, sometimes clients will be lost if improvements are not made quickly so the Turnaround Leader has to evaluate whether financial resources should be used to keep them.

There are five critical ingredients for a successful PI plan:[292]

---

[289] (Slatter & Lovett, 2004, p. 263)
[290] (Roman, 2010, p. 179)
[291] compare (Stalk (Jr.) & Hout, 1990, p. 264)
[292] compare (Slatter & Lovett, 2004, p. 264)

- The people who are going to implement the plan need to understand it and buy into it.
- Behaviors must give priority to corporate objectives even where these may conflict with departmental objectives.
- Improvements must be measurable through key performance indicators.
- Processes that are aligned to the recovery strategy should be improved.
- The focus should first be on processes that are important for the company's survival, and then on those important to rehabilitation.

Process Improvements During the Crisis Stabilization Stage (PI CS)

In the EP component, as well as taking cost-effective control of the direct sales activity, short-term marketing improvements center on decreasing or eliminating current expenditures that have no measurable current or future payout.[293]

Companies in financial difficulties don't have enough money to spend; however, an investment that pays off in the short term and allows the company to save money afterward might be a good investment. The TMT needs to evaluate the ROI carefully in order to free up money to improve such processes.

Process Improvements During the Turnaround Stage (PI TS)

During the Turnaround Stage, the Turnaround Leader should not try to push the limits of a stable process. As long as the process is not underperforming and is running efficiently, it should not be touched unless absolutely necessary. Except for carefully selected continuous improvement initiatives—those that challenge some residual component inefficiencies, or those that help current processes keep up with the times (e.g. upgrades in technology and systems, channels of service)—a stable and efficient process should be allowed to add value and yield results without constant challenges and change.[294] The Turnaround Leader should think about future growth at this stage. After spending precious time and resources finding the optimal ranges and a perfectly balanced approach among effectiveness, efficiency, quality, and customer and employee satisfaction, ensuring steady functioning within these optimal ranges will generate the stability needed for future growth.[295]

Marketing and Sales (MS)

Some marketing improvements can be implemented quickly and without significant financial effort, so they are possible in the Crisis Stabilization Stage and during the EP component. I

---

[293] (Bibeault, 1981, p. 292)
[294] (Roman, 2010, p. 265)
[295] (Roman, 2010, pp. 265-266)

introduce certain actions in this stage and only mention whether a certain action can also be done in the EP component.

The Turnaround Leader should keep in mind that, whereas the implementation of cost- and asset-reducing strategies can be achieved without a major impact on customers, great care should be taken when implementing marketing changes.[296] Changes in the marketing strategy or marketing efforts can easily have a negative effect on customers, so it is important that customers' needs and perceptions of the company are evaluated.

Advertising effort can usually be safely suspended and the money saved used in a number of other ways that should stimulate sales, such as price reductions, commission increases to salespeople, or wider margins for wholesalers or retailers.[297] In some urgent cases, money must be saved at all costs even if it means risking long-term impact.

Symptoms from a Marketing Point of View

A company that is in crisis often has the following symptoms from a marketing point of view:

- The company does not know the competition very well.
- The company does not know who its customers are or what they want.
- The company focuses on achieving high-volume sales as opposed to high profits.
- The company's pricing is inconsistent.
- The products are old and fragmented.
- There are turf wars between sales and manufacturing.[298]
- The targets are too optimistic and not reachable.
- There is no incentive system in place.
- Sales targeting is ineffective or non-existent.[299]
- Management does not know what products or services are the most profitable.
- Sales targets don't exist or are not reachable.
- The sales force is under poor management.
- The quality of the sales force is too low.

---

[296] (Slatter & Lovett, 2004, p. 265)
[297] (Bibeault, 1981, p. 292)
[298] compare (Slatter & Lovett, 2004, p. 265)
[299] compare (Slatter & Lovett, 2004, p. 265)

- Customers' enquiries are not treated appropriately.
- Performance measures are inconsistent.[300]

Marketing and Sales During the Crisis Stabilization Stage (MS CS)

Reducing marketing efforts is a first step in controlling expenses during EP if the company is in urgent need of cash. Of course, marketing expenses cannot be kept down forever. Since the Crisis Stabilization Stage is marked by a cash drain, new investments into marketing are recommended only turning the Turnaround Stage.

The necessary actions that need to be taken in the Crisis Stabilization Stage focus on:

- Reducing costs through minimizing the number of marketing staff, outsourcing non-recurring functions, and choosing the most cost-effective marketing techniques
- Targeting the available funds for marketing efforts at actions that promise the highest return and at products that are in high-growth segments such that investments are made only if there is an opportunity in the market

Two calculations are relevant in evaluating a company's market position:[301]

- A comparison of the size of the business's current product-market segments versus its break-even points
- Assessment of the maximum sales that could be achieved from all other products that the firm has made and still has the capacity to make

These two calculations will provide an idea of whether the business can generate enough sales from its current and/or past products to exceed its break-even point. Hofer furthermore points out that if this is not possible the only other options are major asset reductions or liquidation.

---

[300] compare (Slatter & Lovett, 2004, p. 265)
[301] (Hofer, 1980)

Marketing and Sales During the Turnaround Stage (MS TS)

During the Turnaround Stage, more funds are available for investments in long-term actions, although the actions should still be focused on high-growth segments and products that promise a high return. During the Crisis Stabilization Stage, little effort is put into marketing so considerable costs may be saved and expended on more urgent or important efforts. This situation changes in the Turnaround Stage: here more focus is put on marketing the company and its products in order to make sales in the future and to build a changed picture of the company. In this stage of the turnaround, the marketing emphasis is on increasing revenue growth and profit growth by exploiting existing products and by introducing selected new products.[302]

---

[302] (Bibeault, 1981, p. 350)

The Ten Support Components

The Pre-Turnaround Component (PC)

The Pre-Turnaround Component is not actually part of the turnaround process; its purpose is to ensure that the requirements and prerequisites for the initiation of the turnaround process are in place. The Pre-Turnaround Component starts with the creation of the Turnaround Mandate, which describes very broadly that a turnaround process is being considered and why and how it could be done.

Starting the Turnaround Process (ST)

Starting the Turnaround Process focuses on preparing for the turnaround, and especially on the information a Turnaround Leader needs to make the next steps and to plan the diagnostic review. Finding and appointing a Turnaround Leader is also part of this component.

The Crisis Stabilization Stage (CS)

The Crisis Stabilization Stage is both a stage and a support component. Its purpose is to ensure proper management of processes throughout the most difficult time in the turnaround process.

The Turnaround Stage (TS)

The Turnaround Stage is both a stage and a support component. During this stage the financial survival of the firm in the short term is already secured and strategies that require investments into the future success of the company can be made. The support components ensure proper management of the Turnaround Stage.

Communication Procedures (CP)

Communication Procedures are a crucial part of every turnaround process. This component ensures the proper confidentiality, motivation, and communication at the right time with the right people in order to ensure the highest possible level of stakeholder support and in order to counter one of the main reasons why turnarounds fail: lack of stakeholder support and trust.

Directing the Turnaround (DT)

A formal decision-making component must be in place throughout the process to ensure the company's success in the turnaround. The Turnaround Advisory Board (TAB) is involved with the actual turnaround process but stays at a necessary distance to give the turnaround management the freedom it needs. The TAB must also keep its distance because of its members' personal interests in the company, fear of loss, or other emotional involvement with the company and the turnaround process. The ITMS keeps the TAB at a discreet distance from the TMT but still involves them in major decisions. The ITMS creates shared responsibility among the TAB members, the major stakeholders, and the TMT.

Risk Management (RM)

All of the stakeholders accept additional risk when the company is heading for trouble.[303] The risks that affect a turnaround process are those that arise through the process, but there are also risks that developed long before the turnaround started. By recognizing some of the early warning signs that indicate trouble, companies can eliminate, overcome, or sidestep many of these risks.[304] The Risk Management (RM) component focuses on recording and tracking risk, and it escalates once a risk becomes realistic. The risks associated with a turnaround cannot be reduced to zero, but they can be controlled.

The risk taken also depends on when the turnaround begins. Is the company already in an existence-threatening situation, or is it simply in a stakeholder or strategic crisis? The longer it takes to get the necessary help, the more risk the company takes on because of the increased difficulty of relieving the problem.

---

[303] (Collard, 2002, p. 25)
[304] (Collard, 2002, p. 25)

Planning the Turnaround (PT)

The Turnaround Plan is important in securing bridge financing. If the plan is well thought out and presented the company has a good chance of getting lender support.[305]

The goals the plan sets must be attainable but significant improvements for the company.[306] Involving top managers and even sometimes middle managers in the development of the Turnaround Plan and in setting goals will ensure their support. However, the Turnaround Leader needs to ensure that the timelines are tight but realistic. They, or a specific member of the TMT, will have to be on top of the executives and managers and follow up on their progress at all times, especially during Emergency Procedures and the Crisis Stabilization Stage.

The Turnaround Plan helps the management and the workforce to stay on the same road. This is neither the time nor the place for dotted-line reporting structures, gray areas, or any other form of organizational design confusion.[307] The more the management follows the Turnaround Plan, the better the chance for the company to survive, succeed, and deliver its goals on or ahead of schedule.

During a turnaround execution and post-turnaround stabilization, the success rate is correlated with the TMT's ability to execute the Turnaround Plan and deliver the results quickly.[308]

Change Management (CM)

The biggest enemies of progress are resistance, anguish, pain, and other forms of negative employee emotion or reaction.[309] To manage change:

- The ITMS incorporates essential communication procedures because fear of change is often based on the fear of the unknown.[310] Communication can reduce the unknown and the level of fear.

---

[305] (Bibeault, 1981, p. 215)
[306] compare (Bibeault, 1981, p. 328)
[307] (Roman, 2010, p. 30)
[308] (Roman, 2010, p. 222)
[309] compare (Roman, 2010, p. 33)
[310] compare (Roman, 2010, p. 34)

- The ITMS includes ways to motivate the workforce and sales force.
- It includes open-door policies and the requirements that the TMT are approachable and the Turnaround Assurance Team take ideas from the workforce on how to restructure the company.
- The workforce is involved in the turnaround process.

Communication Procedures (CP)

Proper communication throughout the turnaround process ensures the highest possible level of support from stakeholders for the TMT and the process as a whole. The Communication Procedures support component takes care of informing the right people at the right time about the right things. It includes confidentiality agreements, special dealings with stakeholders, and a Communications Plan.

A Communications Plan is needed because some stakeholders, such as shareholders, may benefit from a restructuring while others, such as employees or suppliers, may be worse off;[311] therefore restructuring a company may have to be done against the interests of a stakeholder. Keeping employees informed of what is going on honestly, openly, and in a timely way will help lower employees' fears, help to gain their full support for the recovery effort, and may also reduce employee turnover and increase their engagement.[312]

The Communication Procedures are guidelines that have evolved out of best practices in order to:

- Minimize the negative impact of the turnaround situation on the company
- Minimize bad press
- Ensure confidentiality at critical points
- Ensure that the right people are informed at the right time

However, not everything needs to be discussed and voted on, nor should it be. Not all employees will be involved in deciding which supplier will provide the next delivery of pens. But

---

[311] (Donaldson, 1994, p. 2)
[312] (Roman, 2010, p. 127)

one needs to be aware that any effort to restructure a company may encounter strong resistance.[313]

Closing the Turnaround Process (CT)

At this point, the company's long battle to regain robust health should be over.[314] The most important goal of the turnaround is survival, but any Turnaround Plan also needs to consider the post-turnaround time and the future growth of the company. When the turnaround process is over, the difficult task of maintaining consistent growth and profitability has just begun.[315]

A turnaround effort can be considered successfully completed even if a relatively large amount of debt is still showing on the books if the earnings before interest (EBIT) are positive, they grow for at least three consecutive periods, and they are achieved in a stable and long-term viable environment. This means that the EBIT is not positive only because of short-term reductions and savings made that will be reversed after the turnaround process, such as the pausing of a maintenance contract or stopping advertising activities. EBIT is a better measure than EBITDA because removing depreciation and amortization does not paint a true picture of the company's ability to operate profitably in the long term.

---

[313] (Simonsen & Cassady, 2007, p. 3)
[314] (Bibeault, 1981, p. 361)
[315] compare (Bibeault, 1981, p. 361)

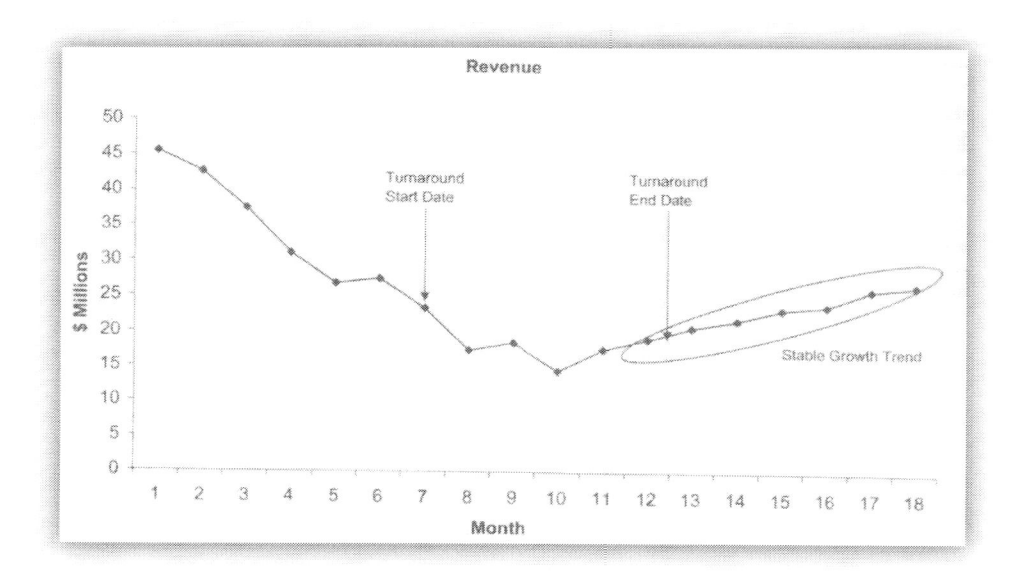

Picture 9 Revenue by month analysis showing post-turnaround stable growth trend

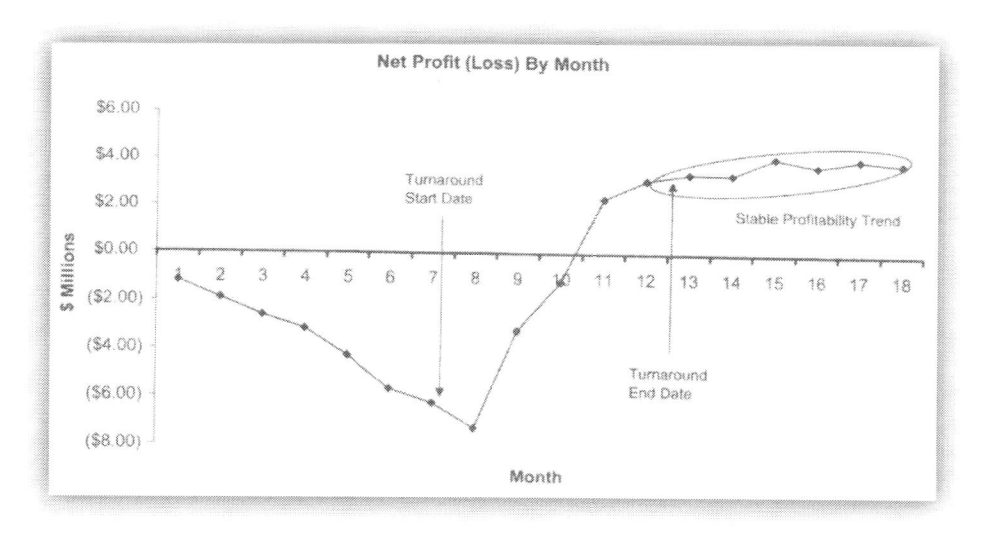

Picture 10 Net profit (loss) by month analysis showing post-turnaround stable profitability trend

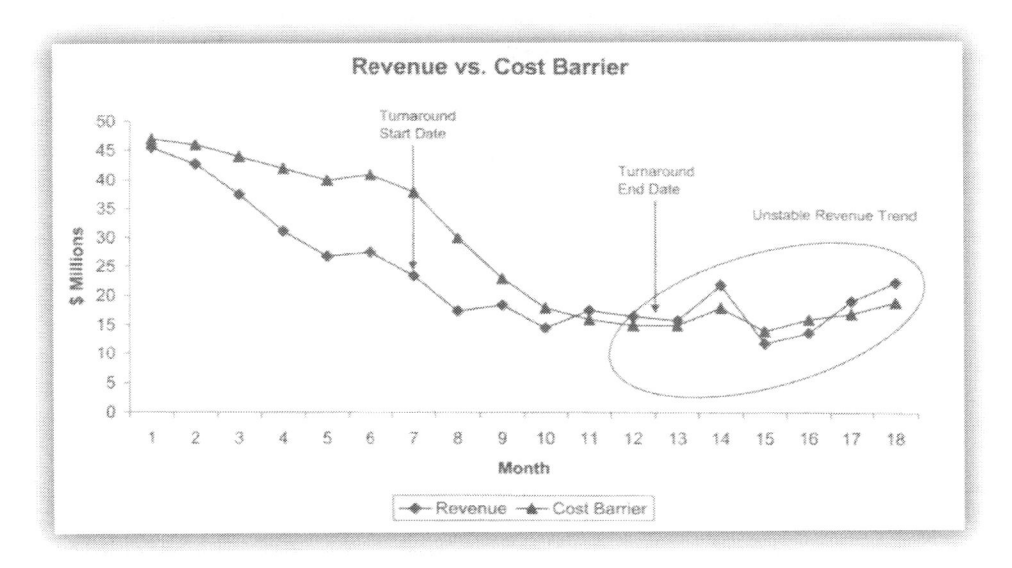

Picture 11 Revenue vs cost barrier by month analysis showing an unstable profitability trend

If a corporate crisis coincides with a general recession in the economy the graphs may be somewhat distorted, as shown in Picture 11. In Picture 12, the revenue trend is not stable at all; it continues to fall below the cost line. In that case, the profit trend needs to be far more positive to show up in volatile sales volumes. However, if the profit (loss) line shows stable—even if minimal—growth, as shown in Pictures 9 and 10.

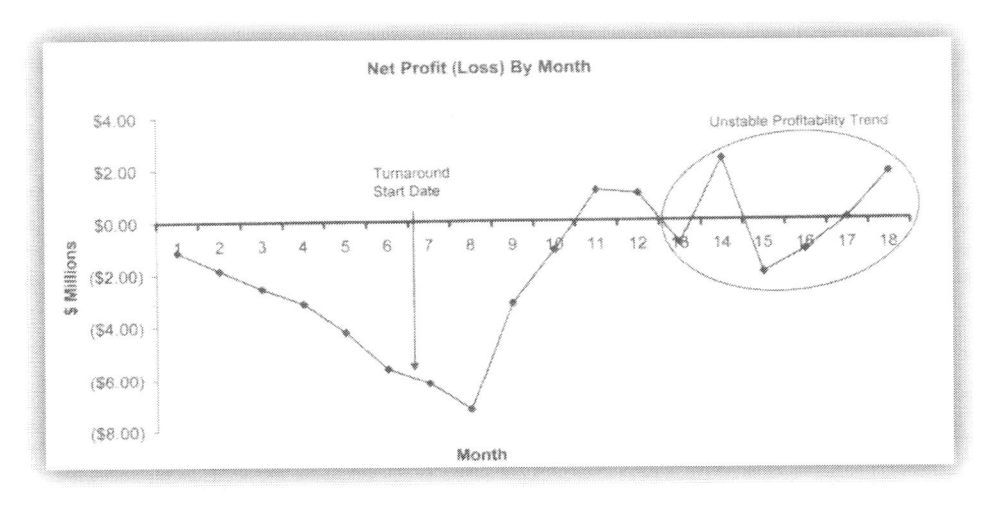

Picture 12 Net profit (loss) by month analysis showing an unstable profitability trend

The Four Stages

There are three major stages in the turnaround or restructuring process: stabilization, reorganization, and restructuring.[316] This standard uses a more organized structure in four stages, each of which includes specific methods for managing a turnaround process. There are two overlapping stages: the retrenchment stage and the recovery stage.[317] The objective of the retrenchment stage is to secure the company's survival and ensure a positive cash flow through, for example, liquidating assets, terminating products, divestments, improving operating efficiencies, and reducing headcount. During the recovery stage, the goal is to get the company to grow and be profitable in the long term. The company enters new markets, acquires other companies, and penetrates other markets during this stage. The four stages used by the ITMS are: the Pre-Turnaround Stage (PS); the Diagnostic Review Stage (DR); the Crisis Stabilization Stage (CS); and the Turnaround Stage (TS).

Pre-Turnaround Stage (PS)

The Pre-Turnaround Stage provides a fairly structured way to start the turnaround. Starting with the Pre-Turnaround Component (PC), a Turnaround Mandate and a pre-turnaround case are created, possible Turnaround Leaders are identified, and the skills that a possible TMT needs to possess are evaluated. In Starting the Turnaround Process (SP), which is the formal start of the turnaround, the Turnaround Advisory Board (TAB) is assembled, turnaround files are set up, a Turnaround Brief is created, and the Turnaround Leader is appointed. In most cases, the power should shortly after be centralized with the Turnaround Leader and a plan for the diagnostic review should be created.

Diagnostic Review Stage (DR)

During the Diagnostic Review Stage, the company in trouble is assessed for its financial situation, strengths and weaknesses, market position, and workforce. A special focus is put on the management in order to determine whether they can support the turnaround process and whether they are the right people for the job.

---

[316] (Davis & Sihler, 2002)
[317] (Robbins & Pearce II, 1992)

The industry surrounding the company is another focus of the Diagnostic Review; here, the analysis combines the political, sociocultural, legal, and economic factors, and the taxes affecting the company. In the evaluation part of the diagnostic review, the collected information is put together to create a decision matrix and the Turnaround Initiation Document (TID). It is also part of the diagnostic review to create the Turnaround Plan based on the recommendations in the TID.

Crisis Stabilization Stage (CS)

When a company is in distress, its cash resources are used up or soon will be. The management often loses control of the company and things can quickly take a turn for the worse. Therefore, in most turnaround situations, crisis management will have to commence immediately[318] and the Turnaround Leader must take rapid control of the situation and implement a strict cash management process.

The objectives of the Crisis Stabilization Stage are:

- To create a window of opportunity by preserving cash in the short term. The time gained can be used to develop a Turnaround Plan and to develop a plan of how to proceed with future cash flows in order to be able to restructure the company financially.
- To show the stakeholders that the TMT has taken control of the situation by reintroducing predictability into the company's operations.
- To implement strategies that generate cash in the short term.
- To manage margin requirements. Companies in distress often forget to keep their costs down and lose valuable margins during inflationary periods.

To make these steps possible, strong top-down control must be implemented throughout the organization by the TMT. The short-term goal is to preserve as much cash as possible. In order to rebuild the stakeholders' trust in the company, it is wise to regularly inform them about the company's short-term cash position, to make forecasts, and to achieve them. Crisis

---

[318] (Slatter & Lovett, 2004, p. 76)

management requires robust leadership; in most cases the Turnaround Leader is forcing a radical mindset change on the organization.[319]

If the Turnaround Leader is not cautious, their enthusiasm for adopting the crisis management procedures set out in this stage can give the impression of achieving early wins, but these may be at the expense of accelerating the downward spiral by further attacking the critical support essential for components to operate.[320] The result is likely to be insolvency.

My definition of the Crisis Stabilization Stage varies slightly from other Crisis Stabilization Stage descriptions found in the literature. The Crisis Stabilization Stage starts when the company is no longer in immediate danger and is already on the way to recovery with all prior actions having been carried out in the emergency stage.[321] The Turnaround Management Society's definition of the Crisis Stabilization Stage starts a bit earlier in the process; from my point of view, stabilizing the company means that the company is still in danger of failing and Emergency Procedures (EP) are only actions begun in the planning or Diagnostic Review Stage in order to avoid the worst. Only certain subcomponents can be started in the EP component since other actions should require prior subcomponents and steps to be completed first.

The long-term planning perspective is not set during the Crisis Stabilization Stage;[322] according to the ITMS, the long-term planning is already done and only the detailed planning of certain stages is left open for adjustment.

In this stage, the goal is to:

- Establish financial and non-financial control procedures
- Install early warning systems for problems that might occur
- Focus on improving profits by concentrating on the profit margin
- Run existing operations more efficiently

---

[319] (Slatter & Lovett, 2004, p. 79)
[320] (Slatter & Lovett, 2004, p. 261)
[321] (Bibeault, 1981, p. 299)
[322] (Bibeault, 1981, p. 300)

Turnaround Stage (TS)

In the Turnaround Stage the company should not lose any more money and should be back on its feet and stronger so more time can be invested and cash-consuming turnaround strategies implemented. In this stage the workforce needs to be motivated with a compensation program in case the turnaround succeeds. The hard cash management controls implemented in the Crisis Stabilization Stage should remain but can be loosened up in some areas, such as marketing. Considerations at this point may include an acquisition or a merger if the financial resources can be secured, new products, or a more cost-intensive product-market shift, and, if the firm's image was badly damaged during the crisis, a corporate name change as a strategic way to distance the firm from that former image. This last strategy is risky but may be necessary.

Operational strategies center on improving manufacturing efficiencies, making maintenance improvements, managing inventory, undertaking development projects, and performing a value analysis. From the process side, quality, supply chain, and customer service can all be improved in the Turnaround Stage.

The marketing strategy will need to adopt the strategic and operative decisions made during this stage, and it may be necessary to develop a new marketing strategy or to at least update the existing one if marketing was not one of the root causes of the crisis.

The Four Processes

Change Control/Out-of-Tolerance Management

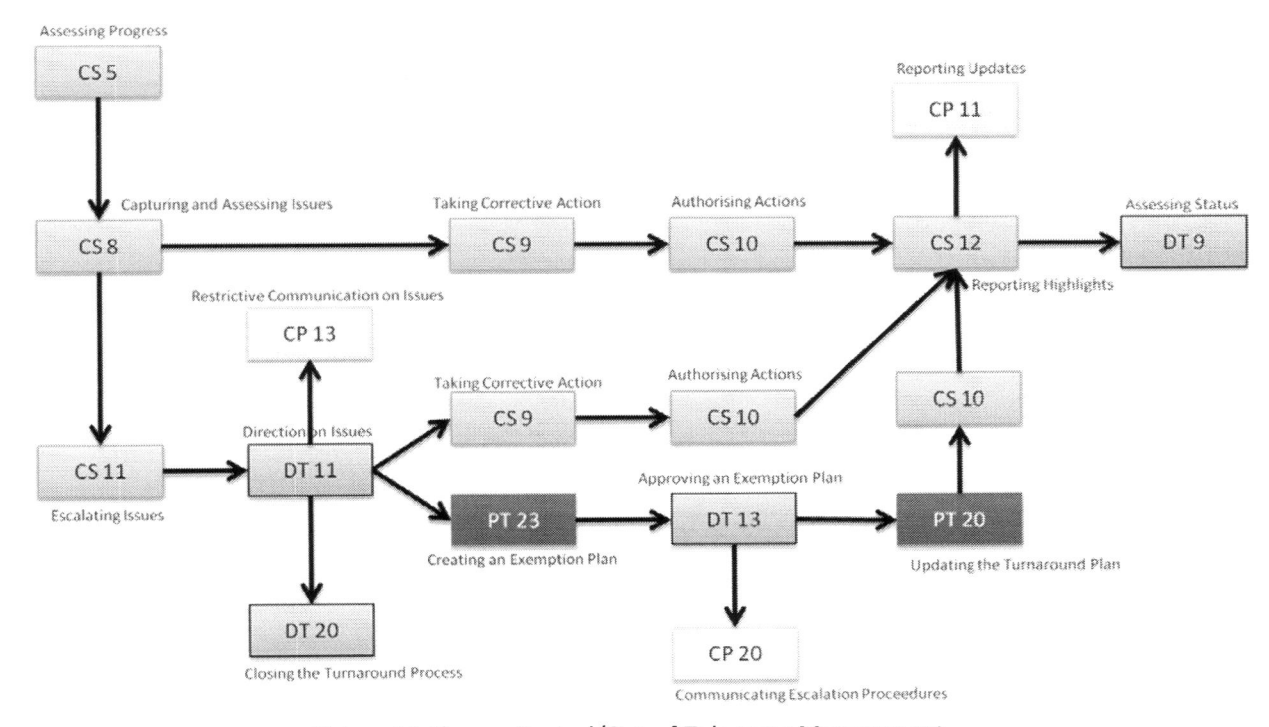

Picture 13 Change Control/Out-of-Tolerance Management

This section of the study explains how the ITMS is used in an out-of-tolerance situation. Consider the example of a subprocess, such as the search for a cheaper supplier for one of the company's main resources, which is planned to take three weeks. This out-of-tolerance process is displayed in Picture 13. At the end of the second week, a planned progress assessment is carried out (CS 5) revealing that no supplier has been found and that it is not likely that a supplier will be found within the next week (CS 8). The Turnaround Leader can either handle the situation directly by agreeing to use the current supplier until a new one is found or, if there is no major impact on any other subprocess, the Turnaround Leader can change the deadline of the search process (CS 9) and order it to be extended (CS 10). However, if the failed search has an impact, such as that the current supplier will stop supplying the urgently needed resource, the issue must be escalated (CS 11), and the TAB will be involved (DT 11). The TAB can decide to close the turnaround prematurely or advise, for example, using a substitute resource or an international supplier (CS 9). If the change is more difficult and has an impact on the Turnaround Plan, an Exemption Plan must be created (PT 23). At this point, some stakeholders may need to be informed of the problem (CP 13). Once the Exemption Plan has been created, it must be approved by the TAB (DT 13) and communicated to stakeholders (CP 20), and the Turnaround Plan should be updated (PT 20). Following the update, the proposed actions in the Exemption Plan can be authorized (CS 10).

Quality Management, Risk Management, Change Management

The Quality Management, Risk Management, and Change Management structures are included in the ITMS, but it is not the function of this version of the ITMS to describe them. However, they function much like the out-of-tolerance management by following the links to the respective subcomponents one makes sure to follow standard procedure.

The Components

Pre-Turnaround Stage Component (PS)

PS 1 – Creating the Turnaround Mandate

Principles

PS 1 concerns the creation of the Project Mandate and is usually the first step in starting a turnaround process. It is often an informal document or an analysis that leads to the Turnaround Mandate.

Context

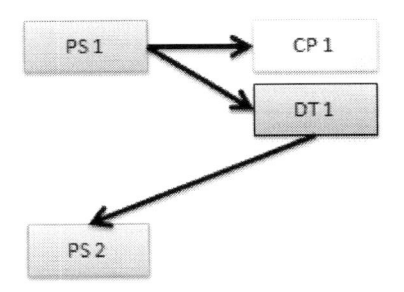

"It's the astute lender or manager that recognizes infallibility and has the foresight to ask for help before serious trouble sets in."[323] To respond to declining performance, a top management team must first acknowledge that a crisis exists and action is needed.[324] Some top managers ignore a crisis and its signs until problems become severe.[325] Once the crisis becomes obvious, the need for a turnaround arises. This subcomponent captures the first step to a structured turnaround process.

---

[323] Collard, 2002, p. 28
[324] Lohrke, Bedeian, & Palmer, 2004
[325] Weitzel & Jonsson, 1989

Description of the Subcomponent

At this stage, it is probably not yet known how the turnaround is going to be carried out and who is going to do it. In some cases, managers have a team of people and a turnaround strategy in their heads immediately. However, in order to maximize the chances of the turnaround process's success, each step of the ITMS needs to be gone though in order to ensure that everything is thought of and analyzed, and every possibility considered. It would not be a very structured approach if one or two managers started a new strategy, picked a couple of people around them to help, and focused all their attention on one or two ideas. Without an unbiased, independent analysis of the whole situation, the chances that these one or two ideas would lead in the wrong direction are high.

The Turnaround Mandate can be an informal document that simply states that a turnaround process is to be considered. It can be a write-up from a conference, an email, or something written on a paper towel. The important thing is that the idea of a turnaround is on the table and to be considered. However, the Turnaround Mandate should describe in basic terms why the turnaround is to be considered and what the problems are that have led to the need for a turnaround.

Information Needs

- What problems led to the need for the turnaround?
- Who will be initiating the turnaround?
- What is the proposed goal of the turnaround?

Responsibility

At this stage, no specific person is responsible for the creation of the Project Mandate since it can be written by an internal manager or an outside stakeholder such as a consulting firm, a bank, or a turnaround management firm.

Outcome

- Turnaround Mandate

PS 2 – Preparing Basic Information

Principles

The company considering a turnaround should be analyzed, at least superficially, in order to gain a first overview of the viability of a turnaround. This initial analysis should include the company and the industry in which it operates.

Context

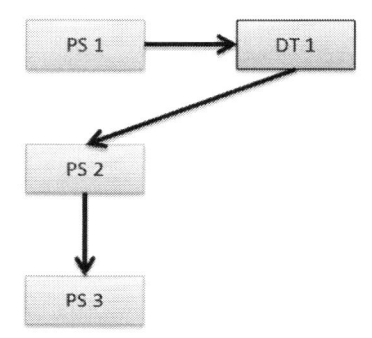

Once a Turnaround Mandate has been approved by the TAB, it must be ratified. During this subcomponent, five basic reports are created that are extended during the following subcomponents.

Description of the Subcomponent

This subcomponent consists of five parts: the creation of a Basic Company Analysis Report, which is best done using a SWOT analysis; a Basic Industry Analysis Report; a Competitor Analysis Report; a Basic Financial Analysis Report; and as a Basic Product Analysis Report.

Basic SWOT Analysis (Basic Company Analysis Report)

In the most general sense, the viability of a company as a whole is viewed by its leaders as a series of strengths and weaknesses.[326] The SWOT analysis can be helpful in establishing a first overview of the organization. SWOT—which stands for Strengths, Weaknesses, Opportunities, and Threats—identifies "the extent to which the current strengths and weaknesses are relevant to and capable of dealing with the changes taking place in the business environment".[327] The analysis helps detect unused potential to gain competitive advantage and identify the general situation of the company in the marketplace.

The threats and opportunities are external forces that the company often cannot directly influence, but it is up to the top management to identify opportunities and turn them into strengths. The strengths and weaknesses can be influenced by the top management and should be targeted by the TMT.

Every company has its own strengths and weaknesses and is faced with its own combination of threats and opportunities.[328]

Strengths (Internal Factors)

- Which products/services have been successful?
- Why and how was the company successful in the past?
- What are the potential synergies that could be used in the future, especially by employing new strategies?
- What are the competitive advantages of the company?
- What makes the company special?
- Does the company have special relationships with suppliers, clients, the government, etc.?

---

[326] Bibeault, 1999, p. 205
[327] Johnson, Scholes, & Whittington, 2005, p. 148
[328] compare (N.A., 2009, p. 7)

Weaknesses (Internal Factors)

- What weaknesses are the company/management aware of?
- What are the potential weaknesses that could arise in the future?
- Which products/services have weak contribution margins, turnover, etc.?
- Which components are highly risky?
- Which components are highly cost-intensive (preliminary level)?

Opportunities (External Factors)

- What are the company's opportunities?
- What are the opportunities for certain products/services?
- Are there any trends that should be followed?

Threats (External Factors)

- What are the threats regarding the overall situation of the company and its products/services?
- What threats are there in market trends?
- What are the competitors doing?
- Are there likely to be any changes in regulations?

Basic Industry Analysis (Basic Industry Analysis Report)

A basic industry analysis gives the TMT insight into how competitive the market is and whether it is growing, stagnating, or shrinking. This analysis involves systematically scanning and collecting information that is relevant to the company, whether it is technological, political, or social.

Managers need to understand the key drivers of change and also the differential impact of these external influences and drivers on particular industries, markets, and individual organizations.[329]

---

[329] (Johnson, Scholes, & Whittington, 2005, pp. 56-66)

Relevant questions include:

- What events could have an impact on the company and the turnaround?
- Are there new market entrants?
- Are there any changes to the law coming up that might affect the market?
- Are there any trends or technological parameters that can affect the company's markets or industry?

The PESTEL framework is very helpful in this kind of analysis. PESTEL—which addresses the Political, Economic, Sociocultural, Technology, Environmental, and Legal factors that might influence an organization—allows the analyst to look into the future and to take into account any changes that might occur. If the future is not easily predictable, scenarios for possible future situations should be used. Typical issues addressed by a PESTEL analysis include:

Political Factors:

- The stability of current regulations and the government
- Taxation law that might apply
- Regulations regarding foreign trade
- Policies regarding social welfare

Economic Factors:

- Interest rates
- Inflation
- Unemployment
- Money supply
- Consumers' disposable income
- Business cycles

Sociocultural Factors:

- Demography of the population

- How income is distributed
- Education levels
- Attitude toward work
- Attitude toward life and leisure
- Distribution of income
- The local lifestyle

Technological Factors:

- New developments
- Speed of technological cycles
- Rates of obsolesce
- Focus of government spending

Environmental Factors:

- Laws designed to protect the environment
- Local customs
- Energy prices and consumption
- Disposal of waste

Legal Factors:

- Product safety regulations
- Health and safety regulations
- Employment law
- Laws regulating the competition

Basic Financial Analysis

In this pre-financial analysis, the TMT usually does not yet have access to the most current company information so the focus at this stage is to analyze the past financial performance of the company by examining its annual reports. If the company does not publish annual reports, a business intelligence department or agency might provide further insight into the company's past performance. This basic financial analysis gives the TMT an idea of where financial problems might lie and whether they occurred suddenly or the company has had a long-term history of financial weakness. It also serves as a pre-assessment of the company in terms of whether it is likely to require some heavy financing or the problems are more strategic in nature. The basic analysis of the financial situation might also give some hint as to the urgency of the situation.

Basic Product Analysis

It is important to find out not only how the products are positioned but also what the margin on these products is, what their lifespan is, how their quality compares to similar products, and where they are made. The products are a very important part of the company's success.

Basic Competitor Analysis

Some basic questions about the competitors in all business areas will help to reveal the strategy that lies behind competitors' actions and help in formalizing the company's own strategy instead of just reacting to competitors' products or services.

Basic questions to answer are:

- Who are the most important competitors and what are their strategies?
- What is the financial power of the competitors?
- What is the potential market share of the competitors?
- How much information does the company already have about its competitors?
- Are the annual reports of the competitors available?
- Are the competitors' home pages and marketing activities known? If so, what are they?
- How many competitors are there?
- How big are the competitors?
- How are the competitors positioned?
- Is there international competition?

The information collected goes into the Competitor Analysis Report, which collects all available information about the company's competitors in all business areas. The Competitor Analysis Report should be updated throughout the turnaround process and populated extensively with all relevant data about the competition during the Diagnostic Review Stage.

Information Needs

Basic information needs to be collected to be presented to potential Turnaround Leaders in PS 3 (The Search for a Turnaround Leader). The basic information includes:

- Problems and reasons for the proposed turnaround
- A broad overview of the company's current financial situation (e.g. a cash flow statement and a balance sheet)
- A broad overview of the competitors and the corporate environment
- A broad overview of the major stakeholders
- Competitive advantages

Responsibility

If no Turnaround Leader has been appointed, the person who initiated the Turnaround Mandate, the CEO, or a project manager of an auditing or consulting firm could be responsible for this subcomponent.

Outcome

- Basic Company Analysis Report
- Basic Industry Analysis Report
- Basic Financial Analysis Report
- Basic Product Analysis Report
- Competitor Analysis Report

PS 3 – The Search for a Turnaround Leader

Principles

If a formal search for a Turnaround Leader or a turnaround firm is not conducted, a suitable person from within the company should be identified.

Context

```
PS 2
 ↓
PS 3
 ↓
PS 4
```

Description of the Subcomponent

Once the information collected about the troubled company and its environment has been approved by the TAB, it can be used to search for a Turnaround Leader.

Leadership requirements for healthy, growing companies differ from those for companies in a troubled situation.[330]

---

[330] (Collard, 2002, p. 26)

Skill	Stable, Healthy or Growth Scenario	Troubled or Turnaround Situation
Focus	On Objectives	Survival, action, problem-solving
Decision making	Deliberate	Decisive, Immediate
Authority	Delegate	Direct Involvement
People	Develop	Recruit talent Communications
Respected for:	Management reputation	Financial credibility
Known for:	Consistency	Ability to shift gears

Picture 14 Leadership requirements for healthy and troubled companies[331]

The search for and evaluation of possible Turnaround Leaders can be time-consuming. The Turnaround Management Society (TMS) can act as an agent in helping troubled companies find the right Turnaround Leader quickly. Going through a third party like the TMS has the advantage of making the search anonymous, so the confidentiality mentioned in CP 1 (Communication Guidelines) is assured. The troubled company can than choose which Turnaround Leader it wants to start negotiations with and confirm their availability.

Negotiations about the Turnaround Leader's compensation, status, general responsibilities, and job description until the official turnaround process starts are carried out in this step as well. The Turnaround Leader must be sure of their direction and sensitive to the ramifications of the turnaround effort, but must also be sufficiently tough and determined to see their decisions carried out.[332]

Internal Versus External Turnaround Leader

Some studies have found that firms that go through a turnaround process successfully are those that have had an external TMT;[333] however, others have found that internal TMTs are usually

---

[331] (Collard, 2002, p. 26)
[332] (Bibeault, Corporate Turnaround: How Managers Turn Losers into Winners, 1981, p. 292)
[333] (O'Neill H. , 1986)

more effective in leading recovery components.[334] Depending on a firm's remaining viability, the situation might require similar or different types of decisions from the top management team than would be required in a healthy firm.[335] Different types of decisions also need to be made at different stages of the turnaround process.[336] Non-executive directors who share financial analysts' points of view or new leaders may be recruited from outside the company largely because of their detachment.[337]

In order to change a company one must change the style of leadership.[338] Therefore an executive team from the outside may be appropriate when extensive change is indicated, particularly since the CEO and management team that managed the company into trouble is likely to lack the skills to bring it back to health. However, a TMT recruited from inside the firm is often out of its element in that it is inexperienced with the company's specific situation.

CEOs who have achieved successful turnarounds have backgrounds in areas such as production or engineering rather than sales or marketing.[339] However, another study shows that most successful turnarounds were led by CEOs with backgrounds in general administration, finance, or legal.[340] Such contrary findings involving functional backgrounds suggest that future demographic research on declining firms should focus on critical situational contingencies that may affect a TMT's ability to successfully formulate and implement turnaround strategies.[341] The contrasting findings show that the functional background of a top management team affects the efficiency with which it executes a certain turnaround strategy.[342]
The Turnaround Leader must have an active manager orientation, be decisive, and be able to isolate problems and find solutions quickly.[343] Managing a renewal strategy requires a special type of manager: an entrepreneur-manager.[344] Entrepreneur-managers are especially skilled at discovering a valuable business proposition for their ventures, communicating and marketing this proposition to all stakeholders within the firm, mobilizing the necessary resources even

---

[334] (Zimmermann F., 1989)
[335] compare (Lohrke, Bedeian, & Palmer, 2004)
[336] compare (Robbins & Pearce, 1992), (Arogyaswamy, Barker, & Yasai-Ardekani, 1995)
[337] (Day & Jung, 2000)
[338] (Collard, 2002, p. 26)
[339] (Zimmermann F., 1989)
[340] (Stanwick, 1992)
[341] (Lohrke, Bedeian, & Palmer, 2004, S. 68)
[342] compare (Lohrke & Bedeian, 1998)
[343] (Collard, 2002, p. 28)
[344] (Simonsen & Cassady, 2007, p. 20)

when they have no authority over them, assembling and motivating a team of experts, and, most importantly, delivering results.[345] The Turnaround Leader needs to be an entrepreneur to some extent and to have entrepreneurial creativity, spirit, and drive.

An entrepreneur-manager should have the following qualities:[346]

1. Skills that Include the Ability to:

- See the big picture and shape strategy
- Communicate and market the strategy
- Manage stakeholders, gain support, and mobilize resources
- Assemble and motivate a team of experts

2. Personal Traits that Include:

- Propensity to take risks
- Passion and inner fire
- Action orientation
- Self-confidence

3. Professional Experience that Includes:

- An established track record that will encourage trust
- Long tenure and varied experience that will help with networking
- Understanding of the industry[347]

An entrepreneurial manager who comes from inside the company has two important advantages:[348]

---

[345] (Simonsen & Cassady, 2007, p. 20)
[346] (Chakravarthy & Lorange, 2008)
[347] (Kramer, 1999)
[348] (Chakravarthy & Lorange, 2008, p. 15)

- Their track record buys the credibility to take risks on behalf of the firm.
- Long association gives them information and access to the company's network of resource holders and power brokers.

Personal traits influence the entrepreneur-manager's ability to proactively seek those with relevant experience within the firm and learn from them.

The Turnaround Leader also needs to be very skilled in communication with stakeholders. A turnaround can essentially be seen as a project and the Turnaround Leader as a project manager. Just as a project manager does, the Turnaround Leader must promote the turnaround to the stakeholders in their place of work and gain their support for the objectives and methods adopted in the Turnaround Process.[349] This standard proposes to have a crisis communication specialist on board for the turnaround, but this person is not responsible for the direct communication between stakeholders and the Turnaround Leader, which is why the Turnaround Leader needs to be skilled and experienced in communication in critical times as well.

The Need for New Top Management

A precondition for almost all successful turnarounds is the replacement of the current top management of the business.[350] Of course, the existing top management team can observe the turnaround process but they should not have the authority to interfere with it. However, the case is different when the crisis is not directly the top management's fault. For example, when the German Bank BayernLB experienced a severe financial crisis in mid-2008 its CEO, Michael Kemmer, was supposed to be fired. However, financial experts believed that he was the right person to "drive the bank into calmer water", particularly because of the support of his employees, around a thousand of whom demonstrated to keep Kemmer and his top management team in office.[351]

---

[349] compare (Turner & Bredillet, 2010, p. 11), (Müller & Turner, 2010, p. 83ff)
[350] (Hofer, 1980)
[351] (Financial Times Deutschland, 2008)

Usually it is necessary to bring in new management to get an independent view of the situation. Since different managers are skilled in different business areas, it is advisable that the new management team consists of people who are skilled in the jobs that need to be done for the turnaround. For example, if the company needs to significantly reduce its costs, it would be useful to bring in someone who is experienced in cost-cutting procedures rather than an entrepreneur/strategist type of manager who would be more suitable in a strategic or a high-growth turnaround.

Consultants

In some turnaround situations consultants who make recommendations to the old management team concerning how to get out of the storm are used. However, the ITMS standard does not fully apply to them since in this system the Turnaround Leader has full decision-making authority. However, the core approach of the ITMS and its recommendations can be adapted and followed by consultants or company managers who do not have a professional TMT at hand.

Responsibility

The company that initiates the turnaround process is responsible for this subcomponent.

Information Needs

- Basic Company Analysis Report from PS 2
- Basic Industry Analysis Report from PS 2
- Basic Financial Analysis Report from PS 2
- Basic Product Analysis Report from PS 2
- Competitor Analysis Report from PS 2
- Is an internal or external Turnaround Leader needed?
- What specifications, knowledge, resources, connections, and experience should the Turnaround Leader have?

PS 4 – Analysis of Required Turnaround Management Team Skills

Principles

This subcomponent gathers the information on the required skills of the TMT.

Context

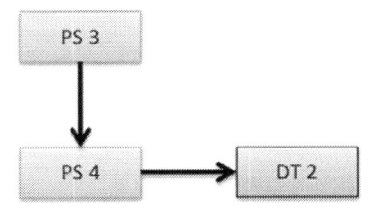

Description of the Subcomponent

Based on the Basic Company Analysis Report, key positions in the company can be identified that should be headed by a TMT member. At this stage, it is not yet clear whether all key positions need to be replaced; that analysis will be done in the Diagnostic Review Stage. However, regardless of the skills of the person currently holding a key position, an analysis is needed of the required skills for that position in a turnaround situation.

There should be experts in the following areas on the TMT:

- Communications
- Finance
- Industry-specific
- Marketing and sales
- Change management/HR
- Trade unions

The members of the TMT should be:[352]

- Willing to experiment with new business models and to explore new capabilities
- Outward-focused and cognizant of changes in their business environments and the new opportunities that these may bring
- Operating managers interested in scaling up an entrepreneurial idea and delivering results
- Action-oriented, self-confident, and not risk-averse

Responsibility

The board of the company that initiated the turnaround is responsible for this subcomponent.

Information Needs

- Basic Company Analysis Report from PS 2
- Basic Industry Analysis Report from PS 2
- Basic Financial Analysis Report from PS 2
- Basic Product Analysis Report from PS 2
- Competitor Analysis Report from PS 2

---

[352] (Chakravarthy & Lorange, 2008, p. 20)

Starting the Turnaround Process (SP)

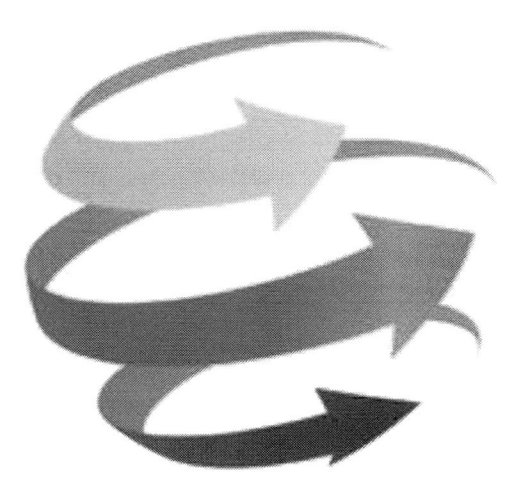

SP 1 – Assembling a Turnaround Advisory Board (TAB)

Summary

The Turnaround Advisory Board (TAB) is an overseeing body that has very limited authority in the daily business during the turnaround process but does have authority over the Turnaround Leader.

Context

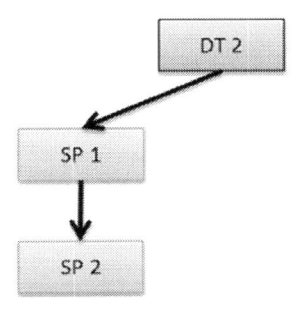

Description of the Subcomponent

Assembling a TAB includes the formal recognition of the stakeholders' representative(s) and representatives of the company's board who are accountable for the turnaround process. In this subcomponent, the job descriptions for these roles are written and agreed upon by the TAB members. The TAB has overseeing authority and may need to help the Turnaround Leader if approval or advice is needed. The TAB is not a discussion board but is there to make decisions quickly, so every member of the TAB needs to have a clear knowledge of what the party they represent wants, how far they can go, and their level of authority to make decisions on their behalf. If a new party enters during the turnaround process (e.g. because it is funding a component), that party may be given a seat on the TAB. From this subcomponent onward, the TAB directs the turnaround.

A stakeholder representative is a person who represents the interests of a particular stakeholder or group of stakeholders. If there are many stakeholder groups, such as important customers and key suppliers, there may be two or more stakeholder representatives; however, it is suggested that there should be as few as possible because conflict between these representatives can endanger the turnaround process and its timeframe.

The stakeholder representative is also responsible for meeting with the stakeholders regularly in order to stay up to date with their opinions and their level of support for the company. Stakeholder representatives can be appointed at two different times based on whether the turnaround process was initiated by one or more stakeholders or by the board of the troubled company.

The major claim-holders' representative is appointed by a group of creditors and has basic decision-making authority. The position enables the TMT to make decisions more quickly and avoids them having to deal with too many creditors at once. The claim-holders' representative is responsible for sticking to the claim-holders' guidelines and for representing their interests. They also works closely with the turnaround communications manager and distribute regular reports to the parties they represent. This approach saves substantial costs and should reduce the complexities that can lead to disagreements[353].

Responsibility

Responsibilities for the TAB to oversee the turnaround process are created in this subcomponent. The subcomponent should be initiated by the company or person who initiated the turnaround process.

Information Needs

- Who are the major stakeholders?
- Will the stakeholders have a voting right? This will make particular sense in large TABs.
- Who will be offered a seat on the TAB?

---

[353] (Slatter & Lovett, 2004, p. 314)

Outcome

The TAB consists of stakeholders. Some positions are required by the ITMS and others are optional. The required members are:

- A representative of the owners
- A representative of the financial investors
- A representative of the employees
- A representative of the clients
- A representative of the major claim-holders.

Optional seats may be given to:

- A supply representative
- A consulting firm

SP 2 – Appointing a Turnaround Leader

Summary

The available candidates are evaluated by the TAB and the Turnaround Leader formally takes charge of the turnaround process.

Context

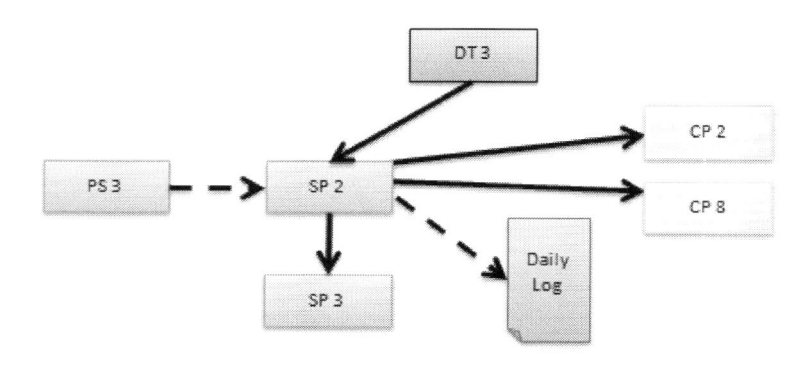

Description of the Subcomponent

The appointment of a Turnaround Leader is important because someone familiar with turnaround situations must lead the turnaround process and be the key decision maker. The objectives of this subcomponent are to:

- Confirm the selected Turnaround Leader
- Establish basic reporting structures (see CP 2 – Confidentiality Assurance)

The Turnaround Leader will need to implement abrupt change and, often enough, unpopular cost-cutting measures. They must have the confidence to face the resulting storm—or at least be able to appear confident whether they feel it or not.[354] They must have the power to

---
[354] (Roman, 2010, p. 70)

announce changes[355] to the Turnaround Plan that may not favor certain stakeholders, to negotiate well with stakeholders, and to convince them to support the turnaround process. The Turnaround Leader cannot let stress and job security concerns diminish performance; thoughts of abandoning ship do not blend well with [the ability] to drive positive change.[356] Appointing the appropriate person for a turnaround is not an easy choice for a company as it often has to choose between a person with extensive industry experience who does not have turnaround experience and a specialized Turnaround Leader who does not have specific industry experience and relationships. A good Turnaround Leader is usually a highly effective general manager, and experience suggests that such people can usually work across all but the most specialized industries.[357]

Once the Turnaround Leader is appointed, it is their responsibility to create and update a Daily Log, which will begin on the day that they start in the role.

One of the Turnaround Leader's first tasks is to evaluate the company's current situation. In severe cases, they will have to make quick decisions to stop the loss of money in order to have enough time to run a deep analysis of the state of the company. One of the challenges for any Turnaround Leader is to ensure that the rescue is built on a robust plan.[358] When the new Turnaround Leader/CEO takes over they need to address the workforce to develop a rapport with the staff and encourage their participation.[359] Therefore a workforce kick-off meeting (CP 8) should be planned.

Responsibilities

The TAB is responsible for this subcomponent. This is also the last subcomponent for which the TAB is directly responsible.

---

[355] (Kramer, 1999)
[356] (Roman, 2010, p. 70)
[357] (Slatter & Lovett, 2004, p. 80)
[358] (Slatter & Lovett, 2004, p. 75)
[359] compare (Khandwalla, 2001, p. 396)

Information Needs

In PS 3 (Search for a Turnaround Leader), available candidates were selected and presented to the TAB. This information is needed in this subcomponent.

Outcome

- Turnaround Leader appointed
- Daily Log, which is the responsibility the Turnaround Leader

SP 3 – Assembling the Diagnostic Review Team

Summary

In order to evaluate the chances and choices for a turnaround, a detailed Diagnostic Review of the troubled company, its business, and environment must be done by experts who are appointed during this subcomponent.

Context

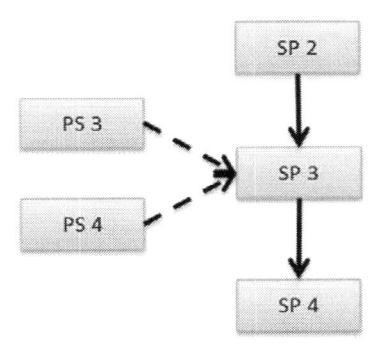

Description of the Subcomponent

This is the first subcomponent that is actually headed by the Turnaround Leader. The skills necessary in the Diagnostic Review Team are evaluated based on the Turnaround Mandate and the Turnaround Leader's experience. There can be changes to the Diagnostic Review Team throughout the Diagnostic Review Stage, but the Turnaround Leader should identify the kinds of people needed to conduct a first analysis of the company.

The members of the Diagnostic Review Team may or may not be members of the TMT; however, some companies that specialize in turnarounds have their own specialists who assess company situations and pass the information to the future TMT.

The Diagnostic Review Team should consist of:

- Industry experts
- Accountants/financial experts
- Experienced turnaround professionals
- Competitive intelligence support (if possible)

The fact-finding must proceed as quickly as possible so a realistic assessment of the current state of the company can be prepared.[360]

Responsibilities

The Turnaround Leader is responsible for this subcomponent.

Information Needs

- Basic company information from PS 2
- Required TMT skills from PS 4

Outcome

The Diagnostic Review Team is appointed.

---

[360] (Collard, 2002, p. 27)

SP 4 – Setting Up Turnaround Files

Summary

In this subcomponent a system is set up for storing and retrieving information created throughout the turnaround process.

Context

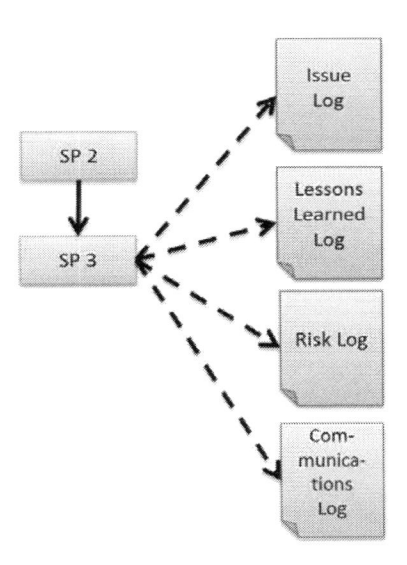

Description of the Subcomponent

One of the key actions in taking charge of a company is ordering the reports and data for evaluation.[361] This should be done as soon as the Diagnostic Review Team has been appointed. In large corporations this component can take some time and, as time is valuable, outside consulting companies might be called in to help collect the information needed for a viability

---

[361] (Bibeault, 1999, p. 204)

analysis.[362] The Turnaround Leader must define clearly all the information they need for their appraisal. While documentation may be the last thing on people's minds in a turnaround, it should be treated with as much care as any other important part of the restructuring process.[363]

It is important that the information created throughout the turnaround process in the form of logs, reports, files, and communications is stored for later review. Files that are created in several different versions should be saved with a time stamp.

An experienced TMT will know what information will be produced, what is critical, and how to store it. It must also be established who is permitted to change the project files and who is permitted to view them at what time. In general, it should not be possible to change a file once it is signed or submitted to another party; if changes are necessary, they should be stored with a new version. All files should be in line with any audit requirements. Documenting the steps and critical actions of a turnaround will ensure that there will be a record of changes made.[364] This is important because law suits might be filed against the TMT if the turnaround processes does not go as planned or as a stakeholder imagined. Having changes documented together with the reasons for a change or deviation from the plan helps to justify decisions that were made.

Creating the Issue Log

During a turnaround process issues raised should be communicated to the person who maintains the Issue Log so they can be recorded. Access to the Issue Log should be controlled by the turnaround support staff and it should be kept in a safe place.

The purpose of the Issue Log is to:

- Number each issue that occurs during the turnaround
- Record the types of issues
- Serve as a summary of all issues
- Record the status and analysis of each issue encountered

---

[362] (Bibeault, 1999, pp. 204-205)
[363] (Roman, 2010, p. 111)
[364] (Roman, 2010, p. 111)

- Record the departments or business units impacted by each issue

The Issue Log is a spreadsheet with the following columns:

1. Number of the issue (so each issue is identifiable, including which component it refers to)
2. Type of issue
3. Author of the issue (who recorded it)
4. The person who recognized the issue
5. Date the issue was identified
6. Date the status of the issue was last updated
7. Description of the issue
8. Priority of the issue
9. Status of the issue (indicating if action was taken and, if so, what kind)

Creating the Lessons Learned Report

The Lessons Learned Log, which serves the company in future situations, should be transmitted to the TMS for storage in the ITMS lessons learned database so other companies can benefit from the experience. It is also a valuable contribution to the community of Turnaround Leaders. The Lessons Learned Log will be transferred in a formal way and stored as an anonymous Lessons Learned Report once the turnaround is over. It should be updated at least at the end of every stage, but preferably more often. Every good and bad incident and aspect of the process that arises during a component should be recorded in the Lessons Learned Log as it happens.

The Lessons Learned Log should include:

- Descriptions of management procedures, decisions, and actions and whether they were good, bad, or lacking
- Descriptions of abnormal events that caused deviations from the planned process
- Descriptions of how special components, strategies, methods, or tools performed
- Recommendations for how the component, strategy, method, or tool could be improved

- Measurement of how much effort was required in terms of money, time, work hours, and so on
- Estimates of how effective or ineffective the planned quality test or reviews were, including a description of why they were good or bad

Creating the Communications Log

The Communications Log documents which stakeholder received what information at what time. In the Communications Log the stakeholders are divided into groups according to their information needs. When information about the company or the turnaround process becomes available the Communications Manager can look up which stakeholders are to be informed. It is the responsibility of the Communications Manager to create the log and keep it up to date.

Creating the Risk Log

The Risk Log is created and filled with the first risks that arise. It contains all available information about risks: their status, analysis of the risks, and possible countermeasures if they occur. From this component on, all risks to the turnaround process or the company, whether they actually happen or not, are entered into the Risk Log. The likelihood of a risk and its potential impact on the company and the turnaround process must be assessed. This Risk Log serves as a reference to a proposed contingency budget and a reminder to the management about what to watch out for and what to check up on.

The discussion of risk demonstrates management's ability to identify and assess risk, to learn from previous experiences, and to reflect the evaluation of the risks in the financial projections through sensitivity analysis.[365] Every company has unique risks that might threaten it. Some risk—such as those caused by the financial markets, the economic situation, competition, and changes in regulations—are not controllable, while others—such as those related to employee behavior, products, and process—are. Taking action when a risk develops is often less desirable than avoiding the risk before it happens. The Risk Log is an effective way to identify and control risk proactively. Effective risk management is a considerable challenge for all businesses, but

---

[365] (Slatter & Lovett, 2004, p. 209)

this challenge is magnified in companies that are undergoing substantial change or transformation since it is not always possible to apply lessons learned from experience.[366]

The Risk Log is a spreadsheet that contains the following columns:

1. An identifier that allows the risks to be grouped
2. The person who identified and submitted the risk
3. The date the risk was identified
4. A description of the risk
5. A category for the risk (e.g. financial, commercial, strategic)
6. The possible impact if the risk becomes reality
7. The probability that the risk will occur
8. When the risk might occur
9. Possible countermeasures if the risk occurs
10. The "owner" of the risk; that is, the person responsible for monitoring it
11. The date when the risk was last updated
12. The current status of the risk (e.g. no change, likely, unlikely, increased likelihood, closed)
13. Actions already taken to mitigate, avoid, or respond to the risk

All risks should be updated whenever the Risk Log is reviewed, which as a minimum should be at the beginning and end of every component and stage. It is the responsibility of the TAB and the Turnaround Leader to check for external risks. The Risk Log is an essential part of the Turnaround Plan.

Example of Business Risks:

Examples of business risks can be found in and grouped into environmental risks, component risks, and information for decision-making risks.[367]

---

[366] (Slatter & Lovett, 2004, p. 210)

[367] (Slatter & Lovett, 2004, pp. 210-212)

Responsibilities

The Turnaround Leader is responsible for this subcomponent. Results must be achieved, measured, documented, recognized, and rewarded promptly.[368] The Turnaround Leader can transfer some responsibility for these activities to the Diagnostic Review Team and the Communications Manager.

Outcome

- Issue Log
- Lessons Learned Log
- Risk Log
- Communications Log

---

[368] (Roman, 2010, p. 191)

SP 5 – Setting Up Turnaround Controls

Summary

The first level of controls is set up in this subcomponent.

Context

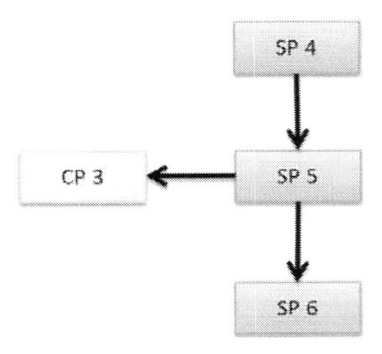

Description of the Subcomponent

This subcomponent is designed to ensure that communication, monitoring, and control frameworks are in place.

Tasks to be carried out in this subcomponent are:

- Identification of the decision-making levels
- Establishment of decision-making procedures
- Establishment of control levels and reporting procedures

The control levels should be consistent with the communications in order to keep important information within the TMT until the TAB has been informed by the Turnaround Initiation Document (TID) and further communication actions have been agreed on. The TID is created in the DR EP stage.

A preliminary control and monitoring framework could consist first of rules that prohibit managers from investing in projects that take more than a certain length of time or require more than a certain level of expenditure without the consent of the Turnaround Leader. Resource orders above a certain limit may also have to be approved.

Responsibilities

The Turnaround Leader is responsible for this subcomponent.

SP 6 – Preparing the Turnaround Brief

Summary

The Turnaround Brief, which is created in during this subcomponent, evolves out of the Turnaround Mandate. Once created, the Turnaround Brief should be discussed with all major stakeholders.

Context

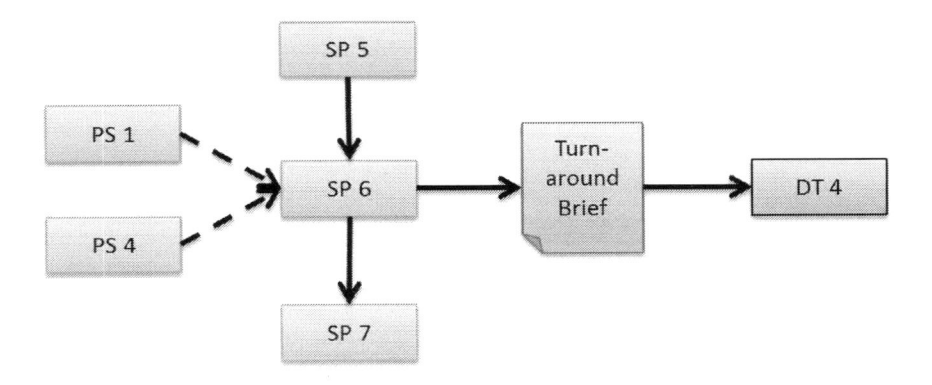

Description of the Subcomponent

The Turnaround Brief spells out the requirements and expectations for the turnaround process. It evolves out of the Turnaround Mandate and helps to determine whether the content of the Turnaround Mandate is still viable. Some of the statements in the Turnaround Mandate may need to be expanded if they haven't been already. The Turnaround Mandate becomes a formal document, the Turnaround Brief, that serves as a reference for the turnaround, establishes the expectations of the stakeholders, and ensures that the business case for the turnaround is in line with the information available at this stage. The Turnaround Brief is updated with the stakeholder representatives' quality expectations—that is, their position on the turnaround, their goals, deadlines, and so on. Once the Turnaround Brief has been created it is discussed with the major stakeholders, after which it may be reworked.

In addition to the information contained in the Turnaround Mandate, the Turnaround Brief sets out the expectations and requirements for the turnaround process, including information on how things will be done, what needs to be done, why, by whom, and when. Not every question can be answered at this point, but the Turnaround Brief serves as a basis for SP 8, when the Diagnostic Review will be planned. The level of detail in the Turnaround Brief will differ from company to company.

Responsibilities

The Turnaround Leader is responsible for this subcomponent.

Information Needs

- Turnaround Mandate from PS 1
- Quality expectations of the stakeholders
- Information about the Diagnostic Review Team from PS 4
- The Turnaround Business Case

Outcome

- Turnaround Brief

SP 7 – Centralizing Power

Summary

In a crisis situation whoever is in charge needs to be able to make decisions quickly. Only a powerful central group can guide the company through the risks and setbacks that are inevitably encountered during a transformation.[369]

Context

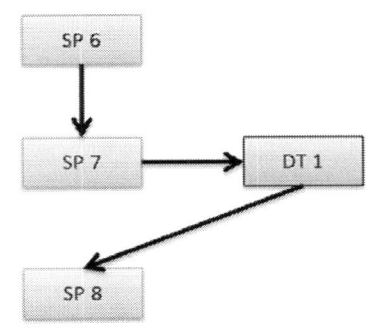

Description of the Subcomponent

This subcomponent is the first major strategic move undertaken by the Turnaround Leader when taking over a turnaround assignment. A cooperative leadership style is necessary in a crisis situation in order for the employees to stay independent so that they can use their full creativity.[370] Centralized leadership frustrates employees but a cooperative leadership style can be motivational and provide a positive atmosphere for employees. Although these values can yield good results when sales numbers are on target and the business is making money, they will come under pressure when financial hardship and insecurity occur.[371] In a turnaround

---

[369] (Day & Jung, 2000)
[370] (Höhn, 1974, p. 111)
[371] (Roman, 2010, p. 108)

situation the locus of power is highly centralized;[372] for the duration of the operational turnaround planning and execution a formalized, authoritative leadership structure must be put in place and enforced.[373] This authoritative structure is only possible by centralizing power.

A TMT needs certain capabilities to overcome a crisis. These are discussed in PS 4 and DR AP 15, which deal with assembling the TMT. These capabilities and skills include the TMT's ability to reach consensus, as well as its competencies and power.

Power involves the ability to exert one's will on decisions that must be made.[374] Therefore, the power that individual members of top management have may affect the decision-making process. The power of top management arises from sources that include formal managerial positions, stock ownership, critical functional expertise, outside board positions, and elite education.[375] If power is exercised too strongly by one individual the outcome of the decision-making process may suffer, lowering the chances of a successful turnaround.[376] The upside is that power centralized in one top manager leads to faster decision-making and aids the management in marshaling the key resources needed to implement a turnaround strategy as quickly as possible. Centralized power is especially important in urgent cases, but it reduces the input of other team members and can affect the quality of decisions.[377]

The need for a unified direction in solving an organization's obvious problems must take precedence over the independence of the functional or divisional heads.[378] Chaos and confusion will recede quickly in the face of the organized structure of a formal hierarchy.[379] Therefore strong centralized leadership is essential to any turnaround process.[380]

---

[372] compare (Bibeault, 1999, p. 330)
[373] (Roman, 2010, p. 108)
[374] compare (Pfeffer, 1999)
[375] compare (Lohrke, Bedeian, & Palmer, 2004) and (Finkelstein, 1992)
[376] compare (Hambrick & D'Aveni, 1992)
[377] compare (Halebian & Finkelstein, 1992)
[378] (Bibeault, 1999, p. 330)
[379] (Roman, 2010, p. 110)
[380] compare (Day & Jung, 2000)

Too many meetings with too many people should be avoided. Everyone will have something to say—even those who are not experts on the matter—but management by group consensus will ensure that no one ends up having any accountability for anything.

For turnaround processes that take a year or longer, mechanisms to prevent abuse by the Turnaround Leader—such as unfair performance appraisals and retaliation—should be put in place with widely advertised channels of recourse for "employees (e.g. escalation paths, investigation mechanisms, formal components for conflict arbitration)".[381]

Responsibilities

The TAB should grant general authority over the company to the Turnaround Leader. The accountability for the turnaround process lies with the TAB, but the Turnaround Leader has responsibility for most subcomponents.

---

[381] (Roman, 2010, p. 110)

SP 8 – Planning the Diagnostic Review

Summary

The next stage, the Diagnostic Review Stage, is planned during this subcomponent.

Context

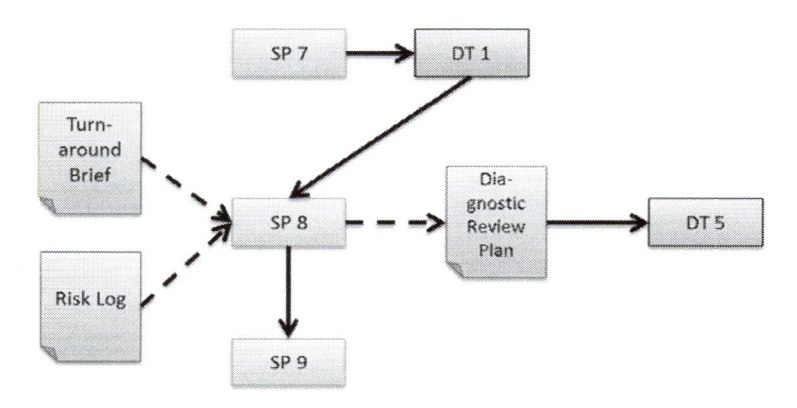

Description of the Subcomponent

In this subcomponent, the Turnaround Brief is expanded to include what needs to be done in the Diagnostic Review Stage, which may include special check-ups that are not part of the ITMS. These check-ups need to be mentioned separately. The aim of the Diagnostic Review Plan is to imform the TAB whether it is worth extending the turnaround into the Diagnostic Review.

Tasks that need to be completed:

- Establish how the work in the Diagnostic Review should be done
- Produce a rough plan of who is going to do what in the Diagnostic Review Stage
- Identify constraints in terms of resources, quality, money, time, and the long-term operations of the company

- Identify any standards and best practices that are available from the stakeholders that should be considered
- Identify legal constraints that could have an effect on the turnaround process
- Determine whether special (human) resources required for the Diagnostic Review need to be brought in from outside
- Give a rough time estimate for the Diagnostic Review Stage
- Define the control and reporting procedures for the Diagnostic Review Stage

All of this information and the Risk Log are entered into the Turnaround Brief, and the Turnaround Brief is handed over to the TAB for approval to commence the Diagnostic Review.

Responsibilities

The Turnaround Leader is responsible for this subcomponent.

Information Needs

- Turnaround Brief
- Risk Log

Outcome

- Diagnostic Review Plan

SP 9 – Proposing Emergency Procedures

Summary

At various times during the turnaround process it will be necessary to implement certain actions quickly in order for the company to survive. This subcomponent is the first time during the turnaround at which information is available about the company and its situation, there is a broad vision of the Turnaround Plan, and the necessity for certain immediate actions has been established.

Context

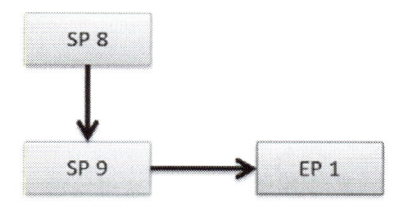

```
SP 8
 │
 ▼
SP 9  ───▶  EP 1
```

Description of the Subcomponent

If the company is in considerable difficulty and is losing money quickly, the Turnaround Leader will have to make quick decisions about how to stop the bleeding before it is too late to conduct a Diagnostic Review. In these cases, this subcomponent triggers the Emergency Procedures component if it is approved by the TAB. There are several points throughout the formal start of the Turnaround Plan at which Emergency Procedures can be started, but the first time in the turnaround process is during the Diagnostic Review Stage; Emergency Procedures should only be used if the near-term survival of the company is at stake and if the decision can be made without much doubt about the consequences—especially if the divestment of a business unit is necessary.

The proposition created during this subcomponent should clearly outline the arguments for the Emergency Procedures proposed and the consequences if the procedures are not implemented immediately.

Responsibilities

The Turnaround Leader is responsible for preparing the arguments for and against the proposed Emergency Procedures.

Diagnostic Review Component (DR)

The Diagnostic Review Component is divided into two phases: the Analysis Phase (AP), in which a corporate due diligence is carried out; and the Evaluation Phase (EP), in which the results are evaluated and possible strategies proposed.

Diagnostic Review: Analysis Phase (DR AP)

DR AP 1 – Committing Resources

Summary

Commit external resources that are needed for the Diagnostic Review.

Context

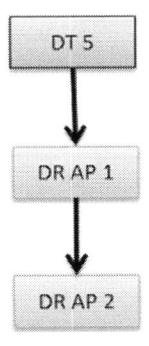

```
  DT 5
    ↓
  DR AP 1
    ↓
  DR AP 2
```

Description of the Subcomponent

This subcomponent is the formal start of the Diagnostic Review Stage. At this point, the resources necessary for a detailed Diagnostic Review should be assigned and committed to their tasks. These resources can be financial in nature but also include support personnel and materials. These may need to be hired or rented from outside the company, depending on the industry. In this subcomponent the availability of the resources needs to be confirmed.

Responsibility

The Turnaround Leader or an assistant is responsible for this subcomponent.

DR AP 2 – Conducting a Viability Analysis

Summary

The viability analysis is the first evaluation of the viability of the company's components, departments, and key employees.

Context

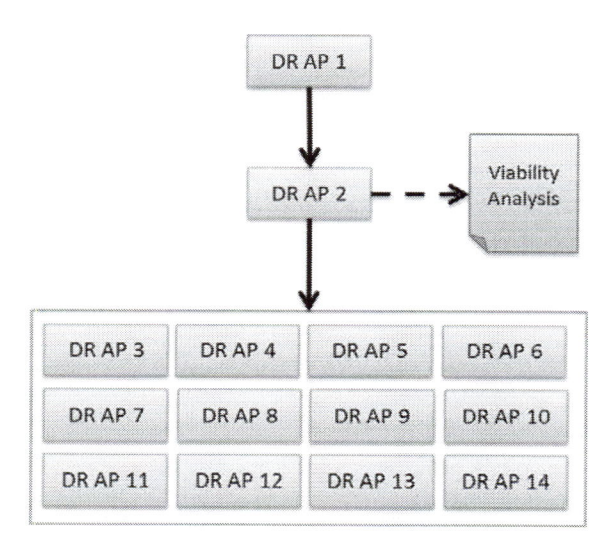

Description of the Subcomponent

A detailed viability analysis is based on two general approaches: segmentation, and evaluation of available resources in terms of financial strength, market competiveness, and people.[382]

Troubled companies usually fall into one of three classes: survival, continuing losses, or declining position.

---

[382] (Bibeault, 1999)

Survival: To fall into this class a company's survival must be seriously threatened. There is imminent danger of bankruptcy if drastic action is not taken.[383] In the US, a company in this class may already be—or will soon be—under Chapter 11 protection.

Continuing losses: The companies in this class are not in imminent danger of failing completely but are experiencing continuing losses. If these losses continue and nothing is done, the company will fail in the foreseeable future. The current losses are adversely affecting confidence.[384]

Declining position: The market share, profitability, and profit margins of companies in this class have been progressively declining. Often, the firm is losing money or will lose money in the foreseeable future if change does not occur quickly. The company's return on equity and on employed assets is near the bottom of its industry group.[385]

Identifying the root causes of failure is a difficult task as they may be very deeply hidden by years of doing business in a specific way and in layer upon layer of paperwork, required forms, established mechanisms, and culture.[386]

For a recovery strategy to be successful it must eliminate the financial crisis, reverse the causes of decline, and overcome the resistance of stakeholders, the constraints of the firm's internal environment, and, in many situations, an unattractive set of industry characteristics.[387] At this point during the turnaround process, the viability analysis still centers on the entity as a whole and not on certain people, products or divisions. Whether a company can be recovered is determined mainly by these six factors:

- The reasons for the crisis
- The severity of the situation
- The stakeholders' view of the company (see DR AP 14 – Stakeholder Analysis)
- The company's internal environment and strategy (see DR AP 4 – Company Analysis)
- The industry characteristics and other external factors (see DR AP 6 – Industry Analysis)
- The cost/price structure of the company (see DR AP 5 – Product Analysis)

---

[383] (Bibeault, 1999, p. 203)
[384] (Bibeault, 1999, p. 203)
[385] (Bibeault, 1999, p. 204)
[386] (Roman, 2010, p. 57)
[387] S.L., Corp. Rec. p. 107

The reasons for decline and the severity of the situation are examined in the following paragraphs.

The Reasons for the Decline

Examining why the company became a turnaround candidate—the reasons for the failure—is necessary in order to outline possible strategies to overcome the decline. Companies suffering from operational weaknesses and poor management or those suffering from an ill-conceived debt burden taken on during an earlier refinancing are much easier to turn around than those where the problem is the result of competitive weakness, severe price competition from competitors with a much lower cost base, or a completely outdated product line.[388] Picture 15 shows the strategies suggested for specific causes.

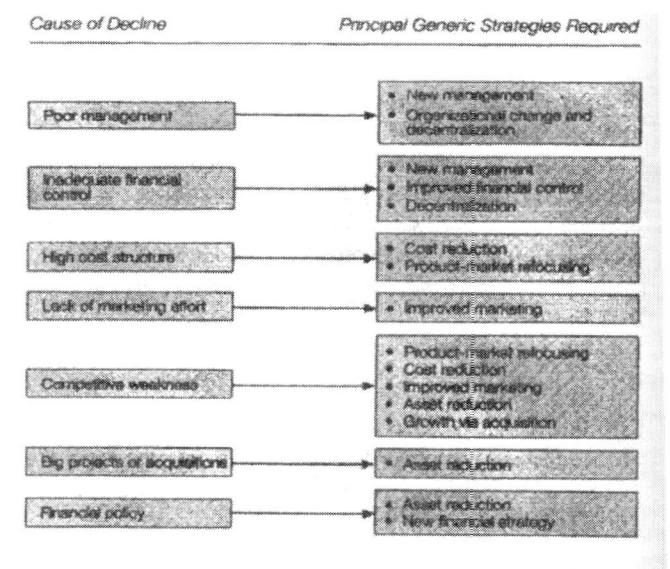

Picture 15 Influence of causes of decline on generic strategies[389]

---

[388] S.L., Corp. Rec. p. 107

[389] (Slatter & Lovett, 2004, p. 108)

The Severity of the Crisis Situation

The simple fact that a company loses money for a couple of months or years is not enough to classify it as being in a crisis situation, but it is sufficient reason to conduct a turnaround. The severity of the crisis facing the turnaround firm is a function of the causes of failure and what stage the crisis has reached (i.e. the degree to which the firm has progressed toward insolvency).[390] Shareholders can usually uncover a pure cash crisis from the firm's balance sheet, but if the management adopts some cash management and conservative gearing policies the crisis can smolder undiscovered for years. It is important to treat the causes rather than only adapting to the change in financial liquidity. If a strong cash crisis evolves, cash management and crisis management strategies must have priority over every other strategy. Strategies such as product-market refocusing and process re-engineering are possible cash-generating strategies, although their effects are often smaller than those of financial restructuring.[391]

If a company is lacking necessary funding, growth strategies and further investments should not be implemented until the recovery of the firm is ensured. Similarly, the severity of the firm's profit crisis (measured by the extent to which the firm is operating at below break-even) determines the extent to which the revenue-generating strategies (product-market reorientation and re-engineering of demand-generating components) will be necessary in addition to a cost reduction strategy.[392] The following shows that even the best cost reduction strategy may not be enough to bring the company back to a break-even level.

---

[390] (Slatter & Lovett, 2004, p. 108)
[391] (Slatter & Lovett, 2004, p. 109)
[392] (Slatter & Lovett, 2004, p. 109)

Figure 5.2: **Influence of Firm's Breakeven on Recovery Strategy**

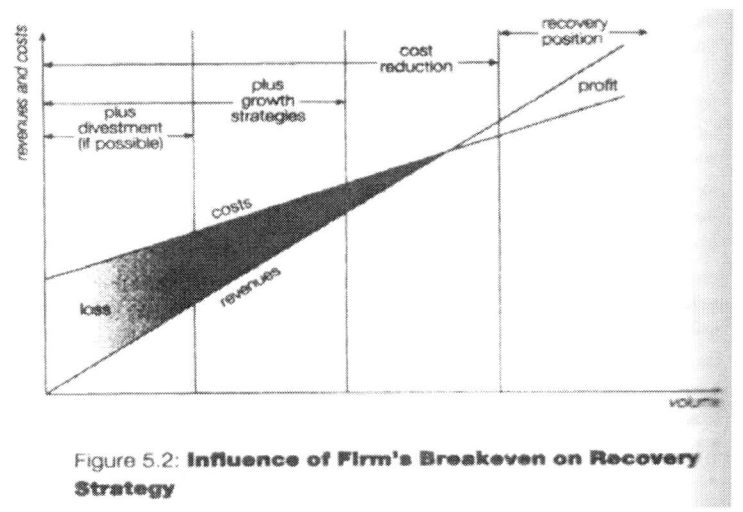

Picture 16 Influence of firm's break-even on the recovery strategy[393]

Segmentation

The first general rule of segmentation is the "rule of three". At any one time, a company, no matter how many formal divisions it has, probably has three types of divisions when viewed from a performance standpoint.[394] In fact, divisions, people, and assets can be classified into three groups: "winners", "maybes", and "losers".

- The company's operating divisions can be classified into viable divisions, divisions that need to be divested, and divisions that are in-between.
- The people in a turnaround company can be classified into staff who should definitely be kept because they are critical to the company, staff who are not critical and can be let go, and staff who are in-between.
- Assets/inventory can be classified into categories that are crucial to the business, categories that can be sold, and those in-between.

That something is classified as "in-between" can mean that the subject needs further evaluation, that not enough information is known, or that a clear classification cannot be made.

---

[393] From (Slatter & Lovett, 2004, p. 110)
[394] compare (Bibeault, 1999, p. 210)

It is important that the three categories differentiate performance in a readily distinguishable and comprehensible way.[395]

The second general rule of segmentation is Pareto's Law. Pareto's law states that a few employees file most of the labor grievances or experience most of the lost-time accidents, that a minority of policyholders file most of the insurance policy claims, and that a small proportion of product line items produces the majority of the sales in most organizations.[396] The concept indicates that in any given population, whether people or products, approximately 20 percent hold 80 percent of the "value" of the population, and the other 80 percent hold only 20 percent of the value.[397] These 80/20 relationships can help management pinpoint where the greatest opportunities for improvement in performance lie[398] by finding the 20 percent that generate 80 percent of the sales, cash, expenses, errors, or whatever. Many companies, particularly those run by founders, refuse to trim back and kill "their babies";[399] the emotional attachment to what they created can quickly get in the way of what is best for the company. To succeed, the management has to strengthen the company's position in those segments that contribute most of what is positive and kill those that generate most of what is negative.

A third type of segmentation technique involves making a detailed classification of expenditures and assets.[400] Assets are classified into those that are absolutely necessary for current operations and those that are based on a future payout. Items that are currently not necessary for the company's operations but have a current payout should go into the "current group", and items that are speculative in nature should be in the "futures group". Examples of the first group are items needed for quality control or automation, while examples of the second group are promotions, public relations, and advertising.

We can combine two types of segmentation by further classifying winners, maybes, and losers into winners, maybe, and losers in the current group and the future group. Losers should be retained only if the rock-bottom expenditure levels, as determined by the current/futures

---

[395] (Bibeault, 1999, p. 210)
[396] (Bibeault, 1999, p. 210)
[397] (Muller, 2011, p. 66)
[398] (Bibeault, 1999, p. 210)
[399] (Bibeault, 1999, p. 211)
[400] (Bibeault, 1999, p. 211)

classification, show a sizable present value or if the Turnaround Leader knows that a poor marketing job is being performed.[401] The same should be done for the items in the maybe group.

The outcome of this subcomponent is the Basic Viability Report.

Responsibility

The Turnaround Leader is responsible for this subcomponent, although the viability analysis is usually done by area-specific or diagnostic review experts.

Outcome

- Basic Viability Report

---

[401] (Bibeault, 1999, p. 212)

DR AP 3 – Financial Analysis

Summary

The financial analysis, a thorough analysis of the company's accounting practices and financial situation, is often done in conjunction with a product analysis (DR AP 5).

Context

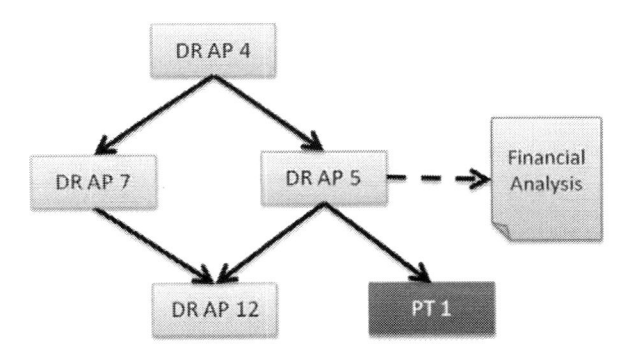

Description of the Subcomponent

The purpose of the financial analysis is to examine the financial condition of the company.

The following questions should guide you in assessing the financial situation:[402]

- How probable is a bankruptcy in the near future if no change to the company's strategy is made?
- How much time is available before the company faces bankruptcy?
- What financial resources could be raised in the short term to aid in the battle?
- What are the industry's current and quick ratios to help assess the company's liquidity?

---

[402] compare (Hofer, 1980)

- What is the size of the turnaround needed to avoid bankruptcy? What are the cash flow projections and cash flow break-even charts? (Cash flow break-even charts and the net income break-even point indicate the size of the turnaround effort that will be needed.)
- How much cash can be freed up by squeezing the firm's inventories and accounts receivable?

One of the first things a Turnaround Leader will do is look at the company's financial statements for the last five years, including the current year or quarter. The financial statements should be broken down by each company and division, each product line, and plant. Many troubled companies do not have such financial breakdowns.[403] The Turnaround Leader and their Financial Turnaround Manager must analyze each line of these financial statements to identify trends and determine how the single positions are related to each other in terms of gains, costs, and volume. The analysis should be compared and discussed with the analysis of external consultants if such consultants are available.

There are about 144 business ratios that can be found in the current literature.[404] We are far from a unique, scientifically based, and empirically confirmed standard.[405] However, business ratios are useful and necessary in evaluating crisis situations[406] and they give us a compressed and simplified picture of reality. Of course simplification also means a loss of detailed information.[407]

Analysis of financial reports is important in revealing information useful for decisions related to the current financial situation and the possible future financial development of the company, but the usefulness of analyzing business ratios in determining a company's financial position is questionable. In an analysis of 12 textbooks, business ratios were identified that are relevant for a crisis diagnosis.[408] There are 20 relevant business ratios that relate the most important financial positions to each other.[409] These business ratios can be used to compare the company

---

[403] (Bibeault, 1999, p. 217)
[404] compare (Hauschildt & Leker, 2000, p. 25)
[405] (Crone & Werner, 2007, p. 57)
[406] compare (Hauschildt, 1996, p. 3)
[407] (Hauschildt & Leker, 2000, p. 21)
[408] compare (Hauschildt & Leker, 2000, p. 19)
[409] (Hauschildt, 1996, p. 3)

with others in the industry and can also provide hints about the company's cost structure, which might need to be optimized. Still, business ratios, which are often derived from the balance sheet, should be treated carefully because of accounting and evaluation choices that the company has made; a close look at how the company calculates these ratios is necessary. Business ratios can draw a misleading picture because of new activities, reductions in accruals, or the generation of liquid funds by selling assets,[410] which are known as "window dressing". There is a basis on which to identify measures that distinguishes between accounting policies that the company follows throughout the year and accounting policies that the company uses to put together the balance sheet.[411]

Existing research focuses on the 20 most frequently used and commonly recognized business ratios.[412] These 20 ratios are introduced on the following pages, along with a norm for each ratio that should be reached in order for a company to be considered healthy. However, just because one or a few of these ratios do not conform to the suggested norm does not necessarily mean that a crisis is at hand. The ideal value of a business ratio will vary from industry to industry and even from company to company, but it can suggest what to look at more closely and where a problem might lie. A clearer picture can be gained by comparing these ratios over a timeframe of three to five years.[413]

The balance sheet and the income statement can provide a snapshot view of the company's financial health. The analysis should consider movement in the revenue and sales volume, including where and how revenue is generated, whether the revenue comes from new business or old customers, and how the volume out (throughput/production) gets the product or service "out the door".

Financial Systems

Looking at financial data in isolation can result in inappropriate or missing information. Many companies in difficulty have one or even all of the following three deficiencies:[414] they don't

---

[410] (Crone & Werner, 2007, p. 56)

[411] compare Rauscher in (Brühl & Göpfert, 2004, p. 236ff)

[412] (Hauschildt & Leker, 2000, p. 32), compare (Bertram & Gottwald, 2006, p. 31f) and Klein in Blöse/Kihm 2006, p. 73

[413] compare Klein in (Blöse, 2006, p. 73)

[414] (Bibeault, 1999, p. 217)

have information; they rely too heavily on accounting statements that do not resemble operating realities; and basic traps in presentation because of faulty conceptualization.

Some features of poor or misleading financial systems include:

- Standard costs that are not up to date, so an analyst cannot find out how big the margin actually is
- Profit-and-loss statements that are kept solely by market, rather than by plant or product line[415]
- Information that is prepared at the wrong level, making it difficult or impossible for management to know what's going on inside their operations[416]

However, even if accounting numbers are as accurate as possible, they will always be approximations that can only come close to the real situation. The accuracy and reliability of business numbers depend on the extent to which purposeful, dedicated effort is expended [on gathering them], and even under optimal conditions business numbers lack real-time and real-world accuracy.[417] The goal is to come as close as possible to seeing the real picture, so a mix of managerial accounting and financial accounting information will bring the analyst closer to the real situation than looking at only one or the other. While there have been abuses in audit reports, these abuses underscore the point that information needs to be checked and re-evaluated.

Symptoms

Symptoms that a company has loose financial controls include:

- The lack of a real and accurate cash forecasting system
- Decentralized responsibility for processing cash receipts, disbursing funds, and maintaining relationships with banks[418]
- The use of banks that are not under the control of federal regulation agencies

---

[415] (Bibeault, 1999, p. 217)
[416] (Collard, 2002, p. 30)
[417] (Bibeault, 1999, p. 218)
[418] (Bibeault, 1999, p. 303)

- The lack of bank records, bank ledgers, activities, and individual accounts
- Management that sees only the traditional accounting measures of company value. They neglect the cash flow from new business generated[419]

Eliminating Creative Accounting Practices

Creative approaches to accounting are usually a clear sign that something is being hidden from the shareholders. Such creative practices must be eliminated if the analyst is to gain a realistic picture of where the company stands.

These are some examples of creative practices that a Turnaround Leader should look out for when analyzing accounting practices:[420]

- Capitalized research costs
- Lease arrangements with "side letters" that remain off the balance sheet
- Capitalized items such as training costs, interest costs on loans, computer set-ups, and software costs
- Lack of routine maintenance on plant and equipment leading to the potential need for major renovation
- Treatment of extraordinary income as ordinary and ordinary expenditures as extraordinary items
- Valuation of inventories at market rather than at cost
- Increasing annual results by up-streaming a greater-than-legal share of a partially owned subsidiary's income
- Inflated valuation of assets
- Improper statement of dividends from subsidiaries
- A "department 99" created to invent customers

---

[419] compare (Collard, 2002)

[420] compare to (Bibeault, 1999, pp. 276-277)

The Balance Sheet

A company in trouble usually has a poor balance sheet position.[421] If this is the case, the Turnaround Leader or the financial expert in the TMT must quickly understand why the company is losing money. Looking at key ratios is not enough. Typical situations that may be present in a troubled company are:[422]

- Overvalued assets, especially intangible assets
- Large write-downs and overvalued inventories
- Capitalized data processing systems
- Capitalized current expense categories
- Capitalized future revenues based on current value
- Uncollectibles in accounts receivable
- Understated liabilities
- Out-of-date inventory listed at its original value

The Turnaround Leader must look closely at every asset category. The company's controllers can help in analyzing the balance sheet account by account. If the controllers don't know the real composition of the accounts, this is where a detailed analysis needs to start.

The financial expert on the TMT can use this component to find assets that can be turned into cash, and the value of some assets, such as land, may be understated in the balance sheet because their last evaluation was made years ago. If a company has a substantial last in, first out (LIFO) inventory account it is also possible that the unit value of inventory is understated from its market value.

The Cash Flow Statement

Analyzing the cash flow statement entails finding the difference between the actual cash flow and the profits in the operating statement. Substantial differences often crop up in companies in the financial services, natural resources, and technology areas.[423] In leasing companies, for

---

[421] (DBB, Corp. Turn., p. 213)
[422] (Bibeault, 1999, p. 214)
[423] (Bibeault, 1999, p. 214)

example, long-term leases are discounted so the actual cash flows are less than once shown. In resource-rich companies, on the other hand, it is common to deplete the resources, which can lead to the company earning more cash than the operating statements show.

Cash flow is the best indicator of business health,[424] therefore a detailed analysis of the cash flow statement with regard to changes in the financial position is important. Such an analysis should give the Turnaround Leader not only a picture of the current financial situation but also a sense of future prospects. If the company has a negative cash flow the goal is to get it to generate a positive cash flow in the short term. Although most companies eventually have enough resources within themselves, external funds will probably be needed to bridge the gap while the company turns assets into cash. It is unlikely that a firm in serious trouble can return to positive cash flow without correcting operational and strategic issues.[425]

Ratios

Degree of Liquidity

The degree of liquidity (DoL) describes the ability of the company to pay its short-term payment obligations with liquid assets (cash). The DoL shows how much of the short-term debt can be paid with liquid assets.

$$DoL = \text{liquid assets} / \text{short-term debt} * 100$$

Quick Ratio

The quick ratio shows how much of the short-term debt is covered by liquid assets and short-term accounts receivable. "This ratio is called the quick ratio because only cash and assets

---

[424] (Collard, 2002, p. 30)
[425] (Bibeault, 1999, p. 215)

quickly convertible into cash are included in the amount available for paying current liabilities."[426] A good quick ratio is about 50 percent.[427]

> Quick Ratio = (liquid assets + short-term accounts receivable) / short-term debt * 100

Current Ratio

The current ratio is a test of short-term solvency. The general rule or standard is that the current ratio for a business should be 2:1 or higher.[428] The ratio is only rarely expressed as a percentage. Short-term creditors usually like to see a company that limits its current liability to half or even less of its current assets because such a ratio creates more safety if each unit of liability is backed up by two units (e.g. euros, dollars) of assets. As creditors are not shareholders and don't share the profits of the company, they are more interested in preserving their investments.

> Current Ratio = current assets / current liabilities

Debt-to-Equity Ratio

The debt-to-equity ratio is an indicator of whether a company is using debt prudently or perhaps has gone too far and is overburdened with debt that may well cause problems.[429] This ratio indicates how many units of liability the company has for each unit of equity. The risk of excessive indebtedness generally rises as debt does.[430] An ideal debt-to-equity ratio is 1:1, although some capital-intensive businesses with a lot of assets, such as public utilities and most financial institutions, operate with higher ratios. In addition, the composition of the debt, not just the absolute amount, is important; a high amount of short-term debt might indicate a danger of sliding into insolvency.[431]

---

[426] (Tracy, 2009, p. 173)
[427] (Baus, 1999, p. 191)
[428] (Tracy, 2009, p. 172)
[429] (Tracy, 2009, p. 173)
[430] (Crone & Werner, 2007, p. 62)
[431] compare (Crone & Werner, 2007, p. 62)

> Debt-to-Equity Ratio = Total Liability / Total Stockholders' Equity

Times Interest Earned Ratio

The times interest earned ratio is a test of the company's ability to pay interest out of its earnings. The ratio should be higher than 1:1. For example, if a company has a times interest earned ratio of 5:1, its operating earnings are five times higher than the interest the company has to pay. Lenders would be very alarmed if a business were barely able to cover its annual interest charges.[432]

> Interest Earned Ratio = Operating Earnings / Interest Expense

Return on Assets

Return on assets (ROA) tells us how much the company earns before interest and taxes are paid on its asset value. This number is compared with the annual interest rate it pays on its borrowing to reveal the size of the firm's financial leverage. If a company's ROA is less than its interest rate, it suffers financial leverage loss.[433]

> ROA = Operating Earnings / Total Assets

Return on Equity

Return on equity (ROE) describes the profitability of the equity in relation to the company's overall return. The ROE should be compared with the average industry values for ROE because normal ROEs can differ quite significantly.[434]

---

[432] (Tracy, 2009, p. 174)
[433] (Tracy, 2009, p. 176)
[434] (Tracy, 2009, p. 176)

$$\text{ROE = Net Income / Stockholders' Equity}$$

Earnings Yield

The earnings yield can be calculated only for companies that are traded on the stock exchange. If the earnings yield of a company is 5.1 percent, the company is earning annual net income equal to 5.1 percent of the current market price of the stock shares.[435]

$$\text{EY = Basic EPS / Market Price}$$

Profit-Turnover Ratio

The profit-turnover ratio describes the profitability of the company independent of its financing structure so it can be compared with other companies. Only companies within the same industry should be compared because suggested profit-turnover ratios vary significantly from industry to industry.

$$\text{Profit-Turnover Ratio = Interest on Debt + Earnings) / Equity}$$

Working Capital Analysis

If the book figure for accounts receivable is higher than the equivalent of 40 to 50 days of company sales, you may be sure that there is work to be done.[436] In a turnaround situation in which the company is no longer making a profit, it is not able to deduct income taxes for uncollectible accounts. The result is that the uncollectible accounts build up, which makes it harder to focus on the accounts that are actually important.

---

[435] (Tracy, 2009, p. 179)
[436] (Bibeault, 1999, p. 274)

Return on Investment

Return on investment (ROI), which relates net income to invested capital (total assets), provides a standard for evaluating how efficiently management employs the average dollar invested in a business's assets.[437] If the ROI increases the stockholders get a higher return on their equity. There is no ROI that is good or bad for all companies. Sound and successful operation results in an optimum combination of profits, sales, and capital employed, but the precise combination necessarily varies with the nature of the business and the characteristics of the product.[438]

$$ROI = \text{Net profit after taxes} / \text{Total assets}$$

Fixed Assets Evaluation

Managers are likely to neglect looking into their fixed assets for hidden capital.[439] If a fixed asset, such as a building, land, or machinery, is already a couple of years old, its book value probably no longer reflects its real value. The Turnaround Leader should evaluate which assets can be sold and for what price if they are not used effectively.

Responsibility

The Financial Turnaround Manager is responsible for this subcomponent.

Outcome

- Financial Analysis Report

---

[437] (Shim & Siegel, 2008, p. 85)
[438] (Shim & Siegel, 2008, p. 87)
[439] (Bibeault, 1999, p. 274)

DR AP 4 – Company Analysis

Summary

This subcomponent involves a thorough analysis of the corporate structure, its strategy, positioning, strengths and weaknesses, and competitive advantages. By balancing company strengths and weaknesses, this analysis weighs up the company's ability to survive.[440]

Context

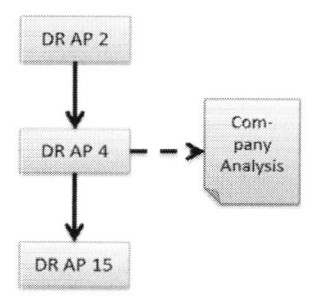

Description of the Subcomponent

CEOs often see the viability of their company's survival as a function of its strengths and weaknesses through answering questions such as these:

- Are we really as good as we think we are?
- How is our customer service compared to that of the competition?
- Do we believe we are good just because our people say we are good?

---

[440] (Bibeault, 1999, p. 205)

Evaluating the Core Business

A strong core business is needed to provide a sufficiently large sales cushion at decent margins to sustain the company while the TMT evaluates and corrects its problems. The most important part of a business is always its core business.[441] The core must have positive cash flow or the ability to be positioned for positive cash flow quickly.[442] However, after reviewing many turnaround cases, I don't necessarily agree with this. I believe that a turnaround can also be successful when the core business is under high pressure to fail and when it does not generate positive cash flow as long as other business lines are successful. In this case, either the divestment of the core business could be considered, so the company's attention would be on one or more of the secondary business areas, or other business areas become supportive and, along with external funding, finance the turnaround. It is not specified how quickly a company must be positioned for positive cash flow. Of course, a core business that does not have the viability to generate any positive cash flow at all is not worth saving, but there may be ways to save the core business, even if it is not generating positive cash flow, by employing financial strategies to accomplish a turnaround. I have not found many companies that have gone through a major crisis situation without their core business being at stake.

Assessment of the Organization Structure

There is no right or wrong structure of a company, although some structures may be more beneficial for one type of business or industry than others. Common organizational structures are:

- The pyramid structure
- The matrix organization
- The flat organizational structure
- The mixed organizational structure

There are a few guiding questions that an assessment of the organizational structure should answer:

---

[441] (Seefelder, 2007, p. 147)
[442] (Bibeault, 1999, p. 207)

- Does an informal structure exist that differs from the formal structure of the firm?
- Is the structure appropriate for the type of business?
- Are there weaknesses in the structure that could have an impact on the desired results?[443]
- Has there been any recent change to the structure and, if so, why?
- Is open and two-way communication supported by the structure?
- Is decision making carried out by people with access to the right level and quality of information?[444]
- Are there too many people reporting to the top management and the CEO?

The Company's Historical Strategy

Organizations that embark on a program of strategic change do not have the luxury of starting with a clean sheet of paper,[445] so any new strategies or changes to an original strategy have to take into account what happened in the past. The company's historical strategy can create short-term parameters for future strategies. How issues have been treated, how business functions have operated, and what the goals and targets have been determine the future development, at least to some extent. A new strategy cannot simply replace an old one from one day to another as, often, a culture will have evolved around a business-wide strategy that will be difficult to change. Companies always have a past that they carry with them—their old customers, existing products, assets, financial resources, employees, expertise, and so on—that can constrain future strategies; however, it should not create boundaries. In any case, the Turnaround Leader should pay close attention to past strategies and practices and the corporate culture.

What is the Firm's Cost/Price Structure?

The cost/price structure is central in evaluating whether the management should focus short-term attention on a marketing improvement strategy, a cost reduction strategy, or both in an

---

[443] (Slatter & Lovett, 2004, p. 123)
[444] (Slatter & Lovett, 2004, p. 123)
[445] (Slatter & Lovett, 2004, p. 111)

effort to make fast progress in increasing profit margins.[446] The cost/price structure is partially a function of the characteristics of the industry in which the firm operates and the reason for the crisis, so a close look at it will rule out certain turnaround strategies. A sensitivity analysis of the company's profit and loss statement will tell the Turnaround Leader a good deal about the firm's cost structure in terms of identifying the profit-sensitive parts of the business. The most important are the parts over which the management has a direct influence: volume, price, and costs. For small changes—say five to ten percent—the value of these three components, the relative importance of pricing, volume-generating, and cost reduction strategies can be ascertained,[447] but the sensitivity analysis does not tell the management which parts to change; this requires good judgment and experience. In the long term, the costs need to decrease independent of pricing.

The TMT should also look for weaknesses that lead to deviations in unit labor costs and procurement costs from the ideal experience curve.[448] The key questions they should ask include:

- How strongly and quickly do the prices of the offered products and services change in the industry?[449]
- How does the company's cost and price curve compare to the cost and price curve of competitors in the industry?[450]

Evaluation of Marketing Effectiveness

This step should be undertaken only if sufficient resources and time are available. It's not uncommon for a company to carry a large number of unproductive salespeople or to be selling low-profit items to low-purchase-level customers. Many audit systems, whether internal or external, can measure the effectiveness of marketing efforts, but the Turnaround Leader should

---

[446] (Slatter & Lovett, 2004, p. 113)
[447] (Slatter & Lovett, 2004, p. 113)
[448] compare (N.A., 2009, p. 9)
[449] (N.A., 2009, p. 9)
[450] (N.A., 2009, p. 7)

consider interviewing key customers personally if time allows. The auditing system should rate marketing efforts and address the following points:

- Does the company acknowledge the primacy of the marketplace and of customer needs in shaping company plans and operations?[451]
- Do plans for long-term growth ensure the long-term profitability of the company?
- Does the marketing department have the right resources and competencies to plan, implement, control, and analyze marketing efforts?
- Are the marketing efforts cost-effective?
- Does the management receive the right information and quality of information it needs to be able to monitor results in order to conduct effective marketing?

Evaluating the Competitive Strategy

The main concern in evaluating the competitive strategy is to determine whether the company can make sustainable profits in the business area that it chooses. The starting point is to define which products or services the firm is selling, to whom, and in what part(s) of the value-added chain the firm is competing.[452] Market position reports will help reveal this information, so each of the various market or product managers should be assigned the task of preparing these reports for review and discussion.[453] A segmentation analysis will help to break the business into its parts and processes in order to reveal whether the current product-market segments and activities are the correct ones given the firm's resources and the characteristics of the external environment in which it operates.[454] One way of examining the current strategy is to have the TMT pretend that they are the competition in order to identify the strategy that the firm should pursue to compete successfully.[455]

Creating Market-Position Reports

---

[451] (Bibeault, 1999, p. 222)
[452] (Slatter & Lovett, 2004, p. 232)
[453] (Bibeault, 1999, p. 221)
[454] (S.L., Corp. Rec. p. 232)
[455] compare (Collard, 2002, p. 30)

The product managers should create a market-position report for each product or market. These reports will be different from business to business, but the basic elements should be:

1. Current and past years' information on the development of the market share, with future projections. The Turnaround Leader should treat these projections carefully, using them as a point of departure for discussion and to evaluate the skills of the product manager.
   - Sales information with future projections
   - Profit information with future projections

2. Explanations of why the market share has changed over the last few years, organized by:
   - Product
   - User group of the product/service
   - Geographic area
   - Distribution channel

3. List of innovations and changes over the last five years in:
   - Marketing strategies (of the company and its competitors)
   - The market
   - The product
   - Price changes

4. SWOT analysis of the products

5. Projections for:
   - Market development
   - Trends
   - Competitive moves

Employee Turnover Rate

A sure sign of underlying problems is rapid employee turnover.[456] It may be high because of inadequate training, poor management style, poor leadership skills, lack of employee development, low salaries, and so on. Management that does not know the turnover rate and how many people the company is losing per year have considerable room for improvement. Solutions include clearly defined job responsibilities, performance expectations, rewards, and scope of authority.[457]

Competitive Advantage

This subcomponent also involves describing the competitive advantages of the company, how new ones can be developed, and how can they be used to overcome competition, and identifying how the key competencies can be used to meet the needs of the customers and to produce benefits for them.

Responsibility

The Turnaround Leader is responsible for this subcomponent.

Outcome

- Company Analysis Report

---

[456] (Collard, 2002, p. 28)
[457] (Collard, 2002, p. 29)

DR AP 5 – Product Analysis

Summary

This subcomponent provides a detailed analysis of each product in the product line.

Context

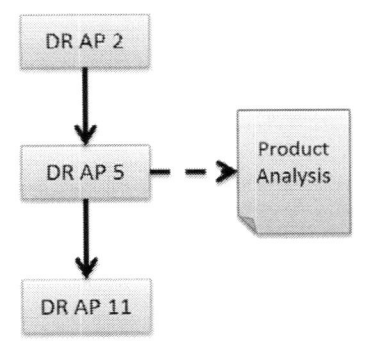

Description of the Subcomponent

Each product line should be analyzed separately. Most companies have a mix of products that are successful and contribute to the company's profit and others that lower profits. Still others may be in-between—not very successful products that are dragged along with the day-to-day business creating overheads that decrease their profitability. On the other hand, these in-between products may create volume that is necessary in order for other products to be profitable, or may be offered just to make other products look cheaper. A careful analysis of a product's contribution to profits and to the overall product portfolio will bring these factors and other aspects of the product to light. In order to find unprofitable products the TMT will also need to verify whether the cost allocations to the different products are correct. Gathering this information can be difficult as troubled companies may not have a clear outline of these financial aspects of their products.

Product line proliferation is one of the more common problems for firms that have run out of control and into a crisis situation.[458] For many companies a growing product line means overall growth, but with growth of the product line comes many requirements that must be met in order to achieve sustainable growth. Sales growth is not a solution to problems that have built up in other areas of the company and may not compensate for inefficiencies; in fact, shrinking the number of products or product lines is usually the surest route to better profits and higher return on investment.[459]

In some cases, products come to market too early, before the need for the product has been created. These are difficult to sell and the return on investment may take a couple years. It is less costly to create awareness of a product or service that meets an existing demand than to develop a new market for them.[460] Firms that set out to exploit their existing products tend to find their major opportunities in two areas:[461] selective marketing strategy and profit improvement.

Analyzing the Price of the Product

This subcomponent helps determine whether the company's product pricing is right. The market analysis carried out earlier to determine where the product is priced compared to its competitors will reveal whether the product is under or overpriced. Underpricing seems to be a perennial problem with troubled companies;[462] if the company's products are underpriced opportunity may lie in the sales force since, with prices lower than the competitor's, the sales force has an easy job and may only be taking orders rather than selling the products' value at a higher price using their persuasion skills.

The pricing analysis should target seven points:

1. How have the sales of the product or product line developed over the last couple of periods? Most products have a life cycle that will cause them to decline after a couple

---

[458] (Bibeault, 1999, p. 286)
[459] (Bibeault, 1999, p. 287)
[460] (Collard, 2002, p. 30)
[461] (Bibeault, 1999, p. 321)
[462] (Bibeault, 1999, p. 284)

of periods. If sales of a product are trending downward the company should spend little or nothing to keep it from dying, focusing instead on products that are at the beginning of their life cycle.

2. Does the product/product line contribute to a positive cash flow? If the old product is still above break-even it should be kept but not considered for a marketing offensive. If the product is not profitable the Turnaround Leader should shut it down. There might be arguments for keeping the product active that need to be discussed but, in the end, it comes down to its profitability. Other arguments should be resisted, particularly in regard to old products at the end of their life cycle that the company is just dragging along because they have always been there. Consider how IBM, originally known as a manufacturer of computer hardware, made a successful transition to a pure software and consulting company by discontinuing or selling off product lines.

3. What is the gross margin of the product/product line? There is no fixed rule about what is satisfactory here. Gross margin is the difference the between net sales price and the total cost of materials, direct labor, and applicable factory overheads,[463] although common terminology, if not definitions in U.S.GAAP and IFRS, often also refers to the difference between sales and cost of sales as gross profit or gross income.[464] In the manufacturing business, to have a profit of at least ten percent on sales before federal income taxes, the gross margin should be no less than 35 and preferably well over 45 percent.[465] If the company's gross margin is low, unless it can raise selling prices (the first place to look) it faces a long struggle to improve operating efficiency because, while the company is fighting to lower its manufacturing costs, its competitors are as well.

4. Who is setting the prices? If the sales department determines how much a product costs then the price is probably lower than it should be. The customer will often pay more with little or no objection despite all the sales department's warnings that raising the price is recklessness.

---

[463] (Bibeault, 1999, p. 228)
[464] compare (Stickney & Weil, 2000, p. 148)
[465] (Bibeault, 1999, p. 288)

5. Is a full product line necessary? If your competitor carries a full line, salespeople will insist that they cannot compete unless they have the full product line as well, because the buyer wants to purchase from one supplier.[466] However, with a full line of products some will sell better than others but all tend to be carried on. Low-margin products should be eliminated.

6. Does the company have too many product variations? Offering custom-made products can be very expensive—more expensive than accounting statements are likely to show—if the products aren't sold in high volume. Many companies offer more and more variations of their products in order to target every possible customer taste and preference, but a crisis situation may require that the variations be cut as keeping customers who don't want the most common version of the product may be too expensive.

7. What is the book-to-bill ratio? A book-to-bill ratio of 0.94 means that for every $100 worth of products shipped (billed) manufacturers received $94 worth of new orders (bookings).[467] As a product line matures and competition comes in, the ratio will drop off even though shipments continue.[468] The book-to-bill ratio should be broken down by product line rather than examined as an overall ratio so products that are trending downward can be identified.

Nature of the Product(s)

Not every turnaround strategy fits every product. Strategies that are designed to generate revenue quickly may not be easy to implement for a product that has a long manufacturing or handling time, such as some capital products. Product-market focusing and price increases, which are often necessary in a turnaround, become increasingly difficult as the product becomes less differentiated and more price-sensitive.[469]

---

[466] (Bibeault, 1999, p. 289)
[467] (InfoWorld, 1991, p. 108)
[468] (Bibeault, 1999, p. 289)
[469] (Slatter & Lovett, 2004, p. 112)

Old Products

Some companies drag along old, low-margin products that have always been offered and that the management believes are necessary to cover overhead costs or contribute more than the financials indicate. Such lines may be doing worse than the financials show and may generate more indirect costs than are charged to them on the accounting books.[470]

Single-Product Companies

Single-product companies have only a very small chance of survival if the product itself is the reason for the crisis. When a single-product company's core product slips, it has very little choice but to milk that product and use the funds to bring out a new product better suited to the market.[471] The strategy is risky but has been used successfully, as when Arctic Enterprises Inc., a maker of snowmobiles, was forced by the decline in industry sales to move to other products.[472]

Product Profitability Analysis

Cost allocation is the process of assigning costs when there is no direct measure for the quantity of resources consumed by a particular cost object. The purpose of all cost allocation methods is to assign shared, or indirect, costs to individual products, customers, branches, or other cost objects (sometimes called cost centers), as defined by an organization.[473] Product costing should be based on what is practical. A product profitability analysis, essential for profit improvements, looks at the contribution of each service or product relative to net operating income.[474] A product economic analysis will show how product costs are physically generated and where the economic leverage lies, as details are usually masked by financial accounting systems.[475]

---

[470] (Bibeault, 1999, p. 287)
[471] (Bibeault, 1999, p. 290)
[472] compare (Bibeault, 1999, p. 290)
[473] (Helms & Grace, 2004, p. 1)
[474] (Ledgerwood & White, 2006)
[475] (Bibeault, 1999, p. 311)

A variety of mechanisms can be used to allocate costs and revenue and determine the efficiency of various business units.[476] Two methods are introduced in this section and explained in detail in the Financial Restructuring component. The first, a traditional cost allocation process, assigns income and costs line by line from the profit and loss account to products, deciding on what basis each line or "allocation unit" should be allocated, such as to direct labor hours or total account balances of a specific product.[477] The basis that is used to apportion costs to cost objects (i.e. the number of material receipts) is called an allocation base or cost driver.[478] The next step is to apply a transfer price to the product or service. After the entire department's overhead costs have been allocated, it is possible to determine the per-unit full cost of the items or activities completed by the producing department.[479] The second method is an activity-based costing, which assigns income and costs based on the resources (such as staff time and infrastructure usage) consumed.[480]

In traditional costing, indirect expenses are usually too aggregated to serve any informational purpose as these large groupings destroy the ability to calculate an accurate cost for any one type of output.[481] Another problem with overhead cost allocation is that excessively broad-bush average rates are applied to calculate costs. Cost allocations often rely on sales-related, volume-based factors, such as direct labor hours or department expenses.[482]

Other important parts of the product analysis are the present and future break-even point of each product, its current and expected market share, and its growth potential.

Responsibility

The Turnaround Leader or, in some special cases where the product is highly complex, a product specialist from the Diagnostic Review Team is responsible for this subcomponent.

---

[476] (Ledgerwood & White, 2006, p. 315)
[477] (Ledgerwood & White, 2006, p. 316)
[478] (Drury, 2011)
[479] (Smith S. G., 2002, p. 40)
[480] (Ledgerwood & White, 2006, p. 316)
[481] (Cokins, 2006, p. 13)
[482] compare (Cokins, 2006, p. 13)

Outcome

- Product Analysis Report

DR AP 6 – Industry Analysis

Summary

The industry is analyzed in this step: industry characteristics, prospects, and technological change rates, along with stakeholders' bargaining power, and the size and growth rate of the market.

Context

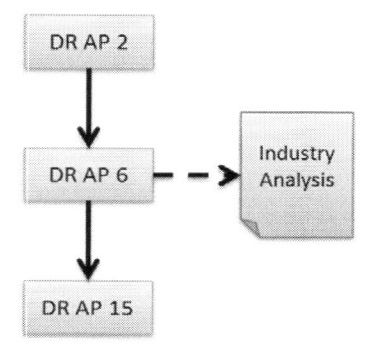

```
DR AP 2
   │
   ▼
DR AP 6  ---> Industry Analysis
   │
   ▼
DR AP 15
```

Description of the Subcomponent

Industry Characteristics

The conditions of the industry in which a company operates always have an influence, whether positive or negative, on the company. There are several factors that influence an industry's profitability that are the same as the factors that influence a turnaround situation.[483] Hence, a company's chances of survival are directly linked to the industry's potentials. The chance of sustainable turnaround in an industry with low profit potential must be lower than in an industry with higher profit potential because, in the latter case, it is easier to attract additional finance for investment and to follow an asset-reducing strategy of divestment since there are likely to be new firms willing to enter the industry.[484]

---
[483] (Porter M., 1989)
[484] (Slatter & Lovett, 2004, p. 112)

One way of measuring governance transparency involves six facets of governance: voice and accountability; political stability; government effectiveness; regulatory quality; rule of law; and control of corruption.[485] The research study, which covered 165 countries, was developed for the World Bank in 1999 and 2002. A diagnostic review team may find this method—evaluating the industry based on these six factors—useful in completing this subcomponent.

Prospects of the Industry

An industry's circumstances, such as its growth rate, have an important comparison value as the growth rate of the market is proportional to the cash usage a company should have. In other words, management should utilize different functional strategies, each of which has a different cash requirement, based on the company's stage of growth. The lack of financial resources, poor management, and lack of financial control that usually characterize turnaround situations may change substantially the traditional pattern of strategic responses expected at different stages of the life cycle.[486] For example, in the growth stage, which is usually a time for companies to invest and to utilize strategies to increase sales, a turnaround situation may dictate the use of other strategies, such as product-market refocusing, cost reduction, and asset reduction.

It is important not to underestimate the potential of an essentially good business in a poorly performing sector and not to overestimate the chances of recovery for a poor business in a highly regarded industry.[487]

Technological Change Rate

The greater the rate of change, the more financial resources are required to bring the firm back to a competitive position because more investments may have to be made in order to keep up with the competition, and because the technology used becomes outdated more quickly than in a company with a slow technological change rate.[488] Hence, a company that operates in an environment with a slow technological change rate is an easier candidate for investment and

---

[485] (Kaufmann, Kraay, & Zoido-Lobatón, 2002), (Fischer, Lee, & Johns, 2004)
[486] (Slatter & Lovett, 2004, p. 111)
[487] (Baden-Fuller & Stopford, 1994)
[488] (Slatter & Lovett, 2004, p. 112)

product-market strategies than one that operates in an environment with a fast technological change rate.

Stakeholders' Bargaining Power

The power that suppliers and customers have over the company can have a substantial effect on the turnaround process. Suppliers and customers affect the turnaround firm in terms of its ability to raise prices and to reduce supply costs. If the turnaround candidate has bargaining power over a supplier, the Turnaround Leader may be able to negotiate new prices for raw materials or other parts that are needed for production.

Size of the Total Market

The size of the total market for the company's products and the size of each product's market segment are essential to be able to determine which products should be pushed and which are already at their limits in terms of growth potential.

Growth Rate of the Market

The growth rate of the market and its market segments are useful in determining whether a market is shrinking and may die out in the near future or whether the company can diversify in a growing market and push advertising. The last five years of market growth should be examined and a projection made for the next five years.

Some factors that can influence the growth of a market should be entered into the Risk Log. These factors include:

- A new emerging industry or market
- Technological developments

External Industry Analysis

The external industry analysis prepared in the Pre-Turnaround Stage (PS) should be combined with the profitability analysis of the firm's products in the Evaluation Stage of the diagnostic review in order to identify opportunities in the market. The criteria for choosing a product-market are segment attractiveness (based on industry analysis), the extent to which the firm has a competitive advantage or disadvantage, and the extent to which it is capable of implementing its chosen strategy.[489]

Responsibility

The Turnaround Leader is responsible for this subcomponent.

Outcome

- Industry Analysis Report

---

[489] (Slatter & Lovett, 2004, p. 232)

DR AP 7 – Competitor Analysis

Summary

A competitor analysis will give the TMT an idea of the strength of the competition, what they are planning, and what the company is up against.

Context

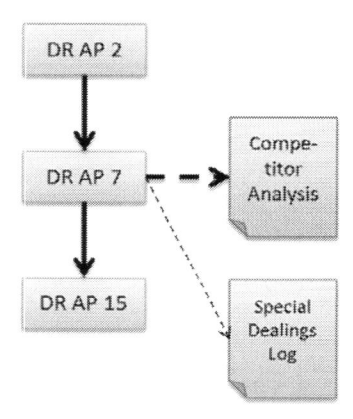

Description of the Subcomponent

Competitors' Strength and Size

The relative strength and size of competitors and the intensity of competition have a direct effect on a company's strategies.[490] If competition intensity is low the company may have more time for changes, but if a competitor is financially strong and has significant market share the competitor may take advantage of the company's weakened condition and run an aggressive price war to drive it out of business.

It is also important to monitor competitors' market share throughout the turnaround process. A report on how the market share of competitors' products has evolved over the last five years

---

[490] (Slatter & Lovett, 2004, p. 112)

should be examined and a projection for the next five years made. Competitive benchmarking is useful at this point. The aim of benchmarking is to improve the performance of an organization, as measured against its mission and objectives. Benchmarking implies comparison, either internally against previous performance and desired future targets, or externally against similar organizations or organizations that perform similar functions.[491] Benchmarking should contain both comparative analysis and recommendations that build upon the findings to help participants embrace best practice.[492]

Two essential questions to answer during this subcomponent are:

- How can competitors offer products similar to ours but sell them for less?
- What worked for our competition and what did not?

If the company has some special agreements with competitors, such as agreements about not entering certain markets, these agreements should be entered in the Special Dealings Log. The Special Dealings Log stores all special agreements made throughout the turnaround.

Responsibility

The Turnaround Leader is responsible for this subcomponent

Outcome

- Competitor Analysis Report

---

[491] (Malano & Dr. Burton)
[492] (Eskew, 1999, p. 2)

DR AP 8 – Prepare Bridge Financing

Summary

If the financial analysis shows that the company will run out of cash before the turnaround process can be started or before cash-generating strategies kick in, bridge financing will be necessary so the company can survive to start the turnaround process.

Context

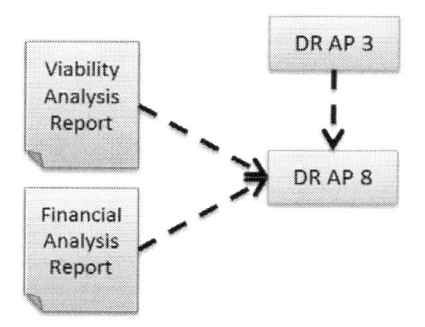

Description of the Subcomponent

For a preliminary viability analysis, a viable core and possibly bridge financing are required to achieve a turnaround. The Viability Analysis Report generated in DR AP 2 and the Financial Analysis Report generated in DR AP 3 will show whether bridge financing is needed.

In only rare cases the viable core generates such a high cash flow that there is little question about where the cash to finance the turnaround will come from. If the company cannot finance the turnaround from its own cash flow, it will have to involve banks or other investors in the turnaround process. Without lender support for bridge financing while a company turns its unproductive assets into cash or debt elimination, the viability of the company is in serious doubt.[493] However, bridge financing should be sought only if the TMT believes in a successful turnaround for the company. If such financing is necessary for a US company, a savvy

---

[493] (Bibeault, 1981, p. 208)

turnaround expert will probably avoid undertaking a turnaround with a poor leader or will seek Chapter 11 protection under the Bankruptcy Act to increase the odds of success.

Responsibility

The Financial Turnaround Manager is responsible for this subcomponent.

Information Needs

- Viability Analysis Report
- Financial Analysis Report
- Company Analysis Report (if available)
- The reports generated in DR AP 3 to DR AP 7 may be needed in order to gain bridge financing

DR AP 9 – Survey Employees

Summary

In this subcomponent the HR Turnaround Manager creates a survey, fields it among the employees, and analyzes the results.

Context

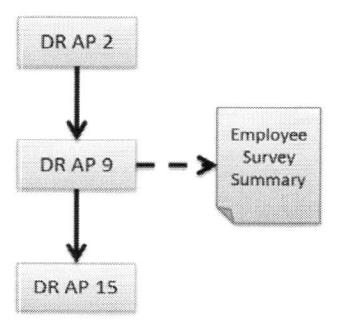

Description of the Subcomponent

The management and employees are asked their options about several important issues:

- Some employees are directly in touch with clients, so they know about their complaints and what they like most about the company. It is these employees who influence the customers to buy a certain product and who drive customer loyalty.
- The management's support for the turnaround and the company is important, and the management can help to reveal hidden problems that have not been discovered yet.
- Employees often see problems before the management, and have ideas that could solve problems quickly or make processes more efficient.
- Employees often know what problems exist; they should also be asked if they know of possible solutions.

- Employees are closer to one operational aspect or another; this closeness and their individual experience with the way components have changed over time will give valuable insight into operational malfunctions.[494]

It is important that such a survey or discussion is kept confidential so that the employees do not need to fear consequences. The turnaround consultant, assuming they are not an employee, will be able to establish an atmosphere of confidentiality and security where employees will share their thoughts freely and without fear of reprisal.[495] The survey should use open-ended questions to get the employees talking about what they have noticed and what is on their minds. Younger or newer employees often notice obsolete policies and systems more than older or more tenured employees. When the information is collected it also needs to be categorized, and additional questions should be aimed at finding out how significant each issue is, which area it is coming from—such as people, policy, culture, or processes—and the time when the negative change was first noticed. The outcome of the survey is presented to the Turnaround Leader.

Responsibility

The HR Turnaround Manager is responsible for this subcomponent.

Outcome

- Employee survey summary, including complaints, ideas, criticism, hopes, expectations, fears

---

[494] (Roman, 2010, p. 19)
[495] (Roman, 2010, p. 58)

DR AP 10 – Management Analysis

Summary

The management analysis determines which managers will support the turnaround process and which have the capabilities and skills needed for the turnaround.

Context

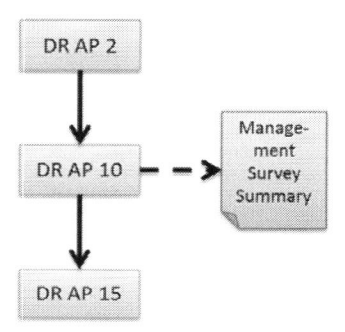

Description of the Subcomponent

If the company's top management team stays on board during the turnaround process, it must quickly and accurately determine the cause of a firm's performance lapse and implement decisions necessary for its prompt recovery.[496] If it does not manage the turnaround properly, the result will be further decline and, eventually, insolvency.[497]

In order to decide which managers can support the turnaround process, the TMT must get to know key managers; much can be gained by observing the people in the organization and by reviewing their responses to requests for information.[498] The essential question is whether the people can perform the turnaround process and whether they can achieve higher standards. The Turnaround Leader has to make this assessment. It is a slow process, but the most accurate.

---

[496] (Lohrke, Bedeian, & Palmer, 2004)
[497] compare (Weitzel & Jonsson, 1989)
[498] (Bibeault, 1981, p. 222)

The management analysis may make clear that good people are working in an area where they don't fit into the turnaround structure or that might be closed. These people should be marked in the Management Analysis Report as top performers who may need to be moved to other departments.

Three criteria should influence the decision about an employee:

- Simple numbers requirements are usually used in decisions about rank-and-file employees, tempered by union seniority rules, affirmative action programs, and company policies.[499]
- A marginal performer is not necessarily a marginal performer in all situations. Their poor performance may be the result of the situation they are in or the work they are doing. A different job or training should be considered to motivate marginal performers. It is easier and cheaper to remotivate and retrain an incumbent with potential than it is to find replacements
- The ability to fire people and the process that must be undertaken to do so varies from country to country. In some countries, a manager can fire a subordinate if he tells him something that sounds right but is wrong. In other countries, people can be laid off only if the company's survival is seriously threatened, and even then the decision concerning whom to fire may not be based on performance but on family connections or seniority.

In a recent study, 40 percent of CEOs had been in their jobs for 22 months, and 20 percent for only 8 months.[500] However, even when top managers have been serving the company for a long time and have unique insights into the industry and the market, they can become "stale in the saddle".[501] When managers become too stale and the company faces major changes in its environment, these managers often fail to formulate a proper reorganization strategy[502] unless the downturn is modest, such as a soft economic recession.[503] If the downturn is long-term—because of old products, for example—studies have shown that short-tenured managers are

---

[499] (Bibeault, 1981, p. 224)
[500] (Challenger, Gray & Christmas, 2006)
[501] compare (Miller, 1991)
[502] compare (Wiersema & Bantel, 1993)
[503] compare (Zimmermann F., 1989)

more likely to implement strategic changes that move the company into new industries or product segments.[504]

Another objective of the management analysis is to determine whether there is consensus among top management. Research has found that consensus in the top management team can have either positive or negative effects on a firm's performance.[505] If no crisis is at hand, a lack of consensus between the members of the top management may have a negative effect on the firm's effectiveness because the management is unable to commit to a strategy.[506] In dynamic environments, however, a low level of consensus may improve decision-making and the firm's performance. In fact, in this situation, a firm's performance can improve[507] as the top management team becomes more heterogeneous in function and the number of relevant issues rises.[508] The dynamism of the environment can also affect whether consensus is positive or negative.[509] In an environment that is not dynamic, the top management would be more likely to agree on a turnaround strategy than if the environment is dynamic.

The management analysis is also useful in addressing and eliminating political games or hidden agendas that could take the turnaround effort hostage.

Management Assessment

The middle management ranks carry the brunt of the turnaround workload. They are also an important group because they are close to the production and administrative groups.[510] This section provides a framework for a preliminary management review.

One of the main causes for a distressed company is the top management. Before a decision on what to do with the old top management can be made, the TMT must individually evaluate the members of the current management. Evaluating management is an integral part of a turnaround situation and is often demanded by outside stakeholders, such as shareholders and

---

[504] (Barker & Duhaime, 1997), (Barker III & Patterson Jr., 1996), (Barker III, Patterison Jr., & Mueller, 2001)
[505] compare (Lohrke, Bedeian, & Palmer, 2004)
[506] (Noble, 1999)
[507] compare (Hoffman & Maier, 1961), (Simons, Pelled, & Smith, 1999)
[508] compare (Hoffman & Maier, 1961), (Hambrick, Cho, & Chen, 1996) r68
[509] (Homburg, Krohmer, & Wokman Jr, 1999)
[510] (Bibeault, 1981, p. 296)

banks, before they will agree to any further financial support.[511] Key goals of a management assessment are to determine the level of support for change, how open they are to discussing their mistakes, and the level of resistance to restructuring. When there is resistance, the solution is obvious: the manager must be replaced. If a manager will support the change and is willing to embrace it, they probably do not need to be replaced.

In general, there are four possible options the TMT need to consider when deciding what to do with incumbent management:

- Hire a new top management team
- Replace the CEO and work with the current management team
- Keep the incumbent top management team but have the TMT lead the turnaround
- Keep the incumbent top management team as advisors during the turnaround process and replace them later

However, before these decisions can be made, there first needs to be an assessment of the senior management team as individuals, their effectiveness as a team, and the effectiveness of the current structure of the organization.[512] This evaluation must distinguish between someone just making a bad call and learning from it and a manager being stubborn and persisting to believe in their poor decisions. Most reasons for a crisis can be traced back to the management. Even if the reasons are environmental, such as an economic crash, one can always draw a line back to the managers who should have anticipated the crash. In this case, however, a replacement may not be necessary.

Reasons why the incumbent management should remain include:

- They may not be responsible for the decline.
- They are willing to learn from their mistakes.
- They have special insights into the industry.
- They can bring guidance and external support to the turnaround process.

---

[511] (Slatter & Lovett, 2004, p. 120)
[512] (Slatter & Lovett, 2004, p. 120)

- Their knowledge of the business is an advantage, especially when rapid change is important.

In developing an opinion on the management, it is more important to look for certain characteristics, particularly those that pertain to the style and approach required in a turnaround situation, than for specific business or industry experience.[513]

The management review in the Diagnostic Review Stage has the following objectives:

- Determine to what extent the management as a whole and as individuals are part of the problem. In some cases, there is only one decision-maker in the organization.
- Determine whether members of the board are there because they are qualified to do the job or for another reason. For example, did they work their way up to the position, or were they given it because they invested in the company or because they know or are related to another person on the board?
- Determine whether the incumbent management team could provide solutions. Sometimes a member of the current management has a solution to the problem but has been overruled by other board members.
- Find out who holds real power or influence within the organization (which may not be consistent with the hierarchy or organization chart); these individuals must become champions of change.[514]
- Assess whether the incumbent management team has the power and capability to implement change.
- Determine whether any members of the management team should leave the company immediately because they cause problems, are not open to change, or may harm the turnaround process in some other way.
- Determine how effective the management is as a team and how effective individual team members are.
- Assess how effective the current organization structure is.[515]
- Assess the management team's willingness to bring about change.
- Assess the management team's ability to learn from its mistakes.

---

[513] (Slatter & Lovett, 2004, p. 121)
[514] (Slatter & Lovett, 2004, p. 120)
[515] compare S.L., Corp. Rec. p. 120

- Assess the management team's openness to discussion.

The following points may be added to this list:[516]

- Is there autocratic leadership, a policy of "divide and rule", or an environment of secrecy? Implementing change or achieving budget is often difficult in a troubled company with these characteristics.
- Does the management have the ability to operate the company efficiently?
- Is there a common objective?
- How is the CEO perceived by the rest of the board?
- What are the board politics like? Who supports whom?
- How successful have they been in implementing change programs in the past?
- Does the structure reflect the needs of the business?
- Does the team appear to be competent and well balanced?
- How long has the management team operated together?
- How many of the team have experienced a turnaround before?
- Do they have the ability to work effectively in a turnaround; that is, can they meet the challenges they are likely to face in the immediate future?
- Do they have flair and vision?
- Do they have the ability to manage the risks resulting from external factors?
- Is there an atmosphere of trust and communication in the management team?
- Are there any conflicts in the management team?
- Is there any evidence of disruptive competition or a lack of cooperation between corporate functions?
- Is information shared (both good and bad) to enable managers to assess the impact of the information on their departments?
- Do they have the capabilities, integrity, skills, and desire to undertake and successfully implement a turnaround?
- What is the role of the non-executive directors?

---

[516] compare (Slatter & Lovett, 2004, p. 122)

Assigning Certain Departments

Certain employees may need a closer look if other analysis shows that they are not doing the job as they are supposed to. For example, this could be the case if the salespeople are only taking orders, not actually selling the products by trying to convince the customer of the products' features and benefits.

Assessment of Individual Directors and Top-Level Managers

A good way to interview management is to prepare an interview questionnaire with open-ended questions. Senior people are usually judged on their ability or lack of ability to adapt to a new culture, rather than on their knowledge or technical ability. The questions to ask depend on the company's situation, its industry, the position of the interviewee, and what in particular the TMT want to find out. The questions should be aimed at assessing each senior manager's "commerciality", personal qualities and objectives, and functional competencies with the goal of determining whether the person is the right person for the job.[517] However, some should be asked to collect ideas, to get new points of view, and to get a feeling for the general culture and atmosphere of the company. Some examples of questions are as follows:

Commerciality:

- Have they demonstrated decision-making abilities?
- Do they see what the problems in the company are and how serious they are?
- Can they explain why the company has not been able to solve the problems?
- Are they entrepreneurial and innovative, or do they just follow orders?
- Do they have ideas about how to improve the current situation and know a way out?
- Are they aware of the competitive advantages the company possesses, as well as its weaknesses and the threats it faces?
- Do they see opportunities for the company?
- Do they know the company's industry well?
- Do they understand the industry's potential, risks, and outlook?
- How well do they know the competition?

---

[517] (Slatter & Lovett, 2004, p. 123)

- Are they aware of how the company's products and services are perceived by its customers?
- Do they know the company's current positioning in the market?
- How motivated are they?

Personal Qualities:

Traits such as integrity, judgment, decisiveness, motivation, leadership, and commitment to change are often key in determining whether the management in place is able to rectify past mistakes and move the company forward.[518]

- How much does the manager want to be part of the restructuring component?
- What is their attitude toward the company and the restructuring component?
- Do they blame others for their mistakes or mistakes that they contributed to?
- Do they have creativity, ideas, and enthusiasm?
- Are there conflicts of interest between their personal goals and the business's goals; if so, how do they handle these conflicts?
- How willing are they to implement change? How far would they go in restructuring the company?
- Do they have the necessary expertise, power, and skills for the turnaround?

Functional Competencies:

Input from specialists is often necessary to provide an accurate assessment of functional competence.[519] However, a rough picture can be drawn by asking colleagues about the competencies of a manager or by going through publications the manager has made and looking at achievements as well as comparing them with what was planned.

---

[518] (S.L., Corp. Rec. p. 124)
[519] (Slatter & Lovett, 2004, p. 125)

Responsibility

The Turnaround Leader is responsible for this subcomponent with assistance from the HR Turnaround Manager.

Outcome

- Management Analysis Report

DR AP 11 – Profitability Analysis

Summary

The Profitability Analysis examines the profitability of the company's departments, processes, and products.

Context

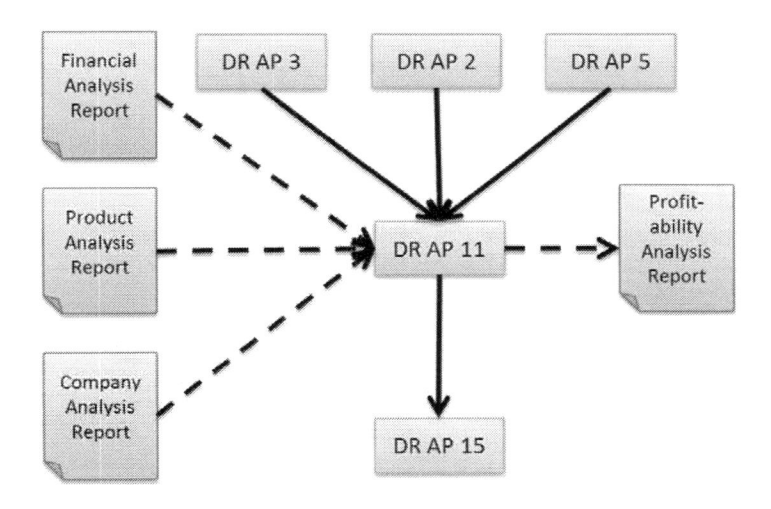

Description of the Subcomponent

The Profitability Analysis is very important in making the right decisions about divesting a business and in controlling such a divestiture. Part of the purpose of the Profitability Analysis is to examine how different divisions are doing business with each other. Especially important is how transfer pricing is managed. Is one division or branch benefiting from the transfer pricing model used more than others? The analysis can reveal a division to be a loser or a winner. If only direct expenses are charged, unallocated expenses may make a unit look profitable when it would actually be losing money if realistic service charges were included.

Business Segmentation

In this subcomponent, the business units are segmented and a profit and loss statement for each product line is evaluated. If the profit and loss statement is not available at this time, product line margins can be used. When segmentation by division is difficult, the use of the direct-costing approach can develop data by business segment on contribution or estimated profit and loss and provide insights into the company's problems.

A detailed probability analysis by product and customer segment should also allocate overheads.

Responsibility

The financial officer for the diagnostic review is responsible for this subcomponent.

Outcome

- Profitability Analysis Report

DR AP 12 – Customer Analysis

Summary

The customer analysis examines what the customers want, their image of the company and its products, and their sensitivity to changes to the firm's products. It includes development of an action plan that captures the discrepancies, ideas, and problems that come up during the process.

Context

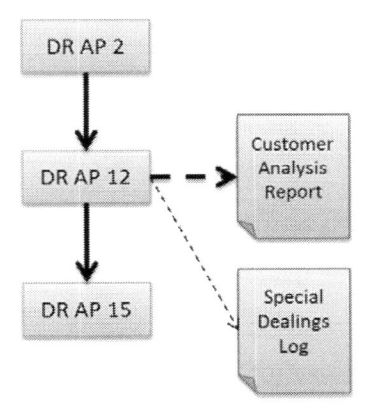

Description of the Subcomponent

Corporate decline forces companies to focus on themselves and by the time the Turnaround Leader arrives there is little talk about customers, who are ultimately the only reason the company exists at all.[520] The senior and sometimes middle management do not really know their customers even though the customers are the ones who ultimately decide whether the company can survive. Information about customers' buying behavior and their perception of the turnaround firm and its competitors is crucial for the preparation of the turnaround plan.[521]

---

[520] (Slatter & Lovett, 2004, p. 266)
[521] (Slatter & Lovett, 2004, p. 266)

Independent market research can often be of help in getting a clear picture of the customers, but such research is not always necessary since a good deal of information already lies within the company. The people who work with customers daily know very well what the customers want, what they are missing, and what their complaints are. The people who work with customers can be salespeople and customer service representatives, but they can also be technical or manufacturing staff. The employees' survey should be designed to mine what these people know about the customers and to uncover ideas that already exist in the workforce. The Turnaround Leader can also talk with some key customers directly. Additional, more extensive market research may be required later in the turnaround process.

The customer analysis needs to be done in order to choose the right process improvements and to arrive at the right strategic decisions. Customer analysis is a quick way to figure out which advertising, financing, warranty, and service programs are working, which are not, and why.[522]

A survey showed that 72 percent of turnaround companies had to eliminate unprofitable customers as part of their turnaround process, resulting in an average of 23 percent of all customers being eliminated.[523] Unprofitable customers are common in troubled companies, and eliminating them can be a quick way to save money.

Companies must ask themselves why they are losing orders. Is it because of the customer or is it because of the company? If it is the company, it is probably no longer meeting the customers' needs. In that case, it is necessary to talk to the customer in order to find out what the problem is and what they need. Most customers do not bother to let a company know why they are not buying its products any longer; they simply stop buying. Companies should ask these customers what could make them change their minds in order to gain insight into their expectations and into whether they are being set by a variety of factors outside the company's control, such as the economy, competitors' advertising campaigns and promises, financing deals, perception of quality, comfort, safety, and so on.[524] Once the company knows what the customer wants or is missing, the Turnaround Leader must evaluate how much the necessary changes cost, whether other clients would be lost because of the changes, and what the other tradeoffs are, then a plan to satisfy customers must be implemented so they will want to purchase again.

---

[522] (Roman, 2010, p. 25)
[523] (Bibeault, 1981, p. 292)
[524] (Roman, 2010, p. 25)

The steps to this kind of customer analysis are:

1. Find out what the customer wants.
2. Find out why customers are not buying your products, perhaps through a short survey that pops up if a customer leaves the website without buying a product, with room for comments in addition to answering the questions.
3. Capture and analyze the responses to discover all of the reasons why customers are not buying your products.
4. Develop an action plan to respond to the reasons discovered.

Responsibility

The Turnaround Leader is responsible for this subcomponent.

Outcome

- Customer Analysis Report

DR AP 13 – Identify Special Dealings

Summary

Special dealings with customers or suppliers are common. Along with new agreements, these dealings should be identified throughout the turnaround process and added to the Special Dealings Log.

Context

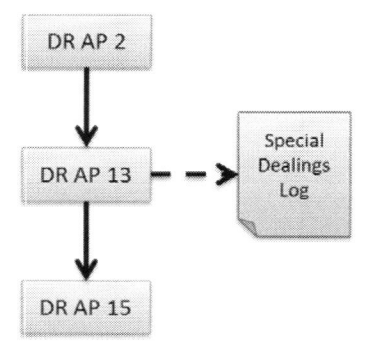

Description of the Subcomponent

In this subcomponent special dealings with customers or suppliers are identified and logged. Diagnostic review team members often encounter such dealings during a review. In that case, the team member should enter the information into the Special Dealings Log.

The Special Dealings Log contains information on:

- Discounts given to suppliers
- Abnormal relationships with customers and suppliers

Responsibility

The Turnaround Leader is responsible for this subcomponent, although an assistant maintains the Special Dealings Log.

Outcome

- Special Dealings Log

DR AP 14 – Stakeholder Analysis

Summary

The support of the stakeholders is crucial in a turnaround situation. Each stakeholder may have a different agenda, so in order to target the stakeholders correctly it is important to target them with the proper information and to ask for their support.

Context

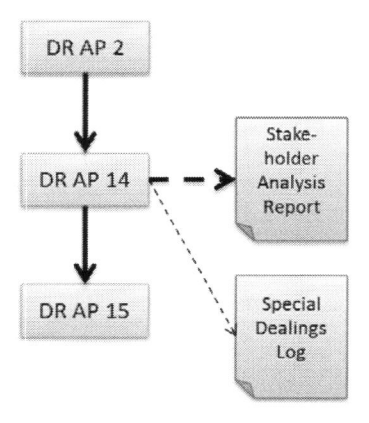

Description of the Subcomponent

Assessment of Stakeholders

It is very unlikely that a company will succeed in a turnaround process without the support of its major stakeholders. Therefore, the TMT should meet as early in the process as possible with representatives of all stakeholder groups, including employees/unions, customers, suppliers, shareholders, investors, and banks. These meetings have the purpose of assessing the answers to several questions:

- What is the stakeholders' understanding of the crisis?
- How high is the confidence in the company, its management, and the turnaround management?
- What are the stakeholders' objectives/agenda?

- How much power does the stakeholder have over the company?
- Can the company survive without the support of the stakeholders?
- How important is the company to the stakeholders?

If suppliers are presented with the right set of open-ended questions—expert advice on how to ask the right questions should be considered—they can indicate what, if anything, makes the relationship difficult, where they struggle, where they see risk in terms of quality, delivery times, and so on, and why.[525] In this way, suppliers can provide insight into how other firms use the company's products or services and where they see possibilities for improvement in a particular part of the process or in their overall relationship with the client.

What is the Stakeholders' Understanding of the Crisis?

Not all stakeholders are involved in the day-to-day business activities of a company, so many don't know the severity of the crisis and may believe the situation to be better or worse than it actually is. This phenomenon is called a "reality cap".[526] Denial is normally associated with management but it often applies to stakeholders as well and all concerned need to acknowledge the reality of the situation in order to give the turnaround process a chance.[527] In any meetings with stakeholders' representatives, it is important to bear in mind that these representatives will talk to their stakeholder groups and have a major influence on their opinions. Therefore, proper communication about the realistic chances of survival and the current situation are important, but the TMT must also maintain a careful balance between giving out sensitive information and holding back too much of the information needed to paint a realistic picture. If the TMT is big enough for a Communications Manager then the first meeting is a good chance to introduce them to the stakeholders to allow them to get to know the stakeholders' concerns and motivations.

How High is the Confidence in the Company, its Management, and the TMT?

The stakeholders' confidence should be assessed with regard to:

---

[525] (Roman, 2010, p. 20)
[526] compare (Bertok, 2004, p. 130)
[527] (Slatter & Lovett, 2004, p. 118)

- The company: Do the stakeholders think the company can survive? Do they think it is financially strong enough to survive the turnaround process?
- The management: What is the stakeholders' level of confidence in the old management? Will they support their efforts? Do the stakeholders have doubts about specific people?
- The Turnaround Management Team: Since the stakeholders do not usually know the TMT, the first meetings give the members of the TMT the opportunity to show their professional leadership and expertise. The TMT must convey that it is a team of experts and rebuild this image each time it meets with the stakeholders. At this early stage, the TMT may not be familiar with every detail of the company's situation, so these first meetings have the purpose of demonstrating its understanding of the industry and the general situation in order to build trust in the TMT and the turnaround management process.

What are the Stakeholders' Objectives/Agenda?

Business intelligence units or companies can be useful at this stage since the goal is to find out everything about a stakeholder before a meeting is conducted. The agenda of each stakeholder can differ sharply from that of the others. For example, a supplier may have the objective of keeping the company alive because it does not want to lose a client for their products, or they may want to let the company die to get out of an old contract at an outdated price. The TMT should find out about existing contracts with these suppliers, their current value, and how they affect the supplier in order to understand their motives.

Another example is a bank that may want to keep the company running because it has other clients that depend on the troubled company. On the other hand, the bank may be interested only in securing its investment in the easiest and fastest way possible by liquidating the company. Its attitude will also be strongly influenced by the level of any security held, the perceived value of that security, and any provisions on its books against the outstanding debt.[528]

---

[528] (Slatter & Lovett, 2004, p. 119)

Unions are usually concerned with the number of jobs that are at risk, work-out increases, and payment decreases. In some countries, unions have a strong influence not only in the company but also over the general public. If they decide to strike, the effect on the company may cause other stakeholders to doubt their opinion of the company and their confidence in the turnaround process.

An equity investor's objectives will reflect the value at which the investment is carried in their portfolio, their ability to invest further monies (which is particularly true of private equity providers whose funds may cap the level of investment permitted in one company), and the relative importance of this investment in the portfolio as a whole.[529]

How much power does the stakeholder have over the company?

If the business's short-term survival is heavily dependent on the support of a particular stakeholder group—to maintain current lending facilities or to pass on a dividend payment, for example—then it is vital that this stakeholder is brought "on side" and involved in the assessment component from the outset.[530] Other stakeholders may have power over the company if finding a new supplier would hurt the current production process or if losing the supplier would hurt its reputation. In this case, it is important to know to what degree the troubled company depends on the supplier and how much it would cost to switch to alternative sources.

What is the stakeholder's attitude toward the company?

The attitude of the stakeholder can vary significantly depending on who initiates the turnaround process. If the turnaround is initiated by the shareholders pressuring the board to change the management, then the primary goal of the stakeholder is usually the recovery of the firm's value and its stock price. If a bank is the major stakeholder that initiates the turnaround, then an asset-reducing strategy designed to repay or reduce the bank's outstanding loans usually has priority (as it does, for example, when a receiver is appointed).[531] If this happens, the long-term survival of the firm may not be the primary objective, so the

---

[529] (Slatter & Lovett, 2004, p. 119)
[530] (S.L., Corp. Rec. p. 119)
[531] (Slatter & Lovett, 2004, p. 110)

Turnaround Leader must ascertain the bank's agenda and the extent of the its support for the recovery strategy.

A turnaround often comes with job losses and job changes. In some companies trade unions have considerable power, and they react to asset reduction and cost reduction strategies by mobilizing their members to participate in strikes or other constraints. Therefore, trade unions have an indirect way of influencing the turnaround process.

Responsibility

The Turnaround Leader is responsible for this subcomponent.

Outcome

- Stakeholder Analysis Report

DR AP 15 – Designing the Turnaround Management Team

Summary

The TMT is put together by the Turnaround Leader. Many of the experts from the diagnostic review team will already have the skills necessary for the turnaround process.

Context

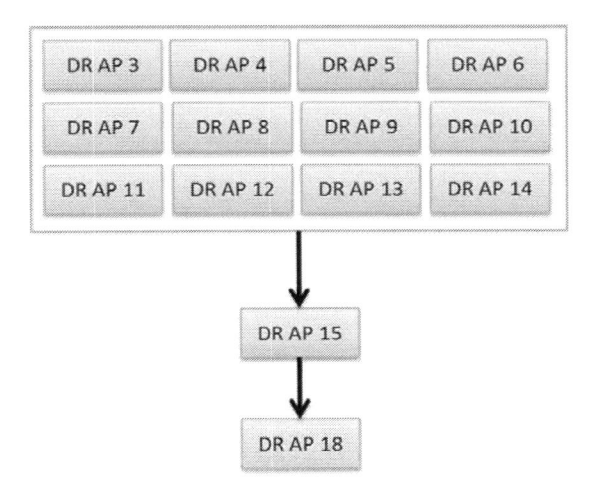

Description of the Subcomponent

Once the project has been analyzed during the DR AP Stage, the TMT can be designed in accordance with the company analysis, the suggested outcome, and its complexity. Putting the right people in place for a turnaround process is the key to success. However, simply having smart people is not sufficient. They need to have proper authority, responsibility, experience, and knowledge to make the right decisions quickly. The TMT also needs to reflect the interests of the stakeholders, to manage the challenges that the company is facing, and to monitor the company's situation for new problems that may occur during the turnaround process that did not exist before and that are not even in the Risk Log. A turnaround process changes the company's proceedings, dealings, processes, and sometimes its business. Until the turnaround process is finished, the company will be on shaky ground that cannot support a risk evolving into an issue that was not anticipated.

The diagnostic review team assembled in SP 3 can serve as a model for the TMT, and some people who were involved in analyzing the company can move on to the TMT since most of the skills needed to evaluate the company are similar to those that the TMT needs for the turnaround process.

The TMT needs to maintain open relations with the company's stakeholders and to be trustworthy in case something does not go according to plan. Banks usually maintain their support of a TMT only if they trust them.[532]

Key roles to be appointed are:

1. HR Turnaround Manager
2. Purchasing and Investment Turnaround Manager
3. Turnaround Spokesperson
4. Turnaround Finance Manager
5. Turnaround Manager responsible for Change Management (in large companies)

Responsibility

The Turnaround Leader is responsible for this subcomponent.

---

[532] compare (Slatter & Lovett, 2004, p. 132)

DR AP 16 – Starting Emergency Procedures

Summary

In some cases, the Turnaround Leader is aware of major cash drains that should be stopped immediately. This component triggers the emergency procedures that are necessary for a formal suspension or closing down of units or products that are losing money or that damage the reputation of the company.

Context

DR AP 16 → EP 1

Description of the Subcomponent

A Turnaround Leader may choose to jump ahead once the following processes are completed and the results are evaluated:

- Viability analysis
- Company analysis
- Product analysis
- Financial analysis
- Profitability analysis

However, such jumping ahead should be done only with the approval of the TAB and when waiting for the end of the formal and complete review would take too long for serious cases of cash drain or funding problems.

Responsibility

The Turnaround Leader is responsible for this subcomponent.

DR AP 17 – Creating the Diagnostic Review Folder

Summary

In this subcomponent the information collected during DR AP is put together and presented to the TAB. This Diagnostic Review Folder will be the main reference for decision making during the turnaround process.

Context

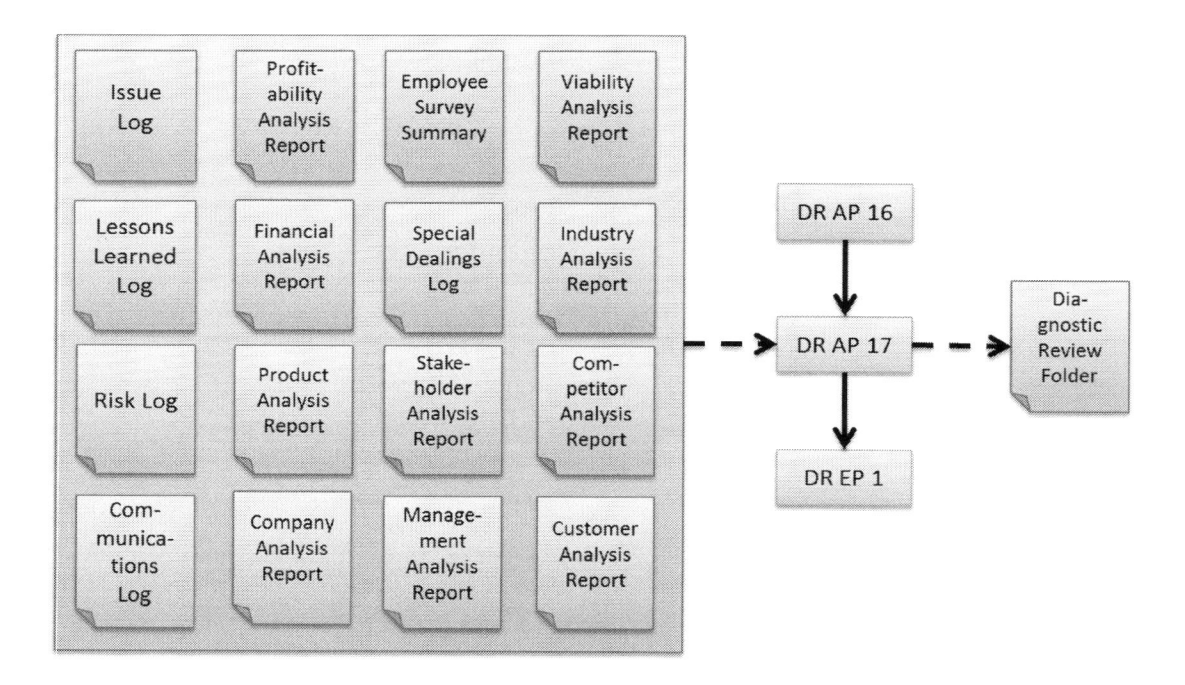

Description of the Subcomponent

In this subcomponent all reports and results collected during the DR AP Stage are put together to be used to draw conclusions and make decisions during the DR EP Stage. The folder is presented to the TAB.

Responsibility

The Turnaround Leader is responsible for this subcomponent.

Requirements

- Issue Log
- Lessons Learned Log
- Risk Log
- Communications Log
- Profitability Analysis Report
- Financial Analysis Report
- Product Analysis Report
- Company Analysis Report
- Employee Survey Summary
- Special Dealings Log
- Stakeholder Analysis Report
- Management Analysis Report
- Viability Analysis Report
- Industry Analysis Report
- Competitor Analysis Report
- Customer Analysis Report

Outcome

- Diagnostic Review Folder

Diagnostic Review: Evaluation Phase (DR EP)

DR EP 1 – Creating an Executive Decision Matrix

Summary

The goal of this subcomponent is to create an Executive Decision Matrix of the company's strengths and weaknesses.

Context

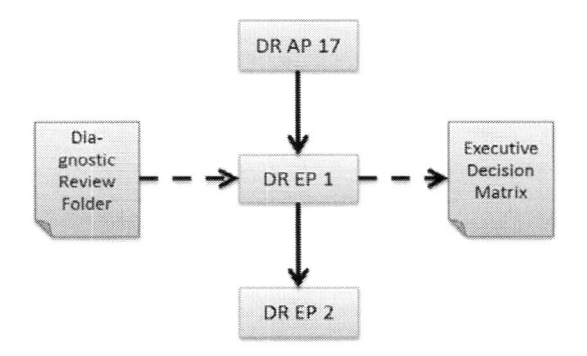

Description of the Subcomponent

Evaluation of the factors considered earlier—the seriousness of the company's situation, the leader's gut feelings, the presence or absence of key viability factors in the turnaround, and the company's finances, competitive position, and people—should all lead to the ability to judge the firm's strategic and operating health. An Executive Decision Matrix helps the Turnaround Leader judge the situation at a high level. This matrix has two dimensions—the operating health and the strategic health of the company—each of which is grouped into five possible outcomes: weak, potentially weak, average, potentially strong, and strong. The TMT decides where to put the company on the strategic and operating scale. The result is a matrix with five x five possible cells related to the company's overall health. A company classified as strong on the strategic and the operational scales is usually not a turnaround candidate unless an outside circumstance is threatening its survival. Firms that have a weak position in both these categories are, of course, turnaround candidates, but they are also the most serious candidates for bankruptcy.[533] Most companies are somewhere between these two extremes, but if both operating and

---
[533] (Bibeault, 1981, p. 225)

strategic factors are weak, liquidation is probably the best option unless the firm has another business in which it can invest.[534]

If the company has a strong strategic position but a weak operating position, the Turnaround Plan should focus on an operating turnaround strategy. However, if the operating position is strong but the strategic position is average, sometimes a turnaround is not needed. In this case, a thorough search for possible strategic repositioning and competitive advantage should be conducted. In the case of a strong operating but weak strategic position, the Turnaround Plan should focus on a strategic turnaround.

A liquidation is sometimes reasonable when the business's strategic position is only average and an operating turnaround is required.[535]

Responsibility

The Turnaround Leader is responsible for this subcomponent.

Information Needs

- Diagnostic Review Folder

Outcome
- Executive Decision Matrix

---

[534] (Bibeault, Corporate Turnaround: How Managers Turn Losers into Winners, 1981, p. 226)
[535] (Bibeault, Corporate Turnaround: How Managers Turn Losers into Winners, 1981, p. 226)

DR EP 2 – Classifying the Situation

Summary

The overall situation of the company is evaluated and the outcome is classified into four possible situations: the company cannot be rescued; it will merely survive the turnaround; it will be able to survive in the short term; or it has a good chance of a sustainable recovery.

This section includes a concluding statement concerning whether the company can merely survive or has a serious chance for long-term or short-term survival. The classification should include an initial assessment, whether it is feasible to implement possible turnaround strategies, and the likely time that is required for implementing the strategies suggested.[536]

Context

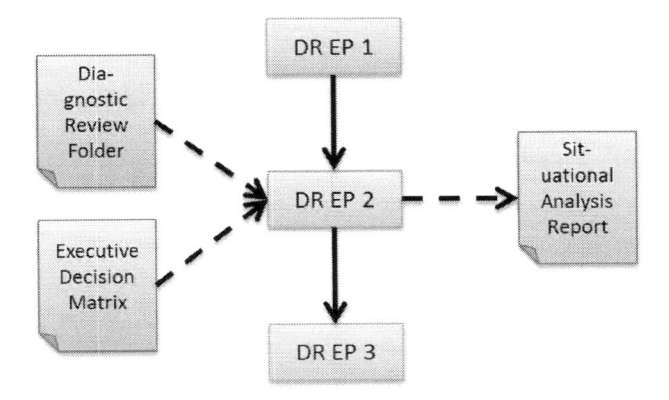

Description of the Subcomponent

Companies find themselves in a variety of situations. Some have six months or less to survive, while others have 12 months or less. With six to 12 months, the time to act is now or the company will be on a downward spiral created by increasing debt, interest rates, decreasing customer confidence, a tarnished reputation in the markets, panicked reactions, and discouraged, scared employees looking for work elsewhere.[537] With six months available for a

---
[536] S.L., Corp. Rec. p. 125
[537] (Roman, 2010, p. 19)

turnaround, actions must be implemented right away to contain the loss of money. In this case, some operational strategies might be moved up to the Emergency Procedures Stage so they can be pushed through right away and without waiting for other subcomponents.

Four Types of Recovery Situations

The chances of a recovery component succeeding depends on a variety of factors, including the TMT, the stakeholders, past mistakes, and the industry's characteristics. It is important for a Turnaround Leader to be able to identify quickly whether the turnaround has a chance to succeed and to keep the four possible results in mind in order to maximize the time available to implement an appropriate course of action and maximize the returns available to the different stakeholders. However, there are some problems with the four classifications since they merely build a conceptual framework. It is especially difficult to recognize the difference between companies that can barely survive from those that can survive short-term, and to distinguish those that can survive only short term from those that can be sustainably recovered. The external environment and internal resources change frequently and no company stays in one business mode forever. Because of rapid technological change and the increased competition that results from slower growth in the world economy, considerable managerial effort—and perhaps some luck—is required to keep a firm in the sustainable recovery box.[538]

Companies that Cannot be Rescued

If a firm is not viable it should be allowed to fail by, for example, leading it to insolvency.[539] Companies that cannot survive even in the short term are called "no-hopers".[540] These companies will inevitably fail and, from an economic point of view, are not worth turning around. These types of companies have one or all of the following characteristics:

- They have very high fixed costs compared to their value added.
- They cannot generate cash by divesting assets because they have only one production facility and/or only one product.
- They suffer from a price war with a competitor that has lower production costs, which leads to a decline of the main business.

---

[538] (Slatter & Lovett, 2004, p. 117)
[539] compare (Pomerleano & Shaw, 2005, p. 103)
[540] (Slatter & Lovett, 2004, p. 115)

- The decline in market demand happened very fast.
- Customers have lost their confidence in the company or its product(s).
- A license that is necessary for the business to survive has been revoked.

Before the company was about to fail, it might turn out that more cash than expected was spent at the cost of the company's survival. This "soft receivership" means that the business is kept running only for the purpose of achieving higher sales prices when the assets are sold off as a known insolvency would lower the prices that can be realized on the asset sales. However, this procedure is not a turnaround process. In such circumstances, the main beneficiaries of the turnaround management's efforts are creditors who enjoy preferential treatment in an insolvency.[541]

Companies that Merely Survive

It is important to distinguish between a company that merely survives and one that has a sustainable recovery. Survival in an economic sense is reduced to a company breaking even and/or earning profits above break-even for a short time. Sustainable recovery means that the company achieves profits above break-even in the long term. It also usually requires a shift in product-market emphasis and growth-orientated strategies such as new product development and/or growth via acquisition.[542] The turnaround process does not necessarily have the goal of achieving sustainable recovery since, if the company is already too badly damaged, it may not be possible.

Once it is clear that the company will survive, the investors must decide if they want to keep their investment in the company and push for a sustainable recovery to achieve competitive returns on their investment or to sell their shares while the company remains afloat. However, a company that has not yet reached the sustainable recovery stage remains in danger of falling back into a crisis in the near future. A "mere survival" firm may become a "sustainable recovery" firm under new ownership since, through a merger, the firm might be able to achieve economies of scale or efficiencies that it would not have if it operated alone.

---

[541] (Slatter & Lovett, 2004, p. 262)
[542] (Slatter & Lovett, 2004, p. 116)

Companies that Survive in the Short Term

Some companies that go through a turnaround process look as if they will succeed in the future but fall back into a crisis a few years later. Following the turnaround process they have a few years with increasing revenues, but if they are not able to build competitive advantage and/or overcome their competitive disadvantages they fall back into insolvency. However, these companies may still be worth turning around if the current investors want to sell the company after the turnaround process.

Companies that Reach Sustainable Recovery

A turnaround candidate that reaches a stage where it can prosper and achieve above-average profits for the long term is sustainably recovered. This is, of course, the best outcome, and it should be the goal unless the objectives are different from the beginning, which would be the case if the firm is only to be made profitable for the short term in order to sell it. Where the causes of the firm's decline are poor management, lack of control, general operating inefficiency, or product-market weaknesses in a subsidiary, sustainable recovery is usually feasible; but if the causes of decline are related to the firm having a weak product-market position in its core business area, sustainable recovery may be impossible.[543] If the company has only one product and weak financial resources, a lack of shareholder support will further weaken the chances of a successful sustainable recovery. If this is not the case, an option is to look for another company to buy the turnaround candidate and invest heavily in the turnaround process in terms of time and money. However, even a fountain of money cannot always cure a firm. A sustainable recovery is usually easiest to achieve in a non-crisis recovery situation since the firm has greater financial resources available to it and a stronger competitive market position on which to build for the future.[544] It is important to start a turnaround process as soon as possible in order to treat the causes of the firm's poor performance before they can eat up the company's resources.

---

[543] (Slatter & Lovett, 2004, p. 116)
[544] (Slatter & Lovett, 2004, p. 117)

Identify Tolerances

There may be some tolerances available in terms of time and finance, and these tolerance levels need to be identified. If there is no tolerance in time and finance, the turnaround process may not be successful.

Responsibility

The Turnaround Leader is responsible for this subcomponent.

Information Needs

- Executive Decision Matrix
- Diagnostic Review Folder

Outcome

- Situational Analysis Report

DR EP 3 – Assessing Options

Summary

In this subcomponent the available options are reviewed by the diagnostic review team.

Context

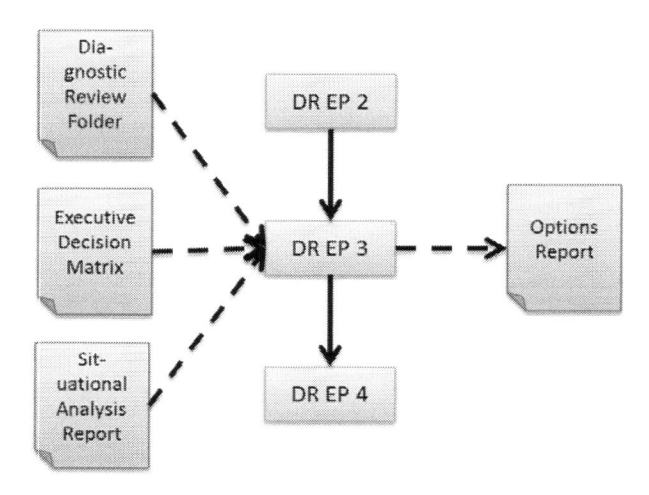

Description of the Subcomponent

Many companies don't recognize the need to restructure until it is too late, when fewer options remain and saving the company may be more difficult.[545] For a turnaround to work there must be enough time, and whether there is enough time must be determined before the actual turnaround process gets started.

The analysis requires a financial plan for the next three months. The forecasts need to be updated daily or at least weekly with up-to-date financial information. In some cases, the company cannot survive without short-term financing. This kind of finance can ensure the company's survival until the restructuring component is finished, but it is usually very expensive

---

[545] (Simonsen & Cassady, 2007, p. 7)

since the company's survival is still uncertain throughout the restructuring component. Answering the following questions can help in the effort to secure short-term financing:

1. Can short-term financing be generated within the firm? If so, how much?
2. Is there a gap between what can be generated internally and what is needed for short-term survival?
3. How much short-term funding is required from external sources?
4. What can the company offer creditors in exchange for short-term funding?

If the company needs short-term financing to service the turnaround process and is not able to generate the cash requirements by themselves, external financing is the only option. If the company cannot attract short-term funding, insolvency or the sale of the business are the only viable options.

Responsibility

The Turnaround Leader is responsible for this subcomponent.

Information Needs

- Diagnostic Review Folder
- Executive Decision Matrix
- Situational Analysis Report

Outcome

- Options Report: The options report outlines the options available to the company and provides financial plans for the proposed alternatives, including possible advantages, disadvantages, and risks.

DR EP 4 – Operative Decisions

Summary

This subcomponent concerns the operative decisions that must be made for the turnaround process.

Context

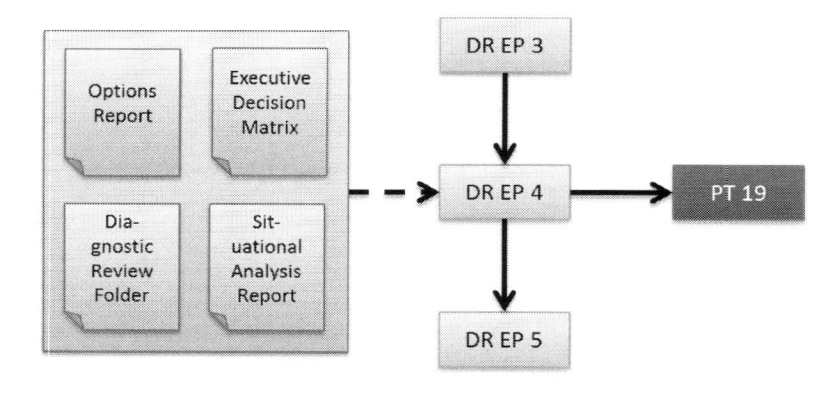

Description of the Subcomponent

At this point, the decision concerning whether cost-cutting methods, revenue-generating methods, and/or asset-reducing strategies are necessary is evaluated:

- If a company is near break-even and has high direct labor costs or high fixed expenses then cost-cutting methods should be used in the turnaround.[546]
- If a company is far from break-even and has low direct labor expenses or low fixed costs then revenue-generating methods should be used in the turnaround.[547]
- If a company is very far from break-even (at 30 percent or less) then asset-reducing methods should be used.[548]

---

[546] (Roman, 2010, p. 170)
[547] (Roman, 2010, p. 170)
[548] (Roman, 2010, p. 170)

- If a company is in an intermediate position with respect to direct labor costs or high fixed expenses then a combination of tactics should be used in the turnaround.[549]

In a study on mature industrial units[550] it was shown that such strategic options as major share gains and the development of new entrepreneurial thrusts are not likely under conditions of shrinking or negative profit margins.[551] Process analysis and value engineering can aid in finding more optimal ways to reduce production costs and optimize the quality outcomes in order to improve the profit margin.

Responsibility

The Turnaround Leader, in consultation with the Diagnostic Review team, is responsible for this subcomponent.

Information Needs

- Diagnostic Review Folder
- Executive Decision Matrix
- Situational Analysis Report
- Options Report

---

[549] (Roman, 2010, p. 170)
[550] (Hambrick & Schecter, 1983)
[551] compare (Roman, 2010, p. 170)

DR EP 5 – Business Divestment Decisions

Summary

In this subcomponent the Diagnostic Review team evaluates whether part of the business should be divested.

Context

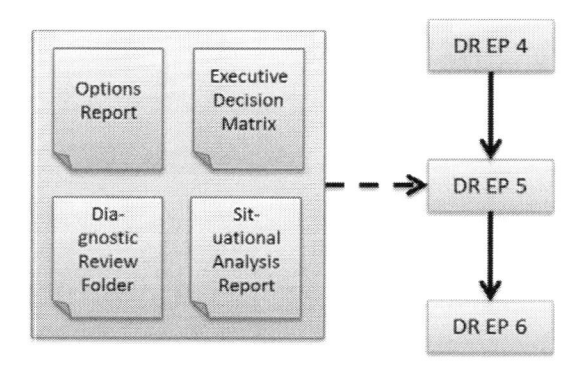

Description of the Subcomponent

The business units should be divided into three categories:

- Category 1 – all business units that are making money and contributing to the company's cash flow.
- Category 2 – all business units that are somewhat positive or almost contributing positive cash flow. The basic criterion for making borderline decisions is that, in serious cases, anything that cannot contribute positively to cash flow within a very short time must go.[552]
- Category 3 – all business units that are not contributing any positive financial resources to the company.

---

[552] (Bibeault, 1981, p. 264)

The next step is to create a 3 x 3 matrix with the three categories of business units above on the horizontal axis and the three categories below as the vertical axis:

- Category A – business units that cannot be outsourced and that are crucial for the business's survival, in that they are part of the company's core business and the company would not be able to survive without them in a strategic or operational sense.
- Category B – all business units that are somewhat important for the company because they give the company some competitive advantage, but they could be outsourced or they are not part of the core business so they are not necessary for the survival of the company.
- Category C – the business units that are not necessary for the company's survival in a strategic sense.

The divestment of a business unit can be done in the EP Component or in the Crisis Stabilization Stage, depending on the urgency of the company's situation.

Borderline Business Units

Companies that are included in category 2B and 2C will probably have to go, depending on the company's situation. If a business unit is in one of these two categories on the matrix, the first question to ask is whether it can be quickly converted into a unit that falls into one of the higher categories by contributing strategically, operationally, or financially to the overall business. The second question is how much money the company would lose by keeping the business unit before the business can be made profitable again. Usually, the loss taken by selling these marginal units is less than the loss the company would incur if it held on to the borderline unit.[553] Therefore, whether the company should divest a business unit now or try to turn it around also depends on the estimate of how long it will take for the business unit to become profitable and contribute significantly strategically, operationally, or financially to the company's health. If financial projections of a turnaround for that business unit suggest that the loss incurred by keeping the business unit up to the break-even point would exceed the liquidation loss, the unit should be divested or liquidated. Non-contributing segments of the

---

[553] compare (Bibeault, 1981, p. 264)

business must be divested and their assets converted to cash that can be used to support the core business during the turnaround.

Further Divestment Considerations

When a business unit is sold during a crisis the management should expect a substantial write down. Therefore, the right communication at the right time is important for stakeholder support, for the public image, and for the sale price of the business unit. A company should try to straighten out such a losing business unit by doing some quick surgery and then sell it as a going concern.[554]

There are four factors for a company to asses when considering divestiture:[555]

- The true value of a divestment/liquidation candidate – The true price is often hard to determine since some business units are difficult to sell because of a lack of buyers, and the price might be known only after a sale actually takes place. In some cases, the value of the resources that will be put to another use is impossible to assess accurately.[556]
- The degree of convertibility – Convertibility describes whether the asset or business unit can be used for other purposes or can be converted into cash. Some assets may have no cash value at all, such as when the cash proceeds recovered in the divestment are less than the cash costs experienced in the divestment of the asset.
- The ease of convertibility – Divestment takes considerable time and effort on the part of management and generates other costs as well. Often, divesting specialized equipment is not very easy because of excess production capacity in an industry.
- The time span for conversion – Whole production plants may need to be sold piece by piece, dragging out the sales component. In addition, some assets may not find a buyer at all but still create costs in trying to find one. The company must also consider how the buyer will pay for the assets and over how much time. An asset paid over a period of years may generate steady cash flow for the seller, but it brings in less cash when it

---

[554] (Bibeault, 1981, p. 266)
[555] compare (Vignola, 1974)
[556] (Bibeault, 1981, p. 266)

is needed the most during the restructuring.

Another issue to consider is whether the business unit in question is a good deal for a possible buyer. If it is established as a going concern, a unit that is supposed to be divested could be worth more to a purchaser than it is to the seller.

Sale Price

When selling a business, a seller seldom gets the desired price. Intangible assets, such as a brand name or patents, are often not sold at the value they hold for the seller. Less than half of divestments sell at book value, but 30 percent sell at less than book value and 25 percent sell at liquidation value.[557] If the buyer knows that the company selling the asset is in financial difficulties, they may try to defer buying until the seller becomes more desperate and lowers the price.

Legal Aspects

If the Justice Department needs to approve the sale because, for example, there are not many competitors in the market, the company can acquire that approval if it can argue that competition will suffer more if it is forced to shut down than if it goes through with the divestment.

Timeframe

For large companies that are not under heavy pressure, the quest to dispose of a poorly performing business unit may take years.

Responsibility

The Turnaround Leader is responsible for this subcomponent.

---

[557] (Bibeault, 1981, p. 268)

Information Needs

- Diagnostic Review Folder
- Executive Decision Matrix
- Situational Analysis Report
- Options Report

DR EP 6 – Planning Assurance

Summary

The purpose of this subcomponent is to determine the expectations for and goals of the turnaround process and to appoint the Turnaround Assurance Team.

Context

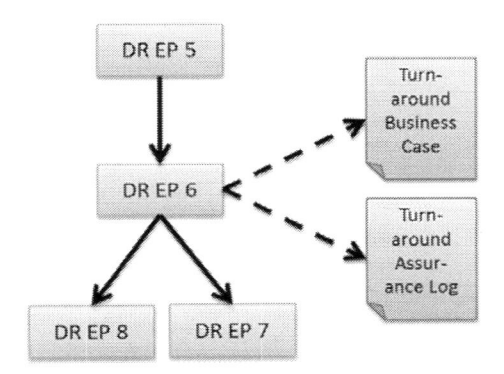

Description of the Subcomponent

Two key success factors for a turnaround are whether it is carried out in accordance with the stakeholders' expectations and whether the company reaches the goals outlined in the Turnaround Business Case. These outcomes will transpire only if the expectations are written down and agreed on at the beginning of the turnaround process. In order to evaluate the success of the turnaround, the procedures for the evaluation must be agreed upon as well by:

- Establishing the expectations of the major stakeholders
- Establishing the turnaround assurance arrangements
- Establishing how change will be dealt with throughout the turnaround process
- Establishing how the success of the turnaround process will be measured
- Establishing responsibilities for the assurance reviews
- Setting up an Assurance Log to document the assurance checks

The Turnaround Assurance Team keeps track of all logs and reports created throughout the turnaround process and assists with administrative tasks.

Responsibility

The Turnaround Leader is responsible for this subcomponent

Outcome

- Turnaround Assurance Log
- Turnaround Assurance Team
- Turnaround Business Case

DR EP – 7 Updating the Turnaround Business Case, Risks, Controls, and Communications

Summary

This administrative subcomponent is mainly concerned with updates to the logs created in prior subcomponents.

Context

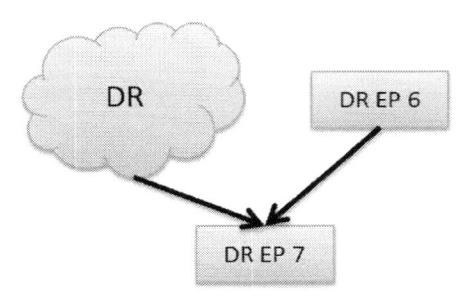

Description of the Subcomponent

The Turnaround Business Case states why the turnaround is being carried out and justifies its purpose. This subcomponent takes the outline turnaround case from the Turnaround Brief and updates the business case with the information that became available throughout the diagnostic review. This revised turnaround case will form part of the TID.

A check of all possible risks also needs to be completed. Is the collection in the Risk Log comprehensive and complete? This task should be checked by the Turnaround Assurance Team.

Updating the Turnaround Case

The turnaround case needs to be updated regularly throughout the turnaround process. The following is a checklist of what should be included and updated in this subcomponent. This should be carried out by the Turnaround Assurance Team or an assistant to the Turnaround Leader.

- The turnaround case should include at least three scenarios for the future turnaround process: the most likely case; the worst case; and the best case.
- Determine whether there are foreseeable external events that can affect the turnaround case and the turnaround process.
- Determine whether any more disadvantages or benefits have emerged.
- Establish how the benefits of a successful turnaround will be measured and recorded for the Post-Turnaround Review component.
- Develop control procedures that are in line with the complexity of the turnaround and the risks.
- Establish day-to-day monitoring procedures to ensure that the turnaround is controlled effectively.
- Ensure that the resources are available to provide the necessary monitoring.
- Populate the Communications Log in CP 4 (Establish Communications for the Diagnostic Review Stage).

Regarding the Risk Log

During the diagnostic review, the diagnostic review team probably became aware of more risks to the company and the turnaround process. These risks should be entered into the Risk Log and risks entered earlier should be updated.

Regarding Controls

The controls set up in this stage should be checked for efficiency.

Communications Log

The Communications Log should be updated if new information that could influence the turnaround process becomes available after it was created.

Responsibility

The Turnaround Leader is responsible for this subcomponent, although the updates are probably done by the Turnaround Assurance Team.

DR EP 8 – Identifications and Estimations

Summary

Based on the results of the diagnostic review and the decisions made during the Evaluation Stage, the TMT identifies actions and makes estimations regarding the turnaround process.

Context

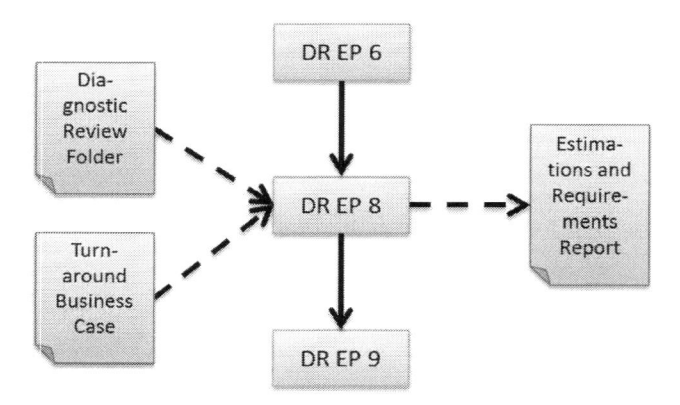

Description of this Subcomponent

In this subcomponent the resource requirements and the timescale of the turnaround process are established. This information, which is stored in the project plan and which serves as a guideline for the Turnaround Assurance Team, is needed in order to evaluate the Turnaround Business Case and so the TAB can control the turnaround process.

The following actions should be taken during this subcomponent:

- Identify and define the ultimate goal of the turnaround process
- Identify the major activities to be performed in order to reach this goal
- Identify the major risks to these goals and activities
- Put in place countermeasures in case the risks should occur
- Estimate the effort required in time and money for each major activity
- Identify what it is possible to accomplish within a certain timeframe and what it is not

- Identify when reviews should be done and major decisions made
- Estimate the costs of the possible outcomes of the turnaround process
- Estimate the best and most likely cases for the level of turnover after the turnaround has been achieved
- Update the Risk Log

It is also necessary to decide which tools and techniques will be used to plan the turnaround, how presentations will be carried out, and what standard will be used for planning.

Estimations and Requirements Report

The Estimations and Requirements Report contains the estimations completed at this stage in terms of activity, money, and time. The change budget and contingency budget form part of the Estimations and Requirements Report.

Creation of a Change Budget

It is also advisable at this stage to consider the possible outcomes of the turnaround strategies and how to finance changes in the strategies. If the company still has enough funds, a change budget should be created in case a change of strategies is required. If sufficient funding is not available, a plan for how to raise additional funds should be outlined and included in the TID. Doing so will allow the TAB to be prepared in case something does not go according to plan.

Creation of a Contingency Budget

A contingency budget is used to finance risks to the turnaround process that become reality. The risks in the Risk Log can materialize quickly so the contingency budget will enable the Turnaround Leader to counteract these threats immediately by putting countermeasures in place.

Responsibility

The Turnaround Leader is responsible for this subcomponent, although the whole TMT participates.

Information Needs

- Turnaround Business Case
- Diagnostic Review Folder

Outcome

- Estimations and Requirements Report (including the change budget and the contingency budget)

DR EP 9 – Preparing the Turnaround Initiation Document (TID)

Summary

The aim of this subcomponent is to produce the TID, which serves the TAB in assessing whether it is viable to proceed with the suggested strategies.

Context

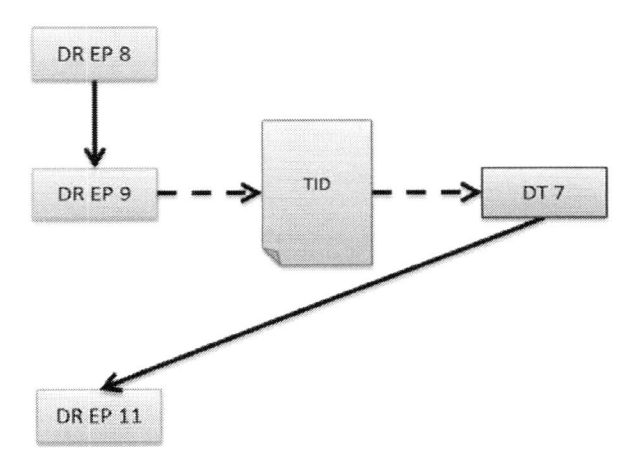

Description of the Subcomponent

In this subcomponent all available information about the company, the industry, and so on, along with the analysis carried out by the TMT and its recommendations, are filed in one place. Thus, this subcomponent puts all the information created in the Diagnostic Review into the TID. The TID provides a benchmark for other management decisions and an information base.

The subcomponent includes a cross-check of the available information in the TID in order to ensure that the information provided is viable and compatible.

It is advisable to create some background information for the TID in case later stakeholders or investors who were not part of the turnaround process from the beginning want to review it. Once completed, the TID is forwarded to the TAB for approval.

Contents of the TID:

- Turnaround Brief
- Turnaround Mandate
- Team structure
- Analysis Folder
- Turnaround controls
- Situational Analysis Report
- Turnaround Case
- Risk Log
- Job descriptions
- Options Report
- Communications Plan
- Control procedures
- Estimations and Requirements Report
- Next stage plan, including goals for the Crisis Stabilization Stage

Diagnostic Review Results

A final Diagnostic Review Report is put together in this stage. It should give all interested parties a picture that is as complete and exact as possible of the company's current position and future outlook in various situations. It includes a current, accurate analysis of the company's financial situation. The report should be read by experienced Turnaround Leaders as outside consultants might overanalyze the situation.[558]

Clearly, the less analysis that is available, the more important the expertise of the reviewer. The stakeholders, whose support is critical to the success of the turnaround process, should understand the trade-off.

---

[558] (Slatter & Lovett, 2004, p. 126)

Financial Situation

The Diagnostic Review Report contains information on the financial situation of the company, including answers to the following questions:

- What is the current financial situation of the company?
- What are the worst-case, most likely, and best-case scenarios for the financial outlook/cash flow forecast for the next three, six, 12, and 60 months?
- What are the possible sources of funding? How likely is each of these sources? Have any sources not been tapped or considered yet? Are there shortfalls? Does the company need more external funding or can it supply the necessary funds itself?
- What are the company's current and future liabilities?
- What are the company's assets worth, and how many of them can be disposed of?
- Are there any accounting errors in the current financial reports, or are these reports outdated?
- What is the company's current financial value?
- What is the net present value of each case?

Risks

The Diagnostic Review Report contains information on the risks to the company, including answers to the following questions:

- What are the risks associated with each option?
- Can the risks be diversified? If so, how?
- Do the risks endanger other parts of the turnaround process? Are the components interrelated?

Strategy

The strategic part is only assessed at a high level at this point in time. However, basic strategic analysis should be presented in the Diagnostic Review Report, including answers to the following questions:

- What is the current strategic positioning of the business?
- Are there assets that can be disposed of in case of a strategic change?

Management Team

The Diagnostic Review Report contains information on the company's management team, including answers to the following questions:

- What are the major changes to be made in order to start the turnaround process?
- If senior management is removed, can outside interim managers fill in at short notice?

Responsibility

The Turnaround Leader is responsible for this subcomponent with assistance from the Turnaround Support Team.

Information Needs

- Turnaround Brief
- Turnaround Mandate
- Team Structure
- Analysis Folder
- Turnaround Controls
- Situational Analysis Report
- Turnaround Case
- Risk Log
- Job Descriptions
- Options Report
- Communications Plan
- Control Procedures
- Estimations and Requirements Report

Outcome

- TID

DR EP 10 – Appointing the Turnaround Management Team (TMT) 1

Summary

In this subcomponent the TMT that was designed in DR AP 15 and the Turnaround Assurance Team are appointed.

Context

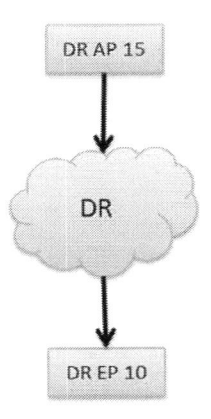

Description of the Subcomponent

The design of the TMT was drawn up in DR AP 15 but its members should be formally appointed. It is within the Turnaround Leader's authority to appoint whomever they wish in order for the team to function smoothly; the TAB should not have a say in this decision. It is also not advisable for the Turnaround Leader to give in to pressure from a TAB member to accept, for example, additional accountants on the TMT, because such team members usually report directly back to their employers rather than only to the Turnaround Leader. This would mean that the Turnaround Leader could not control the flow of information and this lack of control might create a risk to the turnaround process.

Each TMT member must understand the communication procedures and who is responsible for what on the team. Copies of job descriptions should be kept by each team member and the Turnaround Leader.

Another body that should be created at this point is the Turnaround Assurance Team.

Turnaround Assurance Team

The Turnaround Assurance Team is a team of people (or even one person) that checks up on the progress of the strategies and procedures implemented by the TMT. It also ensures that the interests of the principles on which the TAB agreed are kept in mind. The Turnaround Assurance Team is an independent body so no member of the TMT can serve on it. The Turnaround Assurance Team keeps a log of all issues that it encounters.

Specific responsibilities of the Turnaround Assurance Team include:

- Ensuring that the turnaround remains viable
- Observing legislative constraints
- Using applicable standards
- Ensuring that the needs of the creditors' and stakeholders' representative are met
- Ensuring that the external and internal communications work
- Maintaining the focus on the business need
- Ensuring that the right people are doing the right jobs
- Ensuring that the turnaround case is being adhered to
- Ensuring that risks are controlled

Responsibility

The Turnaround Leader is responsible for this subcomponent.

Information Needs

- Design of the TMT

DR EP 11 – Initiating the Turnaround Process

Summary

The TID is sent to the TAB for final approval to initiate the turnaround process.

Context

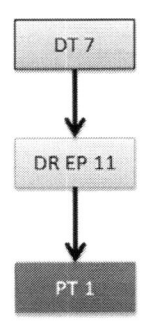

Description of the Subcomponent

Once a crisis occurs, it is usually the banks that initiate the turnaround process.[559] The amount of influence a bank has over a company during a turnaround can vary significantly, from serving in an outsider role to running the company and deciding which strategies should be applied. If the firm is not yet in a crisis situation, it is often the shareholders who act through their representatives to change the company's management before a crisis materializes. A new management team often has more support and power in making recovery actions quickly.[560] A third way of initiating a turnaround is the purchase of a company by an investment committee, a turnaround firm, or another company. In this case, the acquirer usually purchases a major stake in the company and pushes through the efforts it wants. However, the ITMS applies to a more structured turnaround than these. In the cases mentioned above, the entry point into this standard would still be the beginning of the Pre-Turnaround Stage. It is important to start the turnaround at the beginning of the ITMS in order to ensure that all of the important steps are taken and all requirements are set up for the next stages. Until this point, the information required for making the best possible decisions has been collected. Now this subcomponent

---

[559] (S.L., Corp Rec. p. 109).
[560] (Slatter & Lovett, 2004, p. 109)

initiates the turnaround process itself, and the formal planning of the turnaround process can begin.

Responsibilities

The Turnaround Leader is responsible for this subcomponent.

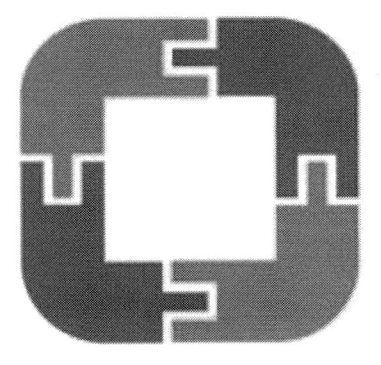

Emergency Procedures (EP)

EP 1 – Planning Emergency Procedures

Summary

The purpose of this subcomponent is to plan Emergency Procedures.

Context

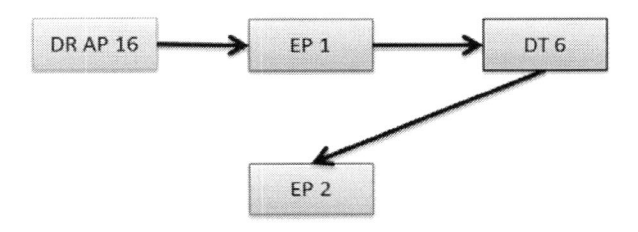

DR AP 16 → EP 1 → DT 6 → EP 2

Description of the Subcomponent

A company that is going through an emergency stage must concentrate its scarce resources on its areas of strength rather than wasting available resources on products or customers that are not profitable and are not key to the company's survival.[561]

Emergency Procedures are usually started while a diagnostic review is still being conducted or when a change in the circumstances for the turnaround makes it necessary to start certain procedures immediately. The plan should include:

- The reason for the Emergency Procedures
- The expected impact if Emergency Procedures are not started
- A formal plan for which Emergency Procedures to conduct
- A plan for the resources needed
- A priority statement for the required resources

---

[561] (Bibeault, 1981, p. 292)

Responsibility

The Turnaround Leader is responsible for this subcomponent.

EP 2 – Authorizing Emergency Procedures

Summary

The Turnaround Leader initiates whatever Emergency Procedures are necessary.

Context

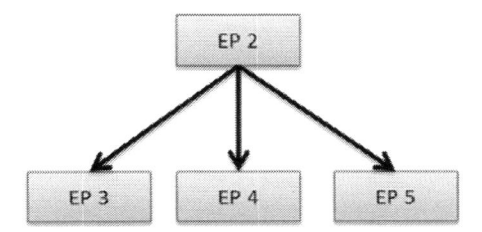

Description of the Subcomponent

In this subcomponent the Turnaround Leader initiates the planned Emergency Procedures that have been approved by the TAB. The actions taken need to be logged in the Turnaround Log for later review, especially actions taken in a hurry that might be questioned later on. It is therefore necessary to take the time to document why a decision was taken at a particular time and based on what grounds.

Responsibility

The Turnaround Leader or an assistant is responsible for this subcomponent.

EP 3 – Stem Major Costs

Summary

The purpose of this subcomponent is to cut major cost drivers that are endangering the turnaround process.

Context

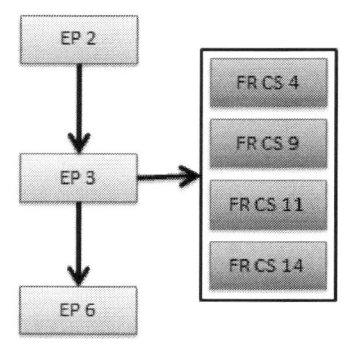

Description of the Subcomponent

If one business process causes a major cash drain, the first action is to analyze the impact of ending it. If ending the process will not endanger the company further, the next step is to stop the cash drain and analyze the impact again. When stopping the cash drain has an unexpectedly significant impact on the company, prior planning should allow the business process to be reinstated quickly. However, cutting costs almost always hurts somebody because somebody was profiting from it. The Turnaround Leader needs to explain clearly why certain costs are cut (temporarily) otherwise employees or customers might be frustrated and leave or withdraw their support for the TMT.

In turnaround processes, soft expenditure in areas such as public relations, community image-building, and advertising is usually cut to the bone.[562] Doing so generally does not have a significant short-term effect on the image of the company.

Responsibility

The Turnaround Leader is responsible for this subcomponent.

---

[562] (Bibeault, 1981, p. 292)

EP 4 – Stop Marketing Activities

Summary

The purpose of this subcomponent is to stop marketing activities that are clearly not necessary to the Turnaround Leader.

Context

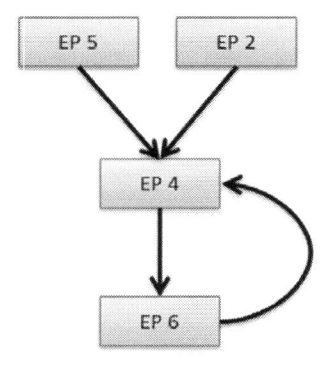

Description of the Subcomponent

Marketing expenses are often long-term orientated with at least the partial purpose of maintaining or establishing the image of the company. These types of marketing expenditure can almost certainly be cut down if cash is critical.

This subcomponent is also triggered if marketing expenses are connected to a product that will be discontinued or to a business unit that will be closed. This does not mean that the whole marketing department should be closed down; the company might need ready-made marketing strategies and materials very quickly at the end of the turnaround process. However, expenses that are related to constant marketing or current activities can most likely be canceled without a significant negative effect on the company's reputation or visibility.

Responsibility

The Turnaround Leader is responsible for this subcomponent or, in a marketing-driven organization, the member of the TMT who is responsible for communications and marketing.

EP 5 – Divestment of a Business Unit in Emergency Procedures

Summary

The purpose of this subcomponent is to undertake urgent divestments or closures of business units.

Context

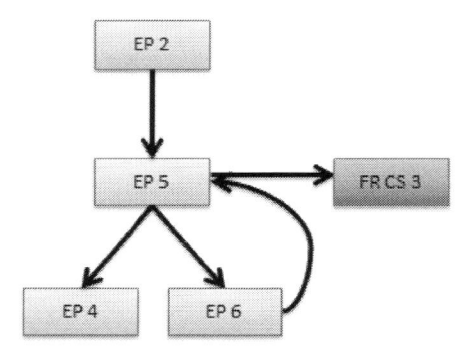

Description of the Subcomponent

Divestment is a form of retrenchment strategy. If the Diagnostic Review shows that some business units, products, or subsidiaries should be divested, the sale or divestment begins in this subcomponent. However, if the divestiture is to be a sale, this subcomponent will lead into the formal SR CS 3 subcomponent in the Strategic Restructuring part of this standard.

In serious crises, the divestment of a business unit can begin as an Emergency Procedure. If the sale or divestment is not necessary to ensure the survival of the business, the divestment should be made in the Crisis Stabilization Stage.

As product demand changes and firms alter their strategies, there will almost always be some portion of the business that is not performing to management's expectations. Such an operation is a prime target for divestment and may well leave the company in a stronger competitive position if it is divested.[563]

Responsibility

The Turnaround Leader is responsible for this subcomponent.

---

[563] (Thomas)

EP 6 – Assessing Progress in Emergency Procedures

Summary

The progress of EP 3 to EP 5 should be checked at regular intervals for its efficiency and adherence to the plan.

Context

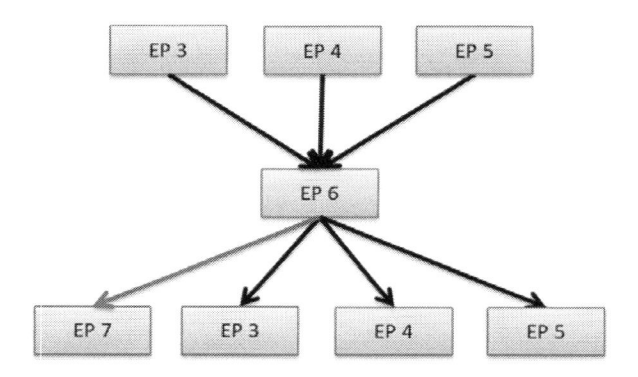

Description of the Subcomponent

In this subcomponent the emergency procedures plan is checked against the actuals. If the Turnaround Leader can fix the problems within their tolerances or can accept new tolerances, this subcomponent leads back to the subcomponent it came from. If the Turnaround Leader cannot fix the problem or must reverse changes quickly, they escalate the subcomponent to EP 7 (Escalating Issues in Emergency Procedures) and inform the TAB.

Responsibility

The Turnaround Leader is responsible for this subcomponent.

EP 7 – Escalating Issues in Emergency Procedures

Summary

Problems for which the Turnaround Leader needs the approval of the TAB are escalated to the TAB in this subcomponent.

Context

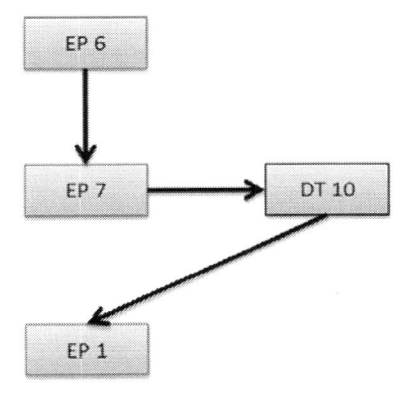

Description of the Subcomponent

If in EP 6 it is established that something has gone out of tolerance in one of the Emergency Procedures subcomponents, the Turnaround Leader must get assurance from the TAB on how to proceed by escalating the issue. The Turnaround Leader is responsible for preparing an escalation document which states the risks of the escalation, and it should be documented in the Turnaround Log.

Responsibility

The Turnaround Leader or an assistant is responsible for this subcomponent.

Outcome

- Escalation document to be presented to the TAB

Planning the Turnaround (PT)

PT 1 – Producing a Rolling Cash Forecast

Summary

The rolling cash forecast serves as a basis for investment decisions.

Context

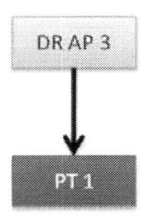

Description of the Subcomponent

Monthly cash flow plans are insufficient in a turnaround because they do not pinpoint the lean cash flow weeks when a company can run out of money.[564] Therefore, a rolling cash forecast must be created. The rolling cash forecast is a detailed daily statement of what inflows and outflows of cash are expected over the next six to eight weeks. After that, the forecast can be made weekly for another six months into the future.

Every feasible source of additional cash must be explored, and all cash that can realistically be anticipated must be incorporated into a detailed cash flow plan.[565] This plan should include only what can realistically be expected as income; it does not make sense to count on income just to make the plan look better. If there is considerable uncertainty about the future financial situation, two or even three plans—good, best-case, and worst-case financial plans—may be created. However, only the worst-case should realistically be counted on. This plan will help the Financial Turnaround Manager know how much money will be needed and when.

---

[564] (Bibeault, 1981, p. 270)
[565] (Bibeault, 1981, p. 270)

Responsibility

The Turnaround Leader is responsible for this subcomponent. The Financial Turnaround Manager is responsible for updating the financial plan and collecting the relevant information.

Information Needs

- All receivables
- All collectibles
- All expenses that are planned

Outcome

- The financial plan

PT 2 – not relevant in this version

This subcomponent is not relevant in this version of the standard.

PT 3 – Setting Turnaround Goals

Summary

At the time of a turnaround—in fact, at any time in the life of a business—success has to be clearly defined so it can be translated into goals, complete with targets and the right metrics by which to measure them.[566]

Context

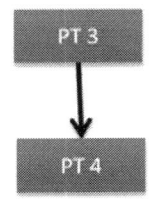

```
PT 3
  ↓
PT 4
```

Description of the Subcomponent

Goals must be set in order to establish a clear vision of where the journey is supposed to go, and to have a clear way of measuring the success of certain stages and the turnaround process as a whole. Success needs to be accurately defined otherwise it will end up as an ever-moving target; the result would be frustration within the workforce and misalignment, which could result in failure. It is also important to celebrate goals that have been reached and to publicly mention people who contributed to the success. Even goals that have almost, but not quite, been reached are worth mentioning since there are always people who have contributed significantly to reaching the goal. (Just because a goal could not be reached does not necessarily mean that the work put in was not good enough; it is possible that the goal was set too high or that other factors out of the workers' control intervened.) The experienced Turnaround Leader can distinguish between goals that are set too high, goals that are reachable, and goals that are absolutely crucial.

---

[566] (Roman, 2010, p. 190)

Stopping for a second and reminding everyone where they used to be and where they are today makes for a great introduction to setting new targets and gaining company-wide support and engagement to reach them.

Responsibility

The Turnaround Leader is responsible for setting turnaround goals.

PT 4 – Identifying, Defining, and Analyzing Activities

Summary

In this subcomponent all necessary activities are defined and analyzed, responsibilities are assigned to these activities, and their dependencies to other subcomponents are documented.

Context

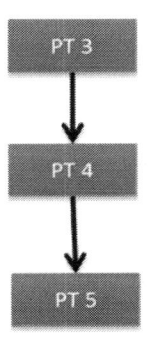

Description of the Subcomponent

The necessary activities for the chosen strategies must be defined and broken down into tasks in order to manage and control the sustainability, quality, and development of the strategies. In addition, by defining the activities everyone involved in the turnaround process can understand them better and work in a coordinated, non-redundant way toward the required outcome. This component is divided into five steps:

1. Identify the activities needed in order to follow the strategies and management components
2. Describe each activity in terms of its goals and quality requirements
3. Provide a logical order for the activities
4. Establish the dependencies (internal and external)
5. Determine which activities can and should overlap in order to save time

The management of risk and quality involved in the activities—and consideration of whether extra activities should be added to the plan in order to manage these risks and the quality of the outcome—is required at this stage, so the Risk Log will need to be updated.

Additional tasks in this subcomponent are to:

- Identify all necessary activities and group them in work packages
- Identify the relationships and dependencies among the different work packages
- Identify the dependencies among the different stages

It is also necessary to identify "key points", which are work packages that must be finished before another stage can start. Key points are highlighted in the Turnaround Plan by, for example, red cubes. The goal is to sort the stages into groups that are as small as possible, keeping in mind whether tasks can be finished first that don't rely on the completion of other stages. The idea behind key points is that, if a stage is running late and another stage cannot start as a result, the late key points can receive the focus of attention in order to solve the issues quickly.

Assigning Responsibilities and Ownership

Each component and subcomponent that contributes to the operational turnaround must have an owner to ensure the execution of tasks, establish the accountability and ownership of the actions taken, and identify the hierarchical structure associated with this execution.[567] The component and subcomponent owners must be assigned and briefed thoroughly. The owners are also often leaders of a team that is executing a particular group of tasks.

Responsibility

The Turnaround Leader is responsible for this subcomponent, although it will involve the whole TMT and possibly internal specialists to identify the activities.

---

[567] compare (Roman, 2010, p. 30)

Updates

- Risk Log

PT 5 – Estimating

Summary

The purpose of this subcomponent is to identify the resources that each activity requires and the time it will take to complete the activities and tasks.

Context

Description of the Subcomponent

The activities and dependencies identified in PT 3 (Identifying, Defining, and Analyzing Activities) are necessary for this subcomponent. The usual approach is a top-down estimate that establishes the time limit within which the turnaround is to be completed; the activities are then allocated the time that they can take. A bottom-up approach would be to estimate the time required for the tasks and activities first, with the timeframe for the whole turnaround then evolving from them.

This subcomponent consists of two steps:

1. Identification of the types of resources required, such as people with special skills, machinery, technology, and travel – Special human resources may have already been requested in DR AP 15 (Designing the Turnaround Management Team), but training may be required for some human resources.
2. Identification of the effort required to undertake each activity by type of resource – Estimating can never be exact, especially when activities are planned to take place over

a long time. In order to reach a good estimate, the activity must be well understood and assumptions must be based on experience. However, a margin of error should be included in the plan. Lessons learned reports from other turnarounds, if available, can be helpful as well. The Turnaround Management Society provides a number of these.

Responsibility

The Turnaround Leader is responsible for this subcomponent, although the estimating should be done by experts in the particular tasks.

PT 6 – Scheduling

Summary

Scheduling follows the establishment of estimates for the time required for each activity, followed by an assessment of the time-related risks inherent in the plan.[568]

Context

Description of the Subcomponent

A plan can show the feasibility of achieving its objectives only when the activities are put together in a schedule that defines when each activity will be carried out.[569]

The tasks to be completed in this subcomponent are to:

- Match the identified activities in PT 3 to the available resources in the same subcomponent
- Schedule the work needs according to the identified dependencies and availability of resources
- Assign cost needs to the resources, including person-days for human resources
- Calculate the cost of all the resources needed
- Confirm stage boundaries for control purposes

---

[568] compare (OGC Office of Government Commerce, 2005, p. 183)
[569] (OGC Office of Government Commerce, 2005, p. 183)

- Confirm the tolerances for the turnaround process
- Review the size of the work packages; if they are too big and they run late other components or work packages may not be able to start

Responsibility

The Turnaround Leader or an assistant is responsible for this subcomponent; although support staff are likely to do most of the work, the Turnaround Leader needs to agree to the dependencies and the due dates as well as the milestones.

PT 7 – Incorporating Risks

Summary

The need for awareness of risk arises in almost every subcomponent of the planning component. In order that these risks are not forgotten or underestimated they must be collected and re-evaluated regularly.

Context

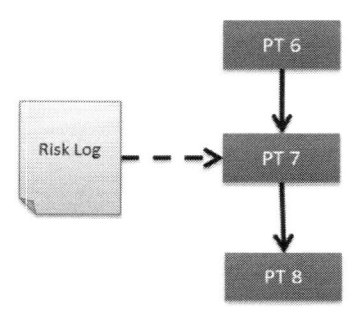

Description of the Subcomponent

This subcomponent should be carried out in parallel to all the other steps in the component as the Turnaround Plan is only a draft until the risks that evolve from it are incorporated. Some risks become obvious only if the activities are compared in a timescale or compared with each other. Each activity and task should be examined for risks that could endanger that and other activities. All identified risks should be entered into the Risk Log. Once all risks have been entered, the Turnaround Leader evaluates whether they endanger the viability of the turnaround process.

The Turnaround Leader is responsible for the analysis of the risks, although other members of the TMT may be better suited to perform specific evaluations. In any case, each risk must be brought to the Turnaround Leader's attention.

Responsibility

The Turnaround Leader is responsible for this subcomponent, although the Turnaround Assurance Team is likely to collect, present, and update the risks.

PT 8 – Creating a Stage Plan

Summary

During this subcomponent the Stage Plan for the upcoming stage is created.

Context

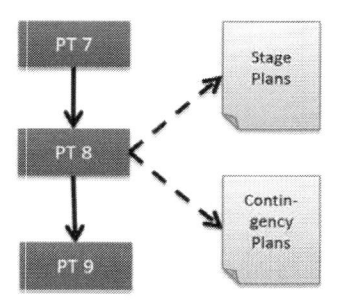

Description of the Subcomponent

The Stage Plan should be detailed enough that the Turnaround Leader can exercise sufficient control. The Turnaround Plan should include an outline of what needs to be achieved during each stage. These stage plans should explain in detail which activities need to be undertaken and by whom in order to reach the stage's goals. The Quality Log and the Risk Log should also be updated regularly, and quality checks should be planned. The required resources should be confirmed again, and the TMT should ensure that everyone involved in the stage clearly understands their responsibilities, tasks, and quality criteria.

Job descriptions should also be prepared in order to ensure that everyone knows exactly what to do. If the stage involves more than one team of people, the team plans should also be prepared at this time. The Stage Plan will also include the previous Stage Plan's Stage End Report.

During this subcomponent the Turnaround Leader should ensure that:

- Each stage is planned in sufficient detail
- Daily controls can be exercised

- The Stage Plan is approved by the TAB
- The TAB understands the Stage Plan, the risks, and the suggested outcome of the stage
- Contingency plans are in place that can turn into an Escalation Plan if needed

Setting Goals

Goals should be consistent, achievable, and sustainable, meaning that they don't change frequently, because the employees should be able to rely on them. If the goals change monthly or weekly from, say, achieving high profit to high turnover and then to achieving data entry goals, the employees won't be able to see the purpose and the whole picture. In fact, goals that change frequently are the result of bad planning. The perfect recipe for disaster comes from a combination of factors:

- Unbalanced, non-prioritized goals, swings in priorities from one extreme to the other, and knee-jerk, panicked reactions from leaders[570]
- The failure of leaders to understand or value the very basic notions of stability, dependability, and consistency in laying out goals for their teams and managing performance[571]
- Leaders who simply push things too far by setting unrealistic targets in complete ignorance of component capabilities, thereby generating unstable, fearful, demotivated environments that are prone to internal conflict and high levels of employee turnover[572]

In addition, the goals must be aligned with the strategy.

Responsibility

The Turnaround Leader is responsible for this subcomponent, although the Turnaround Managers are responsible for the accuracy of the planning for their respective stages.

Outcome

- Stage Plan(s)

---

[570] (Roman, 2010, p. 42)
[571] (Roman, 2010, p. 42)
[572] (Roman, 2010, pp. 42-43)

- Contingency Plans

PT 9 – Setting Stage Targets

Summary

Targets are set on the stage level, the component level, and the subcomponent level.

Context

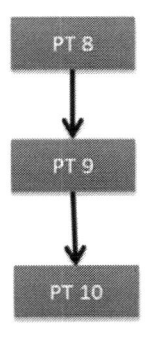

Description of the Subcomponent

The stages and components in a turnaround process must have targets in order for the workforce to know what the goals are and what to focus on. The targets need to be described in detail, as well as what is necessary to reach them. If there are, for example, dependencies to a stakeholder that the targets are linked to, these need to be documented as well. In some cases, a target might turn out not to be reachable simply because a delivery outside the TMT's control was not met rather than due to any failing of the TMT. Documenting these prior deliveries ensures that the TMT is not liable for things outside its control, and it reminds the TMT to address the stakeholder prior to the task or project failing.

Any operational turnaround action in need of fast execution and immediate results needs to have an aggressive bonus plan attached to the milestones, with clear metrics and checkpoints in place, recognizing overachievement in a bold manner.[573]

---

[573] (Roman, 2010), (r92;p30)

Responsibility

The Turnaround Leader is responsible for setting the goals on the stage and component levels, although members of the TMT can be responsible for setting goals on the subcomponent or component levels.

PT 10 – Stage End Meetings

Summary

Stage end meetings are conducted with the TMT to discuss a stage once it has been completed and to discuss the next stage.

Context

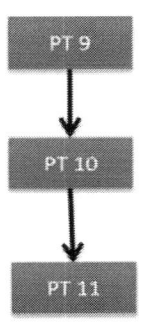

Description of the Subcomponent

After each stage or substage, a stage end meeting is conducted with the TMT to review the progress of the Turnaround Plan. These meetings should be the only time after the company review stage when the whole management (TMT and senior managers) meets. Other than these stage end meetings, every manager should be busy doing their work instead of sitting around in meetings. In some companies the culture encourages frequent meetings, but the fact is that most people lose time in meetings. Turnarounds are not the right time for long and frequent debates.

The stage end meetings are exceptions. They are the forums in which the TMT comes together and analyzes the results of the execution of a stage: roadblocks, solutions, unplanned consequences (good and bad), need for additional support and resources, revised commitments, and so on.[574] The results of these discussions need to be documented clearly in the Turnaround Log.

---

[574] (Roman, 2010, p. 48)

Discussions at these meetings include:

- Whether the turnaround is on time and proceeding according to plan
- The difficulties with and changes made to the past stage plan
- What actions were successful
- How the cash flow evolved

The presentation style at these meetings is not important. Some consulting companies put a lot of effort into making their PowerPoint presentations look as nice as possible, but this is not the time for cosmetics. A Turnaround Leader should be able to read from an Excel spreadsheet, a project management software document, or a Word document; everything else is a waste of time and resources at this stage.

However, communication with stakeholders outside the company should be handled separately, under the supervision of the communications expert on the TMT. They should present the information to external stakeholders in manner best suited to their interests and abilities.

Responsibility

The Turnaround Leader is responsible for the stage end meetings.

Output

Updated Turnaround Log

PT 11 – Defining Exceptions

Summary

A procedure is established to handle exceptions and avoid chaos in a critical situation.

Context

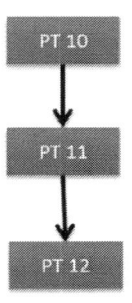

Description of the Subcomponent

In order to know how to deal with exceptions, the Turnaround Leader must know the answers to several questions:

- What is considered an escalation, specific to the turnaround process?
- Who—person or team—should handle the escalation and what should their qualifications be?
- How should the escalation be handled?
- How will the person or team responsible for handling the escalation be reached?
- How much time does the person or team responsible for handling the escalation have for the actions?
- How is the performance of the person or team responsible for handling the escalation measured? What are the targets and goals?

Responsibility

The Turnaround Leader is responsible for this subcomponent.

PT 12 – Setting Key Performance Indicators

Summary

Key Performance Indicators (KPIs) will help in tracking the success of certain components, but it is important to choose the right KPIs for critical components.

Context

Description of the Subcomponent

Establishing KPIs that make sense under the circumstances and are aligned with the strategic plan and its tasks will help to ensure alignment and focus and to control the turnaround process.[575] KPIs should measure key data generated throughout the turnaround process, but if key data is badly chosen and interpreted in the wrong way it can lead to any conclusion, not always the right one.[576] Key data should be quantifiable, livable, comparable, relevant, and current.[577] Choosing the right KPIs is an important task for the Operational Turnaround Manager. The successful Turnaround Leader will introduce KPIs "into the business in a structured and planned way so as to ensure that the most important key success factors are measured and that the workforce understands the KPIs and what they can do to influence performance.[578]

---

[575] (Roman, 2010, p. 45)
[576] (Jankulik, 2009, p. 46)
[577] (Burghardt, 2002)
[578] (Slatter & Lovett, 2004, p. 291) (Slatter & Lovett, 2004, p. 291)

If introduced correctly KPIs can help employees to work on specific goals and to keep their efforts aligned.[579] Workforces react positively and enthusiastically to KPIs that are clearly presented, and develop an appetite for more as they gain a greater understanding of the levers that drive change and create value.

KPIs should adhere to the following principles:[580]

1. The indicator must be important. If the indicator points to a trend, is the trend in relation to improved performance? Would anyone care if this indicator no longer existed?
2. The indicator must be understandable. The employees must be able to understand what the indicator can tell them.
3. The indicator should have the right sensitivity. It should make it easy to spot changes and should reflect important disruptions and errors.
4. The indicator should support analyses and actions. Is the indicator really used by analysts and, if it is, does it draw attention to the improvement of the right components?
5. The data necessary for the indicator should be easily collectible. Are there other indicators that are already in use? Is the expenditure of time to maintain the indicator justifiable?

Responsibility

The Operational Turnaround Manager is responsible for this subcomponent.

Outcome

- KPIs for the key components

---

[579] (Slatter & Lovett, 2004, p. 292)
[580] (Jankulik, 2009, p. 45)

PT 13 – Redesigning the Organization

Summary

In many cases, the organization as it was when the crisis hit will not stand after the turnaround process. It will be necessary to redesign it in order to operate more efficiently and to reflect strategic and operative changes in the organizational structure.

Context

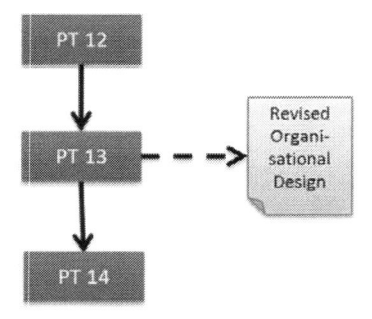

Description of the Subcomponent

A complete redesign of the organization is useful if cash is running out quickly or has already gone and there is no time to go through all the books to identify major cost drivers. A redesign is also useful for an organization that does not have useful books at this stage.

Redesigning the business from the ground up creates an opportunity to address some interesting questions around needs versus wants, as well as the company's core competencies.[581] If a redesign is proposed the top management team and the TMT should come together and design a completely new organization based on the proposed sales. If sales are expected to be 100 million units in Europe, the TMT virtually designs an organization that can provide the 100 million units in Europe efficiently.

---

[581] (Roman, 2010, p. 25)

Sometimes it is useful to look back at the structure of the organization when it used to provide "only" 100 million units. There are major differences between the "now" and the "back then" models: business channels or units that did not exist or are no longer needed, efficiencies that were gained in the interim, new systems, components, and technologies may have changed the very core of the business; therefore, just applying the "back then" blueprint is risky.[582] However, the organization may be able to take the old structure and apply technological advancements to it in order to make it more efficient than it was "back then". Some processes that were done in-house before may also be outsourced.

Responsibility

The Turnaround Leader is responsible for this subcomponent.

Outcome

- Revised organizational design

---

[582] (Roman, 2010, p. 24)

PT 14 – Building a Transition Map

Summary

A transition map describes the current and future design of the organization, along with a way to get there.

Context

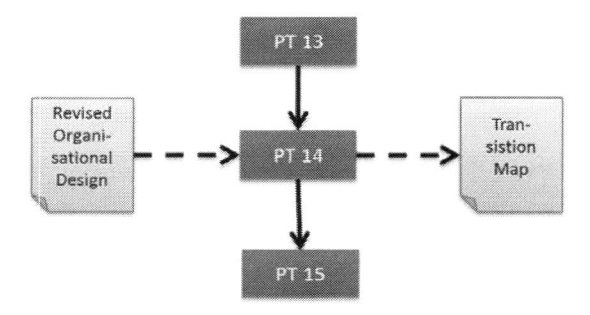

Description of the Subcomponent

The transition map is a high-level draft that explains the current status of the organization and its organizational chart and puts it next to the future design with key actions that need to be undertaken to get there.

EXPL - Current Org	EXPL 2 - Future Design	Key Actions
Headoffice Overhead @ $12M	Headoffice Overhead @ $4.9M	reduce management headcount, redesign org, outsource backoffice functions
Dealership count: 38	Dealership count: 16	identify low performing locations and close; reassign / liquidate inventory
-	Online sales division	create, implement, staff
In-house printing operation	-	outsource
Dealership level organization	Optimized, increased variability	reduced fixed headcount, reassign tasks towards variable
Inventory $ 72 M	Inventory @ 30 M	organize close-out sales events, heavy promo, sell at cost

Picture 15 Turnaround action planning—transition map[583]

The analytics and reasoning behind the numbers chosen as targets are based largely on rightsizing the structure to operate in profitability at the forecasted sales volume.[584]

In changing from one status of an organizational structure to another, a change manager should be consulted to ensure the best possible outcome when the changes are implemented.

Responsibility

The Turnaround Leader, assisted by a change manager, is responsible for this subcomponent.

Outcome

- Transition map

---

[583] from (Roman, 2010, p. 26)
[584] (Roman, 2010, p. 26)

PT 15 – Producing the Financial Plan

Summary

The Financial Plan, which is part of the Turnaround Plan, helps the TMT to negotiate with stakeholders and gives it an overview of the current financial situation as well as the planned income and expenses that are expected.

Context

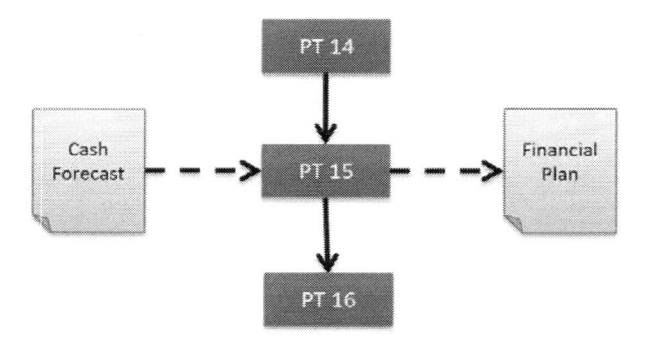

Description of the Subcomponent

The financial forecast forms the basis of any refinancing, financial restructuring, or negotiations for ongoing financial support from stakeholders.[585] It describes the financial implications of the turnaround strategies and the proposed operational actions outlined in the operational part of the Turnaround Plan.

It is vital for the accurate development of a Financial Plan that each action is properly quantified in terms of its impact on profit and cash flow relative to the base case.[586] Each action can have two different levels of financial impact: the risk-adjusted benefit, which has a degree of uncertainty or stretch associated with it; and an impact relative to the target.[587] For example, an action could reduce the costs of a component by four percent risk-adjusted but have a target

---
[585] (Slatter & Lovett, 2004, p. 159)
[586] (Slatter & Lovett, 2004, p. 203)
[587] (Slatter & Lovett, 2004, p. 200)

improvement of an additional five percent. This goal should be included in the financial plan as a risk-adjusted projection and a target projection to gross margin.

If asset reduction strategies require an asset to be sold for less than its book value, they have a positive impact on the cash flow but a negative profit impact.

If an upfront investment is necessary in order to generate a positive cash flow, the net present value of that project should be positive over the life span of the project or the turnaround. There are exceptions in research and development for products that are critical for the long-term survival of the company.

The Base Case

The base case, which is also referred to as "momentum analysis", is a reality check that projects the likely trading performance and financial consequences for the business if no action is undertaken to address the causes of decline and reverse the current trends.[588] It is accepted practice to use daily data for identifying short-term trends, weekly data for intermediate trends, and monthly data for primary trends.[589] The extrapolation of existing trends usually indicates further deterioration in performance rather than the maintenance of current levels of profit or loss, as the business is likely to experience a further downturn in sales if its product-market strategy is not reformulated and costs will remain fixed if no action is taken.[590] The aim of all actions is to increase the performance compared to the base case scenario. Sometimes this will highlight that the business will not survive if dramatic action is not taken, which is why senior management is likely to try to keep it secret from stakeholders. However, doing so is often a fatal mistake since sharing realistic financial information about the company is crucial in order to gain the stakeholders' ongoing support. If the Base Case is not appropriately realistic, the risk-adjusted forecast might be overstated or misinterpreted which can lead to it not being achievable, and further undermining the stakeholders' trust in the TMT's actions.

---

[588] compare (Pring, 2002, p. 181), (Slatter & Lovett, 2004, p. 205)
[589] (Slatter & Lovett, 2004, p. 205), (Pring, 2002, p. 181)
[590] (Slatter & Lovett, 2004, p. 205)

The Risk-Adjusted Forecast

The risk-adjusted forecast forecasts the minimum level of performance that the company must reach in order to survive. It builds on the base case using the financial consequences of the reformulated strategy and of those actions that the TMT believes are certain to be achieved.

The Target Case

The target case is the financial plan that the company should try to achieve. It should be supported by a break-even analysis, activity-based costing, and capacity modeling. The financial models will likely be updated many times because projections and plans change, so the person in charge of these models should keep track of the different versions produced. Management compensation schemes should be adjusted in order to motivate the management to achieve the desired results. The risk-adjusted forecast can be a good basis for the target case. The business plan should include an analysis that clearly reconciles the improvement in the financial KPIs—such as net cash flow, overhead, and sales gross margin—from base case to risk-adjusted forecast and from risk-adjusted forecast to target.

The actions set out in the operational plan should be linked to the targeted financial performance improvements in order to give both management and external stakeholders confidence in the projections, as they are supported by separately identifiable and quantified initiatives developed by the people who will have responsibility for their implementation.[591]

---

[591] (Slatter & Lovett, 2004, p. 206)

	Gross profit £000	Gross Margin %	Initiative Number
Base case	25,000	50.0	
Increased sales at base margin	1,500		S1.01 to S1.04
Procurement initiatives	275	0.5	P1.01 to P1.06
Manufacturing initiatives	1,025	1.9	M1.10 to M1.05
Risk-adjusted forecast (RAF)	27,800	52.4	
Increased sales at base margin	2,500		S1.01 to S1.05
Procurement initiatives	125	0.2	P1.01 to P1.08
Manufacturing initiatives	1,575	2.6	M1.01 to M1.09
Target	32,000	55.2	

Table 2 Reconciliation of base case to risk-adjusted forecast and target[592]

The Financial Plan is updated in the Financial Restructuring component.

Responsibility

The Financial Turnaround Manager is responsible for this subcomponent, although the plan is discussed with the TMT.

Information Needs

- Rolling cash forecast

Outcome

- Financial Turnaround Plan

---

[592] from (Slatter & Lovett, 2004, p. 207)

PT 16 – Producing Operational and Strategic Plans

Summary

Operational and strategic plans for the turnaround are created in this subcomponent. It details how the Operational Turnaround Manager is integrated into the TMT and how process improvements are structured throughout the turnaround.

Context

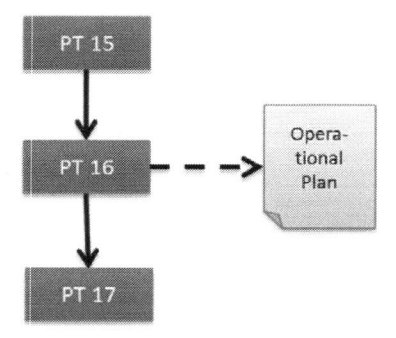

Description of the Subcomponent

The Operational Turnaround Plan should be created by the people who will execute it. If an action plans is developed by a few people only and is then simply handed out to the workforce, it is unlikely to be regarded as realistic and achievable and may simply be ignored because the employees have the feeling that it was developed over their heads.

The Operational Turnaround Plan consists of initiatives that address all of the company's current key weaknesses, which were examined in the Diagnostic Review Stage. The initiatives must produce the competitive advantages that were set for the company and are important in order for it to achieve its goals.

The responsible Turnaround Manager should form a management team that consists of the CFO/responsible finance manager or the chief restructuring officer (CRO) (if in place), and other executives, such as senior operational managers from the business and operational areas, and themselves. Each member creates a plan for creating process improvements in their area. It is vital that they understand the proposed product-market strategy, core capabilities required, and sourcing approach for the business.[593] The responsible Turnaround Manager should be involved with every team in order to delegate the creative activities if necessary. Their primary objectives are establishing and explaining to the core team what is needed to develop the action plans, including their responsibilities, deliverables, and a timetable that meets the overall business plan timetable,[594] and ensuring there are no overlaps or gaps among the different action plans. The Turnaround Leader observes the component and consults regularly with the TMT members on issues. At this stage the Turnaround Leader's primary objective may still be to find funding for the turnaround process so their time should not be consumed by operational matters.

The TMT member responsible for the financial element also needs to critically review the financial implications of the proposed initiatives and to discuss performance measures to be undertaken in order to achieve the strategic and financial goals of the organization. Picture 16 Turnaround management hierarchy—shows a graphic picture of the hierarchy during a turnaround process.

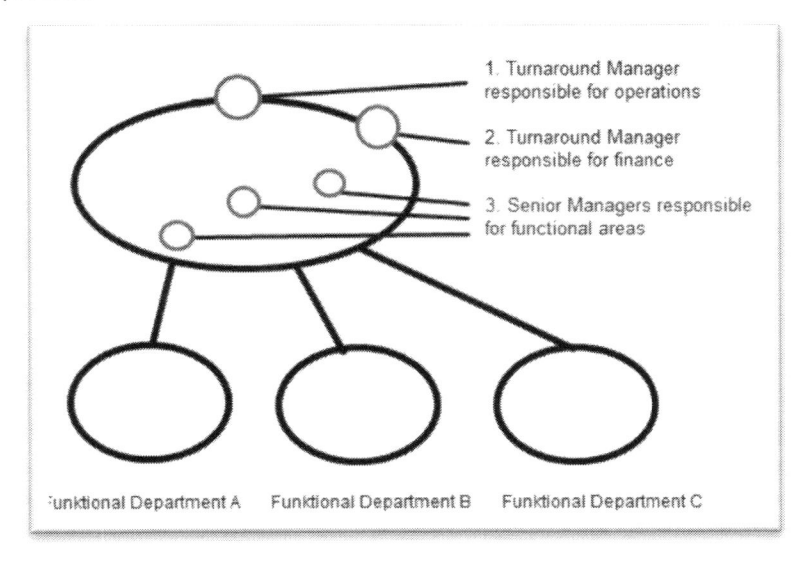

Picture 16 Turnaround management hierarchy

---

[593] (Slatter & Lovett, 2004, p. 200)
[594] (Slatter & Lovett, 2004, p. 200)

It is a good idea to give the executive team a special name, such as "Club X" or "Team Y", in order to build team spirit and to encourage cross-functional solutions and objective-setting rather than isolationist thinking.[595]

The Operational Turnaround Plan must be approved by the TAB before it can be communicated.[596] The Turnaround Leader determines whether the plan is within the targeted timeframe and weighs the costs against the benefits to ensure that both are backed up by careful analysis.

Responsibility

The Operational Turnaround Manager is responsible for creating the Operational Turnaround Plan.

Outcome

- Operational Turnaround Plan

---

[595] (Slatter & Lovett, 2004, p. 200)
[596] see Reporting Updates in the Communication Component)

PT 17 – Producing the Turnaround Plan

Summary

The Turnaround Plan is the backbone of every turnaround process. Its detailed and comprehensive production is a critical success factor. The Turnaround Plan is designed in this subcomponent.

Context

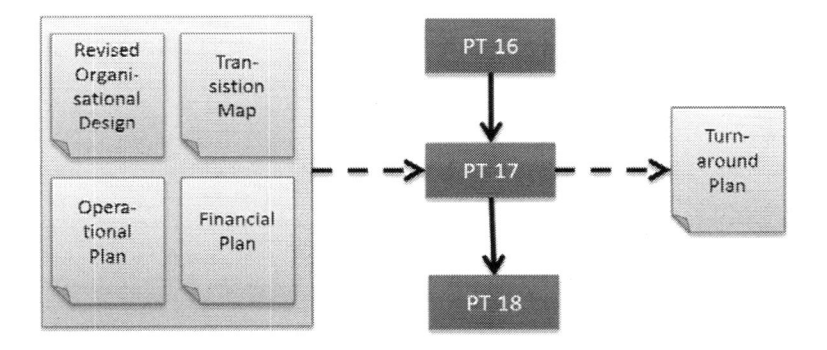

Description of the Subcomponent

A Turnaround Plan is essential for the success of a turnaround, and strategic planning is essential for the survival of an organization.[597] A well-developed turnaround action plan addresses the root causes that led to failure and restructuring so the result will be a stable operation that is positioned for growth, flexible and variable, with components, policies, and culture to match.[598] According to the PRINCE2 manual, good plans cover all aspects of the project, giving everyone involved a common understanding about the work ahead.[599] The Turnaround Plan gives every person involved a clear understanding of what lies ahead and ensures that all aspects of business are covered. When the turnaround is being planned, all functional areas—such as the legal department, the finance and accounting department, human resources, and IT—should be involved. HR can inspect the basis of the decisions, critique

---

[597] (Turner, 2008, p. 18)
[598] (Roman, 2010, p. 57)
[599] (OGC Office of Government Commerce, 2005, p. 171)

them, and educate the Turnaround Leader on possible drawbacks, but ultimately HR helps implement the Turnaround Plan. The same goes for change management and communications specialists; these functional areas have to be on board with the Turnaround Plan and establish operating mechanisms that will ensure proper and timely support of changes and actions undertaken by the turnaround project team.[600]

Planning can save a substantial amount of time and help the people involved to maintain perspective on what gets done, how, by whom, when, in what order, and in what relationship to other activities. The functional departments involved have to define with accuracy the givens, lead times to implement changes, paperwork requirements, and any processes that must be in place in order to ensure flawless execution with minimal cost and risk.[601]

In designing the plan, the TMT should:

- Choose a design and layout for presentation purposes
- Choose planning tools and estimating methods
- Identify the people who will have access to the plan
- Consolidate the stage plans for different activities

How these tasks are accomplished varies based on the complexity of the turnaround process. Estimating can be done using computer tools, experience, discussions, or combinations of these. If a contingency budget and/or a change budget were established they should also be included in the plan.

The person who designs the plan must keep in mind that no one is 100 percent efficient and that people do get sick or experience unplanned events that might defer an activity. The person who designs the plan must ensure that unforeseeable events were not also considered in the estimating subcomponent otherwise these allowances would be entered into the plan twice. According to the PRINCE2 manual, the estimation methods to be used in the plan may affect the design, so decisions about the methods should be made as part of the plan design.[602] It is essential that the Turnaround Plan is a project plan that all involved parties can commit to and

---

[600] (Roman, 2010, p. 51)
[601] (Roman, 2010, p. 51)
[602] (OGC Office of Government Commerce, 2005, p. 172)

stand behind. Roman adds that the best way to ensure this level of commitment and execution is to think of the entire action plan in terms of a project, complete with project manager, task list, resource allocation, and Gantt chart.[603]

The Turnaround Plan has two main stages: the Crisis Stabilization Stage and the Turnaround Stage. The goal of the Crisis Stabilization Stage is to stop losing more money than the company can earn. Profit improvement tactics in the stabilization plan center on rigorous enforcement of margin requirements[604] and on securing both financial and stakeholder support for the Turnaround Stage. The Turnaround Stage then focuses on putting the business back on a firm footing.

The development of the Turnaround Plan is done by the whole TMT, but external consultants can contribute by challenging the TMT's assumptions and thoughts, contributing and analyzing market research, providing independent feasibility studies, and/or providing expertise in specialized areas. Accountants may review the financial part of the plan and develop forecasts, and the advice of lawyers should be sought if intellectual property, competition, environmental, or liability issues are involved.

The style and language of the Turnaround Plan should reflect the culture of the business that the TMT is trying to create and not the style that management consultants or other external advisors usually use.[605]

The preparation of the Turnaround Plan may serve to highlight some issues that cannot be resolved at that time. These issues should be clearly marked and entered into the Issue Log so they won't be forgotten and can be addressed later.

Designing the Target State

Once the industry, competition (both current and future), and product-market segments in which the company currently operates have been assessed and the business strategy has been reformulated, it is useful to articulate or define the desired end-state for the business

---

[603] (Roman, 2010, p. 27)
[604] (Bibeault, 1981, p. 300)
[605] (Slatter & Lovett, 2004, p. 196)

collectively[606] by creating a mission statement or statement of the strategic intent of the company. The new mission statement should include:

1. The proposed product-market positioning – According to the balanced scorecard, this can be done from a customer's point of view. For example, the goal could be: "Company ABC is the best choice for products in the XYZ industry because it has the lowest prices, best service, and highest quality."
2. A summary of the strengths and competitive advantages – This summary should indicate the advantages the company will have over its competitors in order to sustain its viability in the market.
3. Technological perspective – This should indicate what technology will support the company in its direction.
4. Sourcing approach – based on the understanding of its core capabilities and where it will participate in the value chain, the company must determine which activities will be developed internally and which will be purchased or achieved through alliances with other organizations.[607]
5. The firm's organizational approach – This articulates the critical organizational capabilities required to support the business unit strategy as well as the components, organization architecture, and leadership required to make the change succeed.[608]
6. HR policies – These are the key principles regarding the culture, how performance is measured, and how good behavior in line with the company's strategy and goals will be recorded.

The vision articulated in this subcomponent may be revised during the turnaround, but this initial vision can give stakeholders a sense of how the organization's new goals can be achieved.

No plan can tackle every single problem of a troubled firm, and if it does it will fail because limited resources would be wasted on tackling issues that are not "mission-critical". Problems that threaten the existence of the company must be tackled, but the focus should be on the causes, not the symptoms. A recovery strategy based on the symptoms may make the "patient"

---

[606] compare (Slatter & Lovett, 2004, p. 196)
[607] (Hamel, 1990), (Slatter & Lovett, 2004, p. 197)
[608] (Slatter & Lovett, 2004, p. 197)

feel better temporarily, but any long-term recovery strategy has to be based on sorting out the underlying causes of distress.[609]

A successful Turnaround Plan has seven essential ingredients:[610]

1. Crisis stabilization
2. Leadership
3. Stakeholder management
4. Strategic focus
5. Organizational change
6. Critical component improvements
7. Financial restructuring

Successful turnaround situations are characterized by significant actions in each of these seven areas.[611] Generic strategies are outlined in the following sections.[612]

Operational Part

The operational part of the business plan contains an operational analysis and an operational action plan. The operational plan should include a SWOT analysis for every business unit. The goal is to identify areas for improvement as well as opportunities in the market.

The Operational Turnaround Plan addresses the weaknesses and opportunities identified in the Diagnostic Review Stage. The plan breaks down the overall turnaround strategy into quantifiable steps that are measurable and can be tracked.

Implementation Plan

The plan should include a description of the key milestones and key performance measures to be monitored during implementation.[613] This subcomponent triggers the creation of the

---

[609] (Slatter & Lovett, 2004)
[610] (Slatter & Lovett, 2004)
[611] (Slatter & Lovett, 2004, p. 76)
[612] (Slatter & Lovett, 2004)
[613] (Slatter & Lovett, 2004, p. 195)

Communications Plan, which indicates what stakeholders need to be informed about and when throughout the turnaround process.

Risk Summary

The Turnaround Plan includes a summary of the key risks to which the company and the turnaround process are exposed. (The Risk Log keeps track of all risks in more detail.) For all stakeholders, an evaluation of the associated risks is critical in their decisions about whether to support the business.

Responsibility

The Turnaround Leader is responsible for the Turnaround Plan, although they create the plan with the assistance of the TMT and senior stakeholders. If the plan is developed in isolation by the Turnaround Leader working with a small team, or by external consultants, there is considerable risk that it will not achieve buy-in from those who have to implement it.[614] Buy-in is important because the often significant changes that are necessary cannot be made without the workforce's understanding of the severity and urgency of the changes. The employees carry out significant parts of the Turnaround Plan and if they don't understand it their support for the actions necessary may be limited. If this is the case the turnaround will fail, however incisive or appropriate the strategies and plans it contains.[615]

Information Needs

- Revised organizational design
- Transition map
- Organizational plan
- Financial Plan

Outcome

- The Turnaround Plan

---

[614] (Slatter & Lovett, 2004, pp. 195-196)
[615] (Slatter & Lovett, 2004, p. 196)

PT 18 – Completion of the Turnaround Plan

Summary

This subcomponent adds explanations to the plan checkpoints to be used during later reviews of the plan.

Context

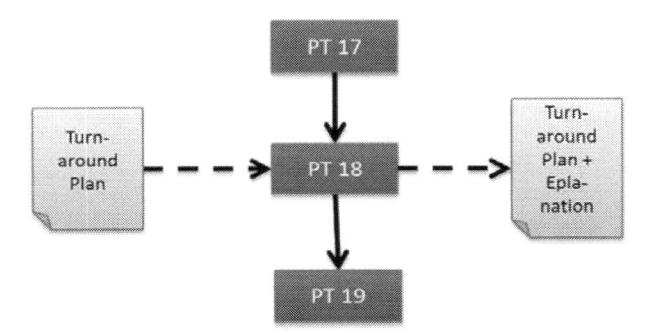

Description of the Subcomponent

The Turnaround Plan has now been put together, but a plan is not fully understandable without proper explanation, which is added at this stage. Basic questions that should be answered to develop these explanations are:

- What is included in the plan?
- What approach was taken?
- What is the suggested approach to implement the Turnaround Plan?
- How and by whom will the plan be controlled and monitored?
- What assumptions were made regarding the Turnaround Plan?

At this point, checkpoints should be created, along with plans for management products, such as Checkpoint Reports, Highlight Reports, and Stage End Reports.

Once the TAB has approved the plan it then becomes its owner, although the Turnaround Leader is responsible for executing it.

Responsibility

The Turnaround Leader is responsible for this subcomponent. The plan should also be reviewed by those parties that contributed to its production.

Information Needs

- Turnaround Plan

Outcome

- Refined Turnaround Plan

PT 19 – Creating a Turnaround Plan Summary

Summary

The Turnaround Plan Summary is a high-level summary of the main activities and an outline of the strategy that the TMT wants to apply to the company. Its main purpose is to support communication with stakeholders during the turnaround process.

Context

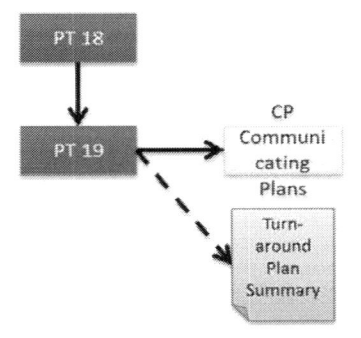

Description of the Subcomponent

The Turnaround Plan Summary is a floating document updated throughout the turnaround process. Its purpose is to give the TMT a summary plan of what will happen. This summary can be distributed to stakeholders and interested parties, but it should also serve as a turnaround overview for employees. The Turnaround Plan Summary outlines at a high level what products the company will produce, what services it will offer, the competitive advantages the company will build, where and in which markets it will compete, and its target customers.

Cost-cutting initiatives, generic strategies, and downsizing operations should also be included in the plan.

Responsibility

The Turnaround Assurance Team is responsible for this subcomponent.

Outcome

- Turnaround Plan Summary for stakeholders

PT 20 – Updating the Turnaround Plan and Turnaround Business Case

Summary

When conditions change, the Turnaround Plan and the Turnaround Business Case might need to be updated.

Context

Description of the Subcomponent

At the beginning and end of each stage, the Turnaround Plan should be updated. The creation of an Escalation Plan may also have an effect on the Turnaround Plan since these changes need to be incorporated. The Quality Log must also be updated when new information becomes available.

At the end of a stage the completed activities, changes that were necessary, actual costs, and the time it took to complete the stage are known—at least to a reasonable extent. This information is incorporated into the Turnaround Plan.

The Turnaround Business Case is critically evaluated at the end of each stage or substage and the risks, time, costs, and benefits are revised. A variety of factors can influence the Turnaround Business Case:

- The costs may have changed during the stage, affecting the overall Turnaround Business Case.

- The timeline may have changed, endangering the final due date for the turnaround process and affecting the benefits of the turnaround.
- The external environment may have changed, affecting the expected benefits, costs, or timeline.
- An Escalation Plan may have some influence on the Turnaround Business Case.
- Suppliers may have changed.
- The availability of external resources may have changed.

Other tasks that should be completed in this subcomponent include:

- Updating the Issue Log if additional issues are known
- Updating additional or changed risks as a result of changes made to the Turnaround Plan
- Assessing the Turnaround Business Case in response to changes made to the Turnaround Plan
- Determining whether the Turnaround Plan will stay within tolerance, especially at the end of a stage

Responsibility

The Turnaround Leader, with assistance from the Turnaround Assurance Team, is responsible for this subcomponent.

PT 21 – Updating Logs

Summary

Updating logs is a regular subcomponent that can be triggered by other subcomponents when the need arises, but also at regular intervals set out in the Turnaround Plan.

Context

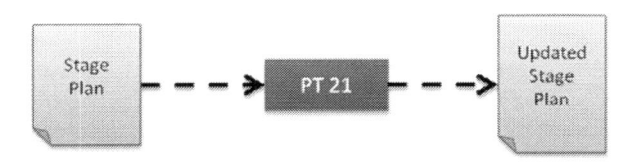

Updating logs can be triggered at any time and within any subcomponent. The initial subcomponent continues while this one is in progress.

Description of the Subcomponent

The logs are updated regularly throughout every stage of the turnaround process. The Risk Log is updated whenever a known risk changes or a new risk arises. Some risks may become unimportant or impossible but this subcomponent ensures that the risks to the turnaround process are regularly reviewed. Whenever the external or internal environment changes, updates to the Risk Log are carried out. The Turnaround Leader is responsible for this subcomponent, although they may delegate the task of reviewing and monitoring risk to a risk specialist or advisor.

- The Issue Log is updated throughout the whole turnaround process.
- The Lessons Learned Log is usually updated only at the end of a stage, but can be updated more frequently if the need arises.
- The Risk Log is updated regularly once a new risk occurs, and the log is reviewed at the end of each component and stage.
- The Communications Log is reviewed for any changes in the shareholder structure and stakeholder priority. Possible new stakeholders are entered into the log.

Responsibility

The Turnaround Assurance Team is responsible for this subcomponent.

Information Needs

- Risk Log
- Lessons Learned Log
- Issue Log
- Quality Log
- Communications Log

PT 22 – Updating the Stage Plan

Summary

Updating Stage Plans is triggered regularly throughout the turnaround process to allow other Turnaround Managers to know the status of the turnaround. It also accounts for small deviations that don't affect other stages.

Context

The Stage Plan is updated whenever a change to a stage occurs, whether it's a change in circumstances or a corrective action.

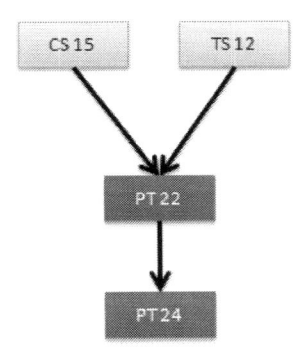

Description of the Subcomponent

Stage Plans must be updated frequently. Whenever an activity is completed, is out of tolerance, or incurs a problem, the Stage Plan should be updated to reflect this. This subcomponent should also be used to hold follow-up meetings between subteams and the TMT, where the subteams present their action plans and key initiatives. The TMT then ensures that the subteams are on track with their work and watches out for overlaps between subteams. By bringing the subteams together, the TMT ensures that all members remain up to date on the progress of the other teams, and engages in cross-functional discussions in order to prioritize and focus on the key initiatives that have a significant impact on the business.[616]

Responsibility

The Turnaround Assurance Team is responsible for this subcomponent.

Information Needs

- Stage Plans

Outcome

- Revised Stage Plans

---

[616] (Slatter & Lovett, 2004, p. 202)

PT 23 – Producing an Exemption Plan

Summary

If deviations from the Turnaround Plan are necessary, an Exemption Plan is created in order to account quickly but in a well-planned way for the change in circumstances.

Context

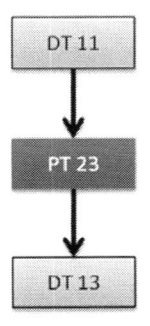

Description of the Subcomponent

As soon as a stage is expected to run beyond its tolerances, an Exception Plan is created. When a version of an Exception Plan already exists for a certain issue in the form of a contingency plan, this is verified for its viability in the new situation and turned into an Exemption Plan. If not, an Exception Plan is created. If the goals of the whole turnaround process are endangered and if the Turnaround Business Case is no longer viable, a turnaround Exception Plan is created if the TAB approves it in DT (Directing the Turnaround). The Turnaround Leader loses the mandate as soon as a stage is expected to run out of tolerance; this component gives it back to them.

The stage, or Turnaround Plan as it once was, becomes invalid and the Exception Plan takes its place once it has been approved by the TAB. The person responsible for configuration management adapts the Configuration Log to the Exemption Plan once it has been approved.

The Exemption Plan is a contingency plan for use if something goes wrong. It should be communicated properly, employees should be trained accordingly, and it should come complete with definitions of change success and failure, as well as checkpoints at important milestones and assigned owners.[617]

Responsibility

It is the Turnaround Leader's responsibility to create an Exception Plan.

Outcome

- Exemption Plan

If it is approved by the TAB, the Exemption Plan takes the place of the Stage or Turnaround Plan in part, depending on whether it is only the stage/component that is expected to run out of tolerance or the whole turnaround process. The Exemption Plan consists of recommended actions and a detailed plan of how to undertake them.

---

[617] (Roman, 2010, p. 35)

PT 24 – Updates to the Turnaround Plan

Summary

Changes to the Turnaround Plan can be made when there are changes in the Stage Plans or when an Exemption Plan is created. They can also be triggered when there is a change within a stage that is within its tolerance.

Context

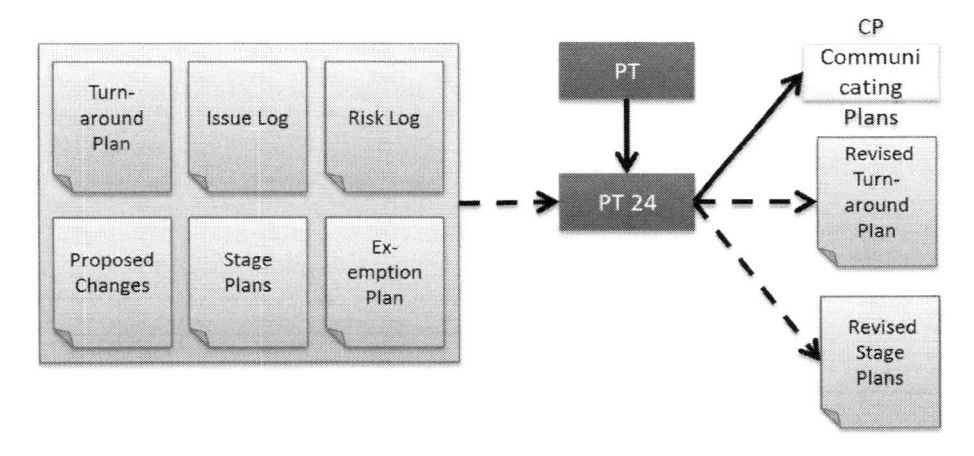

Description of the Subcomponent

In this subcomponent changes to the general Turnaround Plan are made and approved by the TAB, and the Stage Plans are updated to reflect the change. If the changes are due to a change in a stage, the Turnaround Plan is adjusted. If the changes are within the tolerance of the stage and the general Turnaround Plan, the TAB does not need to be informed. This may be the case when general issues affect not only a component but the whole Turnaround Plan.

Responsibility

The Turnaround Assurance Team is responsible for completing this subcomponent. The Turnaround Leader and the TAB approve the changes.

Information Needs

- Issue Log
- Risk Log
- Proposed changes
- Stage Plans
- Exemption Plan

Outcome

- Revised Turnaround Plan
- Revised Stage Plans

Directing the Turnaround (DT)

The turnaround process requires a formal decision-making component to ensure success in achieving the goal.

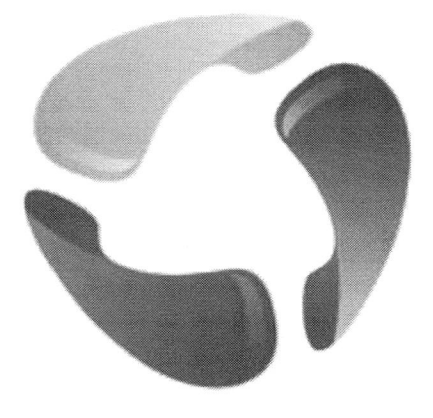

DT 1 – Approval to Proceed

Summary

The company's board approves further investigation into a possible turnaround process.

Context

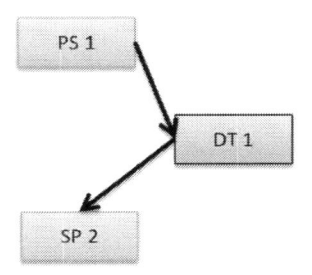

Description of the Subcomponent

In this subcomponent the turnaround is approved or rejected. At this stage there is no TAB, so the company's board performs that function until one is appointed. A turnaround process cannot start without the company's board in any case. The board evaluates whether the proposed turnaround in PS 1 (Creating the Turnaround Mandate) should proceed with the collection of basic information (PS 2) and the search for and evaluation of a Turnaround Leader (PS 3) under CP 1 (Communication Guidelines).

Responsibility

The company's board is responsible for this subcomponent.

DT 2 – Signing Off on PS

Summary

The company board approves the basic company information collected in PS2 and undertakes the search for a Turnaround Leader.

Context

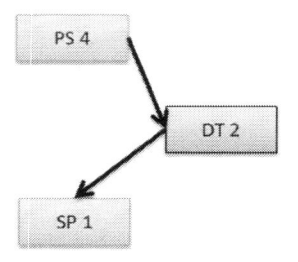

Description of the Subcomponent

The company's board signs off on the Turnaround Mandate and passes the information on to the TAB. This is the last job performed by the company's board alone. The subsequent steps are carried out by the TAB.

The company's board agrees on the basic company information collected in PS 2 and marks what information can be revealed to Turnaround Leader candidates selected in PS 3.

Responsibility

The company's board of directors is responsible for this subcomponent.

Information Needs

- Turnaround Mandate
- Basic company information
- Suggestions for a Turnaround Leader

DT 3 – Confirming the Turnaround Leader

Summary

The Turnaround Leader is appointed.

Context

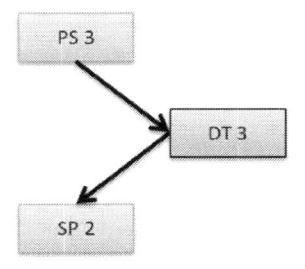

Description of the Subcomponent

Confirming the Turnaround Leader is the first job of the TAB. In this subcomponent the Turnaround Leader and their job role are approved. The company's board should make the decision to appoint a Turnaround Leader with the stakeholders' representatives so that they feel involved and that their interests are reflected.

Responsibility

The TAB is responsible for this subcomponent.

DT 4 – Approving the Turnaround Brief

Summary

The Turnaround Brief is approved or rejected.

Context

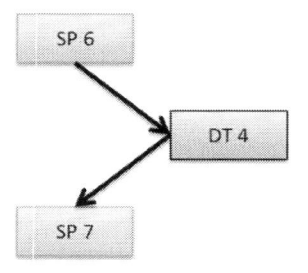

Description of the Subcomponent

The Turnaround Brief is evaluated and accepted or rejected by the TAB. If it is accepted, the next step is to centralize power in the Turnaround Leader so decisions can be made quickly. If it is not accepted it is sent back with detailed reasons for its rejection. The reasons need to be well documented. The Turnaround Leader needs to record them in the Turnaround Log and prepare a new brief.

Responsibility

The TAB is responsible for this subcomponent.

DT 5 – Approving the Diagnostic Review Plan

Summary

The Diagnostic Review Plan is accepted or rejected.

Context

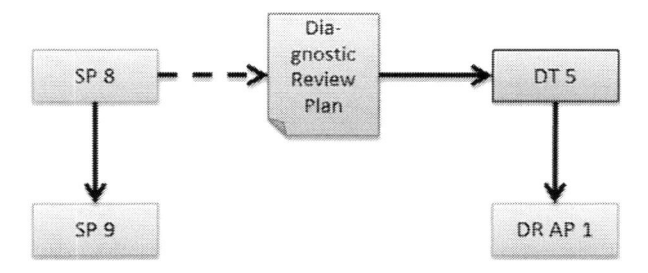

Description of the Subcomponent

The Diagnostic Review Plan is approved by the TAB who make sure that it is sufficiently detailed and does not leave out any areas of the business. If the plan must be reworked, it is sent back to SP 8 (Planning the Diagnostic Review) and resubmitted. The reasons for rejecting the Diagnostic Review Plan must be stated in detail and should be filed in the Turnaround Log.

Responsibility

The TAB is responsible for this subcomponent.

DT 6 – Approving Emergency Procedures

Summary

Emergency situations that require immediate action must be approved by the TAB.

Context

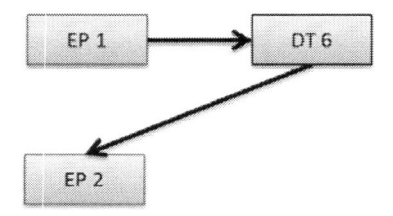

Description of the Subcomponent

If Emergency Procedures identified in the start-up component are necessary in order to save the company, the TAB needs to officially approve them. The approval is documented in the Turnaround Log.

Responsibility

The TAB is responsible for this subcomponent.

DT 7 – Evaluating the TID

Summary

The TAB approves the strategies suggested in the TID.

Context

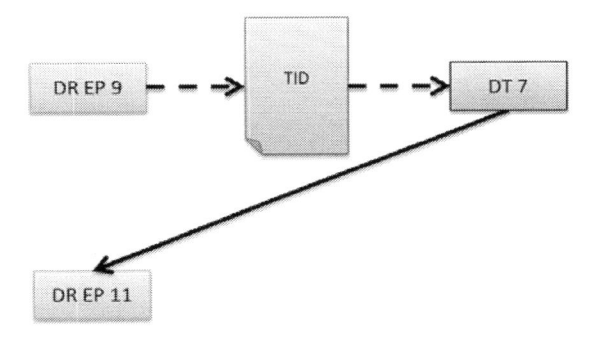

Description of the Subcomponent

The TAB decides whether it accepts the proposed strategies and whether there is sufficient justification to warrant the expenditure proposed in the TID. If the TAB does not agree with the proposed strategies the document is send back to DR EP 9 (Preparing the TID) and reworked.

The TAB also decides whether the company is able to survive an extended strategic turnaround that may involve heavy resources or whether operating strategies are needed to generate more money in the short term. Please see the section "Strategic Turnarounds" for more information.

This evaluation should not take too long; however, the TAB may need some time to go through all of the information. If approved, the turnaround officially starts in DR EP 11 (Initiating the Turnaround Process).

Responsibility

The TAB is responsible for this subcomponent.

DT 8 – Approving the Turnaround Plan

Summary

The Turnaround Plan proposed by the TMT is approved by the TAB.

Context

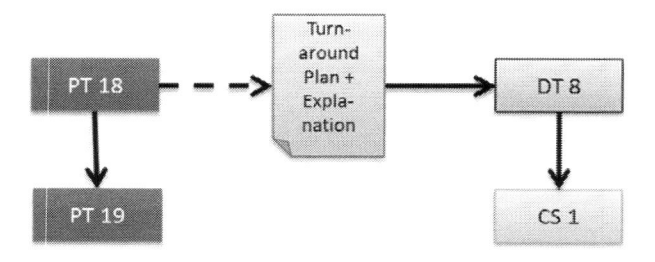

Description of the Subcomponent

Once the Turnaround Plan has been prepared, it is approved by the TAB. There might be some disagreement within the TAB about whether a particular strategy is the right one or the timeframe is appropriate. Such conflicts should be resolved as quickly as possible so the TMT can start work on the turnaround process. If possible, the TAB's vote to support the suggested plan should be unanimous otherwise a stakeholder may not support the turnaround process and may leave the TAB and sue the company. The decision needs to be documented in the Turnaround Log.

Responsibility

The TAB is responsible for this subcomponent.

DT 9 – Assessing Status

Summary

Status updates are provided to the TAB at regular intervals.

Context

CS 12 → DT 9

Description of the Subcomponent

The TAB evaluates the status updates it receives at regular intervals throughout the turnaround process. These updates also serve as a check-up after an Exemption Plan is implemented. The status does not need to be approved in this subcomponent—it is mainly for information purposes—but the representatives of the stakeholders should inform the parties they represent about the updates.

Responsibility

The TAB is responsible for this subcomponent.

DT 10 – Approving Plans

Summary

The Turnaround Plan, including all of its subplans, is approved by the TAB.

Context

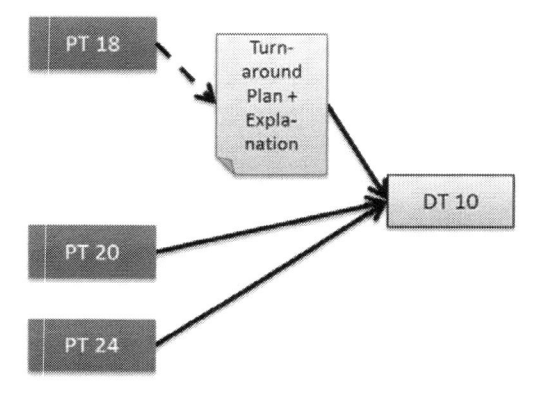

Description of the Subcomponent

In this subcomponent the TAB agrees on the operational, financial, and strategic plans that are part of the Turnaround Plan submitted in PT 18 (Completion of the Turnaround Plan). If the TAB disagrees with some aspects of the plan it is sent back to PT 18.

Responsibility

The TAB is responsible for this subcomponent.

DT 11 – Direction on Issues

Summary

In some circumstances the Turnaround Leader needs to seek approval from the TAB, especially when major changes occur that affect components or tolerances.

Context

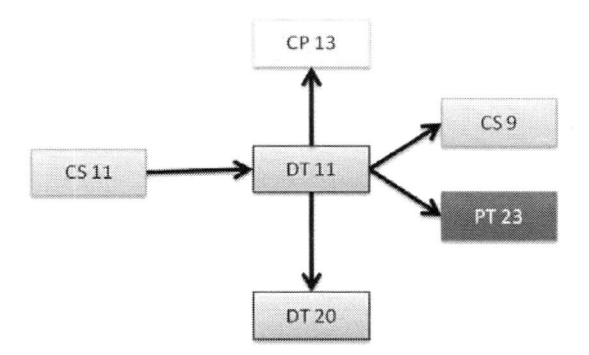

Description of the Subcomponent

The TAB receives a report about issues that have occurred in a component and decides whether to agree on specific actions that can be implemented quickly and don't have a major effect on other components, whether to close the turnaround prematurely, or whether to produce an Exemption Plan. When it chooses an option, the TAB proposes new targets, tolerances, risks, quality limits, and sometimes goals for the turnaround process.

The TAB communicates the decisions that were made and on what basis to all parties involved in the turnaround process.

Responsibility

The TAB is responsible for this subcomponent.

DT 12 – Approving Reorganization

Summary

Major organizational changes are approved by the TAB separately.

Context

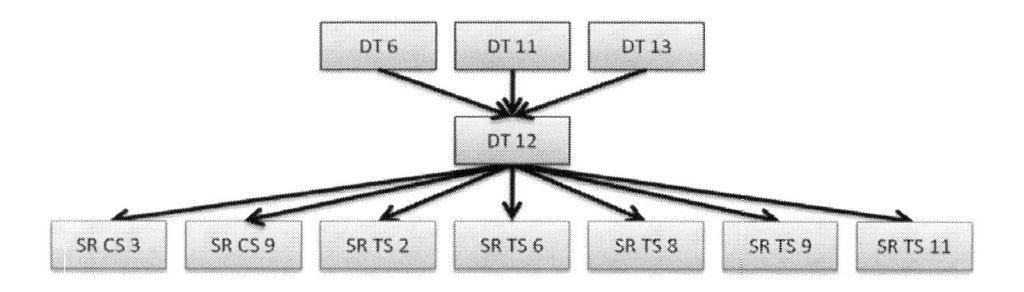

Description of the Subcomponent

A reorganization needs to be approved by the TAB when the changes are so significant that a special subcomponent is created for this decision. Significant organizational changes might include the divestment of a business unit or the acquisition of another business, as well as major changes in the organizational design.

Responsibility

The TAB is responsible for this subcomponent.

DT 13 – Approving an Exemption Plan

Summary

In this subcomponent the Exemption Plan is reviewed and approved by the TAB.

Context

PT 23 → DT 13 → CS 10

Description of the Subcomponent

During this subcomponent the TAB re-evaluates the Turnaround Business Case to determine whether it is still viable under the proposed Exemption Plan, whether a new Turnaround Business Case needs to be written if the main goals of the turnaround change, or whether the Turnaround Business Case simply needs to be updated to reflect the changed conditions.

If the Exemption Plan is approved it is sent to CS 10 (Authorizing Work Packages in the Crisis Stabilization Stage) for authorization of the necessary actions.

Responsibility

The TAB is responsible for this subcomponent.

Information Needs

- Exemption Plan
- Turnaround Plan (for comparison)

DT 14 – Reviewing Process Improvements

Summary

The TAB gets regular updates from the Process Improvements (PI) component.

Context

CS 12 → DT 14

Description of the Subcomponent

Process improvements must be reviewed regularly by the Turnaround Leader. Major updates, such as the completion of particular improvements, are sent to the TAB in a Highlights Report generated in CS 12 (Reporting Highlights in the Crisis Stabilization Stage).

A deadline for the review should be agreed on by the TAB, and the Turnaround Support Team enforces this deadline. The Turnaround Support Team is an administrative support function that assists the TMT in keeping in line with processes and timelines. Feedback from the TAB is included in the plan since the TAB is its owner.

This subcomponent does not necessarily have an output; it ends when the TAB receives the update.

Responsibility

The TAB is responsible for ensuring that they receive the updates and for the review.

DT 15 – Reviewing Financial Restructuring Strategies

Summary

The Financial Plan is reviewed by the TAB.

Context

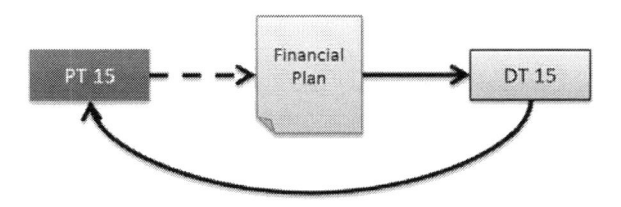

Description of the Subcomponent

The TAB must approve the Financial Plan, after which updates and changes are reviewed in DT (Updating Plans). In large organizations the plan should be reviewed after it has been created in PT 15. In smaller turnarounds the Financial Plan can be submitted with the completed Turnaround Plan, but in both cases it is reviewed if changes occur that are not within the set financial tolerances.

The questions the TAB should consider in approving the financial restructuring strategies are:

- Will the proposed strategies and actions lead to sustainable competitive advantages?
- Is the plan achievable and realistic?
- Will the strategies and actions lead to improved performance by the company?
- Can the company develop the required capabilities to achieve the desired results?
- Will the financial strategies be attractive enough for all stakeholders, or are the stakeholders likely to disagree?
- Are performance measures in place that inform the management early enough if a plan should run out of tolerance?

A deadline for approval should be agreed on by the TAB, and the Turnaround Support Team should enforce it. Feedback from TAB members should be included in the plan since they are its owners.

Responsibility

The TAB is responsible for this subcomponent.

Information Needs

- Financial Plan

DT 16 – Reviewing Operational Plans

Summary

The Operational Plans are reviewed by the TAB.

Context

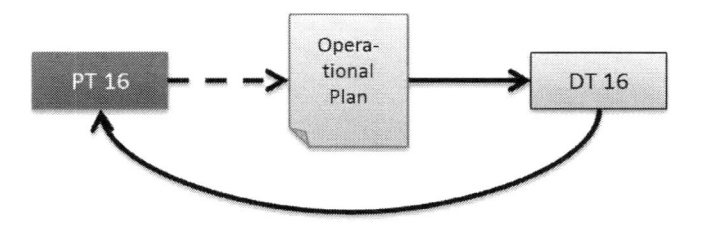

Description of the Subcomponent

The Operational Plans are approved by the TAB as it is the TAB's responsibility to ensure that they are in line with the financial and strategic goals of the business. The TAB must also check the Turnaround Leader's cost/benefit analysis. In smaller turnarounds the Operational Plan can be submitted with the completed Turnaround Plan, but in any case it should be reviewed if changes occur that are not within the set operational tolerances.

The questions the TAB should consider in approving the Operational Plans are:

- Will the proposed actions lead to sustainable competitive advantages?
- Are the plans achievable and realistic?
- Will the strategies and actions lead to improved performance by the company?
- Can the company develop the required capabilities to achieve the desired results?
- Are the Operational Plans in accordance with the proposed actions?
- Will the actions have any effect on the stakeholders?
- Are performance measures in place that inform the management early enough if a plan should run out of tolerance?

A deadline for approval should be agreed on by the TAB, and the Turnaround Support Team should enforce it. Feedback from TAB members should be included in the plan since they are its owners.

Responsibility

The TAB is responsible for this subcomponent.

Information Needs

- Operational Plans

DT 17 – Reviewing Strategic Restructuring (SR) Strategies

Summary

In this subcomponent the TAB reviews the strategic decisions proposed by the TMT.

Context

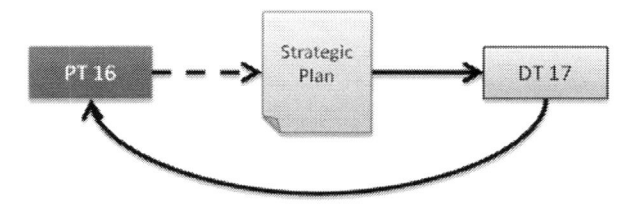

Description of the Subcomponent

The questions the TAB should consider in approving the SR strategies are:

- Will the proposed strategies and actions lead to sustainable competitive advantages?
- Are the strategies achievable and realistic?
- Will the strategies and actions improve the company's performance?
- Can the company develop the required capabilities to achieve the desired results?
- Is the financial plan in accordance with the proposed strategies?
- Will the strategies be attractive enough for all stakeholders?
- Are performance measures in place that inform the management early enough if a plan should run out of tolerance?

A deadline for approval should be agreed on by the TAB, and the Turnaround Support Team should enforce it. Feedback from TAB members should be included in the plan since they are its owners.

Responsibility

The TAB is responsible for this subcomponent.

Information Needs

- Strategic Plan

DT 18 – Assessing Stage Ends

Summary

The end of a stage is approved and controlled by the TAB.

Context

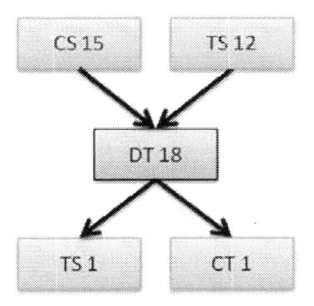

Description of the Subcomponent

At the end of the Crisis Stabilization Stage and the Turnaround Stage, a Stage End Report is sent to the TAB. However, the Turnaround Plan will probably also include substages or milestones that the TAB needs to review. Each closure needs to be formally documented in the Turnaround Log. The Turnaround Plan also needs to be updated once a stage has reached its end.

Responsibility

The TAB is responsible for this subcomponent.

DP 19 – Closing the Turnaround

Summary

The formal approval of the TAB is required for a formal end to the turnaround process.

Context

```
DT 11
  ↓
DT 19
  ↓
 CT 1
```

Description of the Subcomponent

In an ideal scenario everyone approves the turnaround process—the representatives of the stakeholders, the TMT, the owners, and other TAB members. However, it is more likely that someone will be unhappy with the outcome or will not see a particular part of the turnaround as finished as long as their expectations are not met. This is why it is important to formulate as precisely as possible when the end of a turnaround process has been reached.

The TAB agrees to a formal handover of the company's management from the TMT to the new management team. The TAB ensures that the handover is carried out in a controlled manner and that responsibility for all aspects of the business is taken.

The TAB also ensures that:

- Resources used specifically for the turnaround process, including the TMT, are released.
- Formal acceptance from the stakeholder representatives, as well as the owners of the company, is received.

- Necessary actions that are unfinished have proper authority.
- Interested parties are informed of the end of the turnaround process.
- Control mechanisms are in place so the firm does not slip back into crisis.
- If possible, the changes to the firm are sustainable and supported.
- The follow-up recommendations have been recorded and the resulting actions delegated to the appropriate authorities.
- The Lessons Learned Report is approved for distribution to the TMS.
- A Turnaround End Report is approved and sent to interested parties.

Responsibility

The TAB is responsible for this subcomponent.

Crisis Stabilization Stage (CS)

Crisis Stabilization Stage (CS)

CS 1 – Appointing the Turnaround Management Team (TMT) 2

Summary

The TMT is appointed.

Context

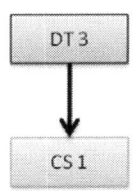

```
DT 3
  ↓
CS 1
```

Description of the Subcomponent

In order to respond properly to a crisis the top management should have certain capabilities, including the required individual power, skills, and abilities to influence strategic decisions, and an ability to reach consensus in order to support those decisions.[618] Existing literature examines how the skills of individual top management team members affect the company's overall competitive position.[619] A good mental capacity will help the team members to handle conflicting priorities, complex situations, and multitasking, while keeping on track and making decisions swiftly and correctly under pressure.[620]

It is the TMT's responsibility to:

- Talk to employees openly
- Explain decisions
- Motivate employees
- Coach employees
- Ensure their teams have everything they need to be successful
- Support their teams

---

[618] compare (Ferrier, Smith, & Grimm, 2002), (Barney, 1991)
[619] (Castanias & Helfat, 2001)
[620] (Roman, 2010, p. 69)

- Mediate in conflict situations
- Remove roadblocks
- Retain employees
- Reward right behavior
- Minimize disrespectful behavior and office politics
- Minimize unproductive attitudes

These leaders must ensure that an employee who is looking for direction will always know where to find their boss, day and night.[621]

Internal Versus External Turnaround Management Team

Most organizations bring in an external turnaround consultant and empower them to lead a department or an important part of the organization for at least the duration of the turnaround, thus making sure roadblocks are removed and execution happens without hesitation or delay. This approach means that there is no need for leadership buy-in, especially if the leadership is temporarily replaced by the TMT.

Research shows that large investors who watch the actions of top managers closely can reduce the self-serving behavior of the top management team and encourage restructuring.[622] Self-serving behavior should be eliminated, especially as it may reduce profitability and the company's stock price,[623] which is why an external TMT might be more useful than internal management in certain situations. When the stock price declines, a company is an easier target for takeover by raiders or competitors.[624]

An internal TMT may be tempted to undertake anti-takeover actions, such as poison pills, even though these mechanisms reduce the stakeholders' wealth and can decrease the chances of long-term survival.[625] For internal employees, no matter how willing they are to support and execute the Turnaround Plan, there is a psychological barrier that will dictate the order in which things are done or the choice of actions to be undertaken.[626]

---

[621] (Roman, 2010, p. 47)
[622] (Bethel & Liebeskind, 1993)
[623] compare (Lohrke, Bedeian, & Palmer, 2004)
[624] (Walsh & Elwood, 1991)
[625] (Sundaramurthy & Mahoney, 1997)
[626] (Roman, 2010, p. 97)

An external Turnaround Leader is not as attached to the company as internal leaders. There are no ties to the company's culture or history to get in the way of critical measures in need of implementation.[627] The external Turnaround Leader is also less likely to have a bias for or against anyone in the organization that might interfere with their ability to be objective about an employee's ability to perform for the company.

Talking about external turnaround consultants, Roman adds "there are no emotional ties to this or that aspect of the culture or the operation since [they] did not implement the project that will now be closed down".[628]

Internal TMT members often say things like:

- "We shouldn't be giving up the centralized processing of returns; we were thrilled back in the day when we first implemented it."
- "It's always been done like that. We can't change it."
- "We can't suggest restructuring in the media department. That's the CEO's favorite."
- "Let's try to cut more from customer service than other departments; the other departments are more important, more strategic (and someone else is managing customer service, not me)."
- "No one will like it!"
- "It's someone else's problem."
- "Let's outsource every department but mine!"
- "How can I make sure my job, function, and span of control emerge intact from the turnaround action?"
- "Is there an opportunity for me to increase my income or span of control? What should I be focusing on to be better positioned in the storm? What should be on the first page of my secret agenda?"

These are psychological barriers that internal Turnaround Leaders might have but external ones don't. It is only normal that employees think of themselves and their own best interests, but it should be clear that the survival of the company *is* in their own best interest.

---

[627] (Roman, 2010, p. 9)
[628] (Roman, 2010, p. 87)

Crisis Stabilization Stage (CS)

Internal Turnaround Leaders can be recruited with help from the HR department, outside consultants, or organizations such as the TMS.[629] However, the people that the HR department recommends may not be the right ones for the job. If not clearly specified, HR will be happy to recommend politically correct people, team players in a traditional way, with good (read as "average") results, and no spark. They may be decent, reliable people who never got into a conflict and never fought too hard for their opinions.[630] They are never late and rarely sick. However, these are not the people who are needed in a turnaround process. The determined rebels are welcome, the ambitious, the overachievers, the ones hungry for recognition and advancement, and the ones who will come in late now and then but always check their email from home in the evening.[631] Finding these special talents isn't easy because they often don't have a very good reputation. They have made enemies. Still, it is these very qualities that make them suitable for the job.

These business rebels often have the following characteristics in their CVs:

1. They change companies often. They take chances that arise and move up on the career ladder. Employees who stay for years in the same position without moving up often lack the necessary drive. They may be good at what they do, but they don't have enough desire to get to the top. They are good soldiers but not the top managers who are needed for the turnaround process.
2. They reach their goals, often even exceed them, and are focused on results.
3. They come up with ideas for how to improve things; they want to drive things themselves and find better ways.
4. Their HR files may have notes about arguments or conflicts with superiors.
5. They are not shy about saying what they think, but they are respectful.

It is helpful to conduct interviews with a turnaround consultant or the Turnaround Leader in this subcomponent. During the interviews, the HR Turnaround Manager will need to identify these skills and be able to dig deeper in order to find the best possible candidate for the TMT.

---

[629] Turnaround Management Society
[630] (Roman, 2010, p. 72)
[631] (Roman, 2010, p. 72)

Appointing Project Managers

Some larger projects can employ a project manager to track the turnaround process and to update the Turnaround Leader on the status of each stage. The project manager serves as a central point of contact for all updates. They are responsible for substages or special components. Roman adds that the project manager should be able to give the Turnaround Leader an update at any given time on the status of execution, on completed items, delayed items, revised dates of completion, resource allocation issues, roadblocks, and bottlenecks.[632]

Responsibility

The Turnaround Leader is responsible for this subcomponent.

---

[632] (Roman, 2010, p. 27)

CS 2 – Authorizing Crisis Stabilization Procedures

Summary

In this subcomponent work packages and substages are authorized by the Turnaround Leader. Other than the Emergency Procedures that might have been triggered earlier, this subcomponent is the first in which real changes are set in train.

Context

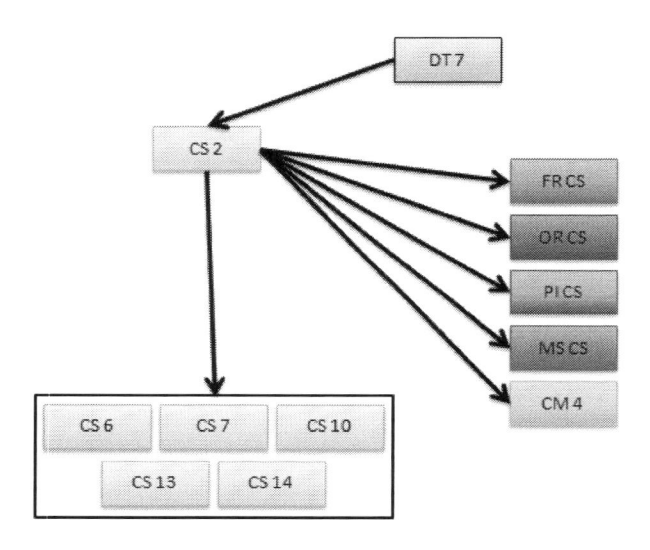

Description of the Subcomponent

Once the turnaround process begins, the Crisis Stabilization Stage involves taking some immediate steps to protect the business such as fostering open communication, establishing a management team, conserving cash, and identifying and safeguarding assets.[633]

Every stage in a turnaround process has a defined start and end. At the start of each stage responsibilities and work packages are assigned, otherwise chaos would endanger the whole component. Some activities depend on each other and others may still be in question at the

---
[633] (Davis & Sihler, 2002)

beginning of a stage or may need special guidance. Therefore, it is important that the Turnaround Leader is aware of all major activities and stages that are starting, are being worked on, or are ending.

CS 2 triggers different work packages throughout the Crisis Stabilization Stage, and the Turnaround Leader is responsible for the timely start of the work packages according to the Turnaround Plan, although they may hand over some responsibility for work packages to project managers or other members of the TMT.

This subcomponent is designed to maintain order and control over the work that is done through the Crisis Stabilization Stage. It involves passing out work instructions and briefing the Turnaround Leader, project managers, and team leaders. In some cases, instructions will need to be revised in order to accommodate change, but only minor changes that are within the authority of the Turnaround Leader are permitted.

In order for the turnaround managers and project managers to work accurately, instructions should be in writing, clearly defining the goals of the activities to be carried out, the activities in the context of the whole component, reporting procedures, timescales, allowed costs, and required efforts.

Responsibility

The Turnaround Leader makes sure that all of the Turnaround Managers know what to do, have a valid plan for their required activities, and understand the inherent risks involved in the activities for which they are responsible. The Turnaround Managers need to do the same with the project managers or specialists who work for them.

CS 3 – Hiring and Laying Off Staff

Summary

In every turnaround process some people will have to be let go and new people hired for certain positions. This subcomponent involves hiring and laying off employees throughout the Crisis Stabilization Stage.

Context

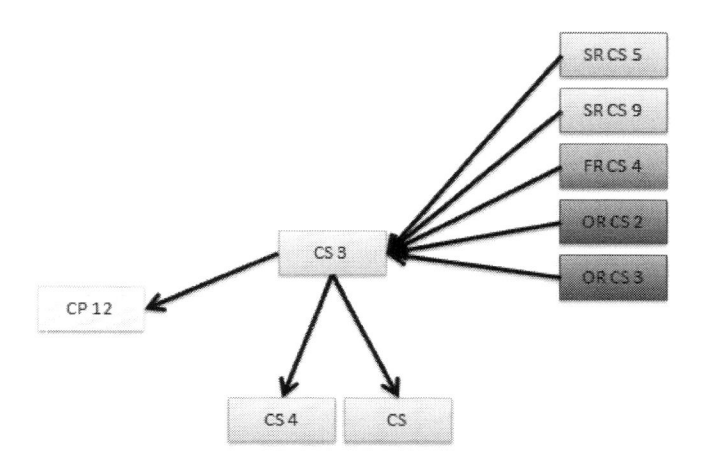

Description of the Subcomponent

Good employees may have left the company long ago, so the TMT deals primarily with employees who either could not find another job or who did not want to leave the company for personal reasons. A good manager will probably have other opportunities and will be disinclined to deal with the stress that a crisis brings with it. The TMT must deal with the employees who remain—exploiting the talents of those who can perform and bringing them to new levels—and recruit talent that is lacking.[634] Existing studies show that firms that have functional deficiencies in their top management teams have great difficulty in attracting talented people to replace managers who have left the company.[635]

---

[634] (Collard, 2002, p. 27)
[635] (Hambrick & D'Aveni, 1992)

People who are not willing to support the turnaround process should be laid off. They deserve good severance, just like the rest of the laid-off workforce, since the need for the turnaround was not their fault; they are products of a malfunctioning environment.[636]

If positions need to be filled with new people, they will need support structures in place to make the transition. Several levels of management attention should be devoted to new key employees (and especially those moving to new positions) during the initial days of their assignments.[637] In hiring new managers, the HR Turnaround Manager should remember that managers who run independent operations must also be adept at problem-solving, decision-making, team-building, and managerial analysis—skills that may not be obvious.[638]

Responsibility

The HR Turnaround Manager on the TMT is responsible for this subcomponent.

---

[636] (Roman, 2010, p. 39)
[637] (Collard, 2002, p. 29)
[638] (Collard, 2002, pp. 30-31)

CS 4 – Improve HR Management

Summary

This is a follow-up subcomponent of the HR management within the company. Some improvements or changes to this department that may be necessary are covered by this subcomponent.

Context

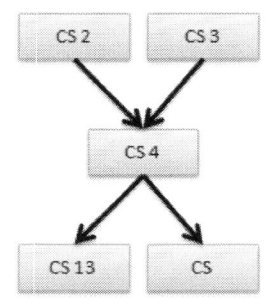

Description of the Subcomponent

The human resources department is a support department in the turnaround process, not part of the decision-making team. Some HR department heads see themselves as TAB members or part of the top management, but during the turnaround process they do not run operational departments or lead teams other than, possibly, change management experts who work to motivate the workforce for the changes ahead and support the implementation of the Turnaround Plan. Employees implement the vision and execute the restructuring, while the HR department makes sure everyone receives fair treatment, decent benefits, reasonable severance, and transition support.[639]

There are many reasons for a company's turnover rate being high. A well-respected HR department can help to slow the loss of good people, reduce the turnover rate, and motivate employees.

---
[639] (Roman, 2010, p. 52)

Good HR management in a turnaround includes:

- Introducing a reward system for lower and middle management
- Writing job descriptions with clearly defined responsibilities for each job in the company
- Defining employees' scope of authority

Responsibility

The HR Turnaround Manager is responsible for this subcomponent.

CS 5 – Assessing Progress in the Crisis Stabilization Stage

Summary

Progress should be assessed regularly. Objective formal reviews of progress can help leaders to spot problems before they become acute.[640]

Context

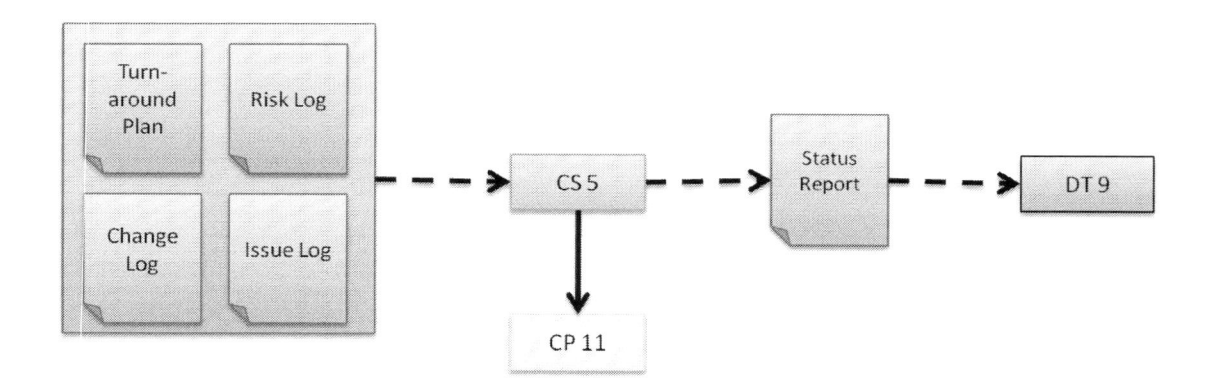

Description of the Subcomponent

This subcomponent is addressed at regular intervals specified in the Turnaround Plan. In order for the management to stay informed and to make the best possible decisions, it needs to know about the status of activities currently underway. Comparing the actual status with what was planned provides a regular assessment of how activities are progressing. In order for the Turnaround Leader to stay focused on crucial activities and activities that are spinning out of control, status updates should be kept to the most important factors as long as the progress is within time and budget constraints and the risks have not changed.

This subcomponent monitors the resources used, costs incurred, and progress against time constraints for the activities on a Turnaround Manager level, and the progress of the stage on a Turnaround Leader level. Completed work packages are received at this stage and other work packages may be started. The Turnaround Plan is updated with the progress or delays, as well

---
[640] (Day & Jung, 2000)

as other information regarding risks (Risk Log), changes (Turnaround Log), and issues (Issue Log).

The information collected during this subcomponent is compiled in a status report that is given to the TAB.

If the turnaround is close to its end, favorable or not, this component triggers CT 1 (Starting Closure Procedures).

Further activities that the Turnaround Leader or the Turnaround Assurance Team must carry out include:

- Determine whether the stage is within the given tolerances and whether it will stay within these tolerances in the foreseeable future
- Review the plans of the Turnaround Managers
- Update the stage plan with actual information
- Review the Quality Log to determine whether quality checks are carried out, what the outcomes are, and that finished activities result in the desired outcomes
- Review the Issue Log to determine whether minor issues have been resolved or have grown
- Assess old and new risks to the Stage Plan
- Determine whether external influences in the company's environment have changed
- Check up on resources that will be needed in the future
- Check the validity of the Turnaround Business Case
- Review and confirm the availability of necessary resources
- Carry out quality checks
- Review entries in the Risk Log, Issue Log, and Quality Log

Meetings in which people from different business units, divisions, or regions compare progress and perspectives make it easier to identify and correct problems.[641]

This subcomponent can also trigger regular status updates for stakeholders. For example, financial results, which are crucial at the beginning, can motivate the workforce. The first

---

[641] (Day & Jung, 2000)

financial results are usually available within the first 60 days after measures have been put in place to contain the loss of money.[642]

Responsibility

The Turnaround Leader is responsible for this subcomponent. They need to identify who should contribute to the decision-making component with data and/or ideas, and which stakeholders need to be involved.[643]

---

[642] compare (Roman, 2010, p. 13)
[643] (Roman, 2010, p. 172)

CS 6 – Implementing Short-Term Controls

Summary

This subcomponent implements short-term controls that are necessary in order to manage the company's cash flow.

Context

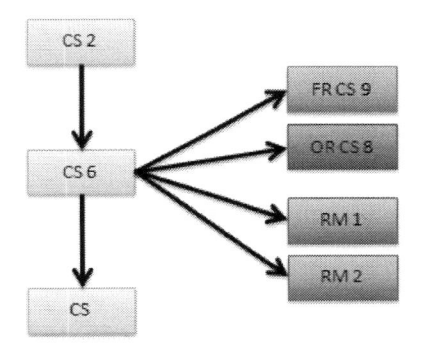

Description of the Subcomponent

Probably the best way for the Turnaround Leader to learn about a business is to be in control of all outgoing cash resources. The Turnaround Leader usually only signs off when most goods are already consumed, but they will get a good feeling for where the money goes and how quickly. They should install upstream management controls so incumbent staff cannot take actions or make decisions that endanger the current situation even more.[644]

Some basic controls should be put in place as soon as a TMT takes over. These include controls on:

- Hiring
- Salary increases and promotions
- Capital expenditure
- Purchasing

---

[644] (Slatter & Lovett, 2004, p. 144)

- New business
- Pricing
- Stakeholder communication

Implementing these controls often involves canceling orders, rescinding purchases, and canceling promotions or job offers to new employees. In some cases, the result of following through with these controls is legal action against the company from suppliers, employees, or customers. The new Turnaround Leader is often in a strong position to negotiate since few outsiders will want to order goods from a company that might not be able to deliver them, or supply goods to a company that might not be able to pay for them.[645]

Seldom is the announcement of a new set of controls enough to implement them; it takes the will of the employees to adhere to them. In a perfect world these controls would be guidelines, everyone would understand why they are necessary and would follow them. However, it is more likely that some managers will ignore them and do their jobs as they did them before. If failure to obey these controls results in a dismissal early in the process, it will underscore the seriousness of the situation and the fact that the controls must be followed.

It is also important that the controls are not too strict; if they are too prohibitive it might result in no one in the firm being able to do anything, bringing the business to a halt. It is the Turnaround Leader's responsibility to find a sensible path between the two extremes and to motivate the employees to obey the controls.

When implementing short-term controls, the company must consider that any emergency planning must include strategies to protect the vital core business from the tribulations and stresses of the turnaround efforts. Of course, if the core business is the problem then it is the support businesses that are participating in financing the turnaround that should be protected.

Accountability and Cash Management

An accountability structure is vital in order to achieve reliable results, to create a Turnaround Plan, and to stabilize the company. Often there is not enough time in a turnaround situation to check existing accountabilities and roles throughout the organization, so it may be necessary to

---

[645] (Slatter & Lovett, 2004, p. 146)

create a new structure that puts key people in charge of prioritized components and deliverables. In times of crisis "cash is king" and the company needs every cent. This situation requires a different mindset, and management must accept that the preservation and generation of cash will often take precedence over the delivery of profit in the short term.[646] According to them, many firms have no systems that ensure proper accountability for cash delivery. Subsidiaries in particular are often accustomed to the parent company providing funds whenever they are needed, so poor cash management capabilities can be the result.

Each department or business unit can select and define relevant metrics, which can be rolled up to reflect the few key measures of profitability, quality, efficiency, output, and so on that reflect the health of a business.[647]

An example of how accountability can be shared can be found in Cisco. Cisco expanded rapidly in 2000 with 23 acquisitions that year, but many of them did not pay off. Therefore, employees who suggested the additional acquisitions were told they would be held personally accountable for a deal's financial results.[648] This reduced the number of acquisitions to two in 2001.

Freeze on All Hiring of Staff

In a turnaround situation it is common practice to put an immediate freeze on issuing offers of employment to new staff and perhaps to rescind offers already made.[649] However, in a crisis situation good people often leave and those who were in key positions have to be replaced. Sometimes other employees can take over the functions of their superiors, as the company may not get around to hiring new people for essential positions and functions. In this case, the decision to use a lower-level employee should be made at a high level within the company or by a member of the TMT. The general decision concerning how many people to hire and when to hire them is down to the Turnaround Leader since they have the overview of the budget. In very big companies, however, the Turnaround Leader cannot sign off on every position; for example, a company with 10,000 employees may need 800 new employees every year to maintain its current staffing level and if it did not hire at all it would not be able to function. In a case such as this, a member of the TMT should take responsibility for human resources and

---

[646] (Slatter & Lovett, 2004, p. 129)
[647] (Roman, 2010, p. 187)
[648] (Rajendar, 2007, p. 35)
[649] (Slatter & Lovett, 2004, p. 144)

sign off on lower-level positions, keeping in mind that a general reduction of the workforce will save the company money that it urgently needs.

Stop Any Salary Increases, Bonuses, and Promotions

An immediate stop on promotions and salary increases will allow the Turnaround Leader to assess both the situation and the people.[650] It is better to delay such decisions to a time when the turnaround is mastered since, no matter how self-motivated and dedicated an individual may be, everyone responds in similar ways to financial and non-financial rewards for performance—or lack thereof.[651] While a freeze on salary increases makes sense, a turnaround situation requires exceptional leadership and a deep understanding of its psychological impact on the workforce. The cancellation of a promised promotion or salary increase can have a severe negative effect on an employee's motivation. In a crisis situation a company struggles with brain drain as good people leave.[652] The best employees are most likely to find more competitive employment opportunities fast, so there is a high risk of turnover in the above-average group of employees. People who are highly motivated—which is rare in a crisis situation—and are good at what they do, usually understand their value and leave the company before it goes bankrupt. Hence, leading the workforce by motivation is extremely important in troubled times. If employees are not motivated and do only as much as they have to because they know they can no longer get ahead in the company, the risk is high that they will fall back into a routine and leave when the opportunity arises.

A bonus program with frequent payouts geared toward key deliverables and milestones on the turnaround path may be even more likely to generate the desired results.[653]

Ban All Capital Expenditure

Control should be direct and personal in smaller firms and centralized in larger firms.[654] Taking control of a company's cash drain usually involves a ban on all capital expenditure until the TMT has a chance to evaluate exactly what the company's financial situation is.

---

[650] (Slatter & Lovett, 2004, p. 144)
[651] (Roman, 2010, p. 222)
[652] (Slatter & Lovett, 2004, p. 222)
[653] (Roman, 2010, pp. 222-223)
[654] (Bibeault, 1981, p. 269)

As long as a Turnaround Plan is not in place, a total expenditure ban—or at least one on items above a certain value—is advisable. Certain expenditures may turn out to be for nothing once the Turnaround Plan is put in place. In a turnaround situation the company's business is focused and some projects are limited or eliminated altogether. It doesn't make much sense to invest in projects that will be put on hold or terminated a few weeks later.

Analyzing and controlling the cash flow of a company has three basic steps. First, the company must take control of the cash flow pipeline, then analyze the total cash flow problem, and finally perform surgery to solve the problem on a more permanent basis.[655]

Purchasing Controls

We deal with purchasing controls separately to the ban on capital expenditure in order to focus on purchasing orders and contracts. The real key to controlling what comes out of the pipeline is to control what goes in.[656] Especially in cash-critical situations, the Turnaround Leader needs to know what goes in and what goes out in terms of orders and cash on a daily basis. If not all cash-related activities can be monitored, the key activities need to be identified. The Turnaround Leader stops anything that could create cash flow problems from coming into the company.

In critical situations the Turnaround Leader must know what has been shipped, what has been collected, and what the balances are in the accounts receivable every day.[657] Often the fact that somebody is looking closely at the finances motivates people to perform better in getting things out the door so they can be added to the shipments, and in following up on receivables.

As with all capital expenditure, purchase orders over a certain amount and purchase contracts over a certain length of time should be brought to the Turnaround Leader's attention and evaluated. Often, purchasing is one of the largest or even the largest cost item for a company so it is critical that the Turnaround Leader has a good overview of what is going on in this area. Purchasing controls are necessary in order to avoid the Turnaround Leader finding out about long-term contractual commitments only after the goods are received. If the Turnaround Leader sees orders before the goods have been received, they may be able to renegotiate terms

---

[655] (Bibeault, 1981, p. 269)
[656] (Bibeault, 1981, p. 269)
[657] (Bibeault, 1981, p. 270)

with a supplier or cancel the order. It is not unknown for a Turnaround Leader to refuse deliveries of goods on order, even if there is a legal contract with the supplier, if they believe the goods are too expensive or not required in such quantity.[658]

New Business Controls

New business controls are similar to purchasing controls. A member of the TMT should review recent orders and contracts and put them on hold or even reject them if the company's Turnaround Plan does not foresee the development or production of the product on order. The last thing a new Turnaround Leader wants is for their subordinates to accept new orders and contracts that are going to be unprofitable, place big demands on working capital, constrain future product-market flexibility, or increase the firm's contractual risk.[659] Imagine if a subordinate signed a two-year contract to deliver a product that will be terminated in the turnaround process; expensive lawsuits that end with the troubled company paying the contractor compensation would be the likely result. Throughout the whole turnaround process, orders above a certain value or timeframe should be approved by the Turnaround Leader.

Pricing Controls

The price of products sold is very important. Since every change in price has a direct effect on the bottom line of the business, price changes and discounts should be approved by the Turnaround Leader. However, if discounts such as end-of-year sales are normal practice in an industry, the company will have to offer the discount or risk not selling anything at all because the competition is following the standard practice of discounting their products. Other price changes that are planned but not yet executed should be suspended until the Turnaround Leader can review them.

Setting up a Control Structure

A control and reporting structure is necessary in order for the controls to be effective. As a result of illegal practices, increased reporting demand, and the failure to give warning of impending difficulties, many companies give their corporate controllers greater authority over

---

[658] (Slatter & Lovett, 2004, p. 145)
[659] (Slatter & Lovett, 2004, p. 145)

their division controllers.[660] Therefore, the division controllers are responsible for the control mechanisms in their divisions and report to the corporate controller.

Responsibility

The Turnaround Leader is responsible for ensuring that the short-term controls are implemented.

---

[660] (Bibeault, 1981, p. 307)

CS 7 – Rebuilding Stakeholder Trust

Summary

This subcomponent triggers several communication subcomponents in order to control the information flow to stakeholders. It can also be triggered from the outside if a stakeholder wants an update on the turnaround process.

Context

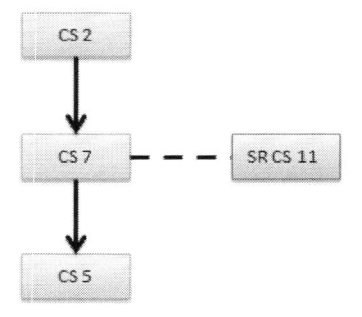

Description of the Subcomponent

The immediate task of the Turnaround Leader is to rebuild stakeholder confidence by re-establishing a sense of direction and purpose. They must move quickly to initiate the development of a rescue plan and communicate it to stakeholders.[661] It is important that the new TMT achieves early wins in order to establish and rebuild stakeholder trust.

Getting Acceptance from Stakeholders

In most cases, one or more stakeholders must agree to the turnaround and to the turnaround strategy that has been selected. Getting such agreement will be easier if regular communications have been maintained with the stakeholders throughout the Diagnostic

---

[661] (Slatter & Lovett, 2004, p. 80)

Review Stage, and the objectives, concerns, or agendas of the key stakeholders have been considered in reaching the recommendation.[662]

Stakeholder Communication Controls

Stakeholder support in a turnaround situation is crucial. No supplier wants to read in the press that a troubled company cannot pay for ordered goods anymore, and no customer wants to hear that they may not get support for products they have purchased. News can be even more destructive if it is wrong. Hence, the kind of information that leaves the company should be controlled in order to maintain the restructuring component's stability. We know that open and frequent communication with stakeholders is central to gaining their support. The measures taken at this stage are not supposed to interfere with that component but, in order to give stakeholders the right information at the right time, the communication flow is first given to, centralized in, and approved by the Turnaround Spokesperson, who is part of the TMT.

Responsibility

The Turnaround Spokesperson or the Turnaround Leader is responsible for communication throughout the turnaround process and for all future communication subcomponents. However, the Turnaround Leader is responsible for overseeing the communications procedure and signs off on major updates to the stakeholders.

---

[662] (Slatter & Lovett, 2004, p. 126)

CS 8 – Capturing and Assessing Issues in the Crisis Stabilization Stage

Summary

This subcomponent, which is triggered by CS 5 (Assessing Progress in the Crisis Stabilization Stage) if issues arise, should be recorded. The issues that occur are assessed in this subcomponent by the Turnaround Leader.

Context

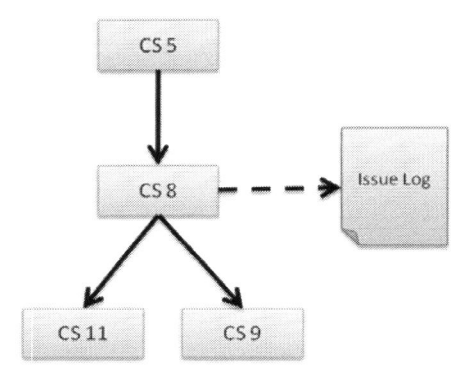

Description of the Subcomponent

Issues that arise throughout the Crisis Stabilization Stage should be captured, assessed, placed in the subcomponent records, and categorized. All relevant data regarding the decision—financial implications, history data, benchmarking data, and so on—should be gathered and structured. As soon as issues are identified, they should be entered into the Issue Log.

Issues are categorized into:

- New risks
- General issues
- Requests for changes

This subcomponent is also the gateway component for all changes in the turnaround process and the environment around it. In other words, all changes go through this subcomponent first, where the issues are evaluated and—if an issue has been dealt with in an appropriate way or if the issue is minor—handled. All data must be accurate to ensure that the conclusions reflect reality.

Each issue is assessed, its impact evaluated, and alternatives suggested and considered. Any issue that does not have an obvious minor impact is recorded and later checked with the Reviewing Stage Status if the issue affects the stage as a whole. All open issues should be reviewed regularly until they are resolved. The impact analysis of an issue should be carried out as soon as possible after the issue is recognized. Issues that have only minor effects should be monitored and reviewed regularly.

A configuration librarian or someone from the Turnaround Assurance Team can be appointed to maintain the Issue Log.

Key questions to be answered during this subcomponent include:

- Which components or activities are affected by the issue?
- Does the issue affect the Turnaround Business Case?
- With regard to the TID, do the objectives or goals change as a result of the solution to the issue?
- Do changes have any effect on existing contacts?
- Who needs be involved?
- Are there any alternative actions?
- Are special actions required in order to protect the stakeholders' interests while the issue is being evaluated?
- Who is needed to evaluate the issue?
- What is the issue's impact on the Risk Log?
- How urgent is the issue?
- What is the cash price for resolving the issue?

If the issue's status is within tolerance and according to plan but with slight deviations, the next step is CS 9 (Taking Corrective Action in the Crisis Stabilization Stage). If serious issues are detected that threaten the progress of the stage and the Turnaround Plan, the Turnaround

Leader has to move on to CS 11 (Escalating Issues in the Crisis Stabilization Stage) in order to get ad hoc direction from the TAB.

In both cases, the Turnaround Leader must formulate a problem statement.

Responsibility

The Turnaround Leader is responsible for this subcomponent.

CS 9 – Taking Corrective Action in the Crisis Stabilization Stage

Summary

In this subcomponent corrective actions are discussed when approval from the TAB is not necessary and resources for the necessary actions are committed and prepared.

Context

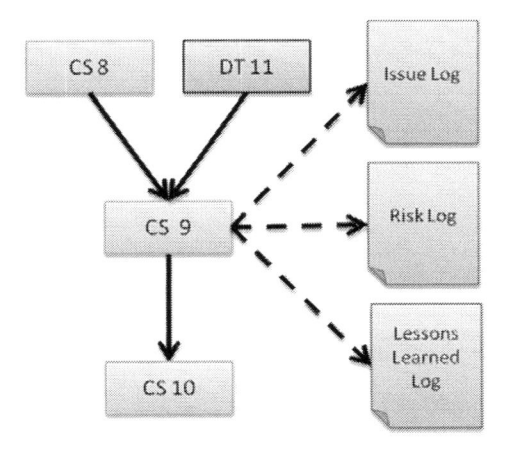

Description of the Subcomponent

Taking corrective action is similar to CS 2 (Authorizing Crisis Stabilization Procedures) as it triggers work packages that have been changed or newly created because of a change in direction or corrective actions. The Turnaround Leader authorizes the work packages in a timely manner in order to correct unwanted changes from the Crisis Stabilization Stage. The changes may be required by the TAB if the issues are major and component-threatening or, in the case of minor issues, if the Turnaround Leader authorized the corrective action. During this component, information about the deviation, such as its cause and effect, is collected in order to identify the most appropriate way of dealing with it. Some of these actions may already have been carried out in earlier components.

During this stage the Risk Log and the Issue Log are updated to reflect the current circumstances. The Turnaround Support Team should adapt the Change Log to reflect the new circumstances if necessary, and the Lessons Learned Log should be updated with the actions implemented to overcome the issues.

If implementation was not already carried out in an Exemption Plan, it should be scheduled to take place immediately and with key controls in place. The controls are there to measure the effectiveness and the result of the decision.[663] The subcomponent is then passed on to CS 10 for immediate implementation.

Responsibility

The Turnaround Leader is responsible for this subcomponent.

---

[663] (Roman, 2010, p. 172)

CS 10 – Authorizing Work Packages in the Crisis Stabilization Stage

Summary

Work planned or discussed in prior subcomponents is authorized.

Context

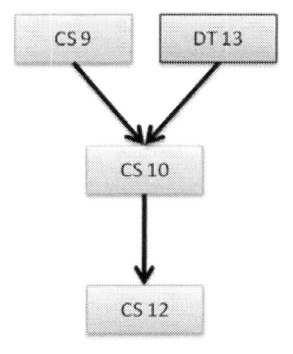

Description of the Subcomponent

This subcomponent concerns the formal authorization of actions that were planned or discussed during an earlier subcomponent. If an Exemption Plan was approved, its implementation starts here as a way of taking corrective action. It will be closely monitored by the Turnaround Support Team and, in some cases, external advisors. If there is no Exemption plan because the issues are still within tolerance, the Turnaround Leader authorizes the actions discussed in CS 9 and work commences in this subcomponent.

Responsibility

The Turnaround Leader is responsible for this subcomponent.

CS 11 – Escalating Issues in the Crisis Stabilization Stage

Summary

The issues that were assessed in CS 8 and that were not fixable within the tolerance given in the Turnaround Plan are prepared and escalated to the TAB.

Context

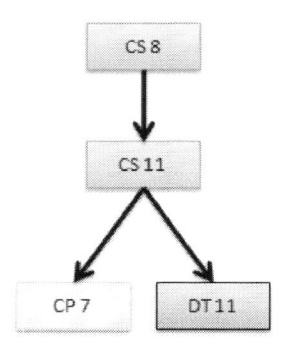

Description of the Subcomponent

Escalating issues is one of the major control methods that the TAB has. As long as an Escalation Report is not issued to the TAB, everything is going according to plan.

The purpose of this subcomponent is to notify the TAB that the Crisis Stabilization Stage may not be running according to plan and within tolerance in terms of time, cost, and goals. Hence, the suggested outcome of the Crisis Stabilization Stage may not be the desired result. The TAB decides whether to close the turnaround prematurely or to agree to proposed changes to the Stage Plan. The reasons for escalating an issue can differ widely, including changes in the availability of resources, estimation errors, changes in the internal or external environment of the company, underperformance, unexpected events or costs, and unexpected outcomes.

This subcomponent can also be triggered by risks that have become more likely. In this stage the Turnaround Leader loses their mandate to run the turnaround process until they receive further direction from the TAB.

Tasks to be undertaken during this subcomponent include:

- Updating the Communications Plan to reflect any changed circumstances in communication procedures and recipients
- Collecting the cause and impact of the deviation. This is usually done in CS 8 (Capturing and Assessing Issues in the Crisis Stabilization Stage)
- Evaluating options to overcome the issues if it was not done in CS 8
- Making recommendations about how to handle the issues that have arisen
- Assembling the Escalation Report

An Escalation Report is created to inform the TAB of serious issues that came up during the current stage or are likely to come up in future. The Escalation Report outlines:

- The causes of the deviation
- The deviation's impact on the Stage Plan
- The deviation's impact on the turnaround process
- The deviation's impact on the risks
- The deviation's impact on the Turnaround Business Case
- Options to overcome the issue or deviation
- A recommendation by the Turnaround Leader on how to handle the deviation

Responsibility

The Turnaround Leader is responsible for this subcomponent.

Outcome

- Escalation Report

CS 12 – Reporting Highlights in the Crisis Stabilization Stage

Summary

Selected highlights and the progress of actions authorized in CS 10 are reported to the TAB.

Context

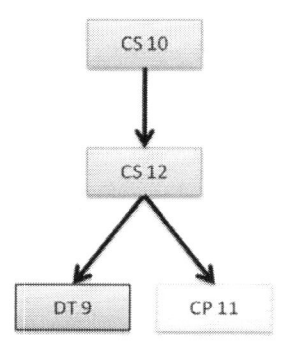

```
      CS 10
        │
        ▼
      CS 12
       ╱ ╲
      ▼   ▼
    DT 9  CP 11
```

Description of the Subcomponent

While the Turnaround Leader is responsible for the turnaround process, the TAB should be informed at regular intervals after the stage status has been assessed and issues have been evaluated. The Highlights Report—a brief report of the results of CS 10 (Authorizing Work Packages in the Crisis Stabilization Stage)—is sent to the TAB and later to the stakeholders. The Communications Plan is reviewed in order to ensure that the Highlights Report is sent to the right people after the TAB has reviewed it.

Responsibility

The Turnaround Leader is responsible for this subcomponent.

Outcome

- Highlights Report

CS 13 – Building an Incentives Scheme

Summary

Any operational turnaround action in need of fast execution and immediate results should have an aggressive bonus plan attached to the milestones, with clear metrics and check points in place, to recognize overachievement in a bold manner.[664] This subcomponent is about building a bonus plan for the workforce to keep them motivated and aligned with the firm's goals.

Context

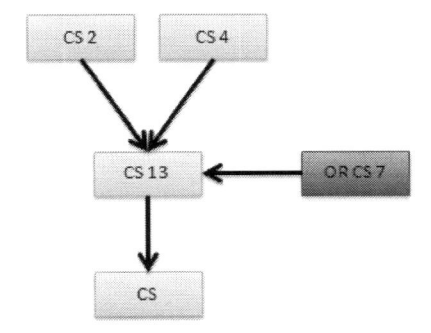

Description of the Subcomponent

During the Crisis Stabilization Stage, an incentive scheme is developed in order to align the workforce to the goals of the turnaround process. In many crisis situations employee morale is low, so it is important to develop a system that maintains the motivation of both management and workforce. When a company's performance is declining, the firm's most talented managers are the first to leave.[665] Some companies have an incentive plan in place; in that case the system is evaluated to determine whether it is in keeping with the turnaround process's goals.

While it seems obvious that programs should clearly and directly reward successful job performance, many firms unwittingly set up compensation structures that reward types of

---

[664] (Roman, 2010, p. 30)
[665] compare (Lohrke, Bedeian, & Palmer, 2004), (D'Aveni R., 1989), (Ferrier, Fhionnlaoich, Smith, & Grimm, 2002)

performance that are altogether different from those outlined in job descriptions and from what is expected by the board of directors.[666]

During a turnaround process the employees will have to reach many short-term goals—such as cost reductions, asset disposal, and inventory adjustments—for which they must be motivated. The trick is to gear the incentive program to those activities—that is, to judge the operating groups on a number of factors, only one of which is profitability.[667]

Motivating through rewards—and, more specifically, financial rewards—is a far faster and more effective way of driving exceptional results than any other type of performance management, and it is what will help keep tasks on track, and delivered on time and within specifications.[668] Also, it is less likely that managers will leave the company when problems arise if their compensation is tied to the program's success.[669]

Extraordinary items that are under the control of management—such as the selling of certain government contracts or the disposal of certain parts of the business—should be taken out of the incentives formula.[670] One way of doing this is to assign a certain pool of money (which is included in the financial plan) to each group leader or department manager for the next few months until the goal is scheduled to be reached. Part of this pool can be assigned to the management team—for example, once staff reductions are completed, once a certain profitability level is reached, or when unprofitable customers are made profitable or their accounts are terminated. Tying incentives to short-term objectives makes a lot of sense and reinforces everyone's desire to get things done.[671] During a turnaround process not all goals are linked to the best interests of stakeholders who seek short-term rewards. In many older incentive plans, the incentive pools are limited to the company's income only after a specified return on equity is subtracted. These older plans are often devised by the top management so they can earn even more money, but the turnaround incentive plan should be written from the bottom up. At the same time, managers who are paid incentives based on gross margin can be more effective than those paid on gross sales.[672]

---

[666] (Collard, 2002, p. 29)
[667] (Bibeault, 1981, p. 332)
[668] (Roman, 2010, p. 31)
[669] (Day & Jung, 2000)
[670] (Bibeault, 1981, p. 332)
[671] (Bibeault, 1981, p. 333)
[672] (Collard, 2002, p. 29)

When explaining the incentive plan, the HR Turnaround Manager should draw a clear picture of the rewards that come with the change and turn it into a positive message with individual benefits.[673] For a reward program to work, the incentive has to come immediately, be substantial enough to trigger changes in behavior, and be tied indisputably to clearly established performance metrics.[674] There are few things worse for the morale and enthusiasm of employees in a company than a bonus program in which they do not honestly believe, or one that they believe will not be paid out before the company closes its books. Ideally, a turnaround program's incentive plan pays monthly, and for the best employees doubling or even tripling their annual income should be possible.

Responsibility

The HR Turnaround Manager is responsible for this subcomponent.

---

[673] (Roman, 2010, p. 34)
[674] (Roman, 2010, p. 49)

CS 14 – Introducing Management by Objectives (MBO)

Summary

The management of the troubled firm must be held accountable for timely results and for performance. Management by objectives is a good way to combine these two important performance factors.

Context

```
CS 2
  ↓
CS 14
  ↓
 CS
```

Description of the Subcomponent

In many organizations managers become non-achievers, perceiving their role as simply defenders of the status quo.[675] They find excuses for why things are not going well, such as that they could not fulfill an order because they don't have enough people or because the team is not motivated. They may say that it took forever to repair a machine that broke down and they couldn't do anything about it. Managers who aggressively perceive and attack problems rather than defensively rationalizing them can cope in a positive manner with an unexpected turn of events: they get repairs made or shift production quickly; they handle late deliveries of parts by improvising, borrowing from another department, or sending a truck out to get the parts from another vendor.[676] The passive attitude that some managers have must be changed, and MBO can help to change the way managers look at their positions and their jobs. When goals are set for specific divisions, they should be broken down into manageable units so the

---
[675] (Bibeault, 1981, p. 349)
[676] (Bibeault, 1981, p. 349)

managers can check up on the status of the effort to attain these goals and provide feedback and rewards. In a successful company performance is checked regularly to find out which employees are not performing according to the standards. A way to deal with these underperformers is to either offer them training or take disciplinary measures.

Responsibility

The MBO structure should be created by the whole TMT, including the HR Turnaround Manager and the Turnaround Leader. The Turnaround Leader is responsible for triggering this subcomponent.

CS 15 – Completing the Crisis Stabilization Stage

Summary

The Crisis Stabilization Stage is closed, and all completed activities are received. That means that completed activities are reported to the responsible turnaround manager in this step. Reports on progress made are passed on to the TAB in DT 18 (Assessing Stage Ends).

Context

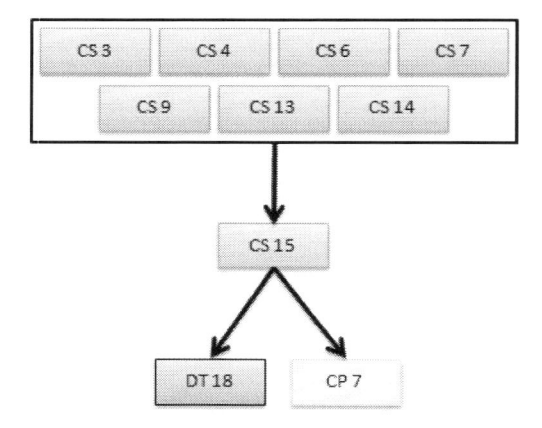

Description of the Subcomponent

Several checks are made to confirm that all activities have been completed:

- Are the Quality Log entries completed?
- Are the records recorded in the right way?
- Have all activities been accepted by the TMT or the team leaders?
- Have the goals for the Crisis Stabilization Stage been checked against the actual outcome as far as possible?

The Turnaround Leader is responsible for this subcomponent and for filing a Stage End Report, which includes the Change Log. The Turnaround Support Team updates the Turnaround Log. The Stage Plan is reviewed for its impact on the Turnaround Plan, and possible impacts are reported to PT 22 (Updating the Stage Plan).

In addition, a configuration audit must be carried out to ensure that the status of the goals has been upheld or to highlight changes. The Lessons Learned Log is updated at the end of each stage to ensure that the knowledge stays within the turnaround process and does not leave with people who were only temporarily engaged in it. Updates may also be necessary to the Communications Plan if the environment has changed. At the end of the stage the results are reported to the TAB and a Stage End Report is created.

Creating the Stage End Report

In the Stage End Report the Turnaround Leader describes why changes to the original plan were made. The report addresses the proposed cost, time required, and achievements of the stage and compares them to the actuals. The Turnaround Leader makes a statement regarding the past stage and the outlook for the forthcoming stages.

Suggestions for the next stage, together with an outline of the next Stage Plan, are created. The next Stage Plan includes the previous Stage Plans and the Stage End Report.

The Stage End Report also includes:

- A summary of all issues raised throughout the stage
- All changes made to the proposed plan
- The use of tolerances
- Actual costs compared to proposed costs
- How many issues were received during the stage
- How many changes were approved during the stage

Responsibility

The Turnaround Leader is responsible for this subcomponent.

Outcome

- Stage End Report

Crisis Stabilization Stage (CS)

Turnaround Stage (TS)

TS 1 – Authorizing the Turnaround Stage

Summary

Work packages and substages are authorized by the Turnaround Leader. This subcomponent is the first one in which actions toward the recovery and long-term success of the company commence.

Context

Description of the Subcomponent

Every stage in a turnaround process has a defined start and end. At the start of each stage responsibilities and work packages are assigned so chaos does not endanger the whole component. Since activities depend on one another and may still be in question or need special guidance at the beginning of a stage, the Turnaround Leader must be aware of all major activities and stages that are starting, are being worked on, or have ended.

TS 1 triggers different work packages throughout the Turnaround Stage. The Turnaround Leader is responsible for the timely and correct start of the work packages according to the Turnaround

Plan, although they may choose to hand some responsibility for work packages to project managers or other members of the TMT.

This subcomponent, which is designed to maintain order and control over the work that is done through the Turnaround Stage, involves passing out work instructions and briefing the Turnaround Managers and Team Leaders. In some cases, instructions must be revised in order to accommodate changes, but only minor changes that are within the Turnaround Leader's remit are permitted.

In order for the Turnaround Managers and Project Managers to work accurately, the work instructions they receive must be in writing and must clearly define: the goals of the activities that are to be carried out; the activities in the context of the whole component; reporting procedures; timescales; allowed costs; and required efforts.

Responsibility

The Turnaround Leader ensures that every Turnaround Manager knows what to do, has a valid plan for the required activities, and understands the inherent risks involved in the activities for which they are responsible. The Turnaround Managers should do the same with their project managers or the specialists who work for them.

TS 2 – Assessing Progress in the Turnaround Stage

Summary

Work packages and actions are checked throughout the Turnaround Stage so progress is assessed regularly. Objective formal reviews of progress can help in spotting problems before they become severe.[677]

Context

See change diagram.

Description of the Subcomponent

This subcomponent is addressed at regular intervals specified in the project plan. In order for the management to stay informed and to make the best possible decisions, it must know the status of current activities. The actual status is compared with the plan to provide a regular assessment of how activities are going. In order for the Turnaround Leader to stay focused on critical activities and activities that are spinning out of control, status updates should be kept to the most important factors unless the activity is out of time or budget constraints, or the risks change.

This subcomponent monitors the resources used, costs incurred, and progress against time for the activities on the Turnaround Manager level, and the progress of the stage on the Turnaround Leader level. Completed work packages are received at this stage and other work packages might be started. The Turnaround Plan is updated with the progress of or delays to the activities, as well as other information regarding risks (Risk Log), changes (Change Log) and issues (Issue Log).

The information collected in this subcomponent is written in a status report that is forwarded to the TAB.

---

[677] (Day & Jung, 2000)

If the turnaround is close to its end, whether favorable or not, this component triggers CT 1 (Starting Closure Procedures).

The following activities also need to be carried out for this subcomponent:

- Determine whether the stage is within the given tolerances and whether it will stay within these tolerances in the foreseeable future
- Review the plans of the Turnaround Managers
- Update the stage plan with actuals
- Review the Quality Log to determine whether quality checks have been done, what the outcomes are, and that completed activities resulted in the desired outcomes
- Review the Issue Log to determine whether minor issues have been resolved or have grown
- Assess old and new risks to the stage plan
- Determine whether external influences in the company's environment have changed
- Check the validity of the Turnaround Business Case
- Review and confirm the availability of necessary resources
- Carry out quality checks
- Review entries in the Risk Log, Issue Log, and Quality Log

In order to identify and correct problems and to compare progress and perspectives, meetings that include people from different business units, divisions, or regions can be very helpful.[678]

This subcomponent can also trigger regular status updates to stakeholders. For example, financial results, which are crucial at the beginning, can be shown to the workforce to help motivate them. The first financial results should be available within the first sixty days after controls are in place to contain the drain of money.

---

[678] (Day & Jung, 2000)

Responsibility

The Turnaround Leader is responsible for this subcomponent. They identify who should contribute to the decision-making with relevant ideas and data, and also which stakeholders need to be involved.

TS 3 – Further Workforce Reductions

Summary

During the Turnaround Stage it may become clear that some employees should be laid off. This subcomponent contains the necessary activities for this purpose.

Context

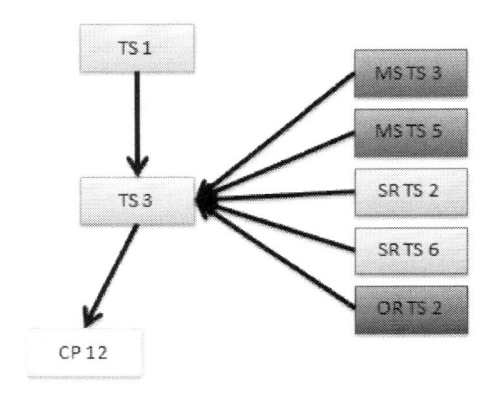

Description of the Subcomponent

Further workforce reductions may be necessary during the Turnaround Stage. By now, the lay-offs that were necessary due to overstaffing and the financial situation should either be completed or about to be completed. Laying people off takes longer in some countries than in others, in which case the "letting go component" should be well underway. At this stage, workforce reductions should focus on employees who are unwilling to support the turnaround efforts. In some cases, it takes a few months to reveal which people are not supporting the TMT or the component. Workforce reductions that are due to the closure of departments or business units should already have been done in CS; however, if they are necessary in TS, this subcomponent contains those activities.

Responsibility

The Turnaround Leader decides which executives need to leave the company. The HR Turnaround Manager is responsible for laying off lower-level employees.

TS 4 – Capturing and Assessing Issues in the Turnaround Stage

This subcomponent is triggered by TS 2 (Assessing Progress in the Turnaround Stage) if issues arise that need to be recorded. The issues that occur are assessed in this subcomponent by the Turnaround Leader.

Context

See change diagram.

Description of the Subcomponent

In this subcomponent issues that arise during a stage are captured, documented in the Issues Log, and assessed by the Turnaround Leader, who is responsible for the stage. However, these meetings should be short. Long meetings drive employee burnout and lead to a sense of powerlessness and lack of control.[679]

Capturing and assessing issues is important to ensure that they are not forgotten. In this subcomponent issues that arise are recorded and categorized, and all data regarding the decision is gathered and structured, including history data, financial implications, and benchmarking data. As soon as issues are identified, they are entered into the Issue Log.

Issues are categorized into:

- New risks
- General issues
- Requests for changes

This component is also the gate component for all changes within and in the environment around the turnaround process; in other words, all changes go through this subcomponent first, where it is determined whether an issue is dealt with elsewhere or within this subcomponent. The data must be accurate so the conclusions are based on reality.

---

[679] (Roman, 2010, p. 84)

Each issue must be assessed, its impact evaluated, and alternatives suggested and considered. Only issues that do not have an obvious minor impact should be recorded and later checked again in TS 2 if the issue affects the stage as a whole. All open issues should be reviewed regularly until they are resolved. The impact analysis of an issue should be carried out as soon as possible after it becomes known and issues that have only a minor effect should be monitored and reviewed regularly.

If a configuration librarian or someone from the turnaround support staff has been appointed, they maintain the Issue Log.

Key questions during this subcomponent:

- What components or activities are affected by the issue?
- Does the issue have an impact on the Turnaround Business Case?
- With regard to the TID, do the objectives or goals change as a result of the solution to the issue?
- Do changes have an effect on existing contacts?
- Who needs to be involved?
- Are there alternative actions and, if so, what are they?
- Are special actions required in order to assure the stakeholders' interests while the issue is being evaluated?
- Who is needed for the evaluation of the issue?
- What is the issue's impact on the Risk Log?
- How urgent is the issue?
- What is the cash price for solving the issue?

If the issue's status is within tolerance and according to plan but with slight deviations, the next step is TS 9 (Taking Corrective Action in the Turnaround Stage). If serious issues are detected that threaten the progress of the stage and the Turnaround Plan, the Turnaround Leader moves on to TS 11 (Escalating Issues in the Turnaround Stage) to seek ad hoc direction from the TAB.

In both cases, the Turnaround Leader formulates a problem statement that describes the problem and its implications for the turnaround process and the company. Data must be accurate so the conclusions reflect reality.

Responsibility

The Turnaround Leader is responsible for this subcomponent.

Information Needs

- Issue Log
- Risk Log

Outcome

- Problem statement

TS 5 – Authorizing Work Packages in the Turnaround Stage

Summary

Work planned or discussed in prior subcomponents is authorized.

Context

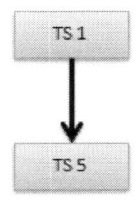

Description of the Subcomponent

This subcomponent addresses the formal authorization of actions that were planned or discussed during a prior subcomponent. If an Exemption Plan was approved, implementation of the plan as a corrective action starts here. Close monitoring is done by the configuration management, as well as external advisors in some cases. If no Exemption Plan exists because the issues are still within tolerance, the Turnaround Leader authorizes the actions discussed in TS 9 (Taking Corrective Action in the Turnaround Stage) and work commences.

Responsibility

The Turnaround Leader is responsible for this subcomponent.

TS 6 – HR Management

Summary

During the Turnaround Stage the TMT increases its focus on developing the workforce and creating an environment that supports talented employees.

Context

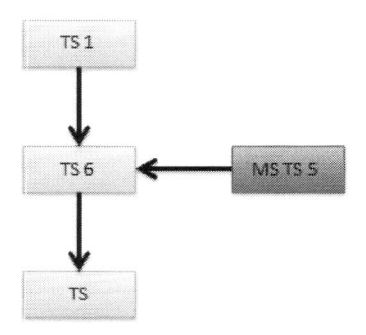

Description of the Subcomponent

In the Turnaround Stage even companies whose decline has stopped lack the money for expansive employee development programs, so training is often done on the job.

Management development at this stage of the turnaround entails two practical requirements in order to make the company grow: adequate training in the management ranks, and the identification of those few individuals who will be needed beyond the original turnaround group.[680] The management team determines who is most committed and most capable of delivering extraordinary results. Selecting these high-potential employees is a subjective task; it is difficult to find people who have potential because those who have it may not have had the opportunity to develop it if their ideas were turned down by incompetent managers or they simply missed their chances. Potential becomes visible only in the right climate for management talent to develop.

---

[680] (Bibeault, 1981, p. 358)

An environment that supports high-potential employees has several important characteristics:

- Political strategies and unfair competition are absent or minimal. An environment rife with politics and competition supports the fight for a position and is a talent-killer. In some organizations one can only grow in the company if one has the right connections and plays along with the internal politics.
- People are not rejected from consideration for senior positions because of unimportant factors such as friendships, ethnicity, gender, or social background.
- There is a high tolerance of individual differences.
- Risk-taking is encouraged and failure, for the most part, is not punished.
- Responsibility is given to inexperienced personnel so they can grow and develop.
- There are "high standards of performance for work, as well as for the evaluation of that work, including disciplined attention to meeting detailed commitments".[681]
- Employees are given the freedom to develop their ideas.
- Moral integrity is upheld.
- People are given opportunities even if they do not have the perfect background for a position, which encourages cross-functional development. An employee may take a position in the company and then find that their true passion is in another business area altogether.
- Management has a profit-conscious attitude.
- Executive development programs support the achievement of a business plan that rewards individuals who accomplish good results.

When replacing employees, the HR Turnaround Manager should keep in mind that the cost of replacing a skilled worker is high, impacting both the operational budget and product quality as a new employee's learning curve has a higher defect rate.[682]

Responsibility

The HR Turnaround Manager is responsible for this subcomponent.

---

[681] (Bibeault, 1981, p. 359)
[682] (Roman, 2010, p. 263)

TS 7 – Decentralizing Power in the Turnaround Stage

Summary

The power that was centralized during the Crisis Stabilization Stage is decentralized again in order to start a transition back to normal management.

Context

Description of this Subcomponent

In large companies some decision-making power that was taken from profit center managers and division heads can be handed back in order to decrease the workload on the Turnaround Leader and to reduce bureaucracy. In small companies the centralization usually continues for a longer time, and full autonomy is handed back during CT (Closing the Turnaround).[683] However, the overall responsibility for coordination remains with the TMT, which follows up on decisions made in the divisions and ensures that department heads are working toward the goals for the Turnaround Stage.

Responsibility

The Turnaround Leader is responsible for this subcomponent.

---

[683] (Bibeault, 1981, p. 330)

TS 8 – Compensation Programs

Summary

Executive compensation is an important part of attracting and keeping effective and professional management teams.

Context

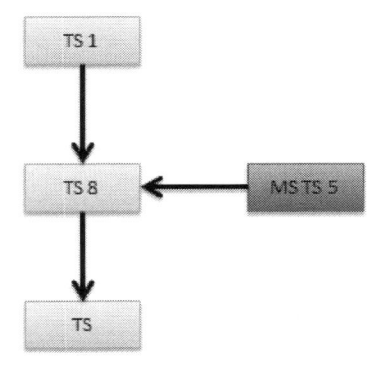

Description of the Subcomponent

Executive compensation has been discussed in several subcomponents; it appears frequently because compensation programs are a primary and direct motivational tool during turnarounds.[684] With the ability to offer a high salary to candidate managers, the Turnaround Leader has more people to choose from. Highly qualified people and people with a good track record of superior performance tend to be very receptive to high compensation and tend to choose such jobs over others, all else being equal. Therefore, offering a high salary allows the Turnaround Leader to attract and hire better people. It is my view that a small team of highly professional, highly qualified, highly compensated, and effective people can achieve more than a larger group of less well-qualified managers.

In hiring new managers or in choosing a compensation scheme for the existing management team, a smaller team with high compensation packages is preferable to a larger team with

---

[684] compare (Bibeault, 1981, p. 332)

lower compensation. The smaller team will have to be more effective to get the job done, but the higher compensation helps ensure the ability to hire good people who are capable of being effective.

Responsibility

It is the HR Turnaround Manager's responsibility to provide the Turnaround Leader with a compensation plan that suits the company's situation.

TS 9 – Taking Corrective Action in the Turnaround Stage

Corrective actions are discussed when approval from the TAB is not necessary. Resources for the necessary actions are committed and prepared.

Context

See change control Diagram.

Description of the Subcomponent

This subcomponent is similar to TS 1 (Authorizing the Turnaround Stage) since it triggers work packages that have been changed or newly created because of a change in direction or a corrective action. The Turnaround Leader authorizes the work packages in a timely way in order to correct unwanted changes from the Turnaround Stage. The changes may be required by the TAB if the issues are major and component-threatening; for minor issues the Turnaround Leader authorizes the corrective action. During this component relevant information about the deviation, including cause and effect, is collected in order to identify the most appropriate way of dealing with it. However, some of these actions may have already been done in earlier components.

During this stage the Risk Log and the Issue Log are updated in order to reflect the current circumstances. The configuration management adapts the Configuration Log to the changed circumstances if necessary. The Lessons Learned Log is also updated with the actions implemented to overcome the issues so knowledge can be gained from the results, whether they are good or bad.

The implementation should be planned immediately if this was not done in an Exemption Plan, and it should include key controls to measure the effectiveness and the result of the decision.[685] The subcomponent is then passed on to TS 10 for immediate implementation.

---

[685] (Roman, 2010, p. 172)

Responsibility

The Turnaround Leader is responsible for this subcomponent.

TS 10 – Not relevant in this version of the Standard

TS 11 – Escalating Issues in the Turnaround Stage

Summary

The issues assessed in TS 4 (Capturing and Assessing Issues in the Turnaround Stage) that are not fixable within the tolerance given in the Turnaround Plan are prepared and escalated to the TAB.

Context

See change control diagram and CP 7.

Description of the Subcomponent

Escalating issues is one of the TAB's major methods of control. As long as an Escalation Report is not issued to the TAB, everything is going according to plan.

The purpose of this subcomponent is to notify the TAB that there is a risk that the Turnaround Stage will not run according to plan and tolerances in terms of time, costs, and goals, so the suggested outcome of the Turnaround Stage may not be the planned result. The causes, which can vary widely, can include changes in the availability of resources, estimation errors, changes in the internal or external environment of the company, underperformance, unexpected events and costs, and unexpected outcomes. The TAB must decide whether to close the turnaround prematurely or to agree on proposed changes to the stage plan.

This subcomponent can also be triggered by risks becoming more realistic. In this stage the Turnaround Leader loses their mandate to run the Turnaround process until they receive further direction from the TAB.

Tasks to be undertaken during this subcomponent include:

- Updating the Communications Plan to reflect any changed circumstances in communication procedures or recipients
- Collecting the causes and impacts of deviations, although this task is usually done in TS 4 (Capturing and Assessing Issues in the Turnaround Stage)

- Evaluating options to overcome the issues, if not done in TS 4
- Making recommendations concerning the issues that have arisen
- Assembling the Escalation Report

The Escalation Report informs the TAB of serious issues that have arisen during the current stage or that are more likely to arise than before. The report outlines:

- The causes of the deviation
- The deviation's impact on the Stage Plan
- The deviation's impact on the turnaround process
- The deviation's impact on the risks
- The deviation's impact on the Turnaround Business Case
- Options to overcome the issue or deviation
- A recommendation by the Turnaround Leader on how to respond to the deviation

Responsibility

The Turnaround Leader is responsible for this subcomponent.

Outcome

- Escalation Report

TS 12 – Reporting Highlights in the Turnaround Stage

Summary

Selected highlights and the progress of actions authorized in TS 5 (Authorizing Work Packages in the Turnaround Stage) are reported to the TAB.

Context

See change control diagram and CP 7.

Description of the Subcomponent

The TAB is informed at regular intervals after the stage status has been assessed and issues have been evaluated. The Highlights Report, a brief report of the results of TS 5, is sent to the TAB and later to the stakeholders. The Communications Plan is reviewed in order to ensure the right recipients receive the information once the TAB has examined the Highlights Report.

Responsibility

The Turnaround Leader is responsible for this subcomponent.

Outcome

- Highlights Report

TS 12 – Completing the Turnaround Stage

Summary

The Turnaround Stage is closed and all completed activities are received. A report on the progress made is sent to the TAB in DT 18 (Assessing Stage Ends).

Context

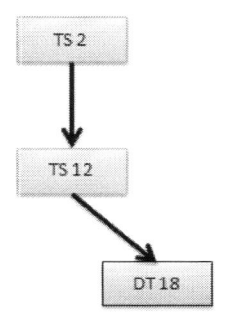

Description of the Subcomponent

Several checks are carried out during this subcomponent to confirm that all activities have been completed:

- Are the Quality Log entries completed?
- Are the records recorded in the right way?
- Have all activities been accepted by the TMT or the team leaders?
- Have the goals for the Turnaround Stage been checked against the actual outcomes, as far as this is possible?

The Turnaround Leader is responsible for this subcomponent and for filing a Stage End Report that includes the Change Log; the configuration librarian is responsible for updating the Configuration Log. The Stage Plan is reviewed for its impact on the Turnaround Plan and possible impacts are reported in PT 20 (Updating the Turnaround Plan and Turnaround Business Case).

A configuration audit is carried out to ensure that the status of the goals has been upheld or to highlight changes. The Lessons Learned Log is updated at the end of each stage to ensure that the knowledge stays within the turnaround process and does not leave with people who were only temporarily engaged in it.

Updates to the Communications Plan may also be necessary if the environment has changed.

At the end of the stage the results are reported to the TAB and a Stage End Report is created.

Creating the Stage End Report

In the Stage End Report, the Turnaround Leader describes why changes to the original plan were made and compares the proposed cost, time, and achievements throughout the stage with what was actually achieved. The Turnaround Leader also makes a statement in the report regarding the success or failure of the past stage.

Suggestions for the next stage, together with an outline of the next Stage Plan, which includes the previous Stage Plans and the Stage End Report, are created.

The Stage End Report also includes:

- A summary of all issues raised throughout the stage
- All changes made to the proposed plan
- The use of tolerances
- Actual costs compared to proposed costs
- How many issues were received during the stage
- How many changes were approved during the stage

Responsibility

The Turnaround Leader is responsible for this subcomponent.

Outcome

- Stage End Report

- Updated Change Log
- Updated Configuration Log
- Updated Lessons Learned Log

Financial Restructuring (FR)

Poor financial performance is usually caused by poor management.[686]

The financial restructuring component described here applies mainly to independent companies, holdings, and parent companies. Subsidiaries of parent companies usually have other sources of financing that are not described in detail in the component.

The overall objective of financial restructuring is to achieve a debt and equity structure that enables the company to implement its turnaround plans, to meet all of its ongoing liabilities as they fall due—that is, to be solvent—and to fund the strategic redirection where appropriate.[687] In normal operations it is the management's responsibility to create value for the company's shareholders, but in a turnaround situation it is the top management's priority to achieve stability first. Only after that does the priority become restoring value. This approach creates concern among the funding stakeholders, but if their money is invested in an unstable environment it is unlikely they will see above-average returns.

The area of financial restructuring is a potential roadblock to any plan so it is critical that any restructuring proposal recognizes the best option available to the stakeholders and clearly shows them that it is in their best interest to support the business plan and the proposed financial structure.[688]

Refinancing can be split into two stages. The first stage is designed to support short-term survival, although some companies may not need such support if the turnaround was started early. The second stage is concerned with the capital structure and its financial reorganization.

The financial restructuring subcomponents are organized along a timeline so some subcomponents can or should begin during the Crisis Stabilization Stage, while others can or should begin during the Turnaround Stage.

Some research suggests that a company can encourage its managers to restructure early, before a significant crisis evolves, by increasing its debt load.[689] However, equity incentives are not widespread.[690] Other existing research suggests that financial restructuring is usually

---

[686] (Slatter & Lovett, 2004, p. 121)
[687] (Slatter & Lovett, 2004, p. 308)
[688] (Slatter & Lovett, 2004, p. 309)
[689] compare (Wruck, 1994)
[690] (Dial & Murphey, 1995)

avoided until a crisis becomes obvious, a takeover is likely, or even bankruptcy is possible in the near future.[691]

---

[691] (Denis, Denis, & Sarin, 1997)

Financial Restructuring During the Crisis Stabilization Stage (FR CS)

In the Crisis Stabilization Stage the focus is on improving cash flow to keep the company alive, able to pay its debts, and perhaps have cash left over to invest during the Turnaround Stage. For companies in this situation, it is essential that their cash be tightly managed from an operational perspective by finding ways to minimize float, such as by changing banking and lockbox configurations, utilizing international cash flow effectively, selectively extending payables, aggressively reducing inventories and receivables, making thoughtful use of leasing instead of direct capital investment, or exploiting a number of other devices for maximizing mileage from working capital.[692]

---

[692] (Bibeault, 1981, p. 303)

Financial Restructuring During the Crisis Stabilization Stage (FR CS)

FR CS 1 – Creating Short-Term Cash Forecasts

Summary

A forecast of the cash requirement for the next few months is created. Forecasting cash inflows and outflows may be the most difficult task a company faces in managing its cash.[693] Urgent cash requirements must be assessed and cash-generating strategies developed.

Context

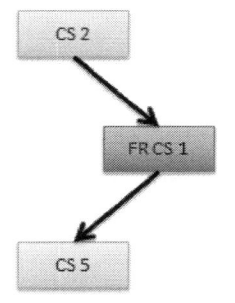

Description of the Subcomponent

After evaluating the company the Turnaround Leader usually works first to generate enough cash so it can survive the Turnaround Stage. Immediate cash requirements may include the need to satisfy a creditor in order to keep them from becoming insolvent or the need to pay overdue wages to keep the employees from striking. These requirements are so important that cash management must take priority over everything else. Without enough cash the company will not survive any other efforts to turn it around. Therefore the company must manage cash on a daily basis.[694] The introduction of proper cash management may be the cause of temporary resistance by some managers since they will feel more controlled and may even feel partially blamed if their spending is restricted. They may even complain that the cash management affects the sales they are supposed to generate, even though this complaint rarely has merit unless the implementation is overenthusiastic.[695]

---

[693] (Plewa & Friedlob, 1995, p. 3)
[694] compare (Vance, 2009)
[695] (Slatter & Lovett, 2004, p. 130)

The Turnaround Manager must undertake four tasks during this stage:

1. Determine the urgent cash requirements of the company
2. Develop an action plan of cash-generating incentives
3. Establish and implement emergency cash management controls
4. Introduce cash rationing

A short-term cash budget plan is created in this subcomponent—a plan for the near future expressed in monetary terms.[696] The cash forecast must be conservative and should not assume, for example, that customers will suddenly decide to purchase double the volumes of the previous month, nor should it "get creative" and shift debt from one seller to another. The forecast should not be too pessimistic, but it should have a pessimistic touch. Banks may raise interest rates and lawsuits can emerge, so these situations should have provision in the forecast.[697]

An adequate cash forecasting system is critical because otherwise the firm could experience problems involving overdrafts, deficiencies, late payments, and reduced levels of earning from idle cash.[698] Cash forecasts are an important part of planning; they are necessary. Cash forecasts not only allow the company to make the required payments for such items as payment of costs, debt repayment, and acquisitions, but also to ascertain the effect that the planned levels of output and their associated costs will have on the firm's cash resources.[699]

The "intensity" of cash forecasts refers to:

- Their time horizon; that is, how far into the future the forecast reaches
- The time period; that is, whether it deals with daily, weekly, monthly, quarterly, half yearly, or annual cash flows
- The number of forecasts; that is, whether it deals with one forecast for each business unit, a consolidated cash forecast for the group, one for each currency, and so on[700]

---

[696] (Droms & Wright, 2010, p. 107)
[697] (Roman, 2010, p. 18)
[698] (Plewa & Friedlob, 1995, p. 3)
[699] (Sneyd, 1994, p. 63)
[700] compare (Coyle, 2000, p. 23)

Within two to three months, the first financial results will begin appearing to indicate whether the turnaround efforts are on the right track.

Assess Immediate Cash Requirements

Detailed short-term cash forecasts are required to assess the urgent cash needs of the firm. A forecast should be prepared one and a half to three months in advance, and a monthly forecast should be prepared for the first half year. Since it is not easily possible to see three months into the future in an unstable situation, the company should consider forecasting the first month on a daily basis and the following two months on a weekly or twice-weekly basis. The forecast should be revised every four weeks in order to always have a rolling forecast for the next three months.

The operating balance sheet must drive these rolling forecasts. Working capital items in the balance sheet are the critical items for the purposes of cash management.[701] Managers often oppose such cash control by explaining that it would take too much effort to create the forecasts; however, almost every company can put proper cash management in place to do so. If the company has internal auditors they can be helpful in monitoring the cash flows on a payment receipt basis along the way; otherwise, external consultants can be useful. If the company was founded under a multi-bank agreement it is essential that the short-term cash forecast clearly identifies the funding through each of the banks so a sensible position on headroom and shortfall against existing facilities can be identified.[702] In order for the TMT to see what kind of cash management initiatives are necessary, the cash flow forecasts should be prepared on a cashbook basis and be based on normal trading procedures. It is also necessary to produce sales forecasts for the same length of time into the future; these forecasts should be created based on a realistic scenario and on a prudent basis, rather than expected sales numbers.

When preparing forecasts, one should keep in mind that external shareholders will not be happy to see results that turn out worse than forecast, so they should not include over-optimistic sales expectations—or at least such optimistic forecasts should only be held internally as best-case scenarios. Although optimistic opportunities can be pursued, they should

---

[701] (Slatter & Lovett, 2004, p. 131)
[702] (Slatter & Lovett, 2004, p. 131)

not be included in the sales forecast if their likelihood is less than 80 percent. This issue illustrates the difference between an external TMT and a TMT internal to the company: a team of internal managers may paint the future of the company as bright because they want to show that it is worth saving and that they should be allowed to try in return for a key position in the company. An external management team will assess the situation thoroughly and not even accept the case if they don't believe the company is worth saving or that it can survive the turnaround. Of course, there is a sensitive middle way that should be found because, if the company's forecast is shown in a worse light than it is actually in, shareholders may be tempted to file for insolvency or withdraw their support for the turnaround.

Develop Cash-Generating Initiatives

Once the company's current position has been evaluated, it is the TMT's responsibility to develop cash-generating initiatives. These initiatives, which can have costs, benefits, and adverse effects on profits, should be assembled into a plan to improve the company's cash requirements. In an ideal situation the Turnaround Leader keeps some initiatives in reserve, but if the cash crisis requires all possible initiatives to be implemented successfully in order to ensure survival in the short term, there is a heightened risk that, without further funding, the stabilization will not be successful. Open communication with stakeholders can lead to banks supporting the firm even in times when initiatives don't have the desired effects, but banks will do this only if they are part of the solution or if they trust the management.[703]

It is the turnaround management's responsibility to run a reality check on all possible initiatives and to priorities them. Cash flow initiatives should be analyzed separately in the cash flow table so that the cash effects of normal trading and the effects of the new initiatives are clear. Furthermore, where this exercise results in a shortfall, the Turnaround Leader enters into early discussions with funding providers to establish whether they are in a position to provide additional cash.[704]

Responsibility

The Financial Turnaround Manager is responsible for creating the cash forecast, but the Turnaround Leader is ultimately responsible for this subcomponent.

---

[703] (Slatter & Lovett, 2004, p. 132)
[704] (Slatter & Lovett, 2004, p. 133)

Outcome

- Cash forecast

FR CS 2 – Injecting Equity

Summary

If it is possible, equity is injected into the company.

Context

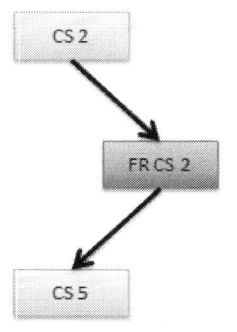

Description of the Subcomponent

The most obvious way for a company to get more money is for its owners to inject more equity. In some situations, injecting equity into a company or a project through the purchase of stock or stock participation can be a more effective mechanism for inducing development than providing debt capital.[705] The owners (or partners) are jointly and severally liable for the company's debt; in other words, each owner is liable for the company's debt to the extent of their own personal capital, and each owner is liable for the entire debt of the company.[706]

The German Bank HSH Nordbank, which got into financial turmoil after the financial crisis of 2008/2009, was twice injected with equity in 2009. The bank is owned by the City of Hamburg, the state of Schleswig-Holstein, and some private investors.

---

[705] (Hamlin & Lyons, 1996, p. 62), (Lyons & Hamlin, 2001, p. 81)
[706] (Laasholdt, 2005, p. 30)

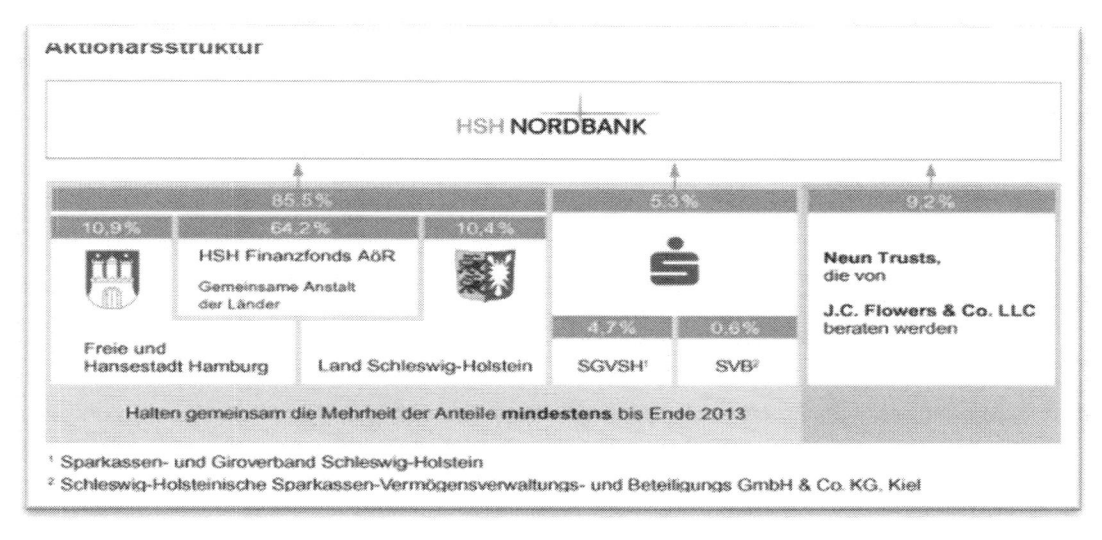

Picture 17 Ownership share of HSH Nordbank[707]

Capital infusions by a company's owners and a company's integration into the acquiring company will affect the troubled company's performance;[708] however, capital infusion may result in worsening performance, while integration seems to benefit it.

Responsibility

The Turnaround Leader is responsible for initiating and overseeing this subcomponent.

---

[707] QuelleSource: http://www.hsh-nordbank.de/de/corporation/unternehmensprofil_3/kurzprofil_4/kurzportrait.jsp
[708] (Castrogiovanni & Bruton, 2000), compare (Fischer, Lee, & Johns, 2004)

FR CS 3 – External Financing

Summary

External financing is considered if the owners of the company don't want to or cannot inject more equity into the company.

Context

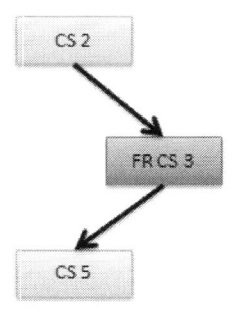

Description of the Subcomponent

Negotiations with Private Equity Investors

Private equity Investors are investors in companies that are not listed on the stock exchange and therefore don't have the option of raising money by giving out shares. When an investor supplies the company with cash they generally want some security in return, which usually takes the form of a share of the company along with the right to influence the strategic direction of both the company and the Turnaround Plan.

The participation of private equity investors usually follows several steps:[709]

1. After the first contact, the private equity investor signs a confidentiality agreement and then conducts an analysis of the potential of the company.
2. If the outcome of the analysis is positive, a Letter of Intent is signed.

---

[709] compare (Crone & Werner, 2007, p. 145)

3. Once the Letter of Intent is signed, the investor starts the due diligence—a deeper analysis of the company, and especially of its value. Subjects of this analysis are the management, the product and market, the business model, finance, and contracts. By using the ITMS the investor can speed up this component significantly; the necessary information has already been collected and analyzed by the TMT prior to starting the turnaround process, so the investor can just check and verify the data and analysis.
4. The Turnaround Plan should already have been created and only minor changes to it should be necessary to accommodate the investor's wishes. If the investor's participation is significant they may get a seat on the TAB and have a say in the turnaround process.
5. Once the investor agrees the Turnaround Plan, the influence and share they receive in return for their investment is outlined in a signed participation agreement.

Mezzanine Capital

The term "mezzanine financing" refers to capital that lies between senior debt financing (the "top floor") and common stock (the "bottom floor"). While it can be used in a variety of industries, as the name implies, it focuses on the broad middle spectrum of business rather than on high-tech, high-growth companies.[710] However, other companies may also consider this type of financing as an available option. This "in-between" money is usually more risk averse than the money from venture capital or leveraged buy-out (LBO) funds.[711]

Mezzanine capital can be described as equity interim financing with profit participation that closes the financing gap between the equity the investor has available and the lending value or loan promised by the financing bank.[712] Additionally, in some cases it takes the form of redeemable preferred stock, but in most cases it is subordinated debt that carries an equity "kicker" that consists of warrants or future conversion into common stock.[713] Mezzanine financing is usually unsecured, with a fixed percentage return which matures after five to ten years. Mezzanine investors generally look for companies that have a demonstrated performance record with revenues of $10 million or more.[714]

---

[710] (Timmons, Spinelli, & Zacharakis, 2004, p. 124)
[711] (Gladstone & Gladstone, 2002, p. 7)
[712] (Mütze, Möller, & Senff, 2007, p. 91)
[713] (Timmons, Spinelli, & Zacharakis, 2004, pp. 123-124)
[714] (Timmons, Spinelli, & Zacharakis, 2004, pp. 123-124)

As one would suspect, the mezzanine lender charges more than a bank but much less than venture capital firms or LBO funds.[715] Even though it is legally treated as debt, mezzanine financing raises the equity ratio.[716]

Mezzanine investors examine the company closely since it must be able to pay the interest, which is usually 15 to 20 percent.[717] In addition to the basic interest there is often a profit-based interest that is paid according to the profit the company makes after the turnaround process.[718]

"As debt, the interest is payable on a regular basis, and the principal must be repaid if [it is] not converted into equity."[719] This is a downside to mezzanine capital since repaying the principal, rather than converting it into equity ownership, may not be possible if the expected growth does not materialize.

There are some common mezzanine financing instruments:

- Junior debt is a debt claim that, according to the inter-creditor agreement, ranks behind senior claims if the firm becomes insolvent.[720]
- Convertible debt is one way of offering upside potential to the debt holder.[721] A convertible debt is one that allows the holder of the security to exchange the debt for shares in the issuing company according to the terms specified in the debt instrument.[722]
- Warrant-linked debt is also a frequently encountered instrument that allows the lender to benefit from equity appreciation, so it justifies a low nominal interest coupon.[723]

Mezzanine financing can be used if bank debt is not available; it is used not only in turnaround situations but also in LBOs, management buy-outs (MBOs), pre-IPO financing, and growth financing. Like private placement, mezzanine financing is characterized by a large number of

---

[715] (Gladstone & Gladstone, 2002, p. 7)
[716] compare (Hess R., 2007, p. 156)
[717] (Crone & Werner, 2007, p. 166)
[718] compare (Hess R., 2007, p. 156)
[719] (Timmons, Spinelli, & Zacharakis, 2004, p. 123)
[720] compare (Kühn, 2006, p. 100)
[721] (Kühn, 2006, p. 100)
[722] (Lewis & Pendrill, 2003, p. 186)
[723] (Kühn, 2006, p. 100)

contractual clauses regarding the achievement of certain performance indicators or limitations on future investment or financing activities.[724]

This subcomponent also includes: writing paragraphs about evaluating the investors' share; producing a participation agreement, a partner's loan, a subordinated loan, a vendor's loan, a profit participating loan, and initial public stock offerings; public placements; and participation rights. These headings have not been included in order to make this book more compact.

Responsibility

The Financial Turnaround Manager is responsible for preparing a portfolio of possible financing solutions from which the Turnaround Leader can choose when the need arises.

---

[724] (Kühn, 2006, p. 99)

FR CS 4 – First-Step Cost Reductions

Summary

First-step cost reductions focus on overmanning and overhead costs, as well as purchasing controls. A cost accounting system, which can help in acquiring an overview of these costs, is implemented in order to control and cut overheads where possible.

Context

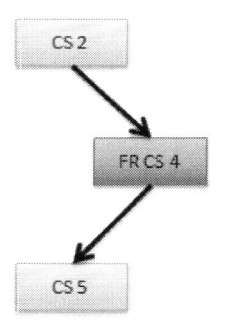

Description of the Subcomponent

During the Crisis Stabilization Stage the primary focus is on gaining control over the company and managing cash flows, but a third emphasis should be put on first-step cost reductions. At this stage it is necessary only to collect data about fairly obvious expenses that are too high, such as:

Overmanning:
> While much has been written about scheduled overtime, little has been published about the effects of overmanning; that is, managing a larger workforce than planned.[725] Overmanning can be described as simply the employment of more people than are needed to do the job with existing equipment, whatever the technically

---

[725] (Laasholdt, 2005, p. 39)

appropriate capital/labor ratio might be.[726] Here, the number of people in any situation affects the quality and quantity of the interaction.[727]

Overhead Costs

A company's indirect costs that cannot be attributed to the direct production costs of a single unit of product are overhead costs.[728] Overhead costs, as a rule, appear only upon the summary of costs.[729] If the company does not have a cost accounting system in place that clearly and accurately outlines overhead costs, a computer-aided cost accounting system should be implemented as soon as possible.

Purchasing

Purchasing cost reductions are sustainable and may result from a change of specification, a change of supplier, or omitting an unnecessary product quality requirement.[730] Purchasing costs must be controlled in order to be manageable, and a cost accounting system can help to control them. Purchasing improvements are discussed further in FR CS 7 (Purchasing Improvements in the Financial Restructuring Component).

Cost Reduction Support

Cost reduction support in the form of controlling the cash flow pipeline and identifying costs by size and type can make an important contribution to the turnaround efforts. Therefore, cost reduction support should be implemented wherever and whenever possible.

Responsibility

The Financial Turnaround Manager is responsible for this subcomponent.

---

[726] (Booth & Jefferys, 1996, p. 66)
[727] (Argyle, Furnham, & Graham, 1981, p. 289)
[728] (Berends, 2004, p. 17)
[729] (Nicholson & Rohrbach, 1919, p. 262)
[730] (van Weele, 2005, p. 38)

FR CS 5 – Debt Restructuring

Summary

Debt restructuring is not required for a turnaround process, but it is a good way to involve stakeholders and to lower interest rates on debt repayments. This subcomponent is triggered individually if the financial situation evaluated in the Diagnostic Review Stage allows or requires it.

Context

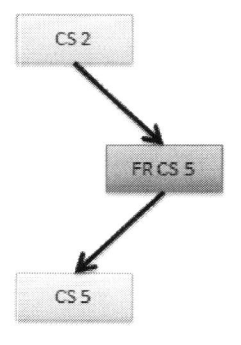

Description of the Subcomponent

Debt restructuring is key to turnaround success for those companies in serious trouble.[731] One form of debt restructuring is conversion of debt into preferred stock. Preferred stock, also called preferred shares, is a hybrid instrument that has the properties of both debt and equity. The data storage provider Memorex, which got into financial difficulties in 1973, used this kind of debt restructuring. A series of extremely aggressive pricing and product actions by IBM had reduced the profitability of Memorex's equipment businesses to the point at which corporate viability was questionable. In 1974 Robert Wilson replaced Spitters as CEO and restructured the company in cooperation with the Bank of America.[732] Bank of America agreed to convert $30 million of the company's outstanding debt into preferred stock, and other lenders converted another $10 million in debt in the same way. The agreement allowed the company to credit

---

[731] (Bibeault, 1981, p. 271)
[732] compare (Johnson L., 2005)

bank purchases of Memorex equipment against its debt and to request that the bank buy even more preferred stock when Memorex redeemed its 5.25 percent convertible subordinated debentures.[733]

In addition to negotiations with lenders to restructure debt, debt reduction through such measures as divestment, cash conservation, and cash concentration[734] can be used to reduce an intolerable debt load.

Debt to Equity Swap

A debt equity swap is quite common in crisis situations.[735] If the original funding for the business was through a loan (promissory note, bonds, mortgage lien financing) the company can offer the lenders partial ownership in the venture in exchange for loan principal by swapping their debt for equity.[736] A debt equity swap is a good way to involve shareholders in the business and to make sure they stay on board throughout the turnaround process. It also improves the profitability of the venture by lowering debt service payments while lowering debt liability on the balance sheet and replacing it with equity.[737]

If ownership of the firm's equity changes significantly—possibly because creditors exchange their claims for new stock—the company can lose the often sizable tax benefit of its net operating loss carry-forwards.[738]

Responsibility

The Financial Turnaround Manager is responsible for preparing the debt restructuring, but the Turnaround Leader is ultimately responsible for this subcomponent.

---

[733] (Bibeault, 1981, p. 271)
[734] (Bibeault, 1981, p. 272)
[735] compare (Ott & Göpfert, 2005)
[736] (Vinturella & Erickson, 2004, p. 237)
[737] (Vinturella & Erickson, 2004, p. 237)
[738] (Jobsky, 1998)

FR CS 6 – Improving Working Capital

Summary

This subcomponent frequently provides the most readily available short-term opportunity to improve the financial position of turnaround companies.[739] Improving working capital is therefore vital for a turnaround candidate.

Context

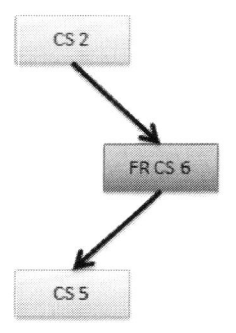

Description of the Subcomponent

Often the working capital has been mishandled, which can lead to an overall situation that has a substantial impact on the bottom line. Therefore, working capital improvements should be triggered even if the financial situation is not in danger. In that case, this component should start in the Turnaround Stage as a low-priority subcomponent or as a follow-on recommendation after the turnaround process. The management of working capital deals mainly with cash, receivables, payables, and inventories.[740]

Increasing Receivables

Receivables can be increased quickly by invoicing customers when goods are delivered. Some companies invoice their customers days or even weeks later, increasing the lead time between

---

[739] (Bibeault, 1981, p. 272)
[740] (Bibeault, 1981, p. 272)

the delivery and payment of goods. Restructuring the payment terms is also advisable if some customers have long payment terms. Some companies have arranged agreements with their customers to pay their invoices only once a year! These kinds of payment policies should be selectively adjusted.

Computer invoicing software can dramatically decrease the lead time and help companies keep track of receivables. Another way to speed up customers' remittances is to set up bank accounts in countries where many customers or major customers are situated.

Short-term borrowing from the bank can be significantly reduced by employing these measures. The result is higher pre-tax profits, lower refinancing costs, a reduction of interest payments, and the obvious increase in working capital.

Studying the accounts receivable will show if the receivables department or finance department is doing a good job collecting debt. The presence of many small balances that are not paid in the receivables and many unmatched credit entries indicates that procedures for matching cash receipts with the proper invoices either don't exist or are not being followed to straighten out discrepancies. Sometimes customers don't pay the full amount of their invoices: they transfer the payment for goods without paying for freight or they allow themselves a discount. The financial department should keep track of these practices and collect the differences. Sometimes the reason behind the customer not paying in full is a mistake the company made or faulty product deliveries. An analysis of the reasons for customers not paying might disclose other mistakes that the company is making that should be corrected in order to keep customers loyal.

Improving Inventory Storage

Inventory levels are often regarded as a buffer between production and sales. Bringing sales and production in sync can reduce expensive storage costs.

Responsibility

The Financial Turnaround Manager is responsible for implementing working capital procedures and overseeing them.

FR CS 7 – Purchasing Improvements in the Financial Restructuring Component

Summary

This subcomponent is often triggered as a follow-up to FR CS 4 (First-Step Cost Reductions).

Context

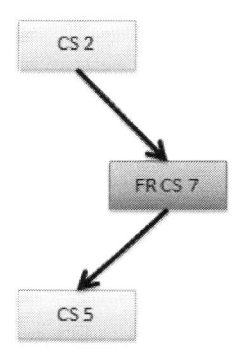

Description of the Subcomponent

Purchasing is frequently a neglected area in distressed companies, but in manufacturing companies it is often the single largest item in their cost structure.[741] The Turnaround Leader should check existing purchasing contracts for the possibility of renegotiating them or canceling them in order to switch to cheaper suppliers. Literature shows that renegotiations have resulted in reductions of up to 15 percent in purchase costs for key components and materials in some turnaround situations.[742] Temporary employees and subcontractors can also be regarded as "purchased goods", and a close look at these contracts may reveal some cost-saving opportunities.

However, if escalation clauses are included, previous management may have miscalculated the costs of performing the contract or have narrowly defined the increased costs that may be

---

[741] (Slatter & Lovett, 2004, p. 149)
[742] (Slatter & Lovett, 2004, p. 149)

recouped under the escalation clause.[743] If this is the case, the turnaround management should try to renegotiate the contracts.

Responsibility

The Financial Turnaround Manager is responsible for this subcomponent.

---

[743] (Slatter & Lovett, 2004, p. 269)

FR CS 8 – Improving Overhead Costs

Summary

This subcomponent is often triggered as a follow-up to FR CS 4 (First-Step Cost Reductions).

Context

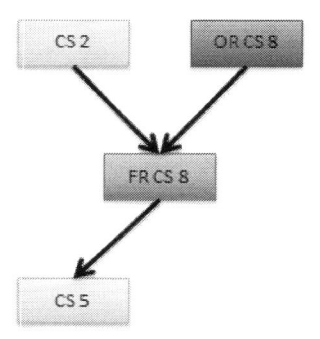

Description of the Subcomponent

At this stage it is necessary and possible to identify only those overhead costs that are clearly not essential and don't add value to the core business of the firm. Some overhead costs are easier to spot then others. The ones that are easy to find are often related to subscriptions, mobile phones, external training, travel, consultants, conferences, trade exhibitions, advertising, and entertainment, as well as employee benefits and motivational incentives such as coupons and company cars. Some overheads cannot be reduced without incurring costs, such as cash penalties for breaking lease agreements. In these cases it is advisable to postpone these items and review them after the Turnaround Plan is established. A careful benefit/trade-off analysis is carried out in these cases to determine whether it makes financial sense to pay to end an agreement early and whether the money required to pay the costs of undertaking such actions is available.

Overhead costs can be reduced by, for example, reducing the number of managers' secretaries.[744] AirTran, for example, had only one secretary for two managers.

Responsibility

The Financial Turnaround Manager is responsible for this subcomponent.

---

[744] (Rajendar, 2007, p. 21)

FR CS 9 – Implementing Emergency Cash Management Controls

Summary

Control over the company's cash flow is quickly established.

Context

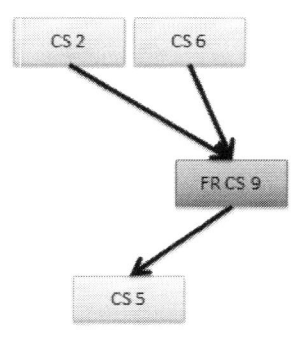

Description of the Subcomponent

This step is taken once the short-term forecast for the company's cash requirements has been created. The financial cash management structure of the company needs to be realigned in order to conserve cash—the highest priority for companies in a crisis situation. The Turnaround Leader should have a system in place to check on the outcomes of the actions it implements using a cash management system (CMS). A CMS has four elements that must be met in order to be effective:

- Strong cash controls must be implemented.
- Managing cash effectively requires resources.
- Forecasting and reporting systems must be in place.
- Cash rationing must be practiced.

The appropriate system for cash control will depend on the size, nature, and structure of the business, but whatever these feature of the business are, the system must provide tight day-to-day control.[745] Strong controls to be implemented include cost, invoicing, purchasing, and inventory controls. These will help control risk and avoid running into surprises. The minimum cash controls installed in a company must include control over disbursements, expenditures, and cash commitments.[746]

Implementing Strong Cash Controls

Centralized cash control is necessary for cash management to work. Small and medium-sized companies usually have a centralized control system, but multinational businesses may be organized differently. Still, to control cash flow during a crisis even large and multinational businesses must have centralized cash management. A complete list of all employees who have the authorization to remit money should be created as part of the control system. This list should be reviewed for authorization limits and for the number of people who are allowed to remit money. Those managers who have the authority to spend money should be involved in the restructuring component. Further, managers should not be allowed to override agreed initiatives, particularly with regard to the settlement of liabilities and the collection of monies from customers.[747]

In order to minimize the number of accounts to be taken care of, a complete revision of the banking arrangements is conducted as well as a revision of automated payments. Doing so helps to ensure that spending is in line with cash forecasts in the short term.

Another form of cash control is to check that delivered goods are invoiced and that the money is received as troubled companies often exercise a low level of scrutiny over bills, but it also includes monitoring transactions and cash components so every order that goes out has the proper authorization.[748] Check-ups on payable bills should be done carefully and often done twice by different people if the amount owed is high. There has never been a troubled company whose accounting department didn't overpay bills from the utility company, the telephone company, or other major suppliers.[749]

---

[745] (Slatter & Lovett, 2004, p. 133)
[746] (Bibeault, 1981, p. 206)
[747] (Slatter & Lovett, 2004, p. 134)
[748] (Bibeault, 1981, p. 305)
[749] (Bibeault, 1981, p. 306)

The control systems should be strong and tight because it is easy to lose control over cash flow. In most cases, it is better to have controls that are a bit too strong than a bit too loose. If controls are only slightly tighter than usual there will be no excessive adverse reaction on the part of management; but an insufficient control system will have to be tightened, after which managers will complain.

Dedicate Resources to Cash Management

The right people—and the right number of people—must be doing the job of controlling cash management. Daily meetings with people concerned with cash collection and weekly meetings with those concerned with forecasting ensure that those who are involved in collecting cash and those who are responsible for incurring liabilities are "on the same page". The people who attend the weekly meetings can then prioritize payments and make sound decisions with a cautiously updated view of the company's financial situation, its demands, and its prospects. "Not only does this component drive the focus to cash management, it also begins to build peer pressure, which is important when the behavior in an organization needs to be changed."[750]

Putting Forecasting and Reporting Systems in Place

Even forecasts that are updated on a weekly basis are not enough to be able to say that an effective cash management system is in place. The weekly cash reports must be checked for any variances between actuals and forecast. Responsibilities must also be reviewed to check if they are still accurate. During the turnaround process, promises may have been given to stakeholders that turn out to be impractical. The impact and quantity of these promises should be minimized in order to restore shareholder confidence. Where the ongoing viability of the company relies on external stakeholder support, it is also important that the formatting of the cash flow and its reporting be agreed upon with the recipient(s) of the report, and that there be an easy way to communicate variances.[751]

Each department or business unit can select and define relevant metrics that are clearly defined and documented.[752] The metrics can be rolled up into a few important measures of profitability, such as efficiency, quality, and output as well as other measures that reflect business health.

---

[750] (Slatter & Lovett, 2004, p. 134)
[751] (Slatter & Lovett, 2004, p. 135)
[752] (Roman, 2010, p. 187)

The selection of key metrics for a business unit must provide a 360-degree view of the respective unit's efficiency, quality, effectiveness, and customer centricity.[753] The goal is to have a system that measures performance but in a way that serves the company as a whole. A stable system is a system that keeps the employees focused on the long-term strategy but is also aligned with shorter-term goals. The measurement system can be, and most likely is, different from department to department, but the whole system is aligned and leads the employees toward the long-term vision.

This type of stability ensures the success of applying a long-term strategy and vision rather than a short-term focus:[754] this month we're all about productivity, next month we're focused on quality, and so on.

The results from the reporting system must be well documented and stored for future reference.

Cash Rationing

Cash rationing is a technique that can be used if the company has several sites at different locations or consists of many subsidiaries in a decentralized organization, and it brings some central control to a multi-company structure. For cash rationing the central controller needs a mechanism to ensure that the division operates in accordance with its short-term cash flow forecast, which has been consolidated into the critical short-term cash flow forecasts used by the company to obtain support from its bankers and on which rebuilt stakeholder confidence is based.[755] In an ideal scenario, the responsible controller only needs to authorize payments that are in accordance with the forecasts. Such a system can operate with a time lag of about a week so any shortfall in receipts in the first week will result in cash rationing by the same amount against the second week's payments. A central contingency should be created by the central controller so if one subsidiary brings in more cash that forecast it can be diverted for redistribution to counteract unforeseen expenditures.

---

[753] (Roman, 2010, p. 187)
[754] (Roman, 2010, p. 187)
[755] (Slatter & Lovett, 2004, p. 135)

Responsibility

The Financial Turnaround Manager is responsible for this subcomponent.

FR CS 10 – Cash-Generating Strategies

Summary

Cash is generated during the Crisis Stabilization Stage.

Context

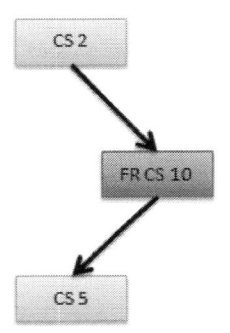

Description of the Subcomponent

An example of how to generate cash in the short term is to reduce the working capital by liquidating surplus stock, improving debt collection, and stretching creditor payments.[756] In some cases it is also possible to sell debt to a debt collector; although the company would receive only a fraction of the debt owed, it would get that cash considerably faster than if it had to collect it itself. There might be an opportunity to increase short-term revenues through provisional events or possibly by increasing prices, but this is not always possible, and it does not always have the desired effect. Capital expenditure that is not essential to the business should be put on hold.

The establishment of a short-term forecast often reveals that there is a gap between currently available facilities and the forecasted cash requirement.[757] During the Crisis Stabilization Stage, the literature provides us with nine alternatives for generating cash in the short term:

---

[756] (S, L, Corp. Rec. p. 79.)
[757] (Slatter & Lovett, 2004, p. 136)

- Extension of creditors
- Reduction of debtors
- Reduction of stock
- Stopping planned expenditures
- Short-term financial support
- Sale of assets
- Divestment of part of the business
- Renegotiated wages
- Employee creativity

The first five of these are considered strategies, while the last four, while not regarded as strategies, are ways to get some liquidity in the short term. As a general rule, cost-reduction strategies do not generate short-term cash flow as either the benefits take time to work through the system (as in the case of better purchasing), or they cost money to implement (making staff redundant).[758]

Extension of Creditors

A good way to free up money is to extend payments to creditors. Suppliers are major stakeholders so they have some interest in the company's survival. In that case, the Turnaround Leader could ask the suppliers for an extension of the payments owed to them, or could try to renegotiate payment terms. However, renegotiations should be conducted so they do not further damage the suppliers' confidence in the trouble company, especially since suppliers often work with credit reference organizations. (If another supplier finds out about the extension it could shorten future payment terms fearing its own payments are at risk.) The Turnaround Leader reminds the suppliers that extending the payment terms is in their own interest as well, since they will lose a customer if the troubled company goes bankrupt. The Turnaround Leader carefully selects the suppliers with which to enter into negotiations, possibly starting with one that depends heavily on the troubled company since it may be more willing than others to comply. Business intelligence (BI) can be helpful if the company has a BI division or if the TMT is connected to a BI company. BI can tell the Turnaround Leader if a credit insurer is involved in the trading terms, as this would mean that the supplier may not be able to extend the payment terms even if it wanted to.

---

[758] (Slatter & Lovett, 2004, pp. 141-142)

The following is a list of practical steps, which I have extended with my own research, to be adopted to extend creditors:

- The Turnaround Leader identifies who is responsible for delivering the initiatives outlined in the short-term forecast.
- All trading terms from all major suppliers are reviewed to identify the largest and most important suppliers, and those to whom the company is the most important.
- The payment routines that are currently in place are reviewed. Sometimes troubled companies pay their suppliers before the payment deadlines, but in a crisis situation liquidity is important so the necessary payments should be stretched to the limit while still being made on time. The exact short-term forecasting ensures that the payment can still be made by the end of its term. Automated payments are reviewed in order to eliminate ones that can be rerouted or stretched.
- It may be easier to negotiate better terms when trading terms with suppliers are not very clear than when they are.
- Existing suppliers are moved to consignment stock arrangements, if possible.
- If better trading terms cannot be reached with existing suppliers, others should be sought out that can offer better terms.

In general, the Turnaround Leader should build good relationships with government bodies through open and frequent communication. Arrangements with government bodies, particularly the Inland Revenue and Customs and Excise in the United States, can often provide scope for conserving cash, and some fairly straightforward VAT-planning steps are normally available to improve a company's cash flow.[759]

If the company does not own the properties it uses, another important supplier is the landlord. If the landlord is not willing to negotiate better terms for the company, perhaps they will agree to shorter payment cycles, such as monthly instead of quarterly payments. However, the Turnaround Leader must be careful in negotiations with landowners since the premiums available in leases often represent major assets.

---

[759] (Slatter & Lovett, 2004, p. 139)

Reduction of Debtors

A quick way to get money into the business is to go through overdue accounts and seek payment. Companies that fall into crisis have often had difficulties dealing with customers who don't pay their bills, especially if there is a dispute involved. Unfortunately, one of the characteristics of a troubled business is that it has often experienced delivery problems or quality problems with its customers that have resulted in payments being delayed or withheld.[760] At least one person should be assigned to the resolution of bad debts and should focus on issues that have led to its non-payment. The Turnaround Leader should ensure that VAT bad debt relief, if applicable in the country, is recovered as soon as disagreements are resolved. Focusing on these issues may wash some money back into the business. Additional cash can be found in the "good" part of the ledger by:

- offering early settlement discounts on good debts (although this is expensive money)
- entering into a factoring or an invoice discounting arrangement with a finance house (also expensive)
- renegotiating trading terms toward a reduced credit period
- prioritizing sales and production to better-paying customers
- asking customers to pay in advance

When as much outstanding debt as possible has been recovered, the Turnaround Leader ensures that the company will not fall back into its old habit of letting disputes slide.

Reduction of Stock

Optimizing inventory management can be another short-term source of money. The focus should be on obsolete and slow-moving stocks of raw materials and finished products. One negative effect of this review can be that the profit and loss account will have to be adjusted in terms of realizable value.

A team consisting of an internal supply and production chain expert and the Turnaround Leader reviews the stock to identify products and materials that can be cleared. A standard process is to identify this stock before moving it to a stock-realization program. It may be possible in some cases to incorporate or redesign surplus raw materials into current products since doing so

---

[760] (Slatter & Lovett, 2004, p. 137)

provides more recovery of cash than the alternative of disposal or scrapping.[761] Another alternative is to return raw materials or products to the suppliers; this is an especially good idea when commodity products are part of the surplus stock. BI may also be able to provide information on other companies that could use the materials without involving the supplier.

Clearance companies or auctions might not be the best way to sell surplus, since disposals to these companies are unlikely to achieve more than ten percent of the original cost. Surplus that is sold will both free up storage room, which can be rented out, and lower administrative costs, so even if the sales price is not high, overhead costs may shrink.[762] It is up to the TMT and the employees to come up with creative solutions to drive money back into the business.

One of the difficulties faced by firms disposing of slow-moving finished goods is that the existing range of products can be weakened or damaged. Therefore the company could try to sell these products through a wholesaler in markets it has not otherwise entered. Selling the product under another name is also advisable.

There is little benefit in converting obsolete stock into an uncollectible debt, but that approach remains common; similarly, selling obsolete stock on a sale-or-return basis leaves the buyer with all the upside and the vendor with all the downside, and no improvement in cash management.[763] Also, companies with excess stock should install an ongoing system to monitor obsolete and slow moving stock.

Evaluation of Sale or Divestment

Divestment of a business is usually the last option if selling the business as a going concern is not possible. Before divesting, a company should try to straighten out a loser by quick surgery and then attempt to sell it as a going concern.[764] To get that troubled business or business unit back to a position where it can be sold can cost much-needed cash. However, if a company can't afford additional cash outflows, liquidating that business may be the only alternative available.

---

[761] (Slatter & Lovett, 2004, p. 140)
[762] (Slatter & Lovett, 2004, p. 141)
[763] (Slatter & Lovett, 2004, p. 140)
[764] (Bibeault, 1981, p. 101)

Borderline Situations

If it is not clear whether a business unit can be sold, the timeframe for turning it into a going concern and selling it should be clearly defined. A date should be set by which the business unit will be liquidated if has not been sold.

Divestment of Part of the Business

The divestment of part of a business can be a source of income for a troubled company. This possibility is discussed in detail in the strategic component.

Sale of Assets

The sale of assets can take several forms. Assets that can be sold include land, machinery, buildings, intellectual property rights, ownerships in other companies, and inventory. In many cases the sale of such assets is a quick way of gaining money.

Employee Creativity

Employees often have good ideas about where the company could save money. Being open with them about the overhead costs for their workplace or area of work can encourage them to come up with ways to save money. For example, if a storage area manager sees that half of their storage area is unused after the reduction of surplus stock during the turnaround process, they may suggest that another company shares it. A team manager may see that the overhead costs for their team are too high because they are paying for legal advice that they never use. While these types of suggestions should be considered carefully, participation in the turnaround process may make employees feel more involved and help them to support unpleasant but necessary procedures.

Stopping or Reducing Planned Expenditure

At the beginning of the Crisis Stabilization Stage, all expenditure will probably be put on hold until a Turnaround Plan is in place. Discretionary expenditure such as advertising campaigns, trade exhibitions, and training—in fact, any spending not directly related to the operation of the business—will usually be put on hold.[765]

Renegotiating Wages

A possible way to save costs is to renegotiate the wages of the workforce. For this step to take place, it is important for the Turnaround Leader to earn the employees' and unions' trust by delivering what they promise and through open communication. While the Turnaround Leader may be able to persuade the company's staff to accept a temporary reduction in salary by bypassing unions, it should not be done without the unions' support. A strike or other actions caused by dissatisfied employees can cost the company in the end. It is difficult to introduce this option early, since trust has to be built first.

Short-Term Financial Support

If the short-term cash forecast shows that the entity cannot survive without external funding, the Turnaround Leader must turn to the stakeholders. The Turnaround Leader's task is to balance the company's need for short-term financing with good relationships with the shareholders. Shareholders are seldom impressed when a company needs to raise money so, at this stage, much depends on the credibility of the Turnaround Leader. If stakeholders think that they are being asked for more money without having a real chance of higher returns, and if they think that their opportunity costs are too high, it is up to the Turnaround Leader to convince them. If the requirement for money is so great that the company must have financing at almost any cost, it would be advisable to review whether the company is really worth saving at all and whether the risk is possibly too high.

The Influence of Banks

The most obvious source to approach for financing is a bank. When a bank grants the company a loan or extends already existing credit, this is called support financing. However, the Crisis Stabilization Stage is not the best time to renegotiate bank loans because doing so will often result in the changes being approved at a high cost to the troubled firm. Therefore, the Turnaround Leader should ask only for the minimum amount that is really needed.

---

[765] (Slatter & Lovett, 2004, p. 141)

The Influence of Shareholders

One possible influence that shareholders have over the turnaround process is illustrated by the cases of Lloyds TSB and the Royal Bank of Scotland (RBS), where equity shareholders were approached for an emergency rights issue. The two British banks, Lloyds TSB and RBS, raised a combined £13 billion through rights issues underwritten by the state in 2008.[766] In the case of Imperial Energy that same year, the Russia-focused oil company signed an irrevocable standby share underwriting facility with Merrill Lynch and ABN Amro's Hoare Govett for a $600m (£300m) share issue.[767]

Joint Venture Partners

If the company is running a joint venture the Turnaround Leader could try to convince the partner(s) to provide some equity, as was the case with CONSOLIDATED Media Holdings and PBL Media, the owner of Channel Nine, an Australian news network,[768] or with Laura Ashley Holdings plc. In 1990, Laura Ashley, which posted a loss of £11.5 million, was saved only by the intervention of the Japanese retailer Aeon, whose infusion of cash in exchange for a 15 percent stake bailed the company out.[769]

Turnaround Leaders are often faced with requests to provide security for short-term financial support but, inevitably, fulfilling this request gives one stakeholder a stronger position while weakening the positions of others. The Turnaround Leader can anticipate ongoing support from external stakeholders if they can devise a stabilization plan under which the stakeholders' position does not worsen while the recovery plan is being developed.[770] However, if the position of one stakeholder is weakened during the restructuring component, the Turnaround Leader may need to offer them more security. This situation should be avoided, not only because of the Turnaround Leader's own exposure to legal action, but also because the shareholder might restrict the Turnaround Leader's flexibility by having more power over the company's assets. The Turnaround Leader must get the best they can with the little they have

---

[766] compare (Duke, 2008)
[767] compare ((Power, 2008)
[768] compare (Hogan, 2008)
[769] compare (International Directory of Company Histories, 2001)
[770] (Slatter & Lovett, 2004, p. 143)

available. If they give everything to the first stakeholder who demands it, other stakeholders would be disappointed and the turnaround process put in even greater danger.

Renegotiating Contracts

Just like credit, supplier payment terms are easier to negotiate when the supplier is eager to get a signature on the contract and a new client secured.[771] However, when the supplier depends on the troubled company as a client the negotiating power of the Turnaround Leader increases. One possibility is to stretch the legal constraints of a contract to its limits. Pushing terms out to the limit makes it difficult to renegotiating payment terms later, so supplier payments should be maintained on schedule and the cash flow managed very carefully. Pushing the limits of contracts should be a last resort, since doing so is likely to damage the firm's reputation and may attract a costly and time-consuming lawsuit.

Responsibility

The Financial Turnaround Manager is responsible for this subcomponent.

---

[771] (Roman, 2010, p. 182)

FR CS 11 – First-Stage Survival Financing

Summary

First-stage survival financing can be triggered in the Crisis Stabilization Stage or through Emergency Procedures if financial survival is critical.

Context

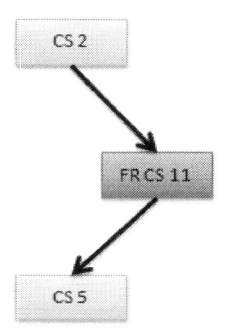

```
CS 2
  ↓
FR CS 11
  ↓
CS 5
```

Description of the Subcomponent

This first stage of financing ensures that the company will not run out of cash before the Crisis Stabilization Stage—and, in some cases, the Diagnostic Review Stage—is completed and the Turnaround Plan and a funding plan have been developed.

Sometimes equity shareholders provide the financing needed in a critical situation, but this approach is risky for them because their money might be used to reduce the debt exposure.

Priority of Interest

Stakeholders can have different kinds of rights to their investments so it is important for the TMT to have exact knowledge of the stakeholders' rights and priorities of interest. Some guidelines will be found in the company's contracts and others are regulated by the applicable law.

Short-Term Refinancing

If a company has access to short-term refinancing the likely outcomes are changed banking terms and/or additional short-term borrowing from banks with which the company has an existing relationship. Additional short-term borrowing is usually possible only with higher interest rates since the bank will adjust to the higher risk of default. Changed banking terms involve postponement of principal payments due, temporary relaxation of existing covenants, extension of maturity dates, and/or all or part of current interest payments due being rolled up into capital.[772]

If a part of the firm is to be sold off, it can be useful to secure some bridge financing since cash flow from the sale of assets or part of the business may take several months to materialize.

Short-term refinancing is done in three steps. The first step is to evaluate the cash that is available to the company. Depending on the detail in which this was done in the Diagnostic Review Stage, availabilities may have to be updated. The plan is then extended with a list of liabilities to each of the creditors, and the cash flow forecasts are updated with actual data. The forecast might reveal that funding—and what kind of funding—is required during the time that it takes to prepare the Turnaround Plan; in that case, the plan needs to include preparations for a longer-term financial reconstruction.

The second step is a difficult one for the TMT and the TAB because they must determine whether the company is able to gain the necessary support from its stakeholders and whether they have enough time to develop a Turnaround Plan. The TAB does not have full information at this point, yet they have a duty to their stakeholders to inform them as soon as important information becomes available. If the TAB and the TMT do not believe a turnaround is possible based on the financial expectations, liquidation should be seriously considered. Decisions made during this time should be documented along with the arguments that led to them. The decisions should be revisited and considered against the actuals as long as no viable Turnaround Plan has been created. The law does not require managers to avoid risk, but they do need to be careful.

---

[772] (Slatter & Lovett, 2004, p. 316)

The third step of short-term refinancing involves requesting short-term support from the major stakeholders. It is important that the stakeholders are not talked into accepting a promise that the TMT and the TAB cannot keep or that they agree to something based on false representation of facts. Either action could have serious consequences for both parties, so transparency is the key to staying legally untouchable.

Furthermore, the size and complexity of the business, the number of funding stakeholders that are involved, and the amount of short-term financing required, as well as other complicating factors, can adversely affect the refinancing component.[773]

Standstill Agreements

A standstill agreement is an agreement between the surety and its principal and/or indemnitors in which the surety agrees to forbear to exercise certain rights against the principal and/or its indemnitors and the indemnity agreement or related documents.[774] These agreements are more common in a multi-banked environment than in bilateral arrangements; although where a series of bilateral agreements exists it is possible that the banks come together through an inter-bank agreement among themselves, leading to a standstill agreement with the firm.[775] Sureties have agreed to standstill or forbearance agreements in the past when the principal needs time to collect bonded contract funds to finance a portion of the next stage of work, to please unpaid subcontractors or suppliers, or to pay overheads.[776] Reaching these agreements can take some time so the Turnaround Leader must make sure that they are not too caught up in the negotiations and that they have enough time to focus on other critical issues. The best thing a Turnaround Leader can do in this situation is to appoint a TMT member to negotiate the terms assisted by further advisors, such as lawyers.

The purpose of the standstill agreement during the period of the standstill is to record evidence arrangements regarding the term covenants, as well as costs and facilities. In exchange, the surety agrees to do nothing or forbear to take advantage of its rights with respect to these acknowledged defaults. The information that the company provides to the surety—or often, in this case, the banks—must be accurate and reliable because a breach or false representation

---

[773] (Slatter & Lovett, 2004, p. 312)
[774] (Klinger, 2008, p. 133)
[775] (Slatter & Lovett, 2004, p. 315)
[776] (Klinger, 2008, p. 133)

of such a standstill agreement can have severe consequences for the troubled company, including the amendment of the agreement, lawsuits for false representation, and loss of trust. Obtaining new sources of funding will probably be almost impossible if a lawsuit about false representation becomes public knowledge.

Sureties have accepted several types of collateral through standstill agreements, including:

- *Real Property:* What makes real property attractive is that it is permanent and its value tends to improve or at least remain steady over time. Real property includes land and attached buildings, as well as rental income from the land.[777]
- *Personal Property:* Sureties have accepted personal property, including life insurance, as collateral. Klinger found that it is more typical for a surety to take a security interest in the personal property rather than to demand outright transfer of ownership.[778]
- *Equipment:* Some typical pieces of equipment that sureties have accepted are loaders, forklifts, backhoes, cranes, and other machinery. The sureties often want to obtain a security interest in all of the principal's equipment as it is often difficult to place an accurate market value on it.[779]
- *Inventory and Materials:* As is the case with equipment, it is often difficult to establish an accurate market value of the inventory.
- *Stocks and Bonds:* Sureties have accepted shares that the troubled company holds in other companies as well as shares in the company itself, regardless of whether the company is publicly or privately held.[780]
- *General Intangibles:* Examples of intangibles are tax refunds, copyrights, trademarks, patents, and rights that evolve out of rights the principal has.[781]

Moratoria

Sometimes it is possible to seek support from suppliers in the form of a moratorium. In order for the moratorium to be successful, it must be in the interest of the stakeholders who have an interest in the firm's survival. Moratoria are often used in cases where there are only a few suppliers to the company and where the supplier seriously depends on the business with the

---

[777] compare (Klinger, 2008, p. 133)
[778] (Klinger, 2008, p. 134)
[779] compare (Klinger, 2008, pp. 134-135)
[780] compare (Klinger, 2008, p. 136)
[781] compare (Klinger, 2008, pp. 136-137)

troubled company. From the supplier's side, a moratorium is a good prospect only if it offers an improved and/or faster chance of survival. The Turnaround Leader must be careful in cases where a supplier is also a competitor; in these cases they should request confidentiality agreements before disclosing the financial situation of the company.

Responsibility

The Financial Turnaround Manager is responsible for this subcomponent.

FR CS 12 – Long-Term Financial Restructuring

Summary

This subcomponent triggers long-term financial restructuring procedures. The objective of long-term financial restructuring is to provide the firm with a solvent balance sheet and the ability to implement the agreed plan while servicing residual or new debt.[782]

Context

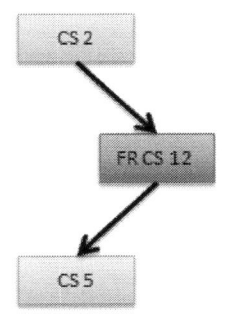

Description of the Subcomponent

Through this subcomponent the firm is put back on a solvent track and creditor confidence is restored. Long-term financing should be acceptable to all stakeholders and should include aspects of motivating the management through financial measures.

It is important for the TMT to understand the position of the stakeholders before entering into negotiations with them. Depending on who they are, equity stakeholders usually have differing interests in negotiating long-term financing:

- Will they get the money back that they injected into the company (whether new money or old money) and is new money really helping the recovery?

---

[782] (Slatter & Lovett, 2004, p. 316)

- Will the financing provide a realistic opportunity for restoring value while providing adequate returns on new monies in the meantime?[783]
- Does the firm have a realistic future in the market in which it competes?
- Is the turnaround management the right team and does the TAB have the right people on it?
- Does the plan provide a better outcome than available alternatives, even when reasonable sensitivity analysis has been applied to the financial measures?[784]

In order to ensure that stakeholders are supportive, the company should make sure that it can answer these questions positively. It is the Turnaround Leader's responsibility to ensure that the stakeholders are on board with the turnaround process and that they feel comfortable with the TMT. Equity stakeholders often take a different view from debt stakeholders in that the priority for providers of debt is to recover their loans with appropriate reward for providing risk support, whereas equity stakeholders are more willing to write-off unsuccessful investments but want to retain the upside of any new money going in.[785]

In some cases there is a swap of debt for equity, as covered by FR CS 5 (Debt Restructuring). If debt is swapped for equity there will probably be some hard negotiations among the shareholders. The debt provider will usually seek an equal ranking on converted debt to new equity injected, whereas the equity providers will want to see a discount on conversion.[786]

Influences on the Financial Structure

Several key factors influence the financial restructuring of a company:

- The current or prior capital structure
- Financial requirements that the company has and will have
- The monetary value of the business and the future value
- Management's credibility
- The claimant's relative bargaining power

---

[783] (Slatter & Lovett, 2004, p. 316)
[784] (Slatter & Lovett, 2004, p. 317)
[785] (Slatter & Lovett, 2004, p. 317)
[786] (Slatter & Lovett, 2004, p. 317)

- Taxes

Typical Financial Restructuring Packages

Typical restructuring packages include:

- Bank debt being converted into convertible loan stock or equity
- Unpaid interest being converted into equity and/or debt
- Outstanding public debt being restructured
- Outstanding preferred stock being restructured
- Debt payments being rescheduled, which may also mean that the interest rates and covenants change
- Fresh money being borrowed
- New equity being issued, which is often done in the form of a rights issue or a private placement

Objectives of the Banks

The banks will usually try to convert as little debt to equity as possible. Their prime concern is to have a high priority debt claim against the company as they earn money from the interest the company pays.

Responsibility

The Financial Turnaround Manager is responsible for this subcomponent.

FR CS 13 – Amendments to the Financial Restructuring Plan

Summary

Changes to the Financial Plan are made as a result of new information or planned changes to the corporate structure that affect the value of the company.

Context

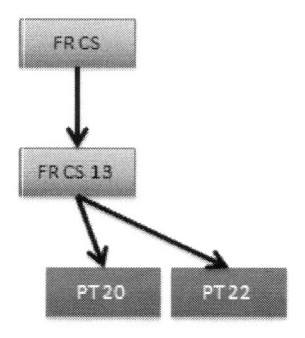

Description of the Subcomponent

Amendments to the Financial Restructuring Plan can occur at any time, especially in regard to the value of the company, which is likely to change throughout the turnaround process. Two important parts of the Financial Restructuring Plan are the company evaluation and allocation of the firm's value.

Company Evaluation

The company evaluation is based on future cash flows, although the true value of the firm is difficult to estimate. Disagreement about the value is likely between the stakeholders and the company's management. In any case, the value should not be overstated.

Allocation of the Firm's Value

Key debt renegotiation issues center on how much value should be given to each creditor and also the type of financial instrument that each creditor is supposed to receive.[787] In these renegotiations the senior debtors are usually interested in cash, but in order to reach an agreement they must often give up on some of their priority positions. In any case, the outcome of these negotiations should be more beneficial for the debtors than insolvency otherwise they would not support the turnaround efforts.

While the focus of financial restructuring negotiations is on the debt-holders, equity investors usually expect to end up with 10 to 20 percent of the company even if it is basically insolvent, since their support is required to approve the new structure.[788]

Cash Forecasts

The cash forecast should be updated regularly. In the first six to eight weeks, a rolling forecast should be produced. After that, a weekly rolling update may suffice.

Responsibility

The Financial Turnaround Manager is responsible for this subcomponent.

---

[787] (Slatter & Lovett, 2004, p. 318)
[788] (Slatter & Lovett, 2004, p. 319)

FR CS 14 – Working Capital Reductions

Summary

In this subcomponent working capital is reduced to generate cash.

Context

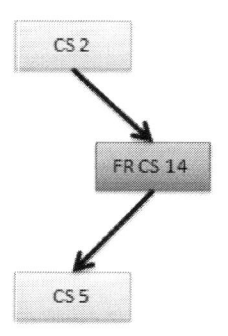

Description of the Subcomponent

While working capital improvements won't generate cash as quickly as tapping a line of credit, but such improvements can unlock dramatic amounts of money from their operations in surprisingly short periods of time with no obligation to pay it back.[789] An improvement in working capital management is a "gift that keeps on giving" because this money can be used to pay back debt, finance an acquisition, buy back stock, or invest into other process improvements or technological updates necessary to stay competitive.[790] Ways to reduce working capital include:

- Standardizing and rationalizing customer and supplier terms
- Setting or rewriting payment and collection policies to manage risk
- Linking accounts payable components and procurement
- Rewarding the sales force for ensuring accurate and timely billing
- Developing a formal dispute-management process for outstanding receivables

---

[789] (Payne, 2002)
[790] (Brigham & Ehrhardt, 2008, p. 779)

- Giving managers new metrics that allow them to monitor the company's progress in terms of minimizing days of sales outstanding[791]

Optimizing working capital management practices consists of efficiently executing the policies and components that impact working capital in the C2C (customer to cash), P2P (purchase to pay) and F2F (forecast to fulfill) cycles. If problems occur in one area, they often occur in another as well. Because its three components—P2P, F2F, and C2C—are inextricably intertwined, trouble signs that appear in one area are often traceable to processes in another.[792]

To employ working capital reductions and policies, the management system must often be upgraded so the cash flow can be controlled. When a company improves its working capital processes, these processes usually remain at their improved levels.[793]

Responsibility

The Financial Turnaround Manager is responsible for this subcomponent.

---

[791] (Payne, 2002)
[792] (Payne, 2002)
[793] (Brigham & Ehrhardt, 2008, p. 779)

Financial Restructuring During the Turnaround Stage (FR TS)

Financial Restructuring During the Turnaround Stage (FR TS)

FR TS 1 – Financial Schemes

Summary

In case of a cash shortage, creative financing schemes might be necessary to support a company's turnaround process.

Context

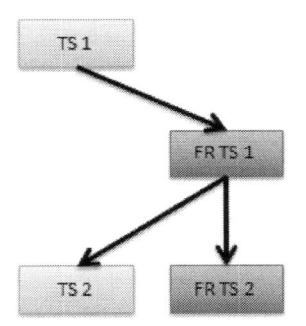

Description of the Subcomponent

This is the first subcomponent of financial optimization in the Financial Restructuring component. At this point in the turnaround process the company's products may not have fully regained the acceptance of the market, but major restructuring strategies are well on the way and in place. Opportunities may arise that should be taken advantage of, regardless of the state of the financial long-term plan. Creative financing through workout arrangements can sometimes enable a company to stretch beyond its apparent financial strength.[794]

There are many creative financing approaches available, but in the context of this subcomponent one example will suffice. Imagine you are running a retail chain and you take over another retail chain that has debt. You could stretch the credit line of the other retail chain after the takeover and secure it with your own inventory to reduce pre-tax earnings from the acquisition. However, if the interest rate for the debt is lower than the earnings from the stores the business still breaks even. Another step could be to make a public offering for equity money,

---

[794] (Bibeault, 1981, p. 341)

thereby retiring the debt in order to ensure that your earnings and return on equity positions are similar to those of other companies in the industry. Of course, this is a risky and specific approach, but it illustrates how management may have to be creative to solve some problems.

Responsibility

The Financial Turnaround Manager is responsible for this subcomponent.

FR TS 2 Financial Guidelines

Summary

This subcomponent establishes the financial guidelines for the Turnaround Stage.

Context

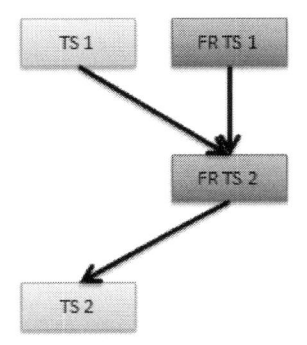

Description of the Subcomponent

The tight financial control and discipline that was put in place in the Crisis Stabilization Stage needs to be kept up in the Turnaround Stage, however, it can be more decentralized.

Companies that achieve a successful turnaround focus on using capital efficiently, and they successfully fight margin deterioration in the face of growth pressures.[795] Therefore, the management must be very disciplined in this fight, and must monitor costs and prices constantly, and rededicate themselves to the balance sheet. Capital efficiency can take many forms, including expanding the use of lockboxes and new remittance procedures to cut receivables, installing and enforcing highly selective guidelines for extending payables, building balance sheet performance factors into personal objectives and management incentive plans, setting objectives for increasing suppliers' warehousing of raw materials, and requiring higher hurdle rates for new capital investment while replacement costs are taken into account.[796]

---

[795] (Bibeault, 1981, pp. 341-342)
[796] (Bibeault, 1981, p. 342)

Responsibility

The Financial Turnaround Manager is responsible for this subcomponent.

FR TS 3 – Forecast and Track Expenses

Summary

Forecasting and tracking expenses is a crucial part of the turnaround process at this point, even though the company is out of the Crisis Stabilization Stage. This subcomponent is designed to maintain the forecasting and, if possible, to extend the forecasting and tracking system.

Context

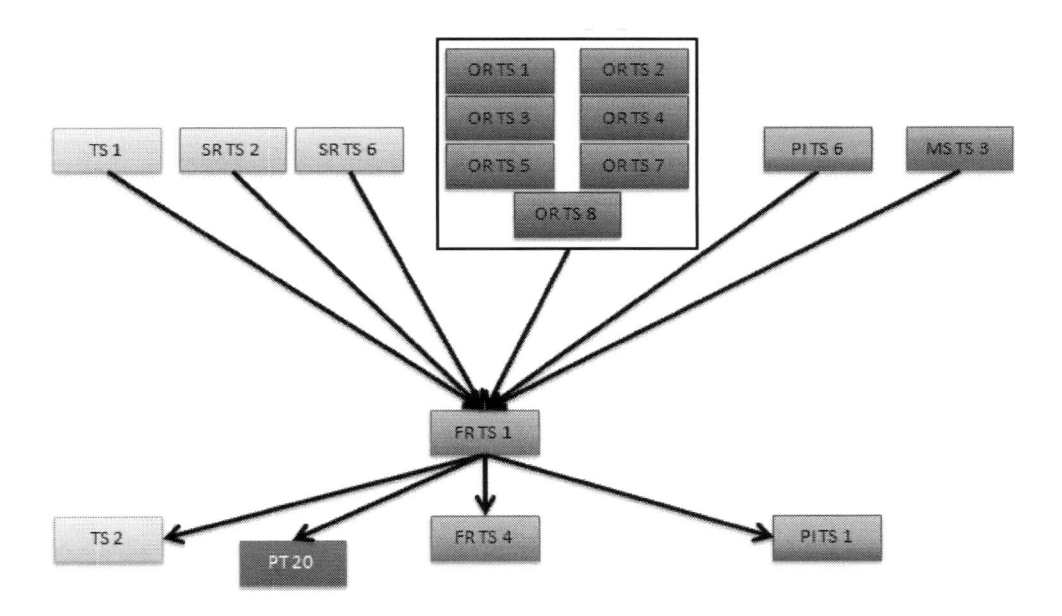

Description of the Subcomponent

Most firms fail to recognize the full scope and cost of their development programs; these programs are sometimes spread over a hundred departments or more.[797] A company in the Turnaround Stage should be able to isolate development costs. In addition to the impact of

---

[797] (Bibeault, 1981, p. 342)

development and sales growth on the income statement, firms often don't take into account the effects of such growth on the balance sheet and working capital.

Forecasting Working Capital

Financial ratios are best suited to forecasting the effect of growth on working capital. These ratios can relate to accounts payable and receivable, inventory turnover, cash, and to either marginal sales increases or average sales levels.

Sales in the Turnaround Stage should be increasing again; therefore the financial management team should make adjustments and prepare for the increase in working capital needed or the company could run into a situation where it does not have enough funds to pay its employees and suppliers before the additional income from the sales increase is available.

Receivables Outstanding Ratio

If the sales volume increases, the accounts receivable is likely to increase as well. The expected increase can be calculated using the day's receivables/outstanding receivables ratio. For example, if the collection period is 30 days, this ratio can be calculated by dividing the accounts receivable by the net sales times 365 days. If the company has sales of one billion and receivables of 110 million and sales increase by 25 percent (25 billion), the receivables will increase by 27.5 million.

Inventory Turnover Ratio

The inventory turnover ratio can be calculated by dividing the net sales by the inventory. For example, company ABC has a sales volume of $1 billion per year and average inventory of $0.25 billion. Inventory turns over four times per year. If a sales increase of 25 percent is expected, the inventory should increase to $312.5 million (an increase of $62.5 million)

Cash/Sales Ratio

If sales increase the company will need more cash for operations. The amount of cash needed is usually expressed in the cash/sales ratio. For example, if a company needs a cash base of $5 million to operate at a sales level of $50 million and sales double to $100 million, the company will need $10 million as a cash base.

LIFO Inventory Valuation

The LIFO method (last in, first out) has been abused by some companies but it can be useful, especially in large companies during inflationary periods, because it improves cash flow and reduces taxes.

The overall implications of the LIFO approach have been misinterpreted by many firms to such an extent that its use has actually hurt the overall position of companies in trouble.[798] The downside of LIFO is that it creates a very inventory valuation by freezing the company's inventory at its level at the time of the switchover. Current costs are matched with current revenues by applying the costs that the company paid for resources at the time of purchase.

LIFO decreases the inventory and the balance sheet resulting in a tax reduction, but it can also result in the company being less creditworthy because the profits are smaller, the losses look bigger, and working capital and net worth look smaller. Since credit and private equity investments are important for a troubled company, LIFO should be applied only if the advantages of the specific situation outweigh the possible disadvantages.

Firms in volatile industries might not find LIFO very useful if their inventory levels vary significantly.

Responsibility

The Financial Turnaround Manager is responsible for this subcomponent.

---

[798] (Bibeault, 1981, p. 343)

FR TS 4 – Financial Modeling

Summary

Financial modeling can help to create future scenarios. During the Turnaround Stage these models can be very useful to plan post-turnaround strategies or even strategies to be used during the Turnaround Stage.

Context

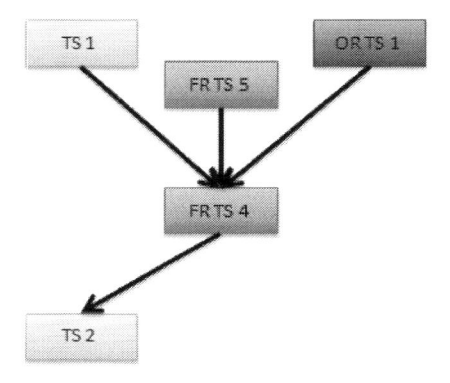

Description of the Subcomponent

The financial model applied to the Turnaround Stage should be kept simple—that is, centered on eight to ten key variables at the most—so the financial or general management has a useful tool for making strategic financial and operating decisions.[799]

Financial modeling is especially important for companies that are listed on the stock exchange. They must maintain a certain earnings per share ratio by having an acceptable debt-to-equity ratio and equity level in order to keep control of the company. This subcomponent should remind the TMT that there are financial modeling techniques available to test future scenarios. The management team should run cases and adjust them to the needs of the company and the shareholders. Financial modeling can also help to create a corporate strategy and to

---

[799] (Bibeault, 1981, p. 344)

communicate the strategy. Then, if it turns out that the company will need additional debt, the management team can contact banks well in advance to show them that they know what they are doing and are not being surprised by sudden capital needs.

Responsibility

The Financial Turnaround Manager is responsible for this subcomponent.

FR TS 5 – Introduce Activity-Based Costing

Summary

Activity-based costing (ABC), a methodology that measures the cost and performance of activities, resources, and cost objectives is introduced. Resources are assigned to activities, and afterwards activities are assigned to cost objectives based on their use.[800]

Context

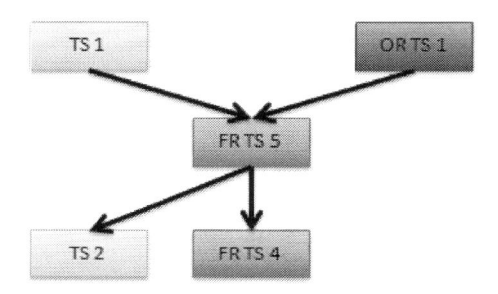

Description of the Subcomponent

The concept of ABC is based on the idea that each activity consumes a certain amount of resources so expenses should be divided between the activities that generated them. Specifically, the expenses that are needed to produce individual units of a particular service or product should be separated from the expenses that are incurred to produce other products or services or to serve other payers.[801] Activity-based accounting systems have been implemented in many organizations, including La Roche, Siemens, RBS, Hoffman, Philips, the BBC, Volvo, and Ericson.[802] ABC is especially useful when large amounts of factory overhead are involved in manufacturing operations.[803]

Using the ABC approach involves financial and non-financial variables as bases for cost allocation. It allows managers to identify excess capacity in their operations, understand the

---

[800] (Baker J., 1998, p. 2)
[801] (Baker J., 1998, p. 2)
[802] (Bhimani, Horngren, Datar, & Foster, 2008, p. 341)
[803] compare (Warren, Reeve, & Duchac, 2009, p. 1108)

true costs of each product, and make informed decisions to improve efficiency.[804] Management decision-makers can utilize ABC information to improve cost-efficiency without negatively impacting the quality of service delivery or continuous quality improvements.

The use of single and multiple department overhead rate methods may lead to distortions.[805] In such cases, traditional overhead allocation bases—such as units produced, direct labor hours, direct labor costs, or machine hours—may yield inaccurate cost allocations.[806]

Zero-Based Budgeting

Zero-based budgeting is also known as priority-based budgeting. Zero-based budgeting emerged in the late 1960s to overcome the limits of incremental budgets. It is a process in which every dollar in a specific budget needs to be justified each year.[807] It works from the premise that projected expenditure for existing programs should start from a zero base with each year's budget compiled as if the programs were being launched for the first time, and it focuses on programs or activities instead of functional departments' line items, which is a feature of traditional budgeting.[808] It forces program managers to justify their projects every year in order not to have projects running that are not useful or that have been going on for too long. Zero-based budgeting is best suited to support activities and discretionary expenses such as costs occurring in research and development, training, and advertising.

Responsibility

The Financial Turnaround Manager is responsible for this subcomponent, but the Turnaround Leader decides whether ABC is to be introduced.

---

[804] (Ledgerwood & White, 2006, p. 316)
[805] (Warren, Reeve, & Duchac, 2009, p. 1186)
[806] (Warren, Reeve, & Duchac, 2009, p. 1186)
[807] compare (Cotts & Rondeau, 2004, p. 75)
[808] (Drury, 2011, p. 375)

FR TS 6 – Balance Sheet Improvements

Summary

This is a follow up subcomponent that was started in the Crisis Stabilization Stage.

Context

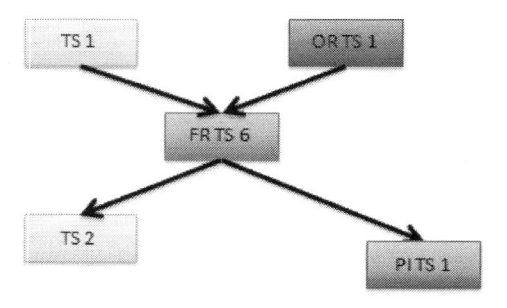

Description of the Subcomponent

Work concerned with the balance sheet that started in the Crisis Stabilization Stage, such as debt restructuring, is continued in this subcomponent; however, the focus during the Turnaround Stage is no longer on asking creditors to defer repayments or ease credit liabilities. This stage is about asset redeployment, by which a firm can significantly ease its liquidity problems and its long-term debt burden.[809] If the company needs additional cash this could be made available by selling more assets or mortgaging property.

Responsibility

The Financial Turnaround Manager is responsible for this subcomponent.

---

[809] (Bibeault, 1981, p. 304)

FR TS 7 – Managerial Accounting Improvements

Summary

In some companies managerial accounting and financial accounting do not work properly, so this subcomponent improves the managerial accounting department, if necessary.

Context

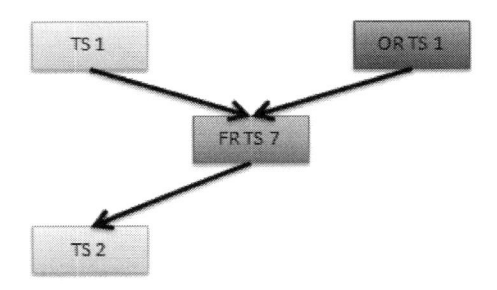

Description of the Subcomponent

In troubled companies the managerial accounting department often does not work well with financial accounting staff and is often in trouble with the top management. In some cases, financial accounting is replaced by managerial accounting or overrules it, which results in misleading information for management.[810] A possible solution to the problem is to give the managerial accounting department the resources it needs to function properly, and for managerial accounting to be separated from the financial accounting staff so that both departments are independent. Thus the financial information does not overrule the accounting information, because the accounting is independent of the financial information the management requests. Some people are designated as financial people and others as managerial accounting people. The results from both departments should then be put together and evaluated by the management team. The following section discusses the information that can be gained from the managerial accounting department that is particularly useful in a turnaround situation.

---

[810] (Bibeault, 1981, p. 307)

Cost Profiles

Categorization of costs helps management to understand them. If such categorization was not already done in the Diagnostic Review it should be done at this point. Sorting the categories from the largest to the smallest will help in making decisions about reducing costs. Some accounting systems show so much information that it takes a Turnaround Manager weeks to find the data they are interested in. If the system is not fully understood by the accounting team it is likely that important information will be overlooked.

Responsibility Accounting

The managerial accounting system should be flexible and provide the required information about every business aspect the department managers are responsible for. A department manager should be able to see what is relevant to each team in their department, along with other information relevant to production. A division head should have access to the combined information of their division, including profit and loss actuals to measure against plan.

Standard Costs

Standard costs, if they are based on company realities, can be a valuable tool in management's evaluation of its winners and losers, and they can replace the use of overall averages that mask reality.[811]

Moving from RoS to RoI

This subcomponent applies only to companies in the distribution business, which focus on return on investment, not return on sales, as a primary measure for performance. Return on sales does not focus on the efficient use of assets and is not an adequate measurement in the distribution business because of this.[812]

---

[811] (Bibeault, 1981, p. 311)
[812] (Bibeault, 1981, p. 338)

Responsibility

The Financial Turnaround Manager is responsible for this subcomponent.

Strategic Restructuring (SR)

Strategic Restructuring During the Crisis Stabilization Stage (SR CS)

SR CS 1 – Creating a Mission Statement

Summary

A mission statement is created for the company.

Context

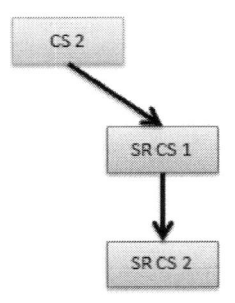

Description of the Subcomponent

The mission statement describes the purpose of the firm and how it wants to fulfill that purpose in a unique way. Many companies' mission statements are not well formulated or thought out. If the current mission statement says only that the goal is to deliver the best products to everybody then the statement is worthless because it does not tell customers, employees, and stockholders where the company is headed.[813]

A proper mission statement should answer the following questions:

1. Why does the customer need the product?
2. What are we doing?
3. Who exactly is our customer?
4. Why should the customer buy our product?
5. How will the products be delivered to the customer?
6. What will we do to complete the product?

---

[813] (Collard, 2002, p. 29)

A proper mission statement explains in a reasonably specific way what the firm intends to achieve. In a turnaround situation the mission statement is a helpful tool in aligning the efforts of the workforce so it is important that it is communicated properly. The mission and value statements do not exist on the pages of marketing materials alone; they should live within the employees and be directly related to everything they do.[814]

Responsibility

The Turnaround Leader is responsible for this subcomponent.

---

[814] (Kamerer, p. 14)

SR CS 2 – Creating a Corporate Strategy

Summary

A corporate strategy is developed for the company.

Context

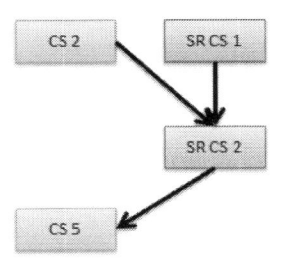

Description of the Subcomponent

The corporate strategy is the set direction for a business in the coming years. It deals with how to operate the company as profitably as possible and the threats to the organization. Developing a corporate strategy requires a deep understanding not only of the capabilities of the company but also of the company's environment. Hill has developed a compact seven-step process for developing a corporate strategy[815] but there is also other extensive research on corporate strategy formulation and its impact on the organization.[816]

In recent corporate strategy literature there has been decreasing confidence in the application of a set of management principles and techniques common to many different businesses, and increased importance has been placed on the role of resources and capabilities in building competitive advantage.[817]

---

[815] (Hill, 2011)
[816] (Johnson, Scholes, & Whittington, 2005), (Porter M., 1989)
[817] (Grant, 2010, p. 450)

Responsibility

The Turnaround Leader is responsible for this subcomponent.

SR CS 3 – Divestment of a Business Unit in Strategic Restructuring

Summary

This subcomponent explains the strategy of divesting a business unit.

Context

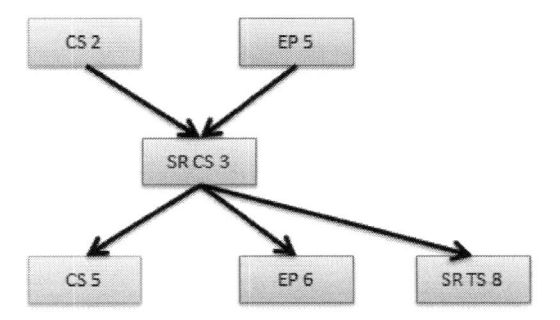

Description of the Subcomponent

Because of the high levels of pressure on the company for liquidity and equity, the literature proposes the divestment of unprofitable business units and/or business units that bind up significant amounts of cash flow needed to refinance the business.[818] If the company does not have enough cash available to plan and survive a turnaround process by its own means and if it is not able raise the required cash at acceptable costs from outside sources, the only solution may be the divestment of a business or business unit.

For small companies such divestment could mean selling off a product to a competitor. The first idea of a manager who has been leading a conglomerate for quite some time but does not have much turnaround experience or knowledge may be to sell the business that is not doing well. In most cases, however, if a company is already in trouble either the price will be extremely low or, in the worst case, no buyer will emerge. In this case, the management may have to sell one of the more profitable companies, divisions, or business units.

---

[818] compare (Jobsky, 1998, p. 334), (Kall, 1999, p. 107), (Buth, 2004, p. 117)

An example of this is the Stakis Hotels Group, a company that evolved in the 1980s and was doing business with hotels, casinos, property development projects, and nursing homes. A turnaround plan was designed that included keeping the hotels and nursing homes and selling the casinos,[819] but it turned out later that the Turnaround Leader was not able to sell the casinos as planned and had to switch to selling the nursing homes, which attracted buyers quickly.

In some cases, when a business unit is sold the remaining firm might not be able to support its debt load even if the cash flow is positive. In this case the debt must be restructured, which generally requires converting loans to shaky equity, or in some cases that the debt is waived. The stakeholders need to support this process because it will appear as a loss on their books. It is important that the TMT puts together a detailed and accurate forecast of the company's cash flow in order to gain stakeholder support for lower interest rates, a debt equity swap, or even forgiveness of some of the debt. The projections should be realistic but should leave plenty of room to hit the targets agreed with the banks.[820] Doing so will go a long way toward solidifying a working relationship built on mutual confidence.

At Humana Inc., which jointly operated hospital and health insurance businesses, management decided to split the businesses through a corporate spin-off because it realized they were strategically incompatible; that is, the customers of one business were competitors with the other.[821] A divestment program such as this makes sense from a company-wide point of view, however, the Turnaround Leader needs to remember that a manager will most likely not come up with a suggestion to divest their own business unit and will probably fight against the proposed plans. Therefore the evaluation of a business unit to be divested should not be done by the people who work there but by the TMT. Companies or business units that no longer fit into the core business and are not contributing a positive cash flow should be divested. If their return on investment is not too bad they could be sold rather than liquidated.

Divestment

The focus of divestment is the sale of significant parts of the business (division or operating subsidiaries) rather than the disposal of current assets or sale of surplus plant and machinery,

---

[819] compare (Slatter & Lovett, 2004, p. 226)
[820] (Bibeault, 1981, p. 216)
[821] compare (Simonsen & Cassady, 2007, p. 6)

which are part of crisis management.[822] The divestment strategy is an important part of product-market refocusing since assets are liquidated while the company cuts down on its products, business areas, and customers. A simple but powerful approach used by some multi-business managers is to sort their individual businesses into three broad portfolio categories: sources of growth (future earnings); sources of current and intermediate earnings; and sources of immediate cash flow.[823] There is also a distinction between an immediate liquidation and a successive liquidation.[824] If possible, one should choose a successive liquidation since liquidating a company successively can help to maximize the cash flow from that unit by lowering market entry barriers.[825]

Divestment can have negative effects on the remaining workforce so it is important to communicate it properly.[826]

Responsibility

The Turnaround Leader is responsible for this subcomponent.

---

[822] (Slatter & Lovett, 2004, p. 85)
[823] (Bibeault, 1981, p. 301)
[824] (Krystek, 1987, p. 260), (Müller, 1986, p. 153)
[825] (DeWitt, Harrigan, & Newmann, 1998, p. 32), compare (Krystek, 1987, p. 260) and (Müller, 1986, p. 153)
[826] compare (Kieser, 2002, p. 33f)

SR CS 4 – Licensing Products

Summary

Licensing products or parts of products can be a way to save costs, to enter new markets, or to gain a strategic advantage.

Context

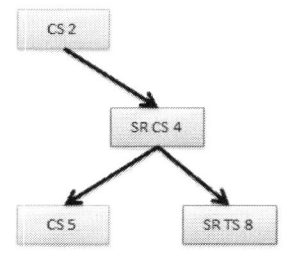

Description of the Subcomponent

In some cases, cash can be generated in the medium term and costs can be saved by licensing a product or service. The company sells the license to produce a product or offer a service to a competitor or a company that operates in a similar field.

In the context of a turnaround, licensing a product is a dramatic way of outsourcing it. The company allows another entity to produce, market, and sell the company's product in a certain market under certain conditions and according to the turnaround company's specifications, and the turnaround company receives a royalty in return. By licensing its property, the company granting the license can take advantage of foreign production without having to invest in it and without taking on managerial responsibilities.[827] Therefore licensing is a quick way of dramatically reducing costs.

---

[827] compare (Lymbersky C., 2008, p. 74)

Responsibility

The Turnaround Leader is responsible for this subcomponent.

SR CS 5 – Outsourcing

Summary

By outsourcing some parts of a production, development, or sales process the company can free up resources, reduce costs, and gain a strategic advantage.

Context

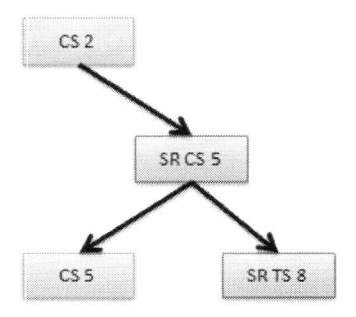

Description of the Subcomponent

Strategic outsourcing, when it is done right, is essential to any successful turnaround.[828] Outsourcing in this context refers to the outsourcing of processes that the company has been doing itself but that can be done just as well by other companies. Such activities can be supportive in nature or they can be core processes.

Activities are outsourced to improve quality, cost, or time. In order to assess which processes can be outsourced, a detailed analysis of the company's processes is carried out looking at the following factors:

- Contribution margin – How much, if any, profit does the activity add to the company?
- Costs – Can another company perform the activity more cheaply and will its overhead costs be lower?
- Added value – Will outsourcing the process bring added value in terms of reputation, profit, expertise gained, and so on?

---

[828] (Roman, 2010, p. 186)

- Competitive advantage – Will competitive advantage be gained?
- Dependencies – If the process is outsourced how high are the dependencies on another company?
- Will outsourcing the activity damage the company's trademarks?

Some firms may be able to move progressively in the short term to outsourced production by outsourcing low-end product(s) and concentrating in-house production on items that are more expensive and of higher quality. The company may also choose to outsource some parts of production by buying partially ready products. Some companies can outsource their HR, accounting, marketing, or IT services to other companies, a choice that gives the troubled company more flexibility if the marketing agency loses its creativity, if a new company emerges with cheaper prices for its services, or if demand falls, especially if the company does not share in fixed costs.

Any calculation of potential savings brought by outsourcing an activity usually fails to identify significant losses of efficiency early in the process.[829] These efficiency losses can occur because the other company needs to adjust to the activity, to set up additional facilities, or to train people to handle the job well. Quality controls may have to be installed to ensure that the products that are bought instead of produced in-house are of acceptable quality.

Outsourcing needs to be treated carefully as it can lead to the company gaining, but also losing, competitive advantages. It can also lead to a loss of customer loyalty and brand reputation. The rationale behind outsourcing is to focus on profitable components where the company has a relative advantage and to outsource the remainder to third parties who can perform them more effectively.[830] Outsourcing was traditionally done with support activities that are not core to the business, such as marketing, IT, and non-critical production stages. More and more companies, however, apply it to core functions as they restructure to focus on only one or two crucial activities in order to be more efficient and to cut costs in areas that can be managed more cheaply by someone else. In a turnaround situation the focus will probably lie heavily on cutting costs since otherwise-allocated capital can be freed up from the sale of assets that are not needed anymore. However, outsourcing makes sense only if someone else can handle the

---

[829] (Roman, 2010, p. 185)
[830] (Slatter & Lovett, 2004, p. 86)

activities more cheaply and the outsourcing makes the company more effective by enabling it to focus on profitable activities in which it has an advantage over its competitors.

Before business existing vendors is started or internal production is terminated, the company should carry out test runs where possible as an added precaution, although time constraints often render such tests impossible. A longer-term solution may be the radical restructuring of the entire company by, for example, transforming the business from a manufacturer and supplier into a brand-holder.[831]

Responsibility

The Turnaround Leader is responsible for this subcomponent.

---

[831] (Slatter & Lovett, 2004, p. 241)

SR CS 6 – Discontinuing Products

Summary

Halting the sale and/or production of certain products or product lines is a strategic decision.

Context

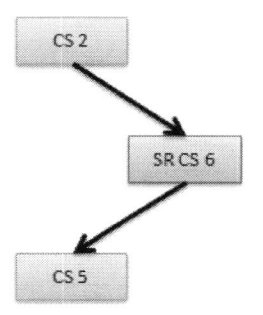

Description of the Subcomponent

When a product or whole product line is discontinued, resources that can be either used as cash savings to pay off a loan or put to better use are freed up. With fewer inventories to be bought more cash is available. With less direct labor to be put into the creation and sale of the product, cash is saved. The company's operations are simplified, saving additional cash from reduced overhead costs, and machinery is either available for other products or sold off.

The decision to discontinue a product or product line should be made after price changes are considered, since changing a price can sometimes make a product profitable again. If the product is aimed at the wrong market and is losing money in its current market, halting production may be the best option until the product can be refocused in SR CS 7 (Product Shift). AirTran reduced its costs by focusing on its most profitable routes and eliminating unprofitable ones.[832]

---

[832] compare (Rajendar, 2007, pp. 18-28)

Responsibility

The Turnaround Leader is responsible for deciding which products, if any, are to be discontinued.

SR CS 7 – Product Shift

Summary

Products are shifted to new markets or market segments.

Context

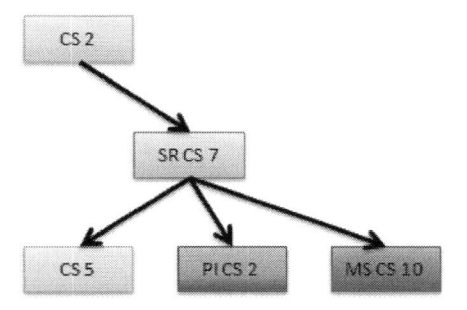

Description of the Subcomponent

Shifting a product from one market to another can be done in the Crisis Stabilization Stage if the product is clearly focused on the wrong market and the shift can be done without major investments in product development, production, or marketing. The Turnaround Leader should consider that a product that is somewhat profitable but could be earning more if directed to another market might be better left untouched in the Crisis Stabilization Stage if the costs of introducing the product into a new market are high enough to bind financial resources needed elsewhere at that stage. In that case the shift should be made in the Turnaround Stage—when more financial resources are freed up products can be strategically refocused.

Studies have shown that managers with short tenures are more likely to implement strategic changes that move the company into new industries or product segments when old products become obsolete than those with long tenures.[833] In the AirTran case, for example, when competitors such as Delta and Southwest were targeting leisure travelers, AirTran targeted business travelers.

---

[833] (Barker & Duhaime, 1997), (Barker III & Patterson Jr., 1996) and (Barker III, Pattersion Jr., & Mueller, 2001)

Responsibility

The Turnaround Leader is responsible for this subcomponent, although what kind of shift makes sense and is necessary should be closely evaluated with the marketing department.

SR CS 8 – Exploiting Existing Products

Summary

Exploiting existing products refers to the evaluation of whether an existing product can be exploited more than it already is by making small changes to the product itself or to its marketing.

Context

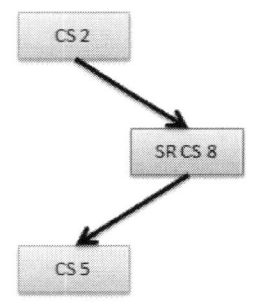

Description of the Subcomponent

It is important to get as much as possible out of existing products. One should not pay too much attention to the theoretical concept of product life cycles; if product life cycles always applied McDonald's would no longer be serving fries. Instead of halting production of its Big Mac, McDonald's develops variations. A product that has never been adapted to changing customer requirements and has never been developed further may lose demand at some point, but the concept of the product life cycle demonstrates that adaptations and changes are necessary, not that all products come to the end of their lives. In some cases, not even adaptations to the product itself are necessary if the way of marketing the product changes. For example, Coca-Cola has not changed much since the first bottle was produced (besides the absence of real cocaine in the drink, of course), but the marketing always adapts to changing conditions.

Another example is Audi, which in 2009 started selling the 2000 model Audi A4 with a facelift but the old technology, branded as the new Seat Exeo.

Responsibility

The Turnaround Leader is responsible for this subcomponent, with the assistance of the marketing department and, possibly, outside consultants.

SR CS 9 – Downsizing

Summary

Downsizing operations is a common strategy to adapt to changed market conditions or demand.

Context

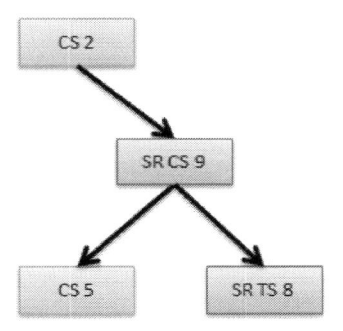

```
         CS 2
          │
          ▼
        SR CS 9
        ╱     ╲
       ▼       ▼
     CS 5    SR TS 8
```

Description of the Subcomponent

If the company experiences a strong decline in revenue, such as from $100 million to $50 million per year, the rule of thumb is that the costs should decrease by half as well. While this kind of decrease is not always possible, it is necessary in order to continue to operate profitably. For example, if a retailer has 20 stores and two production facilities, one way of downsizing would be to close ten stores and one production facility. The owner might end up with 12 stores and one production facility if some stores are critical in terms of representation and brand image, but the costs for those two additional stores would have to be covered by the earnings from the other ten.

A good way to look at downsizing is by taking a look at the history the company. When the company was still growing, it may have had only $50 million in revenue. If it was operating profitably at that time the old company structure could provide clues as to how the organization should be downsized.

There are many financial implications to downsizing to be considered such as whether a cash forecast can be estimated based on the company's current situation. If the company starts with 20 retail locations and after downsizing has 12 retailers left, the cash forecast should be adapted to reflect this as it is unlikely that the revenue with 12 retailers will be the same as it was with 20.

The Downsizing Selection Component

Once the future organizational chart is created, decisions can be made about which facilities to close or sell off. The list should be built in a way that will be as beneficial as possible for the firm, and the localities should be ranked based on productivity and profitability criteria.

One ranking methodology is Expedient Ranking (XPeRank), a methodology for selecting a part of a group of many similar units (e.g. workers as part of a team, retail store locations as part of a chain store, bolts as part of a lot of many similar bolts), based on the combination of multiple performance and/or characteristics criteria.[834]

If ten out of 20 retailers are losing money, the costs of keeping the losing ten exceed their income. The priority is to examine these ten stores and find the ones that can be restructured quickly and the ones that, if they closed, would not have too much effect on others. Let's say we find that one store that is losing money is critical because it is in a premium location where it is generating brand awareness. If other stores could not generate this brand awareness they would sell less as well. If we also find that three other stores are currently losing money but can be restructured quickly to be profitable, we close the other eight and restructure the four as far as possible. In this case, we will have lower overall revenue, say 40 percent lower, but we will also have well over 40 percent lower costs. We might still lose money but we'll lose it at a slower rate, giving us enough time to restructure the stores we need to restructure so they can become profitable. If we still don't have enough money, we may have to use one of the other strategies or close down more stores instead of restructuring them. However, other revenue-generating strategies might kick in, such as opening up an online store, a partnership, and so on.

---

[834] (Roman, 2010, p. 139), for a detailed example of XPeRanking, see (Roman, 2010, pp. 140-158)

Responsibility

The Turnaround Leader is responsible for this subcomponent.

SR CS 10 – Building Competitive Advantages

Summary

Finding new competitive advantages and building on existing ones are important for the business's ability to survive in the long term.

Context

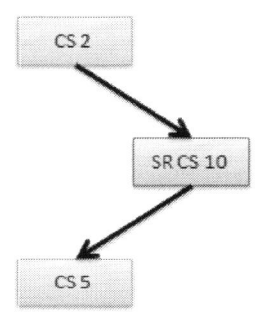

Description of the Subcomponent

A company's competitive position influences its turnaround.[835] Therefore, building competitive advantages is important for the turnaround as well as for the company's ability to survive in the long term. A company without competitive advantages is not likely to survive.

Making a company fit for the future often requires the building of new core competencies which go beyond a single business unit—in terms of the investment that is required and the range of potential applications.[836] In a turnaround situation the whole company is suffering, therefore the competitive advantages need to be developed corporation-wide.

Responsibility

The Turnaround Leader is responsible for this subcomponent.

---

[835] (Hofer, 1980)
[836] (Hamel & Prahalad, 1996)

SR CS 11 – Apologizing to Customers

Summary

Apologizing to customers for prior bad decisions can be a way to regain the trust that was lost.

Context

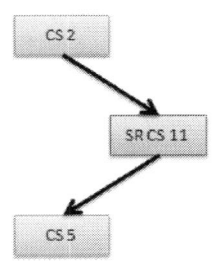

Description of the Subcomponent

Some companies with substantial financial power or a monopoly try to force products or product specifications on their customers. P&G did this when entering the Japanese Market. Cisco did it for a while with telecommunication companies, selling its customers gear that could not easily be integrated with the phone companies' existing switches.[837] In 2003, Chambers, the CEO of Cisco, called top telecom executives to apologize for his past arrogance.[838]

In a lot of countries and cultures an apology is a sign of strength and marks the start of a new beginning and leadership style. Recognizing one's mistakes is the first step to making things better. Most customers will respect this step and might give the management or the company another chance even though they have been disappointed in the past.

Responsibility

The Turnaround Leader is responsible for this subcomponent.

---

[837] compare (Rajendar, 2007, p. 35)
[838] (BusinessWeek, 2003)

Strategic Restructuring During the Turnaround Stage (SR TS)

The stabilization and return to growth strategy should be customer-centric.[839] The strategies proposed in this stage focus on improving customer relationships, gaining new customers and new business, as well as building on competitive strength.

---

[839] (Roman, 2010, p. 267)

SR TS 1 – Revise the Mission Statement

Summary

In some cases, the mission statement should be revised. The purpose of this subcomponent is to ensure that the mission statement created in SR CS 1 remains applicable.

Context

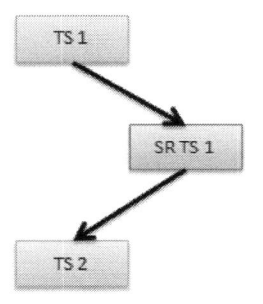

Description of the Subcomponent

During the Turnaround Stage the mission statement may have to be revised to account for changes that were not foreseen at the beginning of the Crisis Stabilization Stage. These changes can include the sale of a business and the adaptation of a product to a new customer segment. In order to be as accurate as possible the changed circumstances need to be reflected.

Responsibility

The Turnaround Leader is responsible for this subcomponent.

SR TS 2 – Growth via Acquisition

Summary

Acquiring another company or business unit can be a quick way out of a crisis situation, but it is also costly and may not be available to businesses that do not have a strong financial background.

Context

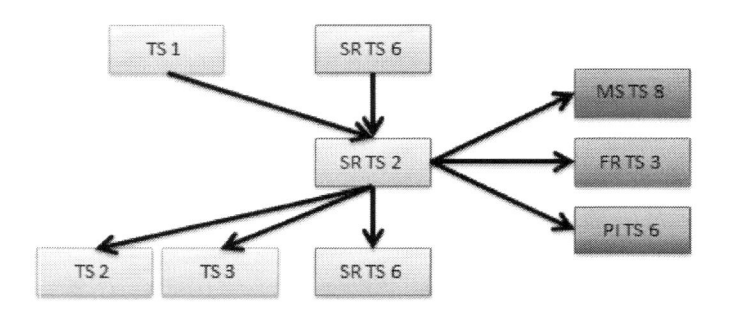

Description of the Subcomponent

We define an acquisition as a strategy though which one firm buys a controlling, 100 percent interest in another firm with the intent of making it a subsidiary business.[840] Acquisitions are often used to turn around companies under no threat of running out of cash any time soon but where growth has been static for some time.[841] However, this strategy is not available to many troubled companies since they are usually characterized by poor financial performance. The benefit of growth by acquisition as opposed to organic growth is the increased speed at which turnaround can be achieved.[842] In some cases an acquisition is one of the medium-term goals of the Turnaround Plan once enough cash has been freed up.

An acquisition target could be a competitor or a company that complements the business. Acquisition of a competitor could be a solution if the troubled company is suffering under an

---

[840] (Hoskisson, Hitt, Ireland, & Harrison, 2007, p. 245)
[841] (compare S.L., Corp. Rec. p. 226)
[842] (S.L., Corp. Rec. p. 226)

extreme price war or if it has no other way of growing in the existing market but needs higher turnover in order to survive in the long term. The acquisition of a complementary company makes sense if the other company is, for example, an essential supplier offering its products at excessively high prices because it has high margins.

Acquiring another firm can be useful if the business can be integrated quickly into the company and if overheads can be slashed.[843] If there is enough time, the company may also buy another firm with several business units but only integrate the useful parts of the other business, disposing of the others (preferably at a profit).

A takeover is a special type of acquisition strategy wherein the targeted firm does not solicit the acquiring firm's bid.[844] In order to take over a company or to merge with another firm a due diligence is necessary.

The following is advice for business acquisitions in this stage:[845]

- Concentrate buying efforts on companies with a significant amount of cash and a high capacity for debt.
- Don't buy a company just to do something; don't overpay and make a deal that is only marginal.
- Take the time to select the right company and don't jump into a deal that just looks good.
- Take the time to evaluate the company and the possible gains from it. Remember that takeovers are also a reason for healthy companies to fail. There is an even bigger chance to fail with a weakened company.
- Don't over-leverage to make acquisitions.

When making a move to acquire another company the TMT should be careful. The failure rate of mergers and acquisitions is somewhere between 70 and 90 percent.[846] A company that is already in a weak position may not have the resources if it needs to invest more than planned to prevent the acquisition from failing.

---

[843] (Bhatia, 2002, p. 226)
[844] (Hoskisson, Hitt, Ireland, & Harrison, 2007, p. 245)
[845] (Bibeault, 1981, p. 339)
[846] (Christensen, Alton, Rising, & Waldeck, 2011)

The dangers of growth by acquisition are the same for turnaround firms as they are for healthy firms. The acquisition price is too high, post-acquisition management is poor, the acquired firm's financial or market position is weaker than anticipated, and so on.[847] However, a firm that has financial difficulties and makes an acquisition during a crisis situation runs a higher risk than a financially healthy company.

Diversification via Acquisition

In industries that are dying out or where the market is highly competitive, the troubled company may choose to acquire a business that is not operating within the same industry. Diversification via the acquisition of unrelated businesses provides the means for entering product-market areas where the profit and growth opportunities are better for the turnaround firm.[848]

Several studies have shown that diversification as a business strategy does not pay off for the shareholders[849] and that the financial gains of the transaction usually go to the shareholders of the company being sold rather than the one making the acquisition. However, these studies have not looked at turnaround candidates. According to Porter, a successful diversification meets three difficult conditions: [850]

- *The Attractiveness Test:* "The industries that are chosen for diversification must be structurally attractive or capable of being made attractive."
- *The Cost-of-Entry Test:* The costs associated with entering the market must be higher than the expected profits.
- *The Better-off Test:* Either the acquired business unit or a business unit of the acquiring firm must be better off after the acquisition.

Porter's studies show that the strategic results of companies that ignored these tests were unfavorable.[851]

---

[847] (Slatter & Lovett, 2004, p. 228)
[848] (Slatter & Lovett, 2004, p. 226)
[849] compare (Slatter & Lovett, 2004, p. 228)
[850] (Porter M. E., 1999, p. 144)
[851] compare (Porter M. E., 1999, p. 144)

The diversification strategy via acquisition is not a very likely one; however, it could be a solution for a company that does not have serious financial issues.

Growth via Acquisition

An acquisition during the Turnaround Stage usually makes sense if the company wants to grow in a certain market. This strategy is seldom available to companies in financial crisis; instead, it is used to achieve sustainable recovery once a turnaround process has passed the most critical stages. It is also available to companies that are in good financial health but in a stagnant position. Growth via acquisition does not necessarily mean that the company is diversifying its product range; it can also be used to acquire a competitor in order to gain more market share or end a price war.

There are several reasons for using an acquisition strategy; however, an acquisition might not always lead to a competitive advantage.[852]

Responsibility

The Turnaround Leader is responsible for this subcomponent.

---

[852] (Hoskisson, Hitt, Ireland, & Harrison, 2007, p. 245)

SR TS 3 – Refocusing

Summary

Refocusing can take three dimensions: focusing on activities and processes; geographic focusing; and strategic focusing.

Context

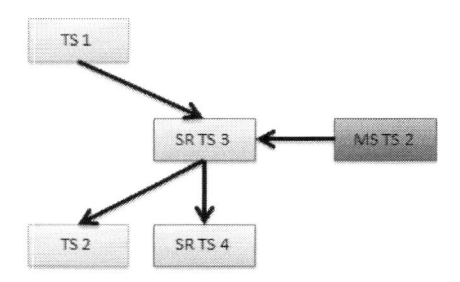

Description of the Subcomponent

Refocusing can be done in any of three dimensions. The first, redefining the business, involves the divestment of subcompanies, businesses, and/or products. The second dimension is the concentration on one or more business activities or processes, and the third involves focusing on certain geographical markets. Regardless of the dimensions the TMT chooses for the troubled firm, it must deploy the two key generic strategies of business redefinition and divestment.[853] The first step is to identify what the future business will be, how likely the company is to survive in these industries, and how much can be obtained by selling off the other businesses.

This identification component is usually not difficult but it must be done quickly. The Turnaround Leader should determine which business units are generating positive cash flow, have a strong management, have the potential to grow, and have genuine competitive advantage. A good way to visualize which businesses are able to survive is to use a policy matrix. The market attractiveness/business position matrix (DPM) can be used to assess the relative

---

[853] compare (Slatter & Lovett, 2004, p. 223)

attractiveness of investing in particular businesses in order to determine appropriate strategic planning goals and funding/manpower.[854] This method plots market attractiveness (vertically) against competitive position (horizontally).[855]

However, the number of factors considered on the arises of the model and the relative weighting are based on the manager's subjective judgments.[856]

Redefining the Core Business

Redefining the core business in a turnaround situation usually involves a fundamental change in the future direction of an organization and a radical restructuring as large chunks of the business are sold off.[857] Undertaking this process also refocuses the business in a certain area and reduces its activities in others.

An example of a company that refocused is British Aerospace (BAe). In the early 1990s, BAe was manufacturing cars (Rover), military aircraft (Tornado jets), airplanes (in a partnership with Airbus), and corporate jets. It was also involved in a construction company (Ballast Needham) and the communications industry (through stakes in Orange). In 1992, BAe found itself in serious trouble and the management quickly realized that, in order to become profitable again, the company had to redefine its business and restructure its operations. The management team knew that its best position and strength was in the military aircraft industry, so the sale of Rover to its former competitor BMW was the logical consequence. To gain even more cash for the necessary restructuring component, BAe sold its corporate jet business and the construction company; it did not need the construction company anymore, and the corporate jet business was hitting a point at which new investments were necessary to develop new products. It sold its stake in Orange in 1994, concluding the refocus.

Another example of redefining the core business as part of a turnaround strategy is the German company ASC. In 1979, a group of investors put Günter Müller in charge of rescuing the company, the core business of which was to develop hi-fi appliances. Müller saw that the client base for its turntables and tape recorders was very small so he put a border around the market.

---

[854] (Dibb, Simkin, & Bradley, 1996, p. 60)
[855] (Wickham, 2000, p. 292)
[856] (Drummond & Ensor, 2005, p. 118)
[857] (S.L., Corp. Rec. p. 221)

He then started to produce language teaching appliances from which he calculated a yearly turnover growth of six to eight percent. About ten years later, Müller had to shift the core business again to digital teaching appliances, and in 2000 he shifted the company to become a software firm.[858]

Concentration on Processes and Activities

To explain this refocusing dimension, consider a vertically integrated company. Coffee is planted and harvested, then it is roasted and prepared. Next, the coffee is distributed to wholesalers and then to company-owned shops. Finally, the coffee is sold in the company's own retail shops.

When the company decides that it should focus its business on only a few steps out of the business line, it is concentrating its focus. There are several examples of companies that have done exactly this in a turnaround situation. For example, Laura Ashley was initially involved in manufacturing and retailing but later focused on retailing only. Lonrho Textiles did the opposite and focused on manufacturing only.

Geographical Refocusing

Many successful domestic organizations hit trouble when they move overseas, and the solution frequently involves a repositioning of the group away from international operations and toward domestic business.[859] In other words, the company goes back to its roots and focuses on those markets in which it was once successful. Companies can be very successful in some markets but fail in others, and the reasons can differ widely. However, a successful market entry strategy often involves a heavy weight of cultural factors in the market selection component.[860] If the firm was running the business itself in the foreign market through a subsidiary, it might be cheaper to export the products or to license them out.[861]

There are three additional reasons why a company may choose to enter a new geographic market, which are to pursue risk diversification, growth in foreign markets, growth in client

---

[858] compare (Schmalholz, 2009)
[859] (Slatter & Lovett, 2004, p. 223)
[860] compare ((Lymbersky C. , 2008)
[861] compare (Nieschlag, Dichtl, & Hörschgen, 2002, p. 216ff)

accounts, and/or economies of scale.[862] For many companies, growing internationally is the only option by which to grow and utilize their full capacities.[863] Foreign business is usually more expensive than local business so a careful calculation that includes all market entry costs is necessary.[864]

Strategic Focus

Companies that underperform over a long period of time are usually facing strategic issues. Strategic problems should always be treated as a high priority because they have an impact on why the company survives in the first place. In order to survive in the long term, a company must serve its customers with a product or service that generates returns that are higher than its costs and its cost of capital.

Troubled companies rarely have robust and viable strategies.[865] Often, a formal strategy has not been clearly articulated and written down, which can result in confusion across the organization. Other companies might have a strategy, but either it is based on unrealistic long-term goals or it doesn't make common sense; sometimes these kinds of strategies are more like slogans than a clear direction. In other cases, the company has a sound strategy in place but lacks the required resources to fulfill it and to gain a competitive advantage over its competitors. These problems must be addressed in a Turnaround Plan. Even though a turnaround needs to be quick as it is often done in an emergency situation, the principles of strategic planning still apply and are central to the long-term survival of the company. Therefore, a Turnaround Plan must be in line with the long-term strategic direction.

It is important not to destroy resources by disposing of divisions, machinery, or people that are important to the company's long-term survival. The strategy should incorporate a simple definition of the goals and objectives of the business and should encompass the "what" and the "how" of the strategy: what products/services is the company going to deliver, to whom, and how? The goals outlined in the strategy must be achievable with current resources. Once this is done, the strategy must be communicated throughout the organization.

---

[862] (Kottier & Bliemel, 2001, p. 621)
[863] compare (Clasen, 1992, p. 294)
[864] (Sloma, 1985, pp. 165-166)
[865] (Slatter & Lovett, 2004, p. 83)

It might be advisable to introduce two strategies: one that is valid for the turnaround time and tackles issues that are important at the time of distress, and a second strategy that focuses on long-term goals. "The strategy for the turnaround time must [...] focus on the key success factors at the heart of the recovery plan since they provide the parameters within which the entire plan must be developed."[866] The long-term strategy must incorporate the changes that are made to the organization in terms of resources, direction, business areas, and capacities and focus on a profitable long-term future. However, the two strategies should be aligned and consistent so the stakeholders know what is important in the short and medium term, and also what the focus in the long term will be.

An important part of developing a strategy is to have a clear understanding of the customers' needs and the product-market mix that defines what products will be sold to which customers. It is often better to be 80 percent right and act than to wait to be 100 percent right and miss the opportunity.[867] Furthermore, the approach must be bold and broad. A Turnaround Leader should not postpone major strategic changes using the excuse of not having enough time for sound analysis.

Redefining the Business

Redefining the business is the most fundamental form of strategic change. The long-term goals and objectives of the organization are changed, the management's mindset changes, and the nature of the business is redefined.[868] This is the case when, for example, an organization was producing products in various business areas and, after the turnaround, focuses on only one business area. It is not unusual for a company to sell parts of its business or to close them down altogether if cash is urgently needed or if the business units are simply not profitable enough. A company that is running multiple components may choose to focus on one process or activity after the turnaround and outsource the others. These are fundamental strategic changes.

Responsibility

The Turnaround Leader is responsible for this subcomponent.

---

[866] (Slatter & Lovett, 2004, p. 84)
[867] (Slatter & Lovett, 2004, p. 84)
[868] (Slatter & Lovett, 2004, p. 84)

SR TS 4 – Product-Market Refocusing

Summary

This subcomponent is about refocusing products towards a new market or market segment. Product-market refocusing involves developing and investing in some businesses while at the same time neglecting or divesting others.[869]

Context

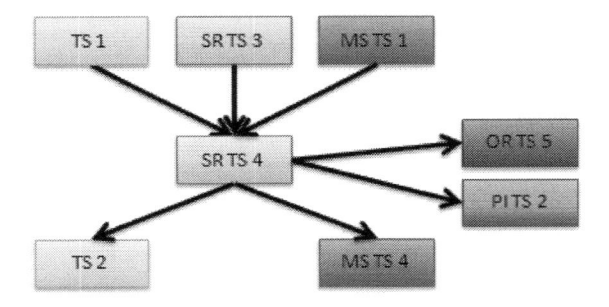

Description of the Subcomponent

If the company has lost its competitiveness in its market or market segment it must focus on a new market or develop competiveness in its old market in order to recover. This subcomponent deals with refocusing the overall product-market strategy. When a company grows too quickly and cannot adapt to the additional workload, their processes or staff must change. When profits decline as sales continue to grow, there is usually a need to refocus the firm's product-market strategy since much of the marginal business the firm has obtained is unlikely to be profitable.[870]

The refocusing component can involve one or more of the following actions:

- Product lines can be added or removed from the company's product portfolio.

---

[869] (Bhatia, 2002, p. 224)
[870] (Slatter & Lovett, 2004, p. 232)

- Customers can be added or removed from the targeted customer segment by redefining who they are in terms of customer type and where they are from (geographic market).
- Marketing can be concentrated on certain products or customers, which will constitute a change in the sales mix.
- The company can leave a market segment.
- The company can enter a new product-market segment.

If the company's core business is viable but the turnaround is urgently needed, the TMT may decide to divest what is unprofitable or does not generate the required return on the capital employed; it may decide to divest a specific business area, remove products, and/or leave a customer segment. This is especially important in cases where time is a factor and where there are not enough time and resources to turn around all business areas in order to achieve a turnaround for the core business. A turnaround is more difficult to achieve where the core business itself is not competitive and unlikely to survive, in which case the chances of successful turnaround are slim and the company is likely to fail eventually.[871] In this case, the TMT may choose to examine whether an acquisition of a competitor, or even a shift into another industry, is possible with the available and obtainable cash.

A focus strategy can give the company some time to achieve sustainable growth again, especially if the targeted segment is too small for a big competitor to compete in or if the turnaround company can provide better service to customers than a bigger competitor.

Shift in Sales Mix

Another less dramatic possibility is to concentrate the marketing efforts on selected products. The same can be done with production priorities. The goal is to focus on segments or customers where the short term potential for profit is the greatest. The literature provides several criteria that can be used to determine which product or products should be emphasized:

- *Sales Volume:* Products that have high sales volumes are usually more attractive because they provide better opportunities for leverage.

---

[871] (Slatter & Lovett, 2004, p. 233)

- *Growth Rate:* **Products that have declining growth rates often have a weak competitive position, are due for replacement, or are at the end of their life cycle.**
- *Brand Loyalty:* **Products that have strong brand loyalty can be cash cows even if they have low sales volumes or growth rates.**
- *Contribution Margin or Gross Margin:* **If the sales volume, growth rate, or brand loyalty are indifferent then the product with the higher contribution or gross margin is preferred.**
- *Speed of Buyer Response:* **Marketing efforts usually have more effect on products such as consumer goods and lead to sales increases. Products like industrial goods are not affected as much by marketing efforts.**
- *Seasonality:* **Some products sell better at certain times of the year.**
- *Manufacturing Cycle:* **The less time it takes to produce and sell a product, the faster the profits can be realized.**

Product/Market Matrix

To assess its current strategic market position a business should determine its position on a product/market evolution/competitive position matrix.[872] If the firm's position is weak it may have no other option than to liquidate or use niche marketing.

A business should also assess its strategic position in its distribution system. The appropriate distribution system for a product often changes as the industry producing it matures. Therefore, a company should always be searching for opportunities and threats from changes in the distribution system of its industry.[873]

Customer Analysis

The process of analyzing customers is similar to the product analysis. In an ideal case a customer profitability analysis is done with each customer, but this approach is seldom possible if the company does not have sophisticated business information systems. Many companies have failed because of inadequate analysis and understanding of where profits and losses are made.[874] Another solution is to segment the customers into groups with similar characteristics

---

[872] (Hofer, 1980)
[873] compare (Hofer, 1980)
[874] (Slatter & Lovett, 2004, p. 235)

such as size, industry, or location. The key is to determine profitability, which is missing in the management accounting systems of most troubled companies. Assessing profitability is important as the largest customers are not always the most profitable because of special rates that the customer has been given, or because the customer buys products with low gross margins. The goal of a customer profitability analysis is to find out how much each customer contributes to the success of the business after overhead costs and after tied up interest charges associated with the customer on the working capital have been deducted.

If the customer evaluation is done with customer groups rather than individual customers, the result of the analysis may not show individual unprofitable customers. A group analysis involves a number of assumptions about allocation of overheads and the appropriate grouping of customers, but whatever assumptions are used—and several alternatives should be used, particularly for customer segmentation—startling results may emerge.[875]

Product-Market Refocusing—the Second Step

Once the right products for concentrated marketing efforts have been selected and the customer to be focused on has been identified, the firm can commence its focused marketing activities. Porter wrote that a firm has three generic strategies available to protect itself against competition within an industry: cost leadership, differentiation, and focus, which is a combination of differentiation and cost leadership. Focus is probably the best strategy for a turnaround firm, since limited resources can be focused on a few products and customers segments. A situation in which the only option was a cost leadership strategy might not be survivable for the company. However, where product differentiation is possible, an aggressive marketing strategy can help to recover a stronger market position, assuming that it is not an out-of-date product. If a new product needs to be developed a lot of advertising activity is usually required. A product differentiation strategy is only possible after the survival of the company has been assured.[876]

Dangers of the Focusing Strategy

There are four primary dangers that the TMT must be aware of if a focus strategy is chosen:

---

[875] (Slatter & Lovett, 2004, p. 234)
[876] (Slatter & Lovett, 2004, p. 235)

- It may cause the firm's unit cost structure to deteriorate as volume and economies of scale are reduced.[877] The result may be increases in fixed and variable costs.
- The choice to employ a focus strategy may not be the right choice for the long term, as is often the case in those situations where focusing means adopting a segment-retreat strategy. In a segment-retreat strategy the firm pulls out of the high-volume, price-sensitive segments where having lower unit costs than one's competitors is not so critical for success.[878]
- If the focus strategy is not implemented quickly enough the company is in danger of failing as, by the time it has focused its resources, any competitive advantage it may have had in the focus segment has been eroded, or their resources have been so depleted that no additional resources are available for implementing the focused strategy.[879]
- The products and customer segment chosen at the beginning of the Turnaround Stage may not be the right choice for future development. Hence, the choice should be re-evaluated when the most pressing stage has been completed, the survival of the company has been assured, and the preparation for the growth stage starts.

Cases in Which Product-Market Refocusing is not Possible

If the company cannot be made more profitable using focusing and cost reductions, the only alternative is to increase sales. However, increasing sales is possible only if the company has operational problems and minor problems with certain parts of the business—such as an inefficient sales team—that can be remedied by hiring better salespeople.

In mature markets the situation is more complicated because in order to increase the market share a significant competitive advantage is required.[880] However, turnaround firms often don't have these strong competitive advantages so a turnaround candidate might fail in that situation.

---

[877] (Slatter & Lovett, 2004, p. 236)
[878] (Slatter & Lovett, 2004, p. 236)
[879] (S.L., Corp. Rec. p. 237)
[880] compare (Porter M. E., 1999)

Product-Market Refocusing

The distressed firm has usually lost focus by adding products and customers while continuing to compete in all of its historical product or market segments.[881] Companies often make 80 percent of their revenues from 20 percent of their customers, so a good deal of business is done at a loss or break-even. In product-market refocusing the company re-evaluates what products it produces, whether they are profitable, and to whom they are sold. Some products are profitable only if a customer buys a certain amount. While it is important to distinguish customers the company serves at break-even in order to hold them for possible future gains or for publicity purposes, even these should be re-evaluated and possibly dropped. In the Crisis Stabilization Stage product-market refocusing involves focusing on profitable customers and products and dropping unprofitable ones.

At Cisco, Chambers (its CEO) changed the growth strategy by pursuing six new markets, including security and net phones. Over half of its $3.3 billion R&D budget in 2002 was spent on emerging markets. As a result, Cisco made headway in most new markets and 14 percent of its revenue in 2002 was earned from emerging markets.[882]

Responsibility

The Turnaround Leader is responsible for this subcomponent, with support from the marketing team.

---

[881] (S.L. Corp. Rec. p. 85)
[882] compare (Rajendar, 2007, p. 35)

SR TS 5 – Strategic Alliances

Summary

Forming an alliance with a suitable partner might be a good way to save resources and gain access to markets that have been unavailable before.

Description of the Subcomponent

An alliance can be understood as a joining of resources in order to reach a certain goal. In a turnaround situation an alliance might be very useful to lower costs and gain access to customers that the company otherwise has no means of reaching.

A turnaround firm should be able to provide a list of possible partners for an alliance.

There is always a risk of losing intellectual property or competitive advantage in an alliance, especially in joint ventures where both companies found a separate entity for the purpose of the alliance; however, the possible gains need to be bigger than the possible risks.

The general process in forming an alliance is:

Developing the Strategy: This involves studying the feasibility, goals, challenges, and possible gains of a strategic alliance. The objectives of the alliance need to be in line with the corporate strategies of both partners.

Assessing the Partner: Possible weaknesses and strengths of the partner need to be evaluated. If more than one partner is evaluated, selection criteria should be used. The motives of the partner need to be properly understood. The firm should make sure that the partner will not take advantage of the weak situation the company is in.

Negotiating the Contract: The objectives of both partners need to be negotiated as well as their goals. The contribution that each partner brings to the alliance needs to be part of this contract, as well as protection of proprietary information, penalties if a partner does not perform, and termination clauses.

Alliance Operations: This step is about getting the senior management of both firms to commit to the goals of the alliance as well as finding the right people to manage the partnership, but it is also about how performance will be measured, agreement of escalation processes, and how results will be determined.

Termination of the Alliance: If the objectives of the alliance have been met, or if the objectives cannot be met anymore, the alliance will have to be terminated. This step describes how the termination would be wound up.

The advantages of strategic alliances are:

- Each partner can contribute what they do best by matching their capabilities.
- The partners can learn from each other.
- The organization might be more likely to survive due to the partner's strength and resources.

Responsibility

The Turnaround Leader is responsible for forming an alliance. The process should, however, be agreed by the Turnaround Advisory Board.

SR TS 6 – Mergers

Summary

Mergers are a strategic solution used to save operating costs.

Context

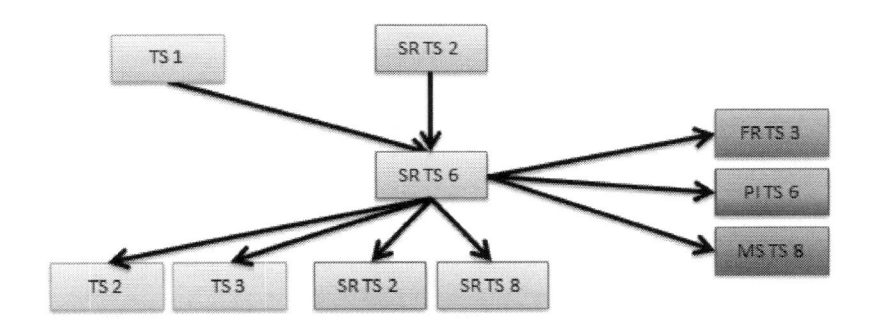

Description of the Subcomponent

A merger is a strategy through which two firms agree to integrate their operations on a relatively equal basis.[883] A merger between two companies can have a substantial impact on the resource requirements of both companies. Since one company often dominates the other, they are sometimes more like takeovers than mergers.

Mergers are typically used when operating costs can be substantially reduced. Chase Manhattan Bank and Chemical Bank used their merger as an opportunity to both reduce operating costs and achieve an important strategic objective.[884]

In a merger, some of the workforce is likely to be laid off. If that is the case, the responsible HR Turnaround Manager needs to decide how these layoffs are to be spread over the two companies. This decision can significantly impact the merger's integration process and how the

---

[883] (Hoskisson, Hitt, Ireland, & Harrison, 2007, pp. 244-245)
[884] compare (Simonsen & Cassady, 2007, p. 6)

stock market values the merger by sending employees and investors a signal about which is the dominant company.[885]

There are cartel laws that might restrict a company's freedom to merge or to cooperate with a competitor.[886] However, this is only the case if the company is quite dominant within its industry.

Responsibility

The Turnaround Leader is responsible for this subcomponent.

---

[885] compare (Dial & Murphey, 1995)
[886] (Krystek, 1987, p. 226)

SR TS 7 – Introducing New Products

Summary

If they can be developed and produced, new products may be a possible strategy to generate new sales.

Context

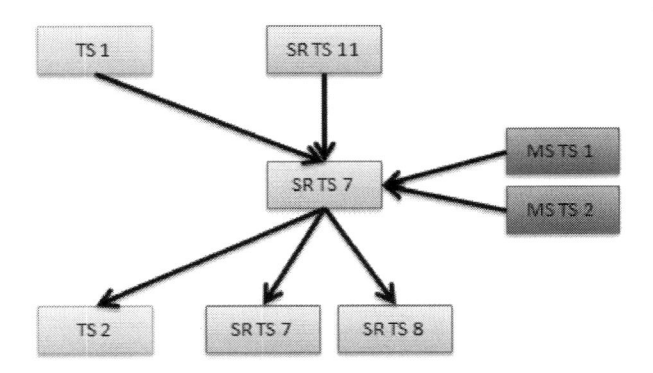

Description of the Subcomponent

Introducing a new product can be a source of new growth for the company, although doing so can entail significant costs associated with developing, producing, distributing, and marketing the product. In a crisis situation, when funding is short, investment in a new product must be particularly carefully considered, but it may be the only way out if the existing products are at the end of their life cycles or if they have non-repairable reputations. A business that has free production capacity, which is a common situation in a troubled company, can use this to produce additional products if they are not too cost-intensive. The urge to increase volume in order to utilize plant and marketing facilities and personnel more economically often leads a company to add new products to a line.[887] Whether an extension of the product line makes sense depends on several factors, including whether they sell through the same channels, appeal to similar consumer groups, move through the same markets, or require similar kinds and equal amounts of selling effort. Often what may seem to be an advantage of more complete

---

[887] (Bibeault, 1981, p. 332)

utilization of facilities and personnel can, in fact, be offset by the difficulties of training salespeople to sell a different type or a larger number of products.[888]

Responsibility

The Turnaround Leader is responsible for deciding which new products should be introduced, while the sales and production departments work on the products.

---

[888] (Bibeault, 1981, p. 322)

SR TS 8 – Re-evaluating the Organizational Structure

Summary

In this subcomponent the TMT analyzes whether the organizational structure is adequate for the changed circumstances.

Context

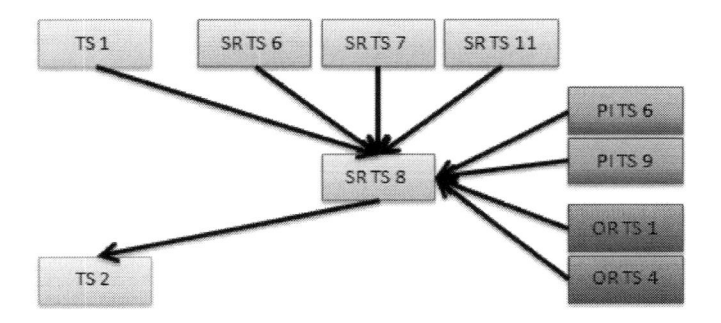

Description of the Subcomponent

The corporate structure may have changed during the Crisis Stabilization and Turnaround Stages, and the old organization of the company may no longer be adequate for the future of the company. Parts of the business may have been closed or sold, or new divisions may have been integrated. Therefore, an analysis of the company's organizational structure is necessary.

Robert Wilson,[889] who reorganized Memorex, scrapped the tightly centralized setup that was installed after he came aboard for a more decentralized structure that split the company into 44 business teams.[890] The result was that field managers had more responsibility for the performance of their units, and two executive vice presidents were hired to care for the day-to-day business so Wilson could focus on long-term strategic planning.

---

[889] (Forbes.com, 2010)
[890] (Bibeault, 1981, p. 360)

Responsibility

The Turnaround Leader is responsible for this subcomponent.

SR TS 9 – Corporate Name Change

Summary

A corporate name change may be a way out of a crisis if the reputation of the old company name is badly damaged.

Context

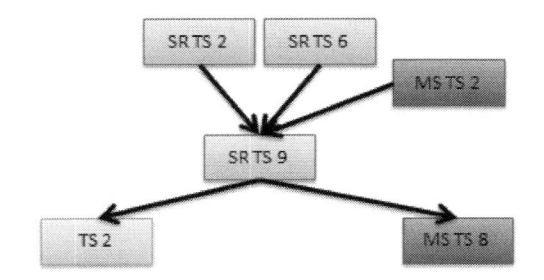

Description of the Subcomponent

This subcomponent can be synced with SR TS 6 (Mergers) or SR TS 2 (Growth via Acquisition). A corporate name change is useful when the company has a poor or irreparable customer image. However, building a new brand name requires considerable advertising expenditure. In 1982, when Datsun changed its name to Nissan in the US market, it spent over $200 million on advertising.[891]

Employees and other stakeholders can be very quick to interpret any change as a serious problem, a crisis, or shareholder pressure, especially when a new majority shareholder enters the company.[892] The situation needs to be properly explained to avoid confusion that can have a negative effect on the turnaround process. Along with changing the brand name a repositioning is usually required, which is quite a communications challenge.[893]

---

[891] compare (Aaker, 1993, p. 336)
[892] (Kapferer, 2001, p. 435)
[893] (Lagae, 2005, p. 80)

Another possibility is to acquire a competitor and use their brand name instead, with the advantage that the brand already exists, is known to at least some customers, and is not as damaged. In this way, the public will not necessarily recognize that the name change is for image reasons. In May 1996, a ValuJet flight crashed in the Everglades on its way from Miami to Atlanta, killing all 110 people on board. As the shock of the crash stayed in the minds of the general public a year after it resumed its air service, the company was renamed AirTran.[894] ValuJet continued operations under its new name and made a successful turnaround by also discontinuing unprofitable routes, modernizing the fleet, and so on.

Responsibility

The Turnaround Leader is responsible for this subcomponent.

---

[894] (Rajendar, 2007, p. 18)

SR TS 10 – Renewing Products

Summary

Renewing products may be necessary in order to keep up with the competition or to gain product features that the competition does not have.

Context

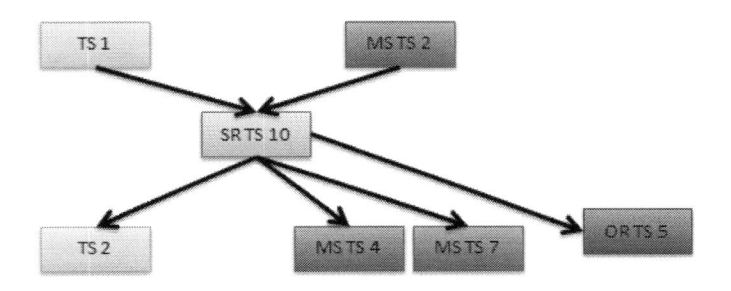

Description of the Subcomponent

Renewing products in order to adapt to changed market needs and developments can be employed in the Turnaround Stage. However, if significant cost-cutting is also an advantage and the investment in the new product pays off quickly, it can also be done in the Crisis Stabilization Stage.

In the case of AirTran,[895] the company invested in new fuel-saving airplanes and enhanced its safety record. One major reason for its profits was the replacement of the airline's obsolete DC-9 aircraft with new, more spacious Boeing 717s for short- and medium-range flights.

It was also part of Opel's (GM's German subsidiary) strategy to launch an all-new design of its middle class sedan, the Opel Vectra, as the Opel Insignia, as the Vectra did not enjoy a very good reputation and had a rather old design. It is not usual for a car maker to introduce new

---

[895] (Rajendar, 2007, p. 20)

cars with a complete design makeover and name unless the old models were not performing well at all.

Responsibility

The Turnaround Leader is responsible for deciding which products should be renewed, while the sales and production departments work on the products.

SR TS 11 – Building up a New Business

Summary

Building or entering a new business can be a strategic action in a crisis situation; it is, however, a fairly expensive turnaround strategy.

Context

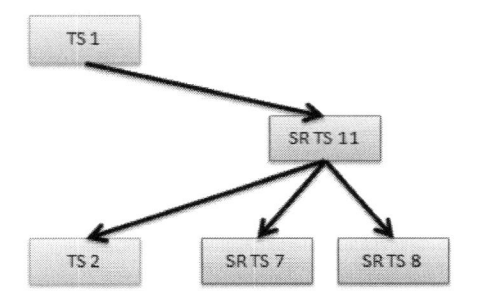

Description of the Subcomponent

Because of its capital requirements, building a new line of business should be done in the Turnaround Stage once cash has been freed up. The autonomous building up of a new business unit is especially difficult in a crisis situation so it is usually limited to areas in which the company has developed perquisites.[896] It is often difficult to find the talented management needed to build a business unit while still restructuring the rest of the company. However, if production or research capacities are free and would not be used or saved otherwise, it is possible to use these capacities for a new business unit.[897] In a recent study,[898] 37 percent of the companies in crisis that were evaluated built new business units. However, the restructuring situation is defined widely, so companies that did not hit serious crisis were included in the study as well.

---

[896] compare (Lafrenz, 2004, p. 130)
[897] compare (Müller, 1986, p. 159)
[898] (Barker & Duhaime, 1997, S. 25)

Responsibility

The Turnaround Leader is responsible for this subcomponent.

Operational Strategies

Operational Restructuring During the Crisis Stabilization Stage (OR CS)

OR CS 1 – not relevant in this version

OR CS 2 – Reduction of the Workforce

Summary

"Sometimes positive cash flow can be achieved solely by headcount reduction, but this is usually not sufficient."[899] This subcomponent addresses the process of reducing the workforce.

Context

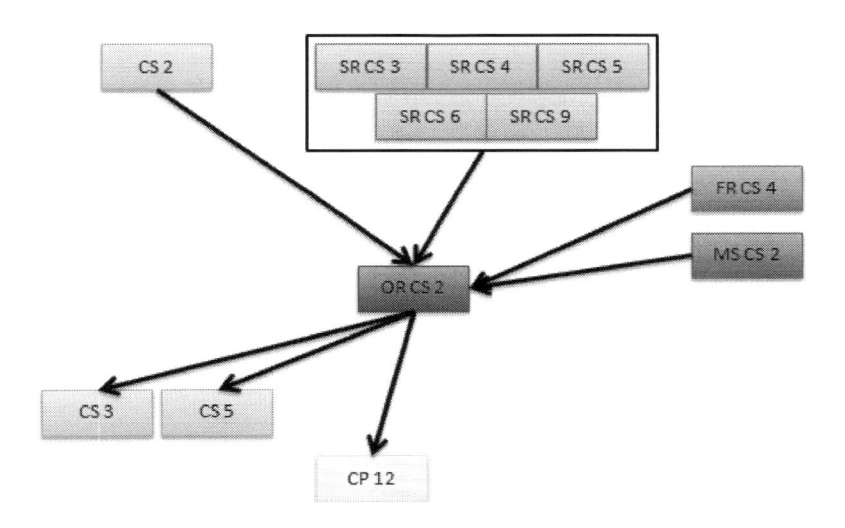

Description of the Subcomponent

At the beginning of the Crisis Stabilization Stage, manpower reductions are the biggest single operating improvement that can be carried out quickly. Most reductions in the workforce are done on a department basis. If cuts must be made across the board in a turnaround, 20 percent of indirect labor and ten percent of direct labor can usually be removed without hurting the business.[900] However, the majority of workforce reductions are done on a functional department basis, so it is necessary to build on the company and workforce analysis done in the Diagnostic Review Stage.

---

[899] (Bibeault, 1981, p. 215)
[900] (Bibeault, 1981, p. 278)

The downsides of workforce reduction are:

- Rehiring is expensive.
- Good people and knowledge leave the company.
- Employees may go to work for a competitor.
- Some employees may try to harm the company once they know they will be laid off.
- Strikes can endanger the turnaround process.

The key is to make the necessary adjustments to the workforce, but to think them through well before implementing them. In addition to deciding how many employees should be laid off, management must decide which employees to target (e.g. white collar vs factory workers, domestic vs foreign employees) and set a timetable for the lay-offs.[901]

Obvious Overmanning

Overmanning is easy to spot, not only for an experienced Turnaround Leader but also for CEOs. Where revenue compared to the volume of products (services) sold declines sharply, overmanning may be suspected. This situation sometimes occurs if the company expands and hires too many people in anticipation of an increase in demand for a product or service. If this increase fails to happen, then overmanning is usually the result. Every industry has certain benchmarks, such as turnover per employee, that serve as guidelines, but the Turnaround Leader should not work too hard to meet these best practice numbers in the early weeks of a turnaround. Instead, they should keep in mind that, if the company exceeds the industry's average workforce for a company of its size, overmanning is probably an issue. However, if the company is significantly overstaffed, the workforce should not immediately be reduced to the average level because those remaining will not be able to handle the increased workload from one day to the next. A gradual decrease is more realistic. One should also consider that a reduction in the workforce will not solve all problems. An overstaffed company usually comes with significant bureaucracy, where people create unnecessary work for themselves in order to justify their jobs, or simply because more people need to be informed and managed than is really necessary. If the workforce is reduced but the bureaucracy and existing workflows are not adjusted, the company could collapse as necessary processes come to a halt. Fine-tuning these parts of the business will be done at a later stage; however, all that can realistically be

---

[901] (Simonsen & Cassady, 2007, p. 10)

achieved at this stage is to take excess capacity out of the system and remove those who clearly do not add value.[902]

At this stage, it is usually only possible to deal with obvious overmanning because the TMT is focusing on developing the Turnaround Plan and putting controls in place rather than making a detailed analysis of how many people are needed for each work process. In addition, at the beginning of a turnaround the Turnaround Leader often does not have the in-depth knowledge required to spot less obvious overmanning, and they need time to determine how many staff are required to run the business in a "safe mode".

The financial aspect of obvious overmanning is also discussed in the subcomponent in FR CS 4 (First-Step Cost Reductions). Letting people go is a very common and effective way to cut costs; however, there are very serious downsides to losing employees. If too many are laid off, and if the lay-offs are not part of a structured improvement plan, downsizing of the workforce can accelerate a downward spiral.

One major problem with laying people off is that it costs the company money that it often does not have. Depending on the country in which the firm operates and on the contracts the company has with its workers, it may have to pay several months' salary to let a person go. In other cases, the company may have to give significant notice before the worker must leave. Because companies often don't have the necessary financing to implement a workforce reduction strategy, some live with their overmanning, accept the losses, and try to save money elsewhere.[903]

In order to minimize severance payments the Turnaround Leader should implement a last in, first out (LIFO) redundancy program so that those people who were hired last are the first to be let go. In most countries these people are not protected by very strict employment laws, so laying them off is easier and cheaper for the company than laying off people who have been there for several years. Some good and newly hired people could be lost in this process, but it might help the firm survive.

---

[902] (Slatter & Lovett, 2004, p. 148)
[903] (Slatter & Lovett, 2004, p. 148)

A special focus should be placed on the overhead workforce. Between 1950 and 1980, the number of non-production workers in the United States' manufacturing industry increased six times as quickly as the number of production workers, and by 1998 non-production workers accounted for 40 percent of all payroll costs.[904] The tendency to retain "staff" workers means that the overhead workforce should be examined carefully for potential cuts.

Reducing the Executive Team

Executive-level cutbacks usually account for the highest percentage of cuts by category.[905] The chief executive is usually dismissed right away in case they are inclined to hurt the company intentionally or to engage in business that is careless and unfavorable to the company. In the US an executive can often be fired on the spot, but in other countries it is not that easy; the executive is often put on gardening leave until their contract expires.

Middle Management Reductions

Middle management cutbacks are seldom easy. The Turnaround Leader will probably have to rely on division leaders and their assessments to determine whom to retain and whom to let go. In one system, division leaders classify their middle managers in ABC categories, where A employees are absolutely critical to the organization, B employees are somewhat important, and C employees are not important, not capable of, or not willing to support the turnaround process. In other jurisdictions and companies with strong unions, the decision might have to be made based on age, years of employment in the company, or family status. It is important not to make the cuts too rough as middle managers will carry the biggest part of the turnaround workload and they are close to the administrative group and production group.[906]

Responsibility

The HR Turnaround Manager is responsible for this subcomponent.

---

[904] (Bibeault, 1981, p. 279)
[905] (Bibeault, 1981, p. 294)
[906] (Bibeault, 1981, p. 296)

OR CS 3 – Restaffing

Summary

The positions of many of the employees who leave or are let go will eventually have to be filled again with skilled and motivated employees.

Context

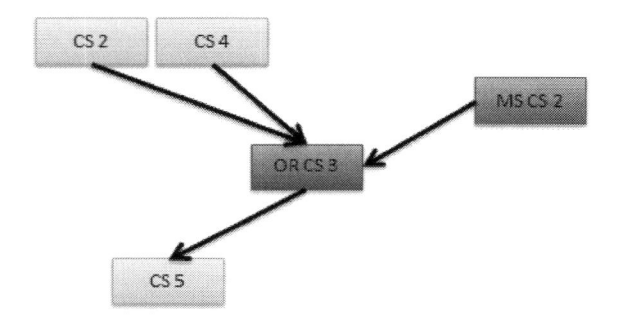

Description of the Subcomponent

Before people are brought in from outside to fill a new position, the TMT should determine whether there are capable people within the organization who have the required skills. It is likely that the motivation and commitment to prove themselves of someone who is promoted will be higher than that of an outsider who does not have emotional ties to the company. Some employees may actually grow beyond their expected potential when they receive such a chance. An outsider has the advantage that they are not influenced by prior negative experiences with the company or demotivated because of the often long decline and uncertainty in the organization. If people who have a proven track record and experience in turnarounds can be brought in, they will know what to expect. Good people seeking a challenge will often be more interested in a firm that is already past the Crisis Stabilization Stage.[907]

To be part of the restaffing from the outside or within the company, potential employees need to bring two things: the right attitude and motivation, and the right competence. The right

---

[907] (Bibeault, 1981, p. 329)

technical competence might be hard to find, especially as rehiring staff and filling positions must be done urgently in a turnaround process, so the right attitude becomes very important. The TMT should be open to cross-functional promotions and consider the advantage of a fresh approach if the employee is highly motivated.

Responsibility

The HR Turnaround Manager is responsible for this subcomponent.

OR CS 4 – Reduction of Inventory

Summary

Reduction of inventory is a way to decrease the capital bound up in stock.

Context

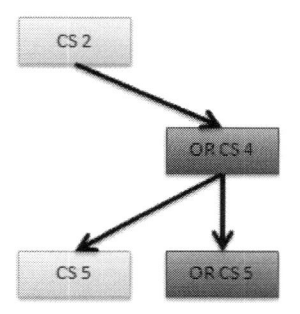

Description of the Subcomponent

A common error in evaluating inventory is the view that the only wasteful expense is associated with having too much inventory, but that is only half the truth as high costs can also occur if the inventory level is too low.[908] A match of sales against inventory positions is necessary in order to identify the right level at the right time of year. A company may encounter a shortage of inventory if a product is selling better than expected. In that case, customers are likely to turn away and buy from a competitor. When there is insufficient inventory, process optimization and an order entry system that matches up the orders coming in with the production schedules and the available inventory can address the problem. If there is too much inventory with the result that the company has to pay for expensive storage space, writing the excess inventory down and selling it for a lower price can help solve the problem.

Responsibility

The Turnaround Leader is responsible for this subcomponent.

---

[908] (Bibeault, 1981, p. 280)

OR CS 5 – Optimization of Inventory

Summary

Having the optimal level of inventory is key to having the least possible capital tied up in inventory while also achieving customer satisfaction.

Context

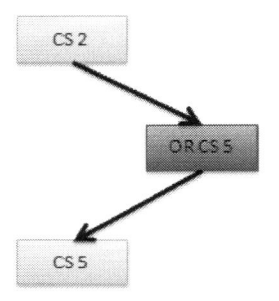

Description of the Subcomponent

A company with half of its stock tied up in items that represent only 20 percent of unit sales, and with its highest volume items selling four times faster than the lowest volume items, has a great deal to gain by reducing its inventories of slow sellers to the point where their turnover rates approach those of the fastest sellers.[909] A reduction of slow-moving inventory at all storage facilities is advisable, but a better alternative may be to concentrate the stock at only one facility from where it will be shipped on demand. Of course, the value of this solution depends on the shipping costs and the delivery time to send the items to the customers.

Customers expect standardized and fast-moving parts and models to be available quickly, so a small stock of these items should be available at all times. Items that are custom-made or sold only rarely don't need to be available very quickly, so they don't need to be in stock in great quantities.

---

[909] (Bibeault, 1981, p. 281)

Another rule of thumb is that the amount of money spent on inventory control should match the product's profit contribution. In order to find out which products to spend money on, the Turnaround Leader arranges the items or goods in order by sales volume per period or profit contribution. The 20 percent of the items that contribute 80 percent of the profit are in the top category that should receive 80 percent of the attention.

Responsibility

The Turnaround Leader is responsible for this subcomponent.

OR CS 6 – Asset Redeployment in the Crisis Stabilization Stage

Summary

This subcomponent focuses on using the available assets as efficiently as possible.

Context

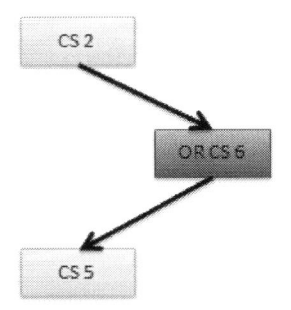

Description of the Subcomponent

In the Crisis Stabilization Stage the redeployment of assets that were sold but are not used in a certain business area focuses on using them more efficiently in another area. The goal is to achieve higher profitability with the assets already at hand and without buying new machinery or other assets. When these assets are evaluated the emphasis should be more on whether the process fits the overall business and has a good rate of return. Company growth, business vitality, and managerial efficiency depend as much on the proper "pruning out" of assets and activities with poor performance records as they do on the inflow of new investments and on the successful operation of those segments that justify retention.[910]

Responsibility

The Turnaround Leader is responsible for this subcomponent.

---

[910] (Bibeault, 1981, p. 300)

OR CS 7 – Reducing Salaries

Summary

Reducing salaries is a way to reduce costs, but the downsides of doing so should also be considered.

Context

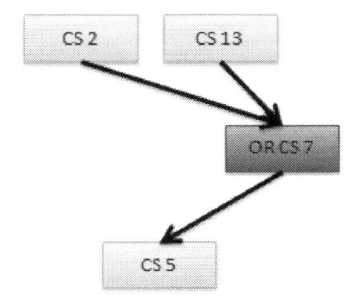

Description of the Subcomponent

Reducing salaries is a difficult task that can demotivate the workforce, but there are cases where lowering salaries, especially for senior staff, allow the company to lower its operational costs. Such a cost-cutting initiative enabled AirTran to lower its costs to 8.5 percent per available passenger mile. To keep up the morale of his staff, Leonard, AirTran's CEO at the time, encouraged open lines of communication and listened to staff grievances about the implications of the cost-cutting measures.[911]

One can also ask for voluntary pay cuts, as some managers with high salaries may agree to a temporary reduction of their salary to keep their goose laying its golden eggs. Others might agree to abandon the right to their bonuses.

---

[911] compare (Rajendar, 2007, p. 21)

Responsibility

The HR Turnaround Manager is responsible for this subcomponent.

OR CS 8 – Reducing Suppliers and Partnerships

Summary

This subcomponent addresses reducing the number of suppliers and partnerships to an optimal number.

Context

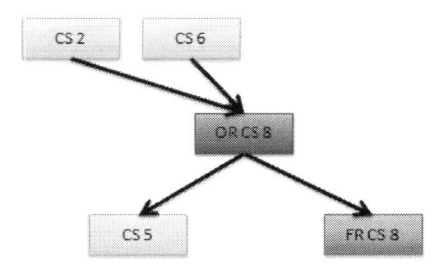

Description of the Subcomponent

Reducing the number of suppliers and partnerships also reduces overhead costs for managing the partnerships and in the buying department. By buying bulk quantities from one supplier, rebates may be negotiable and there should be considerably less administrative effort. However, having only one supplier for a product might be risky for some businesses if the supplier fails to deliver or abuses their power by setting their prices too high.

When Cisco reduced its partnerships, more than 3,000 resellers and 800 suppliers were squeezed out. The reduction was necessary to cut costs and take advantage of volume rebates from the remaining suppliers.[912]

Responsibility

The Turnaround Leader is responsible for this subcomponent.

---

[912] (BusinessWeek, 2003)

Operational Strategy During the Turnaround Stage (OR TS)

Operational strategies in the Turnaround Stage are different from those in the Crisis Stabilization Stage because they are more focused on profit improvements than on limiting losses and downsizing. The operational strategies employed at this stage will be important for the company's ability to survive longer than the turnaround process and for its competitive advantage. Profit improvement is achieved by systematic programs rather than by one-shot cost reductions: remaining plants are made more efficient rather than being shut down on a wholesale basis; manufacturing efficiencies are achieved by brainpower rather than by surgery; inventory management is intensified; and overheads are evaluated on a cost/benefit basis rather than simply being lopped off.[913]

Operational subcomponents in the Turnaround Stage can also be connected to costs that could further destabilize the company as long as it is in the Crisis Stabilization Stage.

---

[913] (Bibeault, 1981, p. 312)

OR TS 1 – Regular Effective Profit Improvements

Summary

This subcomponent addresses optimizing the company's performance.

Context

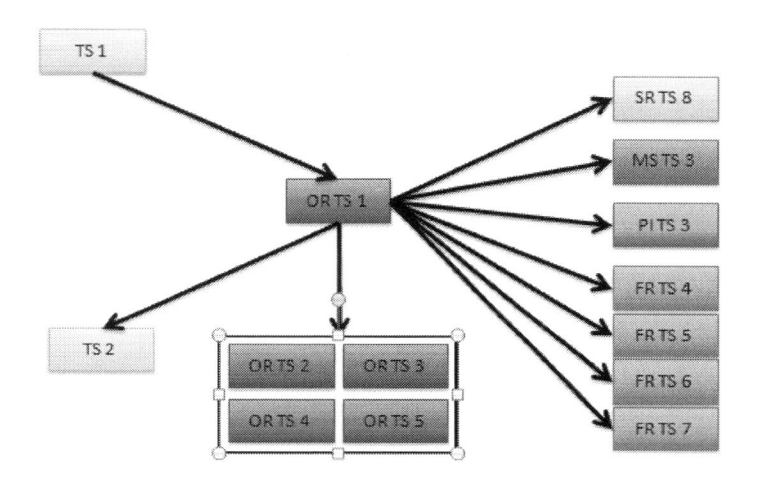

Description of the Subcomponent

Operational efficiency can lead a company to an outstanding profit performance. There are two main reasons why profit improvement strategies could fail: the potential of the improvement and its outcome are misunderstood; and employees are not sufficiently profit-conscious.[914] Regarding the first reason, in many companies the department manager or team manager sees their importance in the company in terms of how many people are below them, so a reduction in headcount would appear to reduce their importance and they would be unlikely to support it. To have a successful turnaround, ego satisfaction must be put aside in order to get down to the hard work of performance. As to the second reason, not all employees are interested in having a big career and working as hard as they can from morning to night. Most employees have important lives outside work and try to get through the day with as little stress as possible. The result is overstaffing because they think, "If I can hire someone to take some workload off

---

[914] (Bibeault, 1981, p. 313)

me I'll do it, and maybe I can get home a couple of hours earlier". If the department head is not constantly on the lookout to keep their department running as efficiently as possible, the department can grow disproportionately to the profit it generates.

In order to be effective, cost improvements need to be carried out regularly. If an edict emerges from the chief executive's office from time to time telling everyone to cut all costs by ten percent by next Monday, then steady and permanent profit improvements simply do not happen.[915]

Cost-cutting should not be too severe, because some arbitrary cost-cutting can result in the removal of profitable activities. For example, when an IT department is eliminated and the activities outsourced to a contractor, depending on the situation, the costs might be higher even if initial projections were positive. Hence, the company should review its cost-cutting activities when the turnaround process is over and for some time later.

A regular profit-improvement program should be implemented in this subcomponent and should include:

- Being willing to undertake major change
- Implementing a profit-conscious culture in the company
- Making employees understand that profit improvements are not a one-time thing but must be done continuously
- Ensuring that profit improvements are comprehensive

One way to get managers to be profit-conscious is to link their careers directly to their ability to cut costs and improve the operational efficiency of the organization. Profit improvements can be spread down the hierarchy of an organization by implementing an effective management by objective (MBO) approach in the Turnaround Stage of the process.[916]

Responsibility

The Turnaround Leader is responsible for this subcomponent.

---

[915] (Bibeault, 1981, p. 314)
[916] (Bibeault, 1981, p. 315)

OR TS 2 – Manufacturing Efficiencies

Summary

This subcomponent deals with improving manufacturing efficiencies.

Context

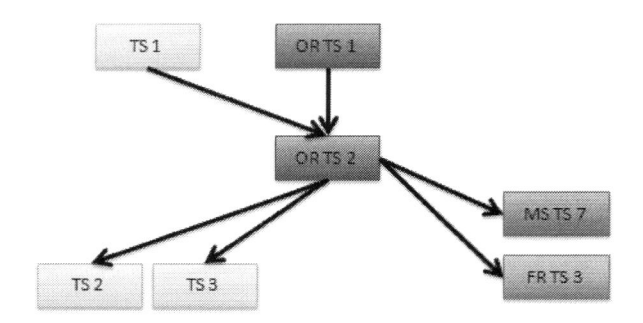

Description of the Subcomponent

This subcomponent is used by manufacturing businesses. Improving manufacturing efficiencies can result in whole new projects that come under the heading of this subcomponent.

Significant labor productivity improvements can be achieved by improving management and applying technology.[917] Possible reasons for ineffective manufacturing processes include over-influential labor unions and technological obsolescence.

For example,[918] in 1978 a steel-rolling mill had a contract crew at 39 workers per shift, which was down from 42 workers per shift a decade before. Each worker cost $30,000 per year. During a strike a decade before, when the contract crew level was 42, 12 supervisors had run the rolling mill successfully for six months. Assuming that the 12 supervisors were more skilled and better motivated and so were equivalent to 14 of the standard crew, we can estimate that the shift was overstaffed by 25 workers, or $750,000 per year per shift. Newer mills were performing

---

[917] compare (Richard & Dorothy, 2010)
[918] (Bibeault, 1981, p. 316)

the same function with only five workers. In addition, the firm had a technological gap of $270,000 per year per shift. Together with the overstaffing, the overpayment amounted to more than $2 million per year for a two-shift operation in this one mill alone.

Responsibility

The Turnaround Leader is responsible for this subcomponent.

OR TS 3 – Maintenance Improvements

Summary

This subcomponent deals with analyzing and optimizing maintenance activities.

Context

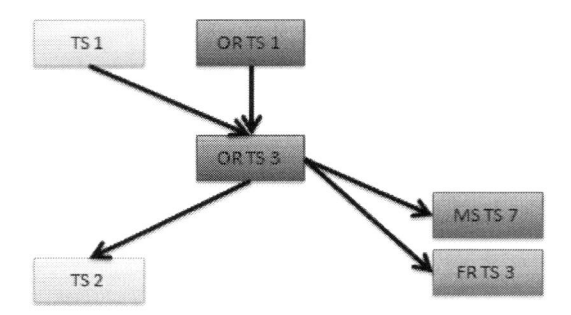

Description of the Subcomponent

In this subcomponent the company's maintenance activities are analyzed and optimized. Improving or outsourcing maintenance can free up cash and improve quality.

As a first step, the current maintenance processes need to be analyzed. Often there are industry requirements and regulations that need to be met, but often the schedule by which machinery is maintained or the facilities where the machinery is maintained are not optimal. The results of the analysis should be benchmarked against competitors' maintenance processes to improve competitiveness.

In the next step, the company should look at what competitors do better, why they have lower maintenance costs, and how they can reach the same level. Sometimes it is possible to outsource maintenance or look for another company to carry it out—one that is cheaper. In some cases it might be better to simply buy new machinery if maintaining old assets is becoming too expensive. Because this subcomponent might require new investment it is recommended to do it in the Turnaround Stage. However, if maintenance is a major cost driver the subcomponent can also be triggered by Emergency Procedures.

Responsibility

The Turnaround Leader is responsible for this subcomponent.

OR TS 4 – Transportation Improvements

Summary

In some companies transportation costs are substantial. This subcomponent addresses optimizing logistics.

Context

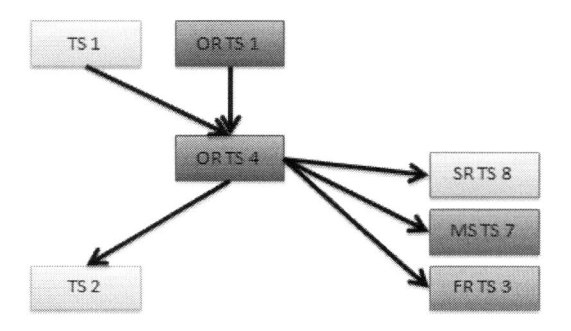

Description of the Subcomponent

If the company has significant transportation costs this subcomponent should evaluate whether the costs are optimized, as the cost savings in transportation can be substantial. If the business is itself a shipping company, improvements could come from improving fuel efficiency or reducing the cost of storage space.

Some firms own their shipping companies. If this is the case, selling the shipping part might bring in some money and save costs. When Neckerman, a big German online store, became insolvent, part of the turnaround plan was to sell the shipping business to DHL. Companies such as Tchibo—a coffee store chain that also sells some electronics, appliances, and clothes with a weekly changing catalogue—need to distribute different goods to thousands of stores every week. This can only be maintained profitably with a highly efficient transportation network.

Responsibility

The Operational Turnaround Manager is responsible for this subcomponent.

OR TS 5 – Inventory Management

Summary

This subcomponent implements an inventory management system. Too much or not enough inventory can both hurt a company's finances.

Context

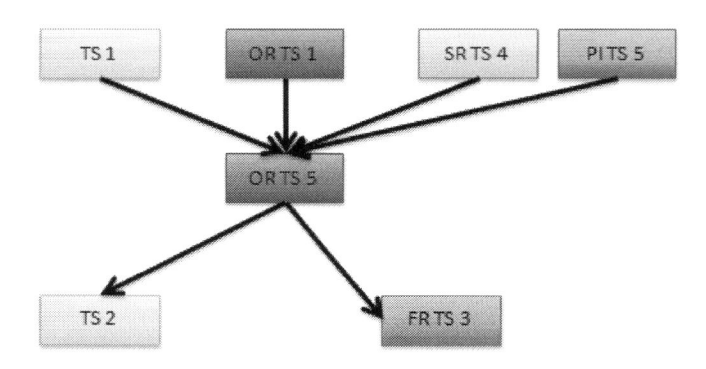

Description of the Subcomponent

A company's inventory determines the health of the supply chain. It requires constant evaluation of internal and external factors as well as efficient planning. A lot of companies have inventory planners; however, the optimal stage is that no inventory needs to be held.

Inventory can be raw materials, work in progress, and output—finished goods that the company has not sold yet. The goal is to have the raw materials required for production delivered just in time and only as many as needed. This requires that the supplier can deliver just in time and on demand. The work in progress can be minimized by an optimal supply chain that ensures no work in progress is lying around. Volkswagen and Toyota have perfectly synced their production chains so that no car is standing around for more than a few minutes. Output can be minimized by adopting on-demand production. Amazon has its own printing company that prints books as soon as they are ordered, but only then. No storage is required because as soon as the book is printed it is sent from the printing facility directly to the customer. In fact, this book you are holding was most likely produced this way, and therefore printed two days before you received it.

The inventory should already have been reduced to the optimum level in the Crisis Stabilization Stage. Proper inventory management should be established in the Turnaround Stage rather than in the Crisis Stabilization Stage because inventory management is usually connected to an enterprise management system that is in turn connected to the production and ordering processes. If an inventory management system is not in place, or if the system used is obsolete, then investment should be made to install an efficient system. This investment is usually only possible at the end of the Turnaround Stage when proper cash flow is established.

Responsibility

The Operational Turnaround Manager is responsible for this subcomponent.

OR TS 6 – Value Analysis

Summary

This subcomponent involves a value analysis carried out in the Turnaround Stage.

Context

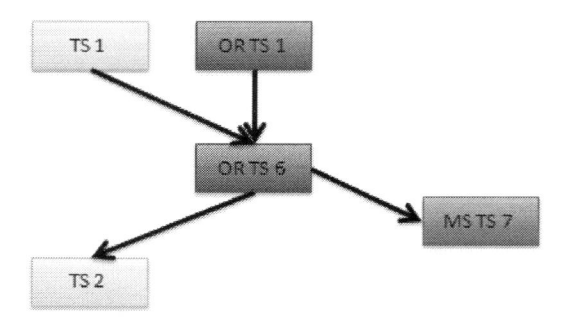

Description of the Subcomponent

A value analysis extends the efficiency efforts from the Crisis Stabilization Stage to the Turnaround Stage. Value analysis was introduced in the USA in 1945 by L.D. Miles at General Electric and in Japan in 1955 as a method to reduce costs.[919] "It provides an efficient mechanism for scrutinizing rapidly and in an organized way all the many thousands of activities that make up overhead, identifying all the areas where cuts can safely be made, and pointing to the right cost/benefit trade-offs where quality is concerned."[920] The techniques used in value analysis involve a search for and evaluation of alternative ways to meet the required performance at the lowest cost.[921]

---

[919] compare (Sato & Kaufman, 2005, p. 8)
[920] (Bibeault, 1981, p. 218)
[921] (Sato & Kaufman, 2005, p. 42), compare (Fandel, Fey, Heuft, & Pitz, 2008, p. 438)

Overhead value analysis (OVA) was developed by McKinsey as a bottom-up approach that is supported by top management.[922] Usually an OVA is carried out at irregular intervals when the competitive position of the company is threatened or in a time of crisis.[923]

There is an international six-step model for OVA.[924] A detailed explanation is not part of this standard since it is already explained in detail by other authors. The Turnaround Management Society can, however, assist you in training and literature requests.

Responsibility

The Operational Turnaround Manager is responsible for this subcomponent.

---

[922] compare (Fandel, Fey, Heuft, & Pitz, 2008, p. 438), compare (Whitney, 1992, p. 205)
[923] compare (Meyer-Piening, Arnulf, 1998)
[924] compare (Have, Have, Stevens, & Van Der Elst, 2010))

OR TS 7 – Asset Redeployment in the Turnaround Stage

Summary

This subcomponent addresses redeploying assets to higher-return areas.

Context

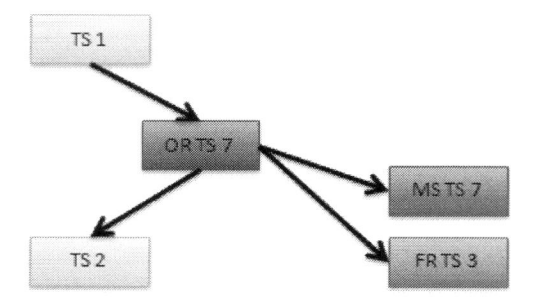

Description of the Subcomponent

Assets that were taken off a process or put on hold during the Crisis Stabilization Stage can be redeployed once the critical time for the company is over. However, asset redeployment in the Turnaround Stage centers on redeploying assets to faster-growth/higher-return areas by offloading poor return-on-investment operations and by making selective acquisitions.[925] Asset redeployment can also generate significant cost savings and cash flow. Assets that are no longer needed for the transformation can be sold and others, such as surplus and idle equipment, might be put to better use.

Responsibility

The Operational Turnaround Manager is responsible for this subcomponent.

---

[925] (Bibeault, 1981, p. 338)

OR TS 8 – Development Projects

Summary

This subcomponent deals with evaluating and classifying development projects.

Context

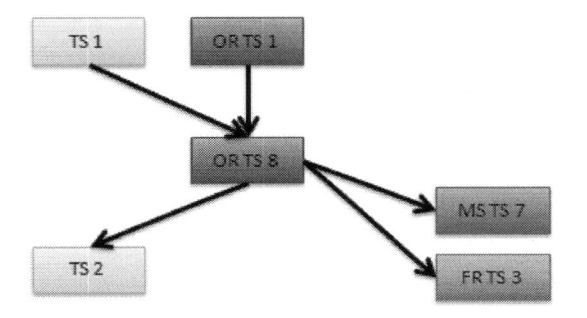

Description of the Subcomponent

The organization and classification of development projects can be difficult, especially in organizations that have many projects going on at the same time.[926] Employees who are engaged in development projects tend to be some of the best. A company that wants to grow internally must have highly qualified and creative employees, while a company that is mainly focused on maintaining the status quo does not need such highly qualified people. The company's culture probably plays a big role in how it deals with creativity and development projects, but the type of task also determines whether it challenges people and makes them creative. People who are naturally interested in finding new ways and creating new solutions need a certain environment and challenge, and if the company doesn't give it to them they are likely to leave. In a crisis situation the company's culture suffers and good people leave because they are no longer supported in the way they need to be. Therefore, development projects must be restarted and new, highly motivated people found to make them successful. Once these people are on board they need to find an environment in which they want to work; this

---

[926] (Bibeault, 1981, p. 347)

kind of environment is difficult for management to maintain because it needs tight controls at the same time as encouraging creativity, imagination, and dedication from innovative people.[927]

In order to deal with a lot of activities and complex problems they should be categorized in groups so the TMT can deal with them at a summary level. Team leaders can then deal with variations within the categories on a more detailed level.

Possible classifications for research projects are those that are in an exploratory stage, those that are in the development stage, and those that are about to be introduced to the market.

Existing business products can be classified into:

- Products that need a modification – these are products that are at the end of their life cycle and need to be revamped by a change in product design or specification.
- Products that are aimed at a new market – these are projects that are aimed at a new industrial or geographic market to extend a current product's reach.
- Cost engineering projects – these projects are designed to improve a certain process or other company activity.

In order to pull together the organization, identification, and allocation of development resources, the company's planning and budgeting systems must be modified to display these project categories.[928] When the overall structure of the development projects is known, the Turnaround Leader can make investment decisions that are oriented toward future growth.

Responsibility

The Operational Turnaround Leader is responsible for this subcomponent.

---

[927] (Bibeault, 1981, p. 347)
[928] (Bibeault, 1981, p. 348)

Process improvements (PI)

Process Improvements During the Crisis Stabilization Stage (PI CS)

PI CS 1 – Cost Improvements During the Crisis Stabilization Stage

Summary

This subcomponent deals with lowering costs by taking out non-value-added activities.

Context

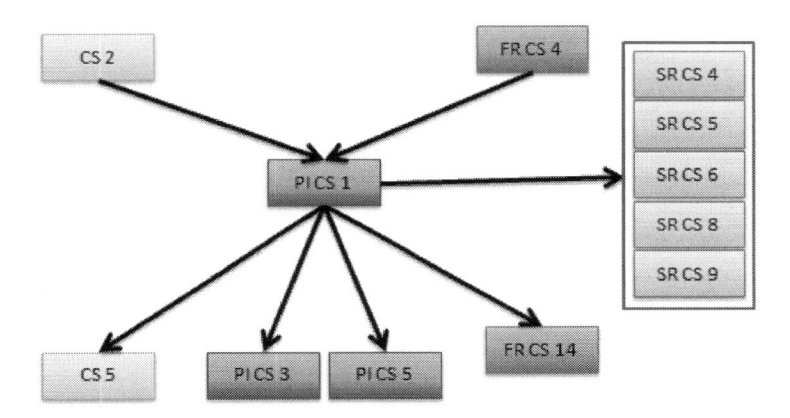

Description of the Subcomponent

When cost improvements during the Crisis Stabilization Stage are necessary, non-value-added processes need to be cut out of the business. Processes and tasks should be eliminated rather than automated wherever possible.[929] In order to spot which activities add value, the company must create and analyze a workflow diagram of all activities. An industry professional will be able to spot opportunities to make cuts quickly.

The first place firms go to for an immediate cost-cutting initiative is not activity process optimization and restructuring, but removing costs from the product.[930] Cutting costs and thereby lowering the quality of a product might not be a good idea, but doing so may be necessary. In Roman's opinion, the product is what made the company successful so it should not be touched; this is true if the cause of the crisis is not connected to the product. However,

---

[929] (Shein, 2011, p. 123)
[930] (Roman, 2010, p. 178)

if the crisis is connected to financial difficulties then product quality may have to be reduced, but first the company should try to lower costs without reducing the price. The challenge is to maintain the highest quality possible while lowering costs and staying competitive in a cost-driven market.[931]

When reducing the quality of a product one should keep several concerns in mind. For example, replacing the outer shell of a mobile phone with cheaper and thinner plastic could save a couple of cents per phone, but the phones may break more quickly resulting in higher return rates, more warranty issues, and maybe even lawsuits, especially if health issues come into play.

Responsibility

The Operational Turnaround Manager is responsible for this subcomponent.

---

[931] (Roman, 2010, p. 178)

PI CS 2 – Quality Improvements in the Crisis Stabilization Stage

Summary

This subcomponent deals with improving the quality of processes.

Context

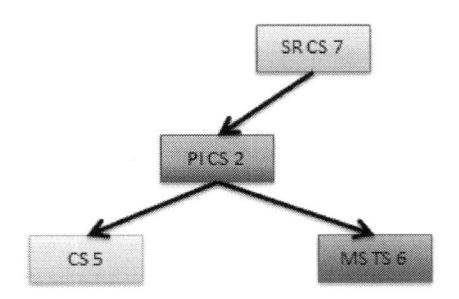

Description of the Subcomponent

In the Crisis Stabilization Stage there is only one reason to improve quality: if the main reason for the decline is poor quality. Unless the firm can provide products or services of satisfactory quality, the turnaround will probably fail.[932] However, improving quality involves financial resources, so it can seldom be done before cash is generated. Once the company has sufficient cash flow available and it is clear that the core products will not be terminated, quality improvements should be implemented to those products. Quality improvements also arise from buying better raw materials and parts so quality is built in, rather than bad quality being inspected out.[933] Quality-focused turnaround strategies are optimal for customer-centric environments.[934]

There are many quality improvement methods, such as Six Sigma, which is suggested as a quality improvement technique for manufacturing businesses and tries to identify the causes of defects and minimize variability. A Six Sigma project performed within a company follows a

---

[932] compare (Slatter & Lovett, 2004, p. 264)
[933] (Slatter & Lovett, 2004, p. 263)
[934] (Roman, 2010, p. 180)

defined order of steps and has specific financial targets such as cost reduction and/or profit increase. The goal of Six Sigma is to make processes as close to perfect as possible with the highest possible quality outcome.

Responsibility

The Operational Turnaround Manager is responsible for this subcomponent.

PI CS 3 – Termination of Products

Summary

Products that are not profitable or fail to fit into the future business plan are terminated in this subcomponent.

Context

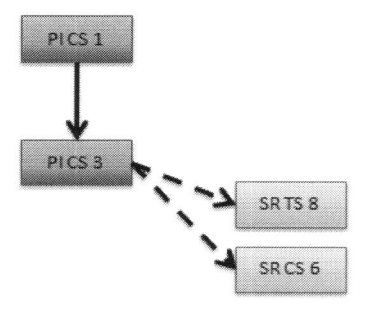

Description of the Subcomponent

Most turnaround situations are characterized by product line proliferation within the product-market segment in which the company competes.[935] Products that are found to be unprofitable and that don't cover the variable costs should be terminated as soon as the turnaround process is started. In this component all products that have a low profit margin but require high capital investments in order to be profitable and products that do not reach a minimum sales level are terminated. If a product is not profitable and sales are going down it should either be terminated or the price should be raised. The latter, however, might have the same effect as terminating the product.

Responsibility

The Turnaround Leader is responsible for this subcomponent.

---

[935] (Slatter & Lovett, 2004, p. 276)

PI CS 4 – Improving Management Information and Performance Systems

Summary

This subcomponent deals with improving the management information and performance systems that are in place, or implementing them if they are not. These systems are very important in order to measure process improvements. Proper management systems also distribute the relevant information to the right parties at the right time in order to make sound decisions.

Context

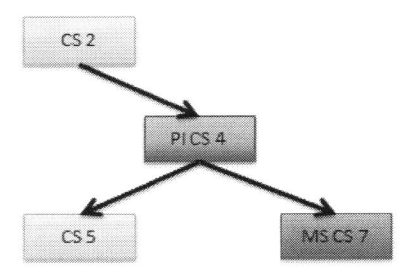

Description of the Subcomponent

This subcomponent should be started only after the Turnaround Plan is finished and the future strategy of the company can be laid out to employees. The goal of the improved management information system is to produce relevant information to support a performance measurement system that measures employees' contribution to the delivery of the Turnaround Plan.[936]

In this subcomponent it is important to understand that the way people behave is usually in accordance with the company's culture, how performance is measured, and the reward system. Every company that is driven by performance needs metrics to set goals and to measure if these goals have been reached.

---

[936] (Slatter & Lovett, 2004, p. 292)

Troubled companies are often characterized by the lack of any meaningful information or the production of information to justify internal behaviors or sustain compensation packages, despite trading realities.[937] If information for external stakeholders such as banks is delayed, is incomplete, or is not sufficiently meaningful, external auditors may be appointed to validate the information. This is especially true if there have already been disagreements with auditors over provisioning policies or the income- or asset-valuation techniques, as the consequence is unreliable information. The following characteristics can be found in companies that are in a crisis situation:[938]

- The information is often financial with little indication of what is causing the company's bad performance.
- True margins are difficult to establish and have a tendency to be overstated because standard costing systems are out of date.
- There are illogical overhead allocations in order to justify non-cost-effective engagements or special projects.
- The management makes decisions based on feelings and opinions rather than on facts.
- Turf wars exist.
- The status quo is not changed, and senior managers try to resist difficult changes.
- There is a fear that measuring performance will reveal problems.
- The management is not motivated to reveal real problems, because the solution would require hard decisions to be made and the current situation would have to be changed.

In order to change the corporate culture and to show that past mistakes belong to the past and are forgiven, the Turnaround Leader should create an environment in which a clean break from historical performance can be made. The new management information system should be designed so employees can fulfill their roles, and the right behavior toward the goals and the organization is encouraged. The system should be transparent but also maintain confidentiality where necessary. Success must be measurable, comparable, and be based on facts where possible. The progress made by employees should be monitored against goals and compared with past performance. The whole workforce should understand the KPIs and what drives them

---

[937] (Slatter & Lovett, 2004, p. 289)
[938] compare (Slatter & Lovett, 2004, p. 290)

so the employees, who often start out skeptical about a turnaround process, grow enthusiastic about seeing the rewards of their efforts.

The new management information system should regularly produce information in accordance with the management's requirements and the communication procedures required during the turnaround. This will enable the Turnaround Leader to use the relevant information to create a performance measurement system and compensation schemes that encourage behavior that is in accordance with the Turnaround Plan.

The Turnaround Leader should be aware that actual performance, as presented through the improved measurement process, is often worse than originally thought, so it is usually beneficial to set targets that are achievable.[939] Once the employees are used to the new performance system, which can take a few months, the targets can be raised.

Inefficient Performance Measuring Systems

Problems with performance measurement systems are often due to poor communication. Symptoms of a non-working measurement system are:

- Employees who believe that the performance measurement system is not important – A new performance measurement system takes time to implement and get used to. Sometimes it even takes two or three launches.[940] However, if the employees don't take the new system seriously it may be because the system has not been communicated well or that is using the wrong measures.
- Unreliable information, especially for non-financial measures – Unreliable information is often the result of trying to implement the performance measurement system too quickly. Open communication and a no-blame culture result in the development of acceptable information in the shortest time.[941]
- The employees don't believe in the system – If employees don't do the job they are supposed to and spend too much time on administrative things they can become skeptical. However, employee skepticism can also result when the system is not

---

[939] (Slatter & Lovett, 2004, p. 292)
[940] compare (Slatter & Lovett, 2004, p. 292)
[941] (Slatter & Lovett, 2004, p. 292)

communicated well and is not understood. In a more serious case, the measurement is not appropriate because goals are set too high or too low.

Responsibility

The Turnaround Leader is responsible for this subcomponent.

PI CS 5 – Purchasing Improvements in the PI Component

Summary

Purchasing improvements can lead to substantial cost savings, better organization, and an improved overview of the firm's costs.

Context

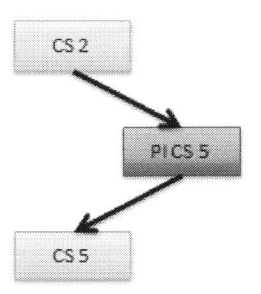

Description of the Subcomponent

The purchasing department plays a key role in a turnaround, and the supply chain specifically. Reducing the costs of services and raw materials that the company requires to run or produce its goods directly affects its competitiveness, the margin, and the sales price that it can offer its customers. The primary function of the purchasing department is to provide the right items at the best price at the right time.

There are various performance measures to determine purchasing performance.

Purchasing Efficiency

Purchasing efficiency does not relate to the amount of goods purchased, but is about how effectively the purchasing department performs against its budget. If the purchasing unit has higher purchasing costs than allocated, it is not efficient enough.

Purchasing Effectiveness

A possible method to assess purchasing effectiveness is to evaluate the inventory turnover ratios. The ratio measures the average number of times the inventory is used, or turned, during a specific period. However, a company may need to account for seasonal effects, in which case this measure is not as accurate.

Purchasing Functionality

Performance can be measured in terms of whether the purchasing department is really supplying the best possible products at the right time and at the best price. Often companies buy items from a certain supplier because it has "always been done like that". It is not unusual that the price paid is even higher than the normal market price. This happens frequently with common technical products such as computers.

A look at the literature and various other studies shows that the following measures are most common in evaluating performance:

- Cost saving
- The quality of the vendor
- The effectiveness of the price
- The flow of inventory
- Delivery metrics

Even though these are the most common measures they are not uniform for every industry and will vary from business to business. Also, the effectiveness of a purchasing department will change over time; regular reassessments should therefore be planned.

In purchasing, three improvements can be achieved through process optimization:

- Central purchasing/bulk purchasing
- Regular changes to lower prices
- Taking cash discounts for fast payments
- Inspecting deliveries

The goals are usually to:

- Reduce inventory investment

- Reduce purchasing process costs
- Reduce costs of products purchased

Central Purchasing/Bulk Purchasing

Handling purchasing requests centrally allows for bulk purchasing and, therefore, lower prices. Central handling also makes it easier to maintain an overview of what and how much is ordered. The disadvantage is increased bureaucracy and longer order cycles.

Regular Changes to Lower Prices

Throughout the turnaround process, the purchasing manager must regularly monitor when prices are changing and ask for lower prices from suppliers when the market price drops. Hedging may also save some money, although if the company is at stake it is probably not in a position to engage in long-term contracts. Conergy, the German solar company, has been in a turnaround situation for years, partly because they agreed to a ten-year overpriced contract for silicon that they could not get out of and that makes it impossible for them to offer their products at a competitive price. On the other hand, Lufthansa, the largest European airline, hedged fuel prices, enabling it to buy fuel at lower-than-market prices during 2007 and 2008, and to offer its flights at prices lower than those of the competition.

Receiving Discounts for Fast Payments

If it has not already done so, the company should establish a regular payment schedule to pay its invoices on time. If the company is in very urgent financial difficulties, paying on time may not be possible and late payment may be used as a way to finance its operations. While this technique should not be used on a long-term basis, if it is necessary the Communications Plan should include information for suppliers in order to maintain good relationships and their trust in the company.

If payments have been late, suppliers should be informed that payments will be made on time. A shorter payment cycle should also reduce costs as the supplier will no longer have to finance the company.

Inspecting Deliveries

Inspecting what the company receives is important in the effort to maintain quality standards and to ensure that the right quantity is delivered. This is discussed in detail in PI CS 6 (Inspecting Deliveries).

Responsibility

The Operational Turnaround Manager is responsible for this subcomponent.

PI CS 6 – Inspecting Deliveries

Summary

This subcomponent puts in place controls to inspect deliveries.

Context

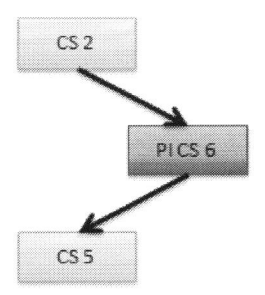

Description of the Subcomponent

Having the supplier locked into a contract with detailed quality stipulations, quality control mechanisms, clearly defined acceptable defect rates, well-documented key measures and tolerances, and penalties for poor quality is probably the safest way to protect the end quality of a product.[942] Product scrap and reject costs are often attributable to poor incoming material control, so only an inspection of the delivered goods can ensure that the materials are the right ones, in the right quantity, and of the quality ordered.[943] Variations in materials can create problems in feeding machines, causing out-of-tolerance assemblies, and even extra material handling, all because of the way the stock is supplied for use at production stations. Material quality is especially important in automated production facilities that need a certain standard to function properly.

Companies try to reduce their costs in many ways, especially in economic downturns, for example by reducing the quality of the goods delivered. If the company does not purchase raw materials, where the quality always stays the same, it must ensure that it gets the quality it

---

[942] (Roman, 2010, p. 180)
[943] (Bibeault, 1981, p. 283)

ordered. One way to do this is to ensure that the contract with the supplier indicates exact quality measures, how these measures will be controlled, and acceptable tolerances. The contract should also indicate clearly who will absorb the cost of low quality products, how the quality control will be carried out, and the process for returning defective products.[944]

The next step is to determine that the quality agreed on in the contract is the same as the quality delivered. The best way to check this is to carry out regular and thorough testing. It is also advisable to have a second possible supplier on standby.

Responsibility

The Operational Turnaround Manager is responsible for this subcomponent.

---

[944] (Roman, 2010, p. 179)

PI CS 7 – Inspecting Deliverables

Summary

This subcomponent puts in place controls to inspect deliverables.

Context

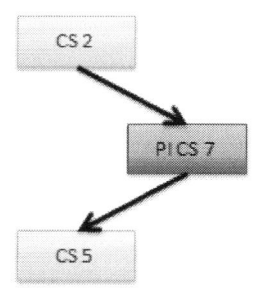

Description of the Subcomponent

Inspecting deliverables ensures that the company knows what is sent to the customer in order to confirm customer satisfaction and to determine whether the company is under-billing. In some cases, this job is done by a person who thinks that someone else will fill out the form that the billing department needs in order to know exactly what to bill for.[945] This kind of process leads to jobs being done without the customer being billed for them. A final inspection or a billing check sheet would help to avoid these problems.

Inspecting deliverables also ensures that the company is not sending out faulty or broken products. In this way, the company will know that if the customer returns a product anyway, it was broken by either the customer or the transportation company.

Responsibility

The Operational Turnaround Manager is responsible for this turnaround process.

---

[945] compare (Bibeault, 1981, p. 283)

PI CS 8 – Collaboration of Executives

Summary

This subcomponent deals with implementing collaboration systems and/or programs that support executive collaboration.

Context

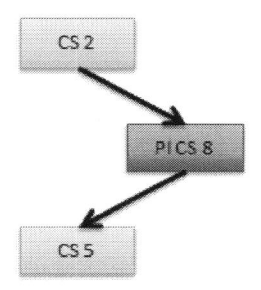

Description of the Subcomponent

When executives collaborate, they think and act together.[946] When department heads collaborate in discussing ideas, products can be produced faster or of better quality.

The collaboration of executives has the following advantages:

- Departments develop a better understanding of what the other departments do, what is important, and why things are done a certain way.[947]
- Duplication can be eliminated.[948]
- A strong sense of team play and belonging can be created.
- Communication is enhanced.

It is not easy to align executives but there are some measures that can increase collaboration. First, the goals of all executives need to be aligned. Even if, in theory, the goals are clear, they

---

[946] (Schell, 1957)
[947] compare (Jankulik, 2009, p. 15)
[948] compare (Rajendar, 2007, p. 34)

may not be for the individual executive. Workshops and team-building events can clear up individual agendas. The workshops should be headed by professional communication and management trainers, and they should bring out and highlight the individual strengths of each executive and encourage respect for one other. There might be disagreements and verbal fights on a daily basis, but the common ground for working together should be respect for each other's accomplishments and strengths.

Another measure to align the executives is by incentives. The incentives should all be aligned to the same goals; however, the requirement is that the overall corporate strategy is clear.

A further possibility is to have senior executives regularly evaluate each other on how well they work together as a team and support other executives. There should not be direct punishments as executives usually have a strong network, and simply because one has a lot of friends on the board or in senior management does not make them a good collaborator. The system should not allow room for abuse by alienating somebody who pushes necessary but unpopular topics. These people are (especially in a turnaround process) very much needed.

Responsibility

The Turnaround Leader is responsible for this subcomponent.

Process Improvements During the Turnaround Stage (PI TS)

PI TS 1 – Cost Improvements in the Turnaround Stage

Summary

This subcomponent deals with implementing cost improvements that require investments that were not possible during the Crisis Stabilization Stage.

Context

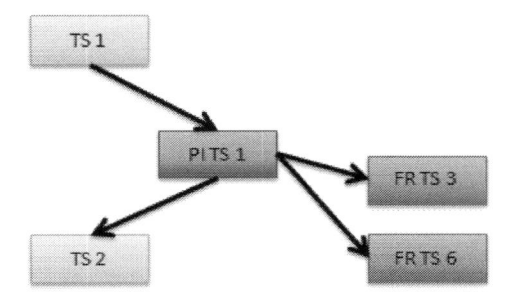

Description of the Subcomponent

Cost improvements carried out in the Turnaround Stage require more analysis of the organization and its processes than cost reductions in the Crisis Stabilization Stage. Cost improvements that result from investments are implemented in the Turnaround Stage and can take various forms in various industries. The Operational Turnaround Manager should propose the right cost improvement strategies for the industry and company within the financial allowances of the firm.

This subcomponent is to start new cost improvements, but also to evaluate the effectiveness and results of earlier cost improvements. For example, it might be that a cost-cutting project has not had the hoped-for effects or that the effects are other than imagined. In that case, the project needs to be re-evaluated and possibly stopped.

Responsibility

The Operational Turnaround Manager is responsible for this subcomponent.

PI TS 2 – Quality Improvements in the Turnaround Stage

Summary

This subcomponent deals with quality improvements during the Turnaround Stage.

Context

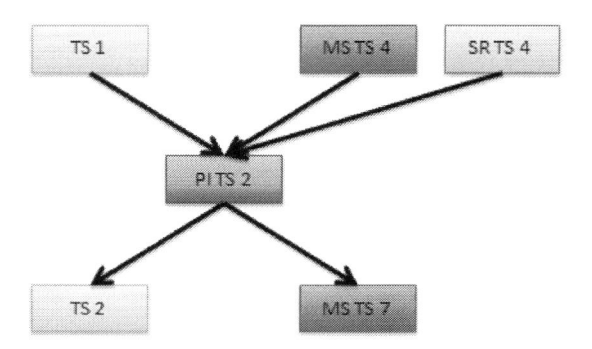

Description of the Subcomponent

During this subcomponent network loops are reduced and reasons for non-conformance are systematically analyzed. This subcomponent is also about taking corrective actions. Often, an easy way to improve the quality of products is to buy better raw materials. When poor product quality is a reason for the crisis, customers will quickly let the company know by actually telling them or by returning goods. In that case, quality improvements are more important than cost reductions. The necessary quality improvements should be addressed during the Crisis Stabilization Stage since they are urgent. The cost of improving the quality of resources in the long term can be high as the cost of quality in a manufacturing business is up to 25 percent of the total manufacturing cost.[949] However, high quality will increase customer loyalty, guarantee a good reputation, and contribute to a growing market share.[950]

---

[949] (Slatter & Lovett, 2004, p. 263)
[950] (Roman, 2010, p. 180)

Responsibility

The Operational Turnaround Manager is responsible for this subcomponent.

PI TS 3 – Improving Operations

Summary

This subcomponent addresses improving operations within the firm.

Context

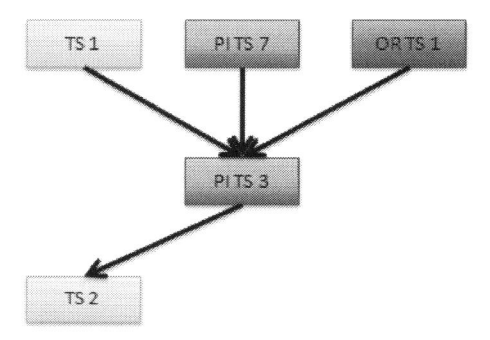

Description of the Subcomponent

Improving the company's operations has several important objectives:

- The use of resources is optimized in order to deliver products within budget and on time.
- Communication among departments is enhanced.
- Manufacturing of products is aligned with customer requirements.
- The lead time of the manufacturing component is aligned with market requirements.
- The cost of purchasing products and raising (if necessary) the quality of purchased products is lowered.
- Operational performance measures are aligned to ensure consistent production of the right product at the right time rather than focusing on achieving maximum efficiency.[951]

---

[951] (Slatter & Lovett, 2004, p. 282)

Characteristics of Inefficient Operations

Troubled companies tend to have several characteristics in common.[952] While not all of these characteristics always exist in every troubled company, most companies experience most of them to at least some extent. If none of these issues are present, it is unlikely that the company's problems are of an operative nature.

- Departments that deal directly with customers are not communicating enough.
- Products are produced for stock and not for sale.
- Products are produced late.
- There are no or few KPIs visible, and the workforce is ill-informed as to required production rates, and so on.[953]
- The supply chain is not working fluently because of problems with suppliers.
- Quality problems result in disputes over invoices.
- Capital expenditure on maintenance is too low.
- Management does not know what the cost drivers are and has unreliable information regarding product costs.
- Employees leave the company as soon as another job becomes available.
- Production planning is inadequate.
- The stock of raw materials is too high.
- When the standard costing system is based on volumes that are too high, work that is in progress might be overvalued.
- There is no procurement.
- Raw material cost is often a high proportion of cost of sales, yet there are usually little or no management processes in place to ensure that supplies are fit for purpose and delivered on time.
- Suppliers are not chosen based on a consistent list of criteria.
- Internal controls are insufficient.
- Products are bought through purchasing authorities.

---

[952] compare (Slatter & Lovett, 2004, pp. 280-282)
[953] (Slatter & Lovett, 2004, p. 280)

- The layout of the production facilities is not efficient and well thought through with the result that there are long lead times. This leads to poor planning of the flow of products through the factory and very high material-handling costs.[954]
- Bottlenecks are not understood or managed.
- The capability of the manufacturing process is not matched to the requirements of product design or the customer.[955]
- There are long downtimes in the production component because changeovers are inefficient. This is also due to poor planning of requirements for tooling.
- If there are high rework levels because of large batch sizes and functional layout it becomes difficult to pick up quality problems when they occur, and many defective products flow through before corrective action is taken.[956]
- Maintenance is not scheduled and is done only when something breaks down, resulting in a lot of downtime.
- The performance measures that do exist are focused on achieving output and maximizing utilization, rather than delivering the right product at the right time.[957]
- Employees are often sick or absent.

Other improvements to operations are suggested in this subcomponent: centralizing the purchasing authority; focusing attention; negotiating payment terms; introducing consignment stocking; buying only what is required; adjusting the resource planning system; and improving packaging requirements.

Centralize the Purchasing Authority

The company should have a central purchasing department as it can often save human resources and allow for bulk buying at special rates from suppliers rather than every department ordering from different suppliers. Buyers can keep an overview of the best sources for products, and the head of the department can be accountable for purchases and spending.

---

[954] (Slatter & Lovett, 2004, p. 281)
[955] (Slatter & Lovett, 2004, p. 281)
[956] (Slatter & Lovett, 2004, p. 281)
[957] (Slatter & Lovett, 2004, p. 282)

Focus Attention

Time and HR resources are critical in a turnaround situation. People are often laid off, and the remaining workforce has to have time to focus on every activity with adequate attention. Therefore, in order to obtain cost improvements and to ensure the delivery of the most important raw materials, the focus should be on these materials and their suppliers.[958]

Negotiate Payment Terms

Negotiating better payment terms, whether on the consumer side or the supplier side, is a critical subcomponent in a turnaround situation. If the company has big customers, shorter payment terms can be negotiated in exchange for preferred-supplier status since a shorter payment cycle improves the cash flow of the company. In some cases, such as Karmann in Germany, the company went bankrupt because some customers, including Mercedes-Benz and BMW, did not pay on time. Other companies use extremely long payment terms because they have a monopoly position. For example, the German book wholesaler Libri delivers books to about 80 percent of all bookstores in Germany and uses its power to dictate payment terms of 180 days for new suppliers that want access to its distribution network.

Introduce Consignment Stocking

When a company moves to consignment stocking some stock risk is passed back to the supplier, which reduces the amount of cash that is necessary for holding stock in the corporation.

Buy Only What is Required

It is not good for the procurement department to be too focused on the purchase price, because the costs of a cheap product over its lifecycle might be higher than for a product with a higher purchase price. If a company is buying too much of a resource the material has to be stored somewhere, which creates costs for the company that have to be included in the selling price. By buying less quantity the company will pay a higher price, but storage will be cheaper and the cash flow will increase. The Turnaround Leader has to evaluate what is best for the company,

---

[958] compare (Slatter & Lovett, 2004, p. 284)

but if the company has high write-offs of raw materials this improvement should certainly be considered.

Adjust the Resource Planning System

Some Resource Planning Systems (MRP systems) use inappropriate parameters such as minimum batch quantities to reorder stock when the inventory level falls below a certain point. This approach effectively decouples the buying obligation from the demand for the item and results in overstocking and a substantial risk of obsolescence.[959] In this case, the parameters should be set to purchase the items based on the actual demand.

Improve Packaging Requirements

A review of the packaging process should be conducted in order to determine whether handling can be decreased and packaging costs reduced, especially with regard to the number of moves, packs, and unpacks between the company and its suppliers.

Responsibility

The Operational Turnaround Manager is responsible for this subcomponent.

---

[959] (Slatter & Lovett, 2004, p. 285)

PI TS 4 – Improve Scheduling Functions

Summary

This subcomponent deals with creating a master schedule and a production plan.

Context

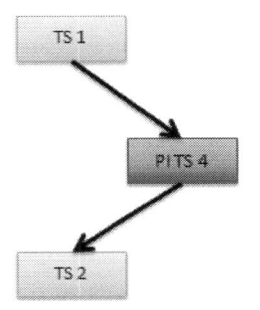

Description of the Subcomponent

The master schedule is an operational plan that is a subset of the larger production plan created in sales and operations planning.[960] The primary input into master scheduling is demand from internal and external customers, which can be expressed in a variety of forms such as customer schedules, customer orders, quotes to customers, samples, promotions, sales forecasts, distribution center replenishment, and more.[961]

Master scheduling must be linked to sales, marketing, engineering, finance, materials, manufacturing, and transportation; in some sense, it is in a pivotal position between these and other important functions.[962] The objective of master scheduling is to balance demand and supply at a mixed level, while capacity planning addresses the supply side of the picture.[963] It serves as a way to find out whether the schedule is realistic and if it is feasible to apply it.

---

[960] (Proud, 2007, p. 29)
[961] compare (Wallace & Stahl, 2005, p. 11)
[962] (Proud, 2007, p. 29)
[963] (Wallace & Stahl, Master scheduling in the 21st century, 2005, p. 12)

The master plan (or schedule) should be created and maintained by a person who understands all areas of the business, particularly the supply and demand sides, and this person should also enjoy the respect of all departments involved.[964] In some cases, the master scheduling function is absorbed directly into the jobs of the line manufacturing supervisors and managers.[965] This person operates as a buffer between the marketing and sales activities and the firm's manufacturing and engineering departments. The master scheduler is a very important position in most turnarounds.

Responsibility

The Operational Turnaround Manager is responsible for this subcomponent.

---

[964] (Slatter & Lovett, 2004, p. 283)
[965] (Wallace & Stahl, 2005, p. 170)

PI TS 5 – Establish Service Levels, Stock Levels, and Lead Times

Summary

This subcomponent deals with calculating target stock levels and implementing a system to maintain optimal stock levels.

Context

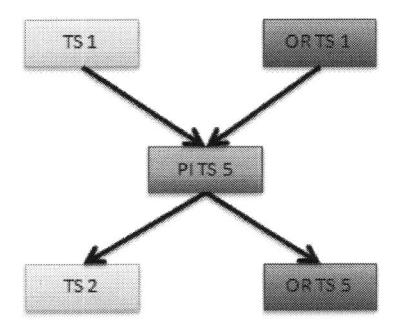

Description of the Subcomponent

The interval between orders for resources can vary widely. Some products will be ordered on a daily basis, others once a week, and some very sporadically. When the interval between orders is known, a target stock level (TSL) can be calculated. The system works by determining the stock on hand after an order has been filled and ordering an amount that brings it up to TSL.[966]

The goal here is to optimize the time between new orders and achieving the required stock level. The more often orders can be placed, the lower the amount of stock that must be available for production and the lower the warehousing costs will be.

From the company's point of view, lead time refers to the time it takes from a customer placing an order to the product being delivered to the customer. By having stock available the company can reduce the lead time for its customers, as a long lead time can result in a customer deciding to cancel an order before it is delivered. For each company and product there is an optimal TSL,

---

[966] (Waters, 2002, p. 621)

which can be calculated based on past experience or by watching market demand closely. Excessively high stock levels that are required to meet the desired service levels are important drivers for a need to cut lead times and increase flexibility in the production process.[967] The following picture shows the target stock level when orders are placed as well as when they arrive.

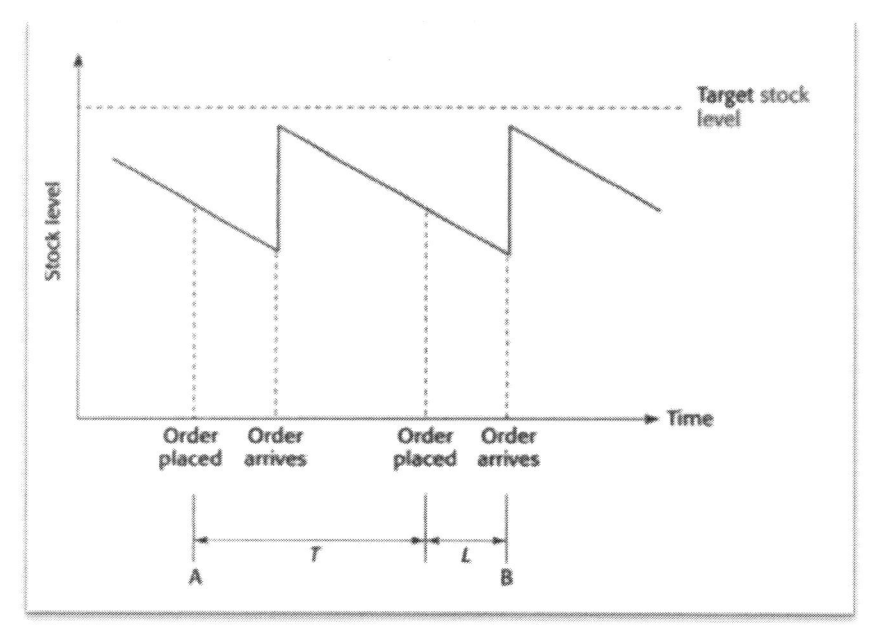

Picture 18 Target stock levels and order times[968]

Responsibility

The Operational Turnaround Manager is responsible for this subcomponent.

---

[967] (Slatter & Lovett, 2004, p. 283)
[968] Source: (Waters, 2002, p. 621)

PI TS 6 – Supply Chain Improvements

Summary

Supply chain management is likely to be needed when customers complain about poor quality, long delivery times, and inconsistent ability to keep promises. Supply chain optimization is an important step in making a business more efficient and in increasing value for customers. Optimization removes the non-value-added steps that have infiltrated or been designed into the series of processes that constitutes a supply chain.[969]

Context

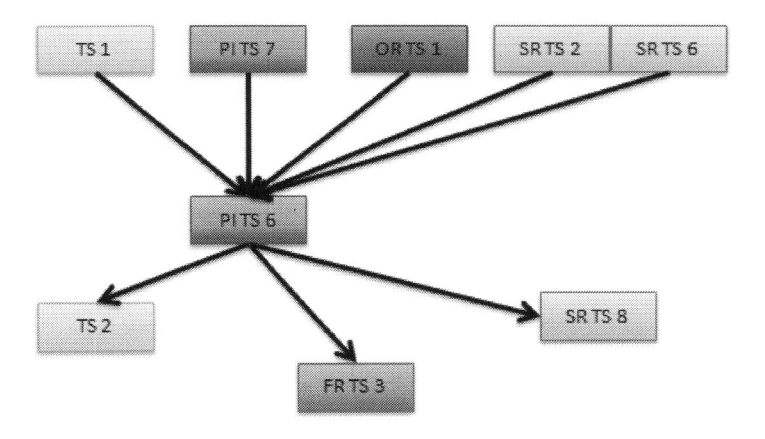

Description of the Subcomponent

While it is not within the scope of this work to describe how supply chain management works, this subcomponent's purpose is to draw attention to the topic and to implement supply chain improvements.

Since 1997, supply chain management has been one of the major issues and challenges that all companies face.[970] The trend in supply chain management is currently leaning toward processes that are easy to understand and overview, alliances, and integrated solutions. A company that

---

[969] (Lysons & Farrington, 2006, p. 109)
[970] compare (Cohen & Roussel, 2006, p. XIV)

does not follow this trend will have trouble keeping up in its market. The objective of supply chain management is to achieve a synchronized and effective response to customer requirements throughout the organization in alliance with other enterprises that form part of the total delivery mechanism, from raw materials to end consumers.[971] The goal is to address cost drivers and to remove functional silos and adversarial relationships in order to increase competitiveness. Strategic alliances can reduce cost structures and the need to monitor processes. In order to optimize the supply chain the TMT needs to be open to working with other companies. Effective supply chain configuration requires building on the business alignment platform established through customer segmentation and customer service propositions.[972]

In a turnaround situation, because of limited resources, the Turnaround Leader must focus their efforts on achieving benefits that the customers value, and discussions with customers should include the evaluation of possible supply chain improvements. The desired outcome, an optimal configuration, will provide the organization with an operational and partnership framework that facilitates delivery of the desired business performance cost-effectively and across multiple interfaces of supply and distribution.[973] Distribution processes and value-added production are synchronized in an optimized supply chain, which often also demands shifting the culture, broader roles, more delegation, and multi-skilling.[974]

The objectives of supply chain optimization are to:

1. Provide the best possible customer service
2. Be cost-effective
3. Achieve the highest possible productivity using the resources available
4. Maximize the company's profits
5. Minimize lead times

The benefits of supply chain management include:[975]

- Increased flexibility to meet the customers' wishes

---

[971] (Slatter & Lovett, 2004, p. 285)
[972] (Gattorna, 2003, p. 49)
[973] (Gattorna, 2003, p. 49)
[974] compare (Slatter & Lovett, 2004, p. 285)
[975] compare (Dam Jespersen & Skjøtt-Larsen, 2008, p. 53)

- Quicker and more precise delivery time
- Greater customer loyalty, resulting in increased sales
- Fewer back orders/sold out situations
- Reduced total costs
- Motivated and focused vendors

The company's top management can increase commitment to optimizing the supply chain by creating a vision that highlights the opportunities and improvements associated with it and keeping everyone working in line with that vision.[976] [977]

Responsibility

The Operational Turnaround Manager is responsible for this subcomponent.

---

[976] Further details about the objectives and factors of supply chain optimization can be found in Lysons and Farrington's *Purchasing and Supply Chain Management*.

[977] More information about the future of supply chain management can be found in Cohen and Roussel's *Strategic Supply Chain Management: the five disciplines for top performance*.

PI TS 7 – Process Value Analysis

Summary

This subcomponent deals with running a process value analysis (PVA).

Context

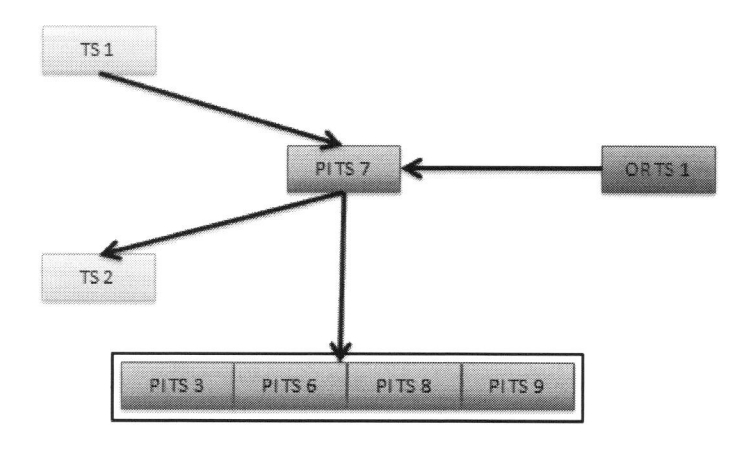

Description of the Subcomponent

The PVA, which offers a systematic way to analyze the costs and value associated with various components, was intended as a bottom-up response to top-down cost reduction programs, many of which involved indiscriminate percentage-based reductions of costs, employees, and programs.[978] It should be carried out in the Turnaround Stage because it can be time-consuming. The PVA is a fairly straightforward approach that involves studying processes and activities in order to understand process flow, and activities that add no value to an output (in the eyes of the customer) become candidates for elimination.[979] The PVA can help save costs, optimize the gains on processes, and increase the company's efficiency. It helps to track down and eliminate activities that add little or no value to the organization.

---

[978] (Davenport, 1997, p. 144)
[979] (Davenport, 1997, p. 145)

The biggest limitation of the PVA is that it can only be applied once to a problem since it does not provide a mechanism for continuous improvement. Davenport found that companies that employ it frequently revert to old practices within a year or two.

Responsibility

The Operational Turnaround Manager is responsible for this subcomponent.

PT TS 8 – Customer Service Improvements

Summary

Satisfied customers are critical for business success. In order to get a business back on track, the company must be able to satisfy its customers by extracting every possible bit of information about them and their complaints. This subcomponent deals with improving customer service and installing customer service processes if they are not already in place.

Context

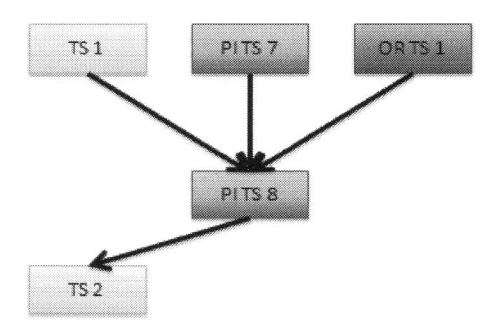

Description of the Subcomponent

In order to optimize customer service, the company must establish some basic requirements, the first of which is to create an escalation process for every non-standard complaint. The complaints should be recorded in a database, and a system to monitor the "voice" of the customer should be installed. Principles that customer service should follow include:

- Customers should be given the same answers, regardless of whom they speak to. All service processes should be standardized.
- Failures that repeat themselves should be analyzed and processes that ensure customer satisfaction should be installed as far as possible. An example would be to establish a warranty for parts.
- All issues that customers have with products should be tracked and categorized.
- Customer feedback should be captured and analyzed.

- Giving gifts to customers should be avoided. It can lead to "pseudo" service calls, whereby some customers will try to get free items without having a real issue.[980] However, the decision concerning whether to give gifts depends heavily on the country in which the company operates. In some cultures gifts are required to do business.

Set Up Escalation Processes

If a customer is not happy with a product or one of its parts fails repeatedly, the customer is likely to be frustrated or upset and demand to speak with a supervisor or someone at an even higher level. In that case, the supervisor or higher-level employee must use their valuable time to deal with a single customer, thereby exceeding the likely margin on the product. An escalation component should be put in place to handle complaints that cannot be handled by customer service personnel.

Large organizations may install an escalation team that handles only these types of complaints.[981] If an escalation team is to be created, it is staffed during this subcomponent. Each response taken by the escalation team should be entered into the complaints database. It should also set up systematic knowledge transfer systems to cross-functional areas based on root cause findings in order to drive improvements in products and services.[982]

Set Up Complaints Database

The complaints database collects all information available from customer complaints, including:

- The product or product part
- How long the repairs took
- The actions the customer service representative is allowed to offer the customer, including guidelines on how to address the issue with a focus on finding and repairing the root cause
- The action taken by the customer service representative
- The mood of the customer

---

[980] (Roman, 2010, p. 92)
[981] compare (Roman, 2010, p. 93)
[982] (Roman, 2010, p. 94)

- Suggestions by the customer

Set Up a VOC System

A VOC (Voice of the Customer) system continuously monitors customers' satisfaction and comments regarding the products, services, and the company itself. There are many VOC systems and ways the customer's voice can be captured, such as by analyzing case studies, conducting surveys, holding focus groups, or developing a Net Promoter Score (NPS).[983] The NPS concept is based on research that shows a relationship between a growing customer base and how loyal it is, since loyal customers are more likely to promote a company's products and services. One method of keeping track of it all is XPe-Track (Expedient Tracking), a matrixed system that reflects in a visual manner the trends of key success indicators (service levels, customer satisfaction) synchronized with special cause events, project launch dates, and campaigns—in short, anything that has a significant impact on customer satisfaction levels.[984]

Responsibility

The Operational Turnaround Manager is responsible for this subcomponent.

---

[983] compare (Hämmerlein, 2009, p. 13), (Reichheld, 2005, p. 39), (Matthews, 2009, p. 70)
[984] (Roman, 2010, p. 100)

*PI TS 9 – Undertake Value Engineering

Summary

Value engineering (VE) improves value without sacrificing function,[985] so this subcomponent should be triggered if a product's value needs to be improved. Since time and resources are required for VE, this subcomponent should be carried out in the Turnaround Stage.

Context

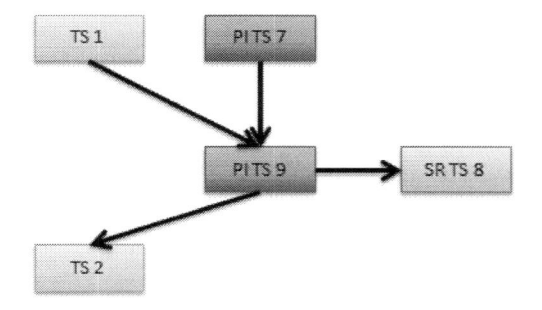

Description of the Subcomponent

Value is the ratio of function over costs, so value can be increased by either increasing function or lowering costs. VE is often a source of substantial cost savings during a turnaround process, particularly for companies that are engineering- or technology-driven. Value Analysis/VE is a complete system designed to define objectives clearly and develop the means to achieve them; it has been proven effective in analyzing products and services at any stage in their development, from concept to production.[986] VE is a management system based on function analysis, analyzing what the product use is. The General Accounting Office estimated that VE efforts save the US government three to five percent of the cost of each program.[987]

---

[985] (Younker, 2003, p. 4)
[986] (Park, 1999, p. 26)
[987] (Younker, 2003, p. 2)

The VE component follows six steps:

1. Information is gathered about who is performing a process, what the process should do, and what it should not do. It is determined which functions are important.
2. It is established how the alternatives will be measured. Are there any other ways to meet the requirements, or are there other processes that can take over the same function?
3. The process is evaluated in terms of what must be done and what it will cost.
4. Ideas are generated about what else the process can do.
5. The alternatives that can produce the requirements and how much the cost savings will be are evaluated.
6. The client chooses between the final alternatives presented.

Responsibility

The Operational Turnaround Manager is responsible for this subcomponent.

Marketing and Sales (MS)

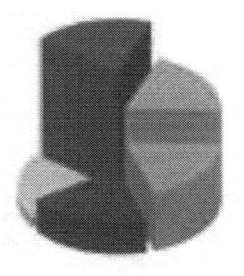

Marketing and Sales During the Crisis Stabilization Stage (MS CS)

MS CS 1 – Implement Sales Forecasting

Summary

The sales forecast is important for the production and finance departments so they can plan accurately and provide the Turnaround Leader with a basis for planning the organizational structure.

Context

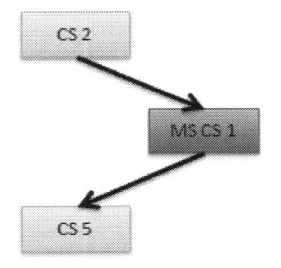

Description of the Subcomponent

In order to work efficiently a manufacturing unit must have accurate demand schedules. The better the demand patterns of the company are understood, the better the planning accuracy will be. A sales forecasting process can be described as a transformation process that has inputs from a variety of sources, one being the forecasting process itself, which is a conversion step similar to physical production; and that has outputs, which are forecasts that are reasonable, reasoned, reviewed frequently, and reflect the total demand.[988]

Sales forecasting is an acceptable estimate based on the company's ability to perform a certain set of actions with a known set of outcomes to arrive at reasonably predictable results.[989]

---

[988] (Wallace & Stahl, 2002, p. 14)
[989] (Webb & Gorman, 2006, p. 68)

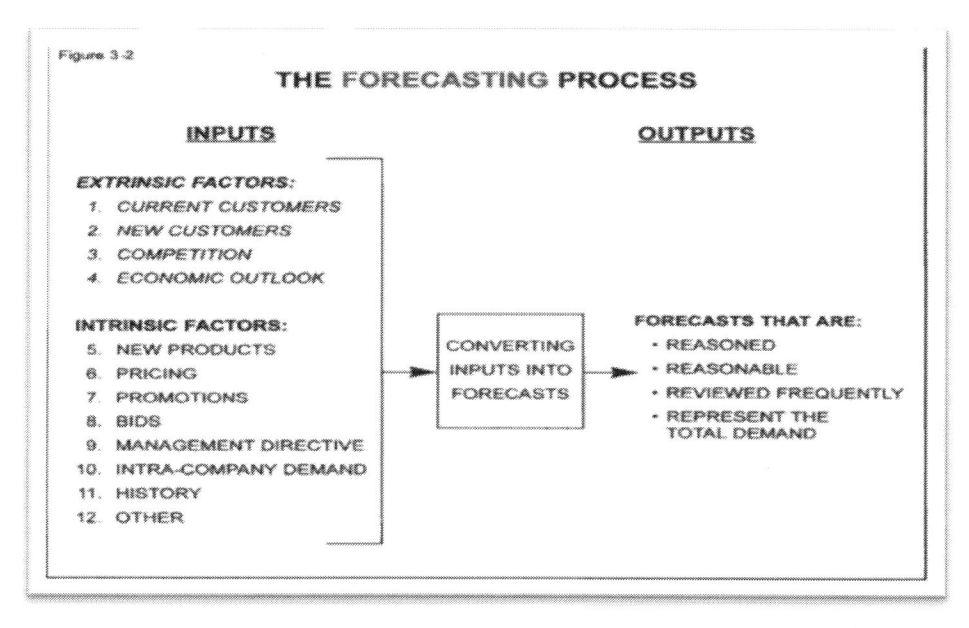

```
                          THE FORECASTING PROCESS
              INPUTS                                    OUTPUTS

    EXTRINSIC FACTORS:
      1. CURRENT CUSTOMERS
      2. NEW CUSTOMERS
      3. COMPETITION
      4. ECONOMIC OUTLOOK
                                                  FORECASTS THAT ARE:
    INTRINSIC FACTORS:                              • REASONED
      5. NEW PRODUCTS           CONVERTING          • REASONABLE
      6. PRICING                INPUTS INTO         • REVIEWED FREQUENTLY
      7. PROMOTIONS             FORECASTS           • REPRESENT THE
      8. BIDS                                         TOTAL DEMAND
      9. MANAGEMENT DIRECTIVE
     10. INTRA-COMPANY DEMAND
     11. HISTORY
     12. OTHER
```

Picture 19 The forecasting process according to Wallace and Stahl[990]

The sales forecast provides the expected level of sales for the company's goods or services during a future period, and it very important for accurate planning and budgeting. Forecasts of future sales and their related costs provide the company with the information needed to forecast financing requirements.[991] Picture 20 Example sales forecasting processshows how a sales forecast should be done.

---

[990] Source: (Wallace & Stahl, Sales forecasting: A new approach, 2002, p. 14)
[991] (Shim & Siegel, 2008, p. 65)

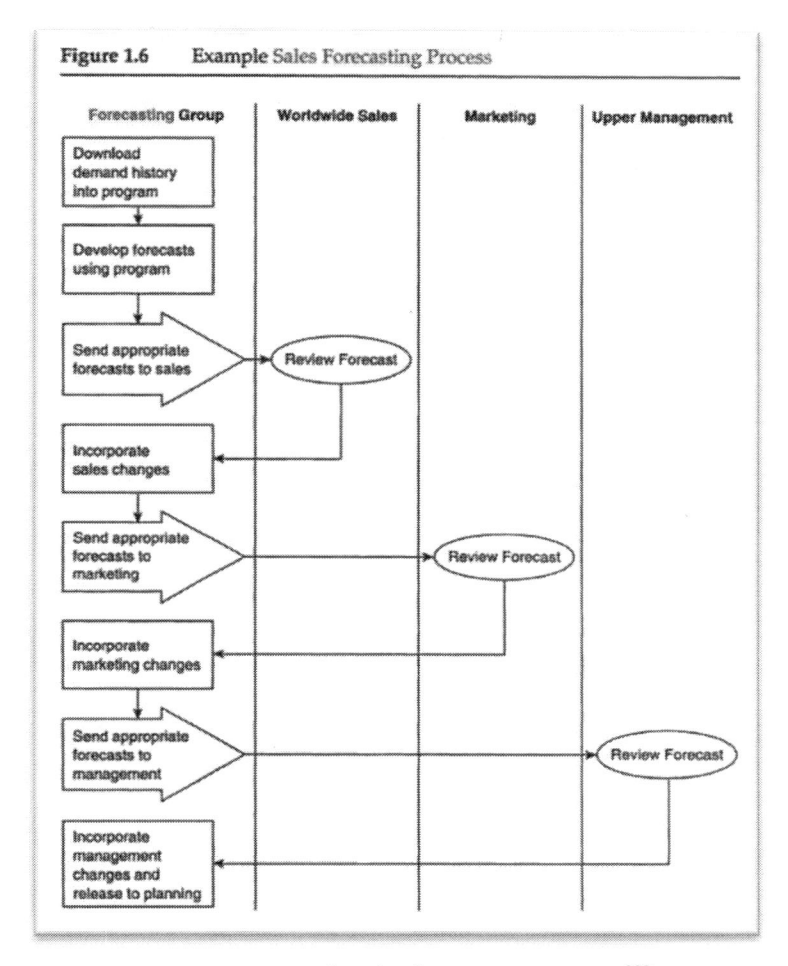

Picture 20 Example sales forecasting process[992]

Sales forecasting is a difficult and inherently uncertain process so it may not yield accurate results very quickly.[993]

Outcome

- Sales forecast

---

[992] Source: (Mentzer & Moon, 2005)
[993] (Slatter & Lovett, 2004, p. 283)

Responsibility

The Turnaround Leader, with the assistance of the marketing and sales expert on the TMT, is responsible for this subcomponent.

MS CS 2 – Evaluating Salespeople in the Crisis Stabilization Stage

Summary

Many companies in turnarounds employ a large number of unproductive salespeople who sell low-profit items to low-purchase-level customers.[994] This subcomponent deals with evaluating salespeople and finding those that are not productive enough.

Context

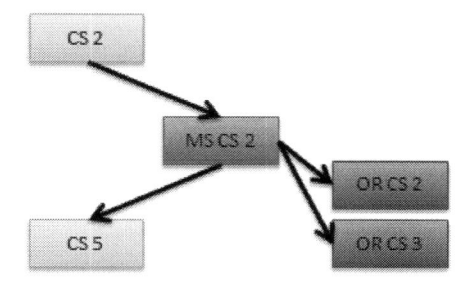

Description of the Subcomponent

The entire sales force should be evaluated at the beginning of the Crisis Stabilization Stage. Reducing the sales force is a way to reduce costs, although the decision to fire the people who actually bring in new business should be made carefully. In some cases, 90 percent of the sales volume is brought in by 40 percent of the sales force. When this situation occurs, sales territories are redrawn and the worst performers are made redundant.[995] A careful evaluation of the sales personnel is required in order to save money and to make the sales force more effective. When salespeople are dropped, executives will often face heavy resistance from sales executives and salespeople, who insist that this is exactly the wrong thing to do.[996] However, if only 20 percent of the salespeople generate 80 percent of the sales, than the sales force can be cut by half. The loss in sales that the lower half generates is likely to be considerably smaller than the money saved by reducing the payroll and increasing the effect and efficiency of team

---

[994] (Bibeault, 1981, p. 323)
[995] (Slatter & Lovett, 2004, p. 275)
[996] compare (Bibeault, 1981, p. 324)

managers who have fewer people to look after. Further savings may be generated by reducing the size of the HR department as a result of the smaller workforce.

There are for five categories of sales performance evaluation:[997]

- Category one relies only on output results such as sales volume, or more subjective measures such as the achievement of sales objectives.[998]
- The second category relies on activities, such as calls made.
- Category three relies on both input and output, and usually combines objective and subjective measures.[999] In this category, evaluations give some measures more weight than others and often use ratios.
- Category four uses both input and output measures against explicit standards, and evaluations are made through supervisory evaluation and statistical methods.
- The fifth category is similar to the fourth, but evaluations are made against the best in the class.

The sales team will be evaluated again at the end of the Turnaround Stage.

Evaluating the Salespeople

The support of the sales director and other sales managers for the turnaround is vital to the turnaround process so it may be necessary to replace the sales management if their cooperation cannot be ensured. After the finance director, the sales manager is the most frequently replaced person during a turnaround process.[1000]

There are six tasks that a sales manager should be able to fulfill:

- Making sure that sales efforts are allocated to the most important products and customers
- Motivating and training the sales force
- Communicating the marketing plan and possibly a new philosophy for the sales team
- Monitoring and evaluating sales performance

---

[997] (Boles, Donthu, & Lothia, 1995)
[998] compare (Baker & Hart, 2008, p. 303)
[999] (Baker & Hart, 2008, p. 304)
[1000] (Slatter & Lovett, 2004, p. 271)

- Evaluating and, if necessary, replacing people on their team
- Understanding the urgency and need for the turnaround, as well as its consequences

A sales manager who is not able to manage these tasks in unlikely to be a successful sales manager in a turnaround situation.

Responsibility

The Turnaround Leader is responsible for this subcomponent.

MS CS 3 – Sales Process Improvements

Summary

Sales process improvements are implemented during the Crisis Stabilization Stage.

Context

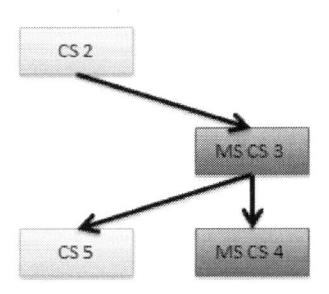

Description of the Subcomponent

Improving sales volume is often not the right focus in a turnaround situation. The sales force may need to focus on the most profitable customers and products instead of trying to sell more to the existing customer base. It may even be necessary to reduce the sales costs by reducing sales efforts. At this point, the TMT should evaluate whether the company can survive with only the current customer base. Some products have a high rate of regular customers who generate a constant and reasonably reliable revenue stream that can keep the company alive until more money can be invested in gaining new customers.

Much of a salesperson's eight-hour workday may be dedicated to traveling between customers. Depending on the industry, many sales are made in person, but in a crisis many of these conversations can take place over the phone or using videoconferencing. Salespeople may argue that face-to-face conversations are key to their success, and this might be true in some cases, but it is also is a good way to justify an expensive company car and time during which no one has direct control over their activity. It is unlikely that real harm would result if these meetings were not held for a couple of months. They should, however, still be regular.

Many of the tactics required to improve the cost-effectiveness of the selling effort are common to all situations; the difference lies only in the instructions to the sales force, not in the activities necessary to achieve a competent sales process.[1001] The bottom 20 percent of any sales activity chews up a disproportionate amount of time and costs and can be neglected or eliminated in favor of reducing costs.[1002]

Sometimes salespeople resist changes that are proposed by the TMT. The Turnaround Leader has a key role in keeping the company together, arguing with respect, and pushing through what is necessary at the right time. The Turnaround Leader must be sensitive to the needs of the sales force but must not become captive to narrow interests.

Responsibility

The marketing and sales expert of the TMT is responsible for this subcomponent.

[1001] (Slatter & Lovett, 2004, p. 71)
[1002] (Bibeault, 1981, p. 290)

MS CS 4 – Focusing the Sales Effort

Summary

In times of scarce resources, the sales efforts must be targeted at the right customers.

Context

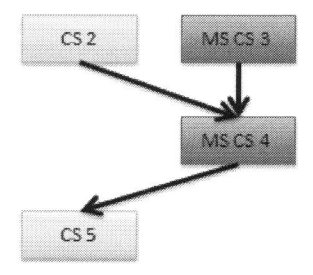

Description of the Subcomponent

This subcomponent ensures that sales efforts are focused on those products and customer segments that contribute the most to the company. Resources are very limited in a crisis situation so they cannot be distributed to all products and services in the same way. In order to use resources effectively, their use must be planned and controlled by conducting an ABC analysis and classification of the customers, or by focusing on specific products.

Conducting an ABC Analysis and Classification of the Customers

An ABC analysis is used to categorize customers by their annual purchases.[1003] Rommel describes "A" customers as those who are crucial to the firm, "B" customers as those who may be very profitable in the future, and "C" customers as those who will never be important to the company because, for example, their sales potential is too low.[1004] 20 percent of the customers (the "A" customers) often account for about 80 percent of retail sales volume.[1005] Typically, this component involves eliminating small and unprofitable accounts. These accounts are ignored,

---

[1003] compare
[1004] (Rommel, 1995, p. 42)
[1005] (Zentes & Morschett, 2011, p. 239)

passed over to wholesalers for servicing, or positively discouraged from ordering by imposing minimum order sizes or surcharges, or by the discounts structure.[1006] Successful companies perform such ABC analyses far more often than less successful ones.[1007]

The ABC analysis can also be based on performance-oriented indicators such as the customer contribution margin. It can be applied to the selection of key accounts and their management, and it may have totally different implications than a sales volume-based ABC analysis.[1008] Picture 21 The ABC analysis and its Lorenz curve.

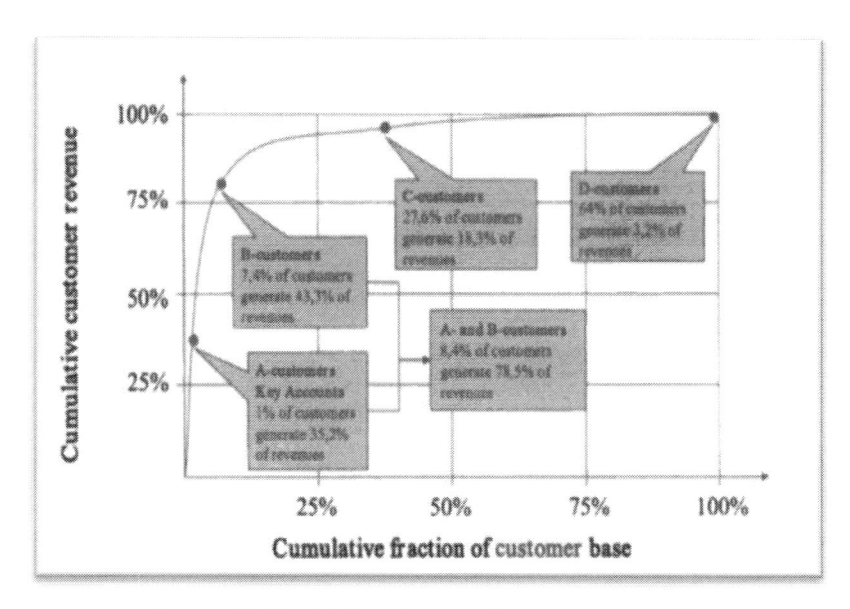

Picture 21 The ABC analysis and its Lorenz curve[1009]

Focusing on Specific Products

The sales personnel only have a certain amount of time for each customer. For example, some estimates have costed the average sales call for industrial companies at approximately $75. One

---

[1006] (Slatter & Lovett, 2004, p. 272)
[1007] (Rommel, 1995, p. 42)
[1008] (Wengler, 2006, p. 73)
[1009] Source: (Plinke, 198, p. 8)

of the most pressing challenges facing today's marketing executives is the achievement of adequate market coverage without pricing the direct sales force out of existence.[1010]

Responsibility

The marketing and sales expert of the TMT is responsible for this subcomponent.

[1010] (Bibeault, 1981, p. 325)

MS CS 5 – Introducing Key Account Management

Summary

This subcomponent is about directing sales promotions to the highest yield accounts. A customer account productivity report and key account management can be of considerable assistance in this matter. Key account management ensures that the most important clients get the information and attention they deserve. In times of crisis, the most important clients become even more so because a group of not-so-important clients may not be able to compensate for the loss of one important one.

Context

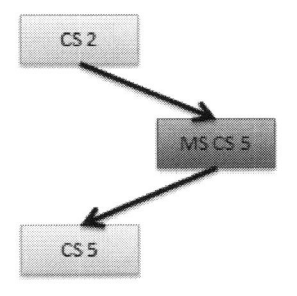

Description of the Subcomponent

Key account management has received considerable attention in the last two decades from research carried out in the area of organizational design in key account management,[1011] its objectives and tasks, and how its performance is measured.[1012] [1013]

Key account management ensures that the most important clients get the information and attention they deserve. For most companies, the 80:20 rule applies when analyzing customers: the majority of purchases are made by a few major customers.[1014] Key account management

---

[1011] compare (Cannon, Gundlach, & Narayandas, 1997), (Kempeners & van der Hart, 1999)
[1012] compare (Belz, Müllner, & Zupancic, 2010), (Bradford & Weitz, 1999), (Putzmann, 2003)
[1013] (Krieger, 2005, p. 106)
[1014] (Slatter & Lovett, 2004, p. 273)

refers to creating long-term relationships with other firms,[1015] producing a detailed plan for the customer accounts (account planning), managing the multiple relationships that may exist between supplier and customer, ensuring that good relationships are maintained, and achieving the sales and profit targets set in the account plan.[1016] On the other side, key account managers, whether they like it or not, should be held responsible by the customer for the delivery of what they have promised, so the company need a process of two-way communication to collect information they get from the customer, as well as good and poor performance indications from the customer.[1017] In a healthy company, key accounts will all be profitable customers, but during a turnaround process it is not unusual for some major customers to be unprofitable (although the incumbent management may not know this).[1018] Some customers, especially large customers, still fail to provide enough revenue to cover overhead costs.

The senior management is responsible for a number of processes in successful key account management.[1019] It is usually the key account managers' responsibility to provide information for these processes so they should know how they work and what they can contribute to them.

The following is a list of the strategic activities for key account managers:[1020]

- Selecting attractiveness criteria and key customers
- Managing the customer portfolio
- Considering implications of customer strategies
- Allocating and prioritizing resources
- Assessing and managing risk to the company
- Sponsoring key customers
- Coordinating across boundaries
- Enabling organizational learning

[1015] (Blythe, 2005, p. 253)
[1016] (Slatter & Lovett, 2004, p. 273)
[1017] (Woodburn & McDonald, 2011, p. 239)
[1018] (Slatter & Lovett, 2004, p. 273)
[1019] (Woodburn & McDonald, 2011, p. 238)
[1020] compare (Woodburn & McDonald, 2011, p. 238)

Key account managers have a duty to add value to customers and their own organizations by managing change. Therefore, there is another set of activities:[1021]

- Analyzing key accounts, developing strategy, and planning
- Developing relationships with customers
- Developing business and capturing opportunities
- Selling and negotiating
- Pricing
- Developing new products
- Customizing products and services
- Managing the product mix
- Developing marketing programs
- Developing the supply chain
- Developing transaction handling
- Providing customer training
- Developing internal relationships
- Providing information

The following is a list of operational activities:[1022]

- Selling
- Processing orders
- Manufacturing operations
- Serving customers
- Delivering to customers
- Collecting payments

A good deal of sales activity belongs at the operational/transactional level and may be carried out by the field sales force or telesales rather than by the key account managers.[1023]

[1021] compare (Woodburn & McDonald, 2011, pp. 238-239)
[1022] compare (Woodburn & McDonald, 2011, p. 239)
[1023] (Woodburn & McDonald, 2011, p. 239)

Responsibility

The marketing and sales expert on the TMT is responsible for this subcomponent.

MS CS 6 – Sales Force Motivation

Summary

Sales force costs are up to 40 percent of sales and, for many firms, the largest part of the sales and marketing budget is spent on the sales staff's incentives, salaries, information systems, and other expenses as well as other support structures and systems.[1024] Putting this spending to the best possible use requires a highly motivated sales force.

Context

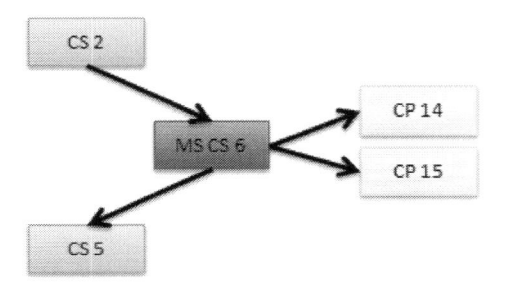

Description of the Subcomponent

In a crisis situation, the sales force may have taken a beating from the top management; high pressure, threats, and salary cuts are not unusual. In order to get the best results from the sales force they need to be motivated to do their jobs as well as possible. Therefore, the leadership skills of the Turnaround Manager responsible for the sales team are important for motivating the sales force. The sales force must act in line with the strategic direction of the company, so the purpose of an effective sales-incentive scheme is to push them in the right direction.[1025]

Recognizing the sales force for their efforts to stay in line with the strategy is a way to ensure the short- and long-term direction of their actions. Most sales forces are paid by results through a combination of a base payment and incentive or commission payments.[1026] Only a very few

---

[1024] (Zoltners, Sinha, & Zoltners, 2001, p. XIII)
[1025] (Newby, 1998, p. 17)
[1026] (Newby, 1998, p. 17)

organizations have incentive schemes, even though the need should be obvious.[1027] Incentives are rewards for successful sales force performance.[1028] They are important because a sales force that gets paid a commission is usually more committed,[1029] and a poor sales compensation plan design is frequently a reflection of senior management confusion about strategy and alignment.[1030]

The incentive scheme should encourage the sales behavior set out by the TMT, and incentives should be based on long-term results. Under normal circumstances short-term incentives would be counterproductive,[1031] but the situation is slightly different in a turnaround so it may require some short-term actions that call for short-term sales improvements. Sales force incentives can work wonders where a quick increase in sales volume is necessary as part of a recovery strategy;[1032] however, extreme inducements can lead to actions that may not meet customer needs or help the firm achieve its goals.[1033]

If incentives are based on revenue the sales force may demand price cuts and will often choose to decimate corporate margins if empowered to reduce prices.[1034] A profit-incentivized sales force, on the other hand, may also have a tendency to focus on quick sales without regard to building a long-term relationship with the client.[1035] In any case, incentives do not work if the performance criteria cannot be measured.[1036]

The TMT can also offer training to motivate the sales force. However, if training is not introduced and carried out correctly, it can lead to demotivation. One Turnaround Leader told an entire sales force that they would all be taking a training program.[1037] The employees were upset; for many of them it was the first time they had been told they needed training. However, the Turnaround Leader immediately introduced the person who was going to do the training and five minutes later, after a string of the dirtiest jokes imaginable, nearly all of the sales force

---

[1027] (Slatter & Lovett, 2004, p. 273), (Bibeault, 1981, p. 291)
[1028] (Zoltners, Sinha, & Zoltners, 2001, p. 291)
[1029] compare (Newby, 1998, p. 18)
[1030] compare (Cichelli, 2010, p. 4)
[1031] (Zoltners, Sinha, & Zoltners, 2001, p. 291)
[1032] (Slatter & Lovett, 2004, p. 273)
[1033] (Zoltners, Sinha, & Zoltners, 2001, p. 290)
[1034] (Newby, 1998, p. 20)
[1035] compare (Newby, 1998, p. 20)
[1036] (Zoltners, Sinha, & Zoltners, 2001, p. 284)
[1037] (Slatter & Lovett, 2004, p. 274)

wanted to take part.[1038] In the end, the training was a much-needed morale-booster in an uncertain time.

Responsibility

The marketing and sales expert on the TMT is responsible for this subcomponent, but the Turnaround Leader plays an important role in motivating the sales force by addressing them directly.

[1038] (compare (S.L., Corp Rec. p. 274)

MS CS 7 – Monitoring the Performance of the Sales Force

Summary

This subcomponent deals with installing a system to monitor the performance of the sales force.

Context

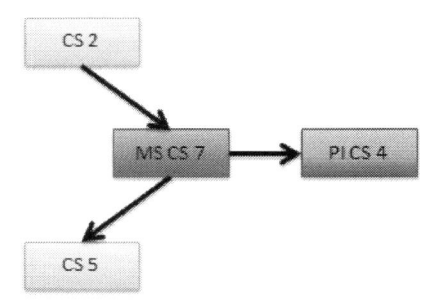

Description of the Subcomponent

Monitoring the sales force is necessary to improve it, but it should be done in a way that does not seem to the salespeople like an attempt to control them. It is important that salespeople have fun doing their job and that they can be creative; that the management trusts them and respects their competence is very important to them.[1039]

In order to monitor the sales force in a crisis situation, the sales management team should have the following responsibilities:

- Analyze actual product line sales against budget on a monthly basis, although in the depth of a crisis weekly analysis is necessary. "If volume and price variances can be separated, so much the better, but this assumes a reliable standard costing system, which is absent in the majority of turnaround situations."[1040]

[1039] (Wayne, 2008, p. 33)
[1040] (Slatter & Lovett, 2004, p. 284)

- Identify and monitor the five to ten most important accounts in terms of their contribution to the company's profits.
- Identify and analyze sales trends if this was not already done in the business's normal activities.
- Monitor the impact of promotional campaigns.
- Implement simple sales force controls, such as the achievement of sales targets by territory, weekly call/order reports showing daily calls and orders, the following week's call schedule, and so on.[1041]

Changing call patterns requires very close control because salespeople don't always act in the best interests of the firm; they typically like to call on friendly customers, on customers with whom they have a good personal relationship, or on customers who are based close to their home.[1042]

Responsibility

The marketing and sales expert on the TMT is responsible for this subcomponent.

[1041] (Slatter & Lovett, 2004, p. 284)
[1042] (Slatter & Lovett, 2004, p. 275)

MS CS 8 – Promotional Costs

Summary

This subcomponent deals with evaluating and targeting promotional activities.

Context

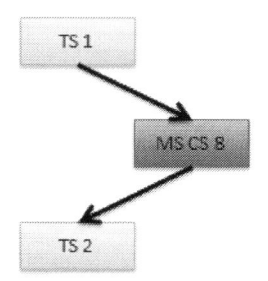

Description of the Subcomponent

Most troubled companies' promotional costs are out of line.[1043] Troubled organizations cannot afford to invest in promotional activities that are not targeted at the right people and at the right time. Most companies are saddled with the heritage of 100 percent promotional coverage that comes largely from the "smother 'em" marketing concept of consumer goods marketers who want to sell their full lines to anyone through every outlet.[1044]

As with many things, Pareto's law usually applies to promotional and sales activities, and the TMT often finds that 20 percent of sales activities do not result in any useful outcome, and the top 20 percent of the sales force accounts for 80 percent of the turnover. Until the Turnaround Management Team has time to conduct a detailed analysis, the sales team should focus on the top 20 percent of customers, get rid of the bottom 25-30 percent, and disregard the middle. Closer to the end, or as a follow-up recommendation of the turnaround process, the sales management can decide whether these customers are activated again. Promotions should be

---

[1043] (Bibeault, 1981, pp. 290-291)
[1044] (Bibeault, 1981, p. 291)

focused on the products that are winners and extended to the customer accounts that are the most profitable.

Responsibility

The marketing and sales expert on the TMT is responsible for this subcomponent.

MS CS 9 – Price Changes

Summary

Price changes can have a significant effect on the business's bottom line and so should be considered carefully. This subcomponent is triggered if the TMT is considering changing the price of the firm's products, if additional funding is needed, or if the product evaluation during the Diagnostic Review came up with optimal prices that differ from those being offered.

Context

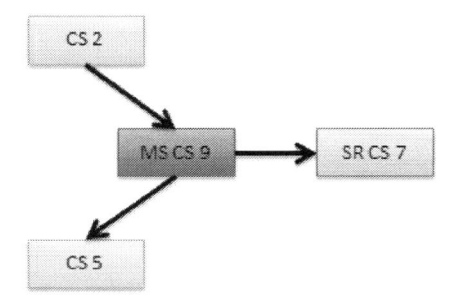

Description of the Subcomponent

Price changes can be implemented more quickly than any other strategy available to the Turnaround Leader.[1045] Price adjustments can be made in the Turnaround Stage, but they are more likely in the Crisis Stabilization Stage because they can help to generate cash flow or decrease inventory.

This section also addresses the difference between list prices and a discount structure. The Turnaround Leader should evaluate, based on the nature of the product and the distribution channel, what to change if they want to change the price structure of the company.

The net price of products sold directly to the customer tends to be more important than a high discount on the original price. The customer cares only about what they have to pay. If the

---

[1045] (Slatter & Lovett, 2004, p. 266)

company sells its products through a distribution network, as is usually the case in the publishing industry, for example, the distributor may be more willing to push the product if there is a high discount on it. A discount structure that is uncompetitive by only 2.5 percent of the end-user selling price on a highly differentiated product can make a big difference in the distribution channel's interest in selling it.[1046] A discount can lead to an increase in sales quantity, but the cost-price structure of the company determines whether discounts are possible at all.

Managers sometimes think that additional sales can be successfully added to the normal sales volume even at prices that are too low to cover a proportional part of the overhead costs.[1047] They also argue that the theory of increasing volume to offset high fixed costs, which is quite popular in business school textbooks, is not applicable in real life. In break-even accounting, expenses are classified into fixed and variable costs, but in real life it is not always that easy since overheads are not always a fixed expense, especially not in the long term. Not taking account of overhead costs when trying to set the right sales price can be a deadly mistake. Except in rare and well-controlled exceptions, marginal business taken to keep the operation going incurs the same overhead costs as the regular business and, by adding to the complexity of the total operations, it often requires more than normal overhead.[1048] If overhead costs cannot be lowered, it is possible to sell the product at a price that contributes only a little to the overhead costs; however, this can only be a short-term measure and must not become a regular action if the company does not want to go bankrupt. Managers often believe that a firm needs to grow if it wants to cover its fixed costs, but costs can often be cut significantly in order to increase the margin. Raising the price of a product is a good idea where there is reason to believe that doing so will only slightly reduce the sales volume.

In a study of 220 companies, only seven percent believed that the prices of their products (capital goods, components, and materials) were below the average market price, while 89 percent believed that their prices were about average or higher than average.[1049] One consequence of this belief is that whether industries enjoy reasonable or tight profit margins may depend on historical factors over which the present generation of marketing managers has

---

[1046] (Slatter & Lovett, 2004, p. 270)
[1047] (Bibeault, 1981, p. 285)
[1048] (Bibeault, 1981, pp. 285-286)
[1049] (Skinner, 1975, p. 72)

little control.[1050] Applied to a turnaround situation, this shows that a company could try to increase prices and make others in the industry follow suit with the result that some products that are sold at break-even might become profitable and would not have to be scrapped. The decision concerning whether a product or product line should be discontinued should be made after price changes are decided.

Increasing the Price

Increasing prices is common and effective in turnaround situations.[1051] Increasing the price of a product or service can be achieved by raising the price or ceasing to offer discounts. Raising the price is the quickest and safest method of increasing price as changing discounts is more complex, has a greater impact on distributors, and requires more detailed cost and market information than is often available at the start of the recovery stage. Although raising the price is usually easy, there are serious questions to consider, especially in price-sensitive markets.

Firms in a crisis situation usually have prices that are too low because the prices were incorrectly assessed by marketing agencies or the sales force, but also because of timidity or neglect. A price increase, if one is necessary, is likely to help the company's profitability. Underpricing occurs four times as often as overpricing, making the job of the sales force too easy and turning them into order takers instead of employees who use their skills to sell the products.[1052]

1. *Determine Products that Should Have a Price Increase.*

The first question to consider when evaluating whether prices should be increased is whether an increase should apply to only one product or a few. The same percentage price increase on all product lines is unlikely to be appropriate, so the TMT should compare the prices of the competitors' products with the current and proposed prices of its own and carry out a price elasticity analysis.[1053] (A quick price elasticity analysis should always be done before increasing the price, even in the Emergency Procedures Component, although in that component time pressure means that the decision will have to rely on the management's experience and perception of the market.) Some helpful points to consider when evaluating price increases are:

[1050] (Bibeault, 1981, pp. 285-286)
[1051] compare (Slatter & Lovett, 2004, p. 266)
[1052] (Bibeault, 1981, p. 284)
[1053] compare (Slatter & Lovett, 2004, p. 267)

- Products that already have high margins can often stand a further price increase more easily than low-margin products since their competitive position is likely to be stronger.[1054]
- Products that are not purchased often have a tendency to be less price-sensitive because the customer is less likely to recall the original price.[1055] In the case of windshield washer fluid, for example, people seldom buy the product and, when they do, don't remember the price they paid the last time they bought it. The product has since been priced several times higher than before, with no measureable decrease in demand and with a fat profit margin that has helped in the promotion of other items where there is price competition and margins cannot be as wide.[1056]
- If there are not too many competitors and the competitors are not strong, price increases may be easier and more successful.
- If the costs to a buyer of switching to a competitor are high, prices are often less elastic.

2. How Much Can the Price be Raised?

For almost all products there is a maximum price after which demand decreases sharply. The potential premium that can be charged over the mean market price depends not only on the nature of the product but also on the competition; however, 10 to 15 percent is at the high end of the spectrum.[1057] If a customer wants to buy a product for 100 euros and finds a product that costs 109 euros, the customer will probably still consider it; but there is most likely a limit to the extent to which a price can be raised. At a certain point the company will lose customer goodwill.

3. When Should the Price Be Raised?

Price increases should take inflation into account, so prices should be increased every 12 months regardless. If the price has been increased recently it will be more difficult to justify an additional increase. More frequent adjustments to the price are possible if there are high fluctuations in exchange rates, or economic shocks.

[1054] (Slatter & Lovett, 2004, p. 267)
[1055] compare (Slatter & Lovett, 2004, p. 267)
[1056] (Bibeault, 1981, p. 286)
[1057] (Slatter & Lovett, 2004, p. 268)

Most companies' terms of trade state that the price of services or goods can be increased at any time, which means that the price can change even if an order has already been received and not yet delivered. However, it is not advisable to raise the price of orders that have already been received since doing so may upset the customer. If the firm has excess inventory and urgently needs more cash it may wish to give its clients advance notice of an upcoming price increase in the hope that they will buy more and that the excess inventory will be liquidated.[1058]

4. What About Contracts with Clients?

If the company has contracts with some clients, the TMT should look for escalation clauses that allow them to be renegotiated. However, as a client usually does not have an interest in the company failing before its contract is fulfilled, the TMT might have some leverage.

The biggest resistance to raising prices often comes from the sales force since they may believe that a higher price will make selling the products more difficult. This objection is especially likely if their bonuses are tied to the performance of the sales team. However, sales force complaints are normal. When the sales department willingly agrees to a price increase, one can be sure that the proposed price increase is still too low.[1059] I have come across sales departments who support price increases if they understand the reasons behind them, but a meeting with the sales managers should always be conducted prior to increasing prices to evaluate their position and build their trust in the management.

When the TMT does not have a great deal of experience in a particular industry and its products, it is very important for the management to listen to the salespeople and evaluate their points of view before changes are made. If the price increase was the wrong decision or based on incorrect assumptions, the Turnaround Leader can almost always lower the price again to previous levels. In any case, it may take a while before customers become accustomed to the higher prices, which can explain a sudden drop in sales right after the price increase. I call this effect "customer adjustment time".

[1058] (Slatter & Lovett, 2004, p. 268)
[1059] (Slatter & Lovett, 2004, p. 270)

Lowering the Price

A price can be decreased by either offering discounts or keeping the price steady while the costs go up and competitors raise their price.

Changing Discounts

There are two kinds of discounts: settlement discounts and volume discounts. Changes in a firm's discount structure tend to lead to more customer reaction than changes in list prices.[1060] Discounts should be cut only if the company wants to discourage certain customers, such as unprofitable customers, from buying the firm's products. Unprofitable customers can be large customers who demand extremely low prices because of their order quantity or very small customers who order only very small quantities. In the case of small customers, the administrative costs of keeping the client can sometimes be higher than the profits they offer.

Dismissing discounts is therefore not a good idea in implementing an overall price increase, especially in the Crisis Stabilization Stage of a turnaround, because it might make the remaining customers even more upset and push them to buy from a competitor.

Responsibility

The Turnaround Leader is responsible for this subcomponent.

[1060] (Slatter & Lovett, 2004, p. 269)

Marketing and Sales During the Turnaround Stage (MS TS)

MS TS 1 – Overall Marketing Strategy

Summary

This subcomponent deals with evaluating the existing marketing strategy and adapting it to the Turnaround Plan or creating a new marketing strategy.

Context

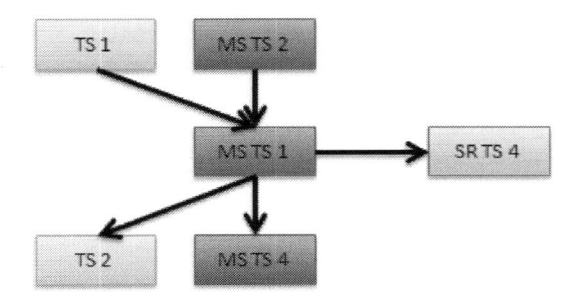

Description of the Subcomponent

An overall marketing strategy is developed in this subcomponent. If there is already such a strategy in place, it is re-evaluated and adjusted according to the Turnaround Plan. How to create a new marketing strategy or change an existing one would be a book in itself, so this subcomponent should be attended to by experts and is only to be seen as a trigger to further actions that are not part of this standard.

The overall principles of marketing strategy for companies in the Turnaround Stage include:

- Only expend products and markets in a sizable, manageable manner in order to stay efficient and competitive. If the expansion is done too quickly costs get out of hand and the expansion will throw the company back into a crisis.
- Obtain and hold niches in end-use markets where it is possible to maintain a profit performance superior to that of the competition and to avoid retaliatory action from very large competitors.[1061]

[1061] (Bibeault, 1981, p. 356)

- Utilize the company's competitive advantages.

Outcome

- Overall marketing strategy

Responsibility

The Turnaround Leader is responsible for this subcomponent.

MS TS 2 – Understanding the Customers

Summary

This subcomponent examines what customers want and do not want, what they know about the company, and how they see the company and its products.

Context

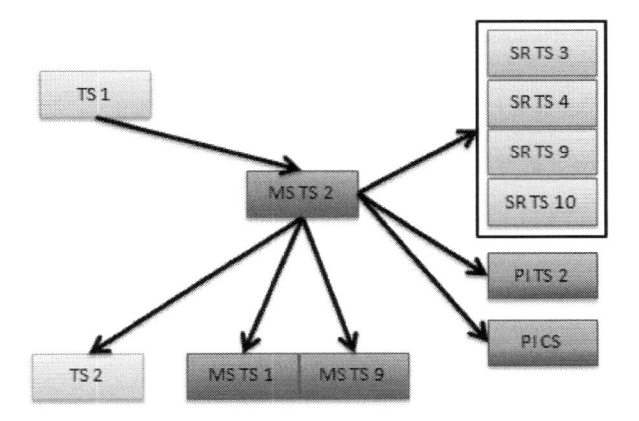

Description of the Subcomponent

Once the company is stabilized again and is starting to generate some free cash flow, extensive market research about its customers can provide an extensive view of the customer base and point out specific research that may be important for future strategic decisions, such as research into new markets, changes in the market, and cross-market influences.

A product-market analysis can lead to selective marketing for a certain product in order to target the customer better.[1062] Knowing what the customer wants and does not want is important for the development of new products, gaining a competitive edge over the competition, and improving customer service.

[1062] compare (Bibeault, 1981, p. 351)

Responsibility

The marketing and sales expert on the TMT is responsible for this subcomponent.

MS TS 3 – Improving the Cost-Effectiveness of Marketing

Summary

Marketing activities are direct expenses so they should be as effective as possible. This subcomponent examines and optimizes the costs associated with marketing.

Context

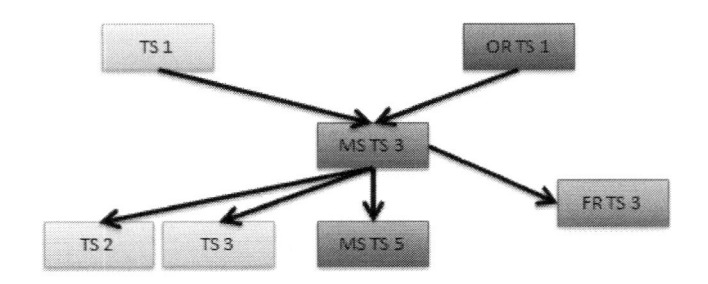

Description of the Subcomponent

It is important that the product-market strategy be examined or, if there is no such strategy, developed. Five areas should be examined closely: the costs of the sales force; marketing and management costs; promotion and advertising costs; distribution costs; and service costs.

1. The Costs of the Sales Force

The costs of the sales force can be broken down into both fixed and variable. A sales force that works on commission is a variable cost, except for the fixed income, fringe benefits, and other expenses.[1063] A third element of costs associated with the sales force is overheads, which are one of the main targets for evaluation during a turnaround process. Reducing overheads associated with the sales function usually involves such actions as reducing the size of the sales force or eliminating regional sales offices, since controls over items like travel and entertainment expenses are rarely sufficient to make much of an impact on profitability.[1064]

[1063] compare (Harvard Business Press, 2009, p. 185)
[1064] (Slatter & Lovett, 2004, p. 279)

2. Marketing Management Costs

What's true for the sales force is also true for the marketing team. However, the variable costs might not be that significant in this department so the focus should be put on exceptional expenses and overhead costs. Exceptional expenses are, for example, studies commissioned by the marketing department and contracts for public relations activities that it has with external agencies.

3. Promotion and Advertising Costs

Marketing and advertising sometimes have little direct effect on sales efforts but serve instead as a future investment. In some businesses (e.g. mail-order houses) the lag effect is minimal, but in others, such as capital goods and industrial projects, the time between the initial marketing expenditure and the collection of sales revenues is measured in years.[1065] If the company's short-term survival is at stake, these costs may be cut so available resources can be invested in keeping the company afloat. The promotion and advertising costs also depend on whether the TMT is preparing the company for a quick sale or implementing measures for a long-term, sustainable recovery. There are great dangers in taking the short-term approach and most successful recovery situations point to a balance between the short-term demands of survival and the need for longer-term actions to achieve a sustainable recovery.

The TMT should also compare the advertising costs and how they are allocated with how competitors spend their advertising budget. In this way, the TMT can find out where their focus lies and possibly adopt the strategy or even find a niche.

If the company cannot afford to push the marketing efforts on all products, it should focus on the few highly profitable ones. One of the most common areas for improvement in companies that have declined is their advertising expenditure, which is often spread too thinly over a large number of products so the advertising message is drowned out by competing messages from competitors' products.[1066] Another strategy that could be considered is the tide and flood strategy, where a few products are pushed with the maximum amount of expenditure available,

---

[1065] (Slatter & Lovett, 2004, p. 278)
[1066] (Slatter & Lovett, 2004, p. 279)

but only one at a time. In practice, product A would receive all marketing efforts for about six months, then product B for six months, followed by product A again.

4. Distribution Costs

For firms that have significant distribution costs, a quick reduction is seldom possible. A comparison of distribution providers and a call for tenders could be made. The TMT needs to keep in mind that changes to the distribution system can have an effect on inventory levels, bounded capital, and cash flow of the company. The point to remember is that manufacturing and distribution costs are interdependent, and that the balancing of inventory-carrying costs against production costs is a key management decision.[1067]

5. Service Costs

The company must be careful in cutting costs that customers will be aware of; for example, a reduction in service levels cannot feel favorable to the customer. In a crisis situation, cutting marketing costs can be useful because the time it takes to implement the cuts is very short and savings can be realized quickly.

Responsibility

The marketing and sales expert on the TMT is responsible for this subcomponent.

[1067] (Slatter & Lovett, 2004, p. 280)

MS TS 4 – Product Line Refocusing

Summary

This subcomponent refocuses the products to a different market, terminates further products, or introduces new products.

Context

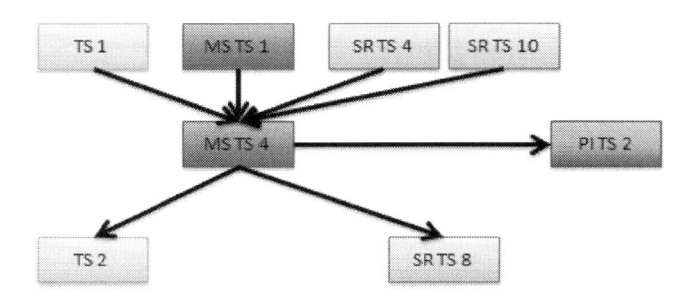

Description of the Subcomponent

Most companies in a turnaround situation suffer from product line proliferation within the product-market segment in which they compete.[1068] The proliferation often takes the form of offering the same product with many variations in the same market segment.

Products that are custom-made for specific clients are often not profitable unless the whole operation is set up to suit these clients. The same goes for products that need to be adapted or changed frequently. In addition, products that do not cover their variable costs should be terminated right away. Much of this has already been done in the Crisis Stabilization Stage, so now the TMT needs to examine whether products that cover their variable costs remain profitable once overhead costs are added, because the overhead costs may have been reduced to a minimum as a result of the turnaround action. As a result, some products may have become profitable, while others may still not be profitable once the fixed costs, such as administration, are taken into account. The products that still do not provide a healthy contribution to the

---

[1068] (Slatter & Lovett, 2004, p. 276)

business should be eliminated. The contribution lost by cutting one product should be recouped by persuading the customer to switch to a standard product instead, or the lost contribution can be recouped in increased sales and profit from the reduced product line since, with fewer products, the firm should be able to concentrate its efforts and sell more of the products that remain.

When some products are terminated, the sales force will probably protest. Their argument is usually that the firm's sales of its biggest-selling products are dependent on also selling other products that are possibly not profitable. That is, however, rarely the case. The TMT needs to evaluate the connection between the different products in the product analysis carried out in the Diagnostic Review Stage. To counter the arguments, the Turnaround Leader can demonstrate that the most important customers don't buy all the products, especially not the ones that are to be terminated. If a big customer buys only unprofitable products, the customer is probably not worth keeping if they are not willing to switch to a standard product. Few companies have been negatively affected by not offering a full spectrum of products.[1069] By terminating one or more product, the company will free up capacity that can be used to produce more of the profitable products, or free up resources and investments by selling assets. The Turnaround Leader should keep in mind that carrying a full line may be a valid strategy for a healthy market leader but almost never is for a firm that is losing money.[1070]

Refocusing can also mean the introduction of a new product. If the company was not producing the right products for the right market it can either change the market or change the product in order to serve the market more effectively. For example, if a company that produces milk products does not adapt as customers become increasingly fat-conscious by producing more fat-free or low-fat milk, it could introduce a new product such as a low-fat, low-calorie milkshake to complement the product line and to adapt to the changing preferences of the customers.

Responsibility

The marketing and sales expert on the TMT is responsible for this subcomponent.

[1069] compare (Slatter & Lovett, 2004, p. 277)
[1070] (S.L., Corp. Rec. p. 277)

MS TS 5 – Evaluating Salespeople in the Turnaround Stage

Summary

This subcomponent re-evaluates the sales force according to the changed circumstances in the Turnaround Stage.

Context

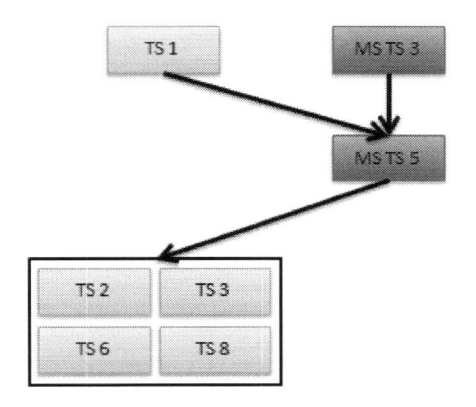

Description of the Subcomponent

The sales force should be re-evaluated close to the end of the Turnaround Stage because products, the motivation to support the products or the company, or other circumstances that influence the effectiveness of the sales force may have changed during the turnaround process.

Since the TMT has probably introduced many changes to the sales force it is likely that some people could not or did not want to adapt, especially if there were new and increased control mechanisms. Most people don't like being controlled so the word control should be avoided when discussing employees. Guidance may be a better choice of word. Also, most people don't like to be told what to do, when, and who they need to do it with. Salespeople, for example, like to choose who to call, when, and how often. However, this freedom is only possible with people who bring results; others may need that guidance, whether they like it or not. It takes a few months to determine which people are able to adapt to the new management style so this second evaluation determines how people are dealing with the new management, incentives, and controls.

Responsibility

The marketing and sales expert on the TMT is responsible for this subcomponent.

MS TS 6 – Placeholder for the Introduction of Yield Management

Summary

This subcomponent is a placeholder for the introduction of yield management, but not part of this work.

Context

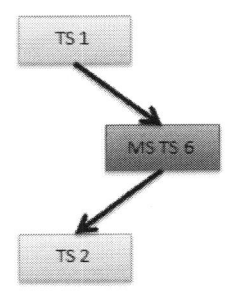

Description of the Subcomponent

One way to gain profit with existing products is to introduce yield management. Yield management allows a product to be sold with slightly altered functionalities or features for a higher or lower price, while the original product stays the same.

Responsibility

The marketing and sales expert on the TMT is responsible for this subcomponent.

MS TS 7 – Reviewing the Price Structure

Summary

This subcomponent starts a review of the products' price structure.

Context

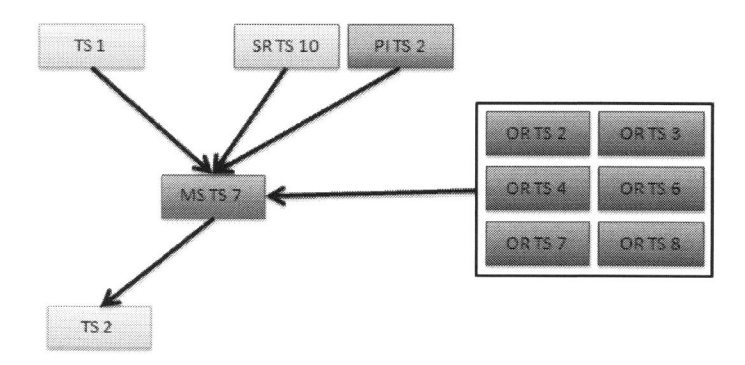

Description of the Subcomponent

If the prices of the company's goods or services have been changed there should be a formal review of the price changes in the Turnaround Stage to evaluate their effect in terms of increased/decreased sales quantity, lost or gained customers, and changes in profits made.

Responsibility

The marketing and sales expert on the TMT is responsible for this subcomponent.

MS TS 8 – New Corporate Design

Summary

If necessary, a new corporate design should be developed when the turnaround process is finished.

Context

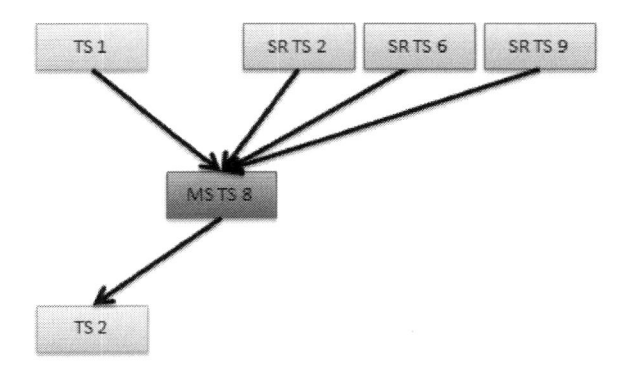

Description of the Subcomponent

This subcomponent is not triggered in every turnaround situation, but it may underscore a new fresh start that the company wants to make.

Since a change in corporate design is expensive, it is suggested only toward the end of the turnaround process. In the rare cases where the company's survival depends on a name change, this subcomponent can be triggered by Emergency Procedures. However, in the case of AirTran's turnaround, a new corporate design was developed alongside the purchase of new airplanes, a new customer target, and a fresh new look, all of which added positively to the overall picture of the company. In that case, the new planes had to be painted anyway, and the changed customer target (business class) demanded a new visual image.

Responsibility

The Turnaround Leader is responsible for this subcomponent.

MS TS 9 – Famous Customers

Summary

This subcomponent examines the importance of well-known customers for marketing purposes.

Context

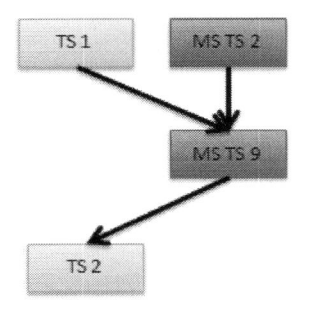

Description of the Subcomponent

Well-known or famous customers can help to restore the image of the troubled company, so they are important for turnarounds. This subcomponent examines how these customers can be helpful.

In some cases, well-known customers can provide influential references. These references can also be beneficial if the company is traded on the stock market because they help the company get attention and support from shareholders.

At Cisco, Chambers, the CEO, knew that gaining well-known customers would not only help to drive earnings but also help to increase the company's presence in the media. On the sales side, Chambers pressured staff to do a better job of pursuing stable telecommunications customers, such as the four "Baby Bell" local phone companies. This had long been a company weakness, and Chambers knew that Cisco needed more big-name customers if it was to regain Wall Street's confidence.[1071]

Responsibility

The marketing and sales expert on the TMT is responsible for this subcomponent.

[1071] compare (Rajendar, 2007, p. 35)

Change Management

CM 1 – Fresh Start

Summary

The change management consultant on the TMT and the Turnaround Leader should create an atmosphere that suggests a new start.

Context

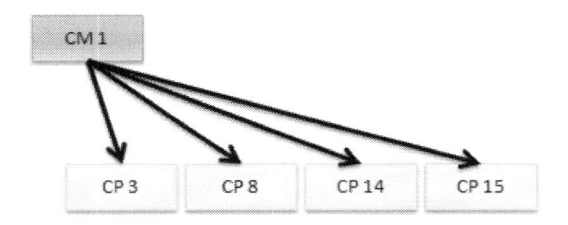

Description of the Subcomponent

Around 70 percent of all change initiatives in companies fail.[1072] It is therefore important to manage change early on.

Change management can be tough going, especially when things have been done a certain way for a long time or are part of the company's culture. For example, some managers may be against removing a free service that has always been offered to customers but does not add value to the company, because they believe that too many customers will be lost by removing this benefit. However, resistance often occurs simply because things have been done the same way for a long time. "The operational turnaround consultant is the ultimate change agent; they should have experience implementing unpopular, against-the-grain changes and be focused on immediate, attainable financial results."[1073]

A fresh start requires a kick-off meeting with the workforce and the TMT, an open-door policy where the TMT is approachable, and a team of experts who listen to the concerns of the workforce, motivate them, and try to help with concerns. Sometimes even the long-promised

---

[1072] compare (Beer & Nohria, 2001, p. 2)
[1073] (Roman, 2010, p. 11)

replacement of a broken LCD screen or office chair can help to show people that change is coming.

Responsibility

The change management consultant on the TMT is responsible for this subcomponent.

CM 2 – Corporate Culture

Summary

Turnaround situations often require a new corporate culture to support new values. This subcomponent triggers a change in the corporate culture.

Context

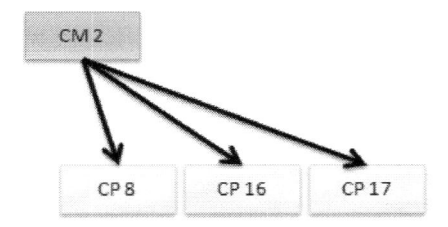

Description of the Subcomponent

To overcome a corporate crisis it is very likely that the culture of a company must change; often, even if it was not part of the problem, it was at least not preventing it. A company's mission and value statements are the elements that define its corporate culture.[1074] Hence, changing the corporate culture is also connected to SR CS 1 (Creating a Mission Statement). Furthermore, some actions that are necessary in order to save the company might go against the old culture and create misunderstandings, demotivation, and conflict if the culture is not adapted to the new strategy.

If the crisis was due to exogenous factors and the company did not respond quickly enough, the culture may have suffered under the crisis as well. In both cases, the culture needs to be changed.

It is rare that changing corporate culture can be initiated from within.[1075] The change management should be led by an outside consultant or the Turnaround Leader because it

---

[1074] (Kamerer, p. 14)
[1075] compare (Rembor, 2004)

requires out-of-the-box thinking, and people from inside the organization have been exposed to old habits and to how things have been done in the past.

Bad Corporate Culture

Bad corporate cultures share several traits:

- Employees are afraid to express their own ideas and they don't want to present or speak up. They meet after meetings to discuss their real opinions.
- Open and honest conversations are not encouraged.
- Public humiliation is often present. Employees who stand up for their beliefs are at risk of being publicly disciplined for making a mistake or having a different way of thinking. Employees may have been fired or turned down for promotion for expressing unorthodox opinions or for criticizing the leadership.
- Employees are not willing to make decisions on their own, and look for ways to stay out of trouble or find out what their supervisor wants to hear from them. In that case, errors go unreported, unrealistic plans are based on impossible assumptions, and processes are in place to please the boss and deliver their vision, regardless of how costly and inefficient that may be.[1076]
- Employees work a considerable amount of overtime because of insufficient training, high failure rates, or bad planning.

Responsibility

The change management consultant on the TMT is responsible for this subcomponent.

[1076] (Roman, 2010, p. 77)

CM 3 – Managing Resistance

Summary

People tend to greet change in any form with the same vast array of weapons, armed and ready to fire: objections, threats, disruptions in routines, accusations, resignations, strikes, acts of sabotage, and so on. These reactions happen when change is not managed through a change management process.[1077]

Context

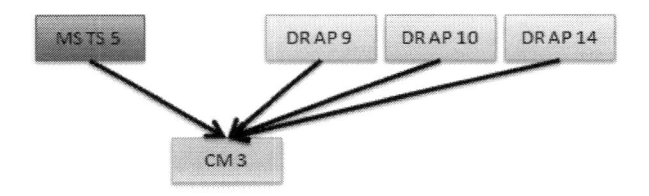

Description of the Subcomponent

Resistance to change is almost normal. However, the TMT cannot force a corporation to turnaround, to want to change, and to support the turnaround process. The company needs to want to survive. In order to minimize the fear of change and the resistance that follows it, the TMT should define the threats, prioritize them, avoid too much force, and remove obstacles, but also force compromise where required.

Define Threats

Employees who have been with the organization for a number of years tend to resist change, while newly hired employees tend to be more open-minded to new ideas and take a more critical view of the business.[1078] Experienced turnaround professionals should have a sense of what employees will perceive as threats as turnarounds are extreme in terms of the changes they present, often making everyone nervous, ready to defend themselves and protect their jobs. To avoid losing their jobs, people can be highly creative in terms of how they block a

---

[1077] compare (Roman, 2010, p. 33)
[1078] compare (Roman, 2010, p. 58)

change. Therefore, the TMT should think carefully about who might be threatened by their communications. An expert in communications for turnaround situations can be very helpful in this regard.

This is not the time to forget that companies are made up of people; feelings drive people to act, and no process can ever supersede that.

Prioritize Threats

Some managers have an ego problem when change is proposed because, to them, change means they did something wrong or were not good enough. Rather than admit this, some may prefer to see the company fail rather than change. "In that case, the failure wouldn't be about 'me' but [...] about 'us', and there is instinctual safety in that."[1079] If the failure occurred because of the manager's actions they may have to be replaced, but if the failure is not due to the manager but they perceive that they are being labeled a failure or are being exposed or humiliated, they will have to be motivated in some way, for example by increased compensation or prestige if the change efforts are successful.

Avoid Force

Telling a manager to stop resisting change or to threaten them with repercussions if they do not change is counterproductive, but it is one of the most frequently used methods of halting defensive behavior to order.[1080] Defensive behavior is instinctive, so the TMT must address the existing objections, engage in open conversation, and ask questions. The goal is to gain understanding and the support that comes from free will. Therefore, "if a systems change is the initial threat, implementing the new system can become a goal [that] pays, say, a 25 percent bonus upon completion with zero business disruption and zero delay".[1081]

Having highly motivational leaders is a good way to get people moving. If team leaders do not support the turnaround process they may have to be replaced or motivated. They should be directed gently towards what is coming up and asked to think about their teams, who will need

---

[1079] (Roman, 2010, p. 37)
[1080] (Roman, 2010, p. 37)
[1081] (Roman, 2010, p. 38)

their support if they have problems with the change process, and about their goals, which will lead to the comeback.[1082]

Remove Obstacles

Getting buy-in from some employees can be difficult. Some may not want to change, even after discussions, because they are simply too stubborn, too political, or too rigid. Others are simply strong believers in the old corporate culture and don't want to change, while still others are only concerned with their own good and are not interested in the company's fate. In that case, they become part of the problem and a burden to the turnaround process. If they are not recognized or ignored roadblocks could form that make the change even more difficult. For those who can be convinced, the compensation system must mirror their efforts in the turnaround and change component. At the same time, "the buy-in must be real; it is the true buy-in, heart and soul, combined with achievable rewards, that will generate the creative, impactful, and immediate results needed to reverse the fall".[1083]

Force Compromise

Sometimes exaggeration can be useful in gaining employee support, but it is important that the threat is believable. At United Airlines, the top management made the crisis sound more severe than it was in order to gain support from the unions. Early in the negotiations the management threatened to break up the airline, which would have meant thousands of employees losing their jobs if an agreement could not be reached.[1084] The unions were further convinced by a restructuring plan, evaluations, and financial projections, and they agreed to what the CEO wanted.

Responsibility

The change management consultant on the TMT is responsible for this subcomponent.

[1082] (Roman, 2010, p. 38)
[1083] (Roman, 2010, p. 39)
[1084] compare (Simonsen & Cassady, 2007, p. 7)

CM 4 – Implementing a New Corporate Culture

Summary

Companies in trouble sometimes have a questionable corporate culture, and a new culture that encourages open discussion may be necessary. The change management expert on the TMT should help to create a new corporate culture.

Context

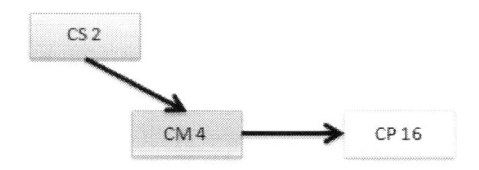

Description of the Subcomponent

Implementing a new corporate culture is time-consuming. New values cannot be placed into people's heads overnight.

In this subcomponent the change management consultant analyzes the existing corporate culture in discussion with the TMT, and new values and goals are prepared. The change management consultant should then outline a way to change the corporate culture to a motivating and highly effective work environment by encouraging open discussions and prioritizing clearly.

Encourage Open Discussions

Open discussions with the leadership should be encouraged since employees should be able to express their fears and worries openly in regular meetings. These meetings with the management can bring up ideas, as the changes implemented in the turnaround may encourage employees to come up with ideas about how to improve things even more. If employees' opinions are ignored their motivation will most likely suffer, which can lead to a negative atmosphere and employee disengagement.[1085]

Prioritize Clearly

If work teams are not able to make decisions quickly it may be because priorities are not clear, so the priorities set out by the TMT should be clearly communicated to all staff. The workforce must understand these priorities and act accordingly. One sign of unclear priorities is long meetings in which it is difficult to make quick decisions. If this is the case, the root causes should be examined and addressed. They could be related to poor alignment of goals and objectives, conflicting priorities, or "meeting addiction". [1086] Long meetings can be counterproductive.

Responsibility

The change management expert on the TMT is responsible for this subcomponent.

[1085] (Roman, 2010, p. 83)
[1086] (Roman, 2010, p. 84)

Risk Management (RM)

RM 1 – Laying Off Employees

Summary

This subcomponent is a support subcomponent that deals with the risk of laying off employees.

Context

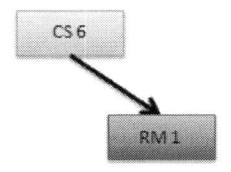

Description of the Subcomponent

When turning a business around, there will be changes to what people do, how they do it, and whether they will still be working for the company at the end of the turnaround process.[1087]

The risk to the company must be managed when employees are laid off or fired since employees who know that they will be let go may try to hurt the company. In some countries it is possible to fire a person immediately; in others the employee must be notified months in advance, potentially giving them enough time to sabotage the company or to lower their performance level. The best way to minimize the risk is for the released employee to be escorted out of the building once they have been given the news. Even then a lawsuit may follow, and the employee often has the right to be paid for the next few months or until their contract expires.

If the employee is needed for a few more months, they may be asked to sign a contract that guarantees them a bonus if no harm to the company can be traced back to their actions.

Responsibility

The Turnaround Assurance Team, together with the HR Turnaround Manager, is responsible for this subcomponent.

[1087] (Blayney, 2005, p. 191)

RM 2 – Establishing and Monitoring Control Systems

Summary

This subcomponent is triggered regularly when control systems are put in place or evaluated.

Context

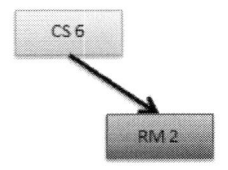

Description of the Subcomponent

The early establishment of control systems helps the management to avoid unnecessary surprises during the turnaround process. Although mistakes and surprises are unavoidable, it is possible to control and minimize their impact. Unless a turnaround process is configured to accommodate these unwelcome surprises, it can all too easily turn out to be incomplete midway through.[1088] The same goes for operations in a healthy company. This subcomponent monitors the effectiveness of the control mechanisms put in place.

Responsibility

The Turnaround Assurance Team is responsible for this subcomponent.

[1088] (Day & Jung, 2000)

RM 3 – Managing Conflict

Summary

This subcomponent deals with managing conflict and controls the risk associated with it.

Context

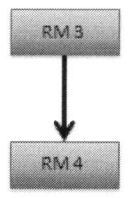

Description of the Subcomponent

"Before any corporation can have external success, it has to achieve some degree of internal tranquility."[1089] Conflict exists in every company, whether it's a start-up, a company growing quickly and profitably, or a firm in a crisis situation. For example, a natural conflict exists between the sales department and the credit department; salespeople have an interest in selling products to as large an audience as possible while the people in the credit department may not want to offer credit terms to a certain customer group. A similar conflict may occur between the marketing manager and sales if the marketing manager wants to sell a product for a high price in order to maintain its premium status. Other conflicts may arise between marketing and production departments. In a crisis situation, however, conflicts must be managed in a professional way so they do not interfere with the turnaround process.

If conflict has been rampant in the firm for some time, department heads are probably more open to having some sort of order and stability imposed from above.[1090] One way of overcoming conflicts among department heads is to move them all into one big office and have them operate from there. This approach helps them to become united as a management team and to resolve conflicts more easily and quickly. This worked well at American Microsystems where

---

[1089] (Bibeault, 1981, p. 331)
[1090] (Bibeault, 1981, p. 331)

Glenn Penisten, the CEO, had the executive group work together day and night for a couple of weeks.[1091] In the face of an external threat teams usually pull together, so the Turnaround Leader could create an external threat by showing how the competition is threatening the company's existence.

A Turnaround Assurance Team member should be able to evaluate the impact that conflicts can have on the turnaround effort and to escalate them to the Turnaround Leader if necessary. However, the team member should first try to resolve the conflicts themself. If conflicts cannot be solved quickly, they should be entered into the Risk Log.

Responsibility

The Turnaround Leader is responsible for managing conflict on a company-wide basis. The Turnaround Assurance Team or a complaints manager can help resolve conflicts on a department level.

[1091] compare (Bibeault, 1981, p. 331)

RM 4 – Updating the Risk Log

Summary

This subcomponent updates the Risk Log.

Context

Description of the Subcomponent

The entries in the Risk Log should include a current status. If a risk is very likely to occur, the status should be set to "immediate"; if the risk is likely to occur, the status is "possible"; and if the risk is not very high, the status is "unlikely".

Even though the Risk Log is supposed to be used to monitor risks, there is no certainty that nothing unforeseen will happen. "Any company in turnaround can positively count on surprises", which might be positive or negative.[1092] The Turnaround Assurance Team updates and monitors the risks entered into the Risk Log. When the status of a risk changes to "immediate" or "possible" the Turnaround Leader should be informed.

Responsibility

The Turnaround Assurance Team is responsible for updating the Risk Log.

[1092] (Collard, 2002, p. 27)

Communication Procedures (CP)

CP 1 – Communication Guidelines

Summary

Communication guidelines serve as preliminary guidance on who needs to know about the proposed turnaround efforts until a complete Turnaround Plan can be created.

Context

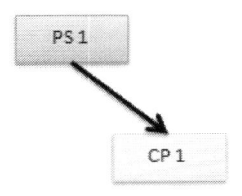

Description of the Subcomponent

Before a Communications Plan can be created, communication guidelines should serve as the basis for whom to inform about what and when. "[A] comprehensive strategy is needed for the successful implementation of a communications plan—one that addresses issues freely and provides an open-conversation environment."[1093]

Communication to the right people helps to ensure that employees will not be left to imagine what is going on, which might be worse than the reality. Avoiding important topics can create the feeling among the workforce that the really significant or dangerous things are not being said, which might result in them not believing the TMT. Meetings behind closed doors are likely to trigger rumors, but the Turnaround Leader should restrict access to meetings because not everyone always needs to be informed about everything and meetings need to be kept short.

Studies have shown that institutional investors (e.g. pension funds) and other large block holders can affect TMT decision-making.[1094] "[S]mall shareholders have only limited abilities to

---

[1093] (Roman, 2010, p. 127)
[1094] (Lohrke, Bedeian, & Palmer, 2004)

affect the actions of the top management. Even though large investors have more influence, they cannot sell off their large investment without reducing the stock price."[1095]

Also, "some claimholders, such as shareholders, may benefit from a restructuring, while others, such as employees or suppliers, are made worse off".[1096] Therefore, communicating the right thing in the right way to the right audience is important to the success of a turnaround.

Output

- Communication guidelines

Responsibility

The TAB is responsible for this subcomponent.

[1095] (Kochhar & David, 1996)
[1096] (Simonsen & Cassady, 2007, p. 3)

CP 2 – Confidentiality Assurance

Summary

The parties that discuss the possibility of a turnaround should sign confidentiality agreements.

Context

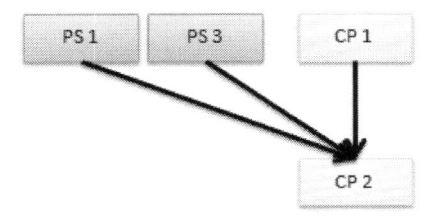

Description of the Subcomponent

The purpose of CP 1 (Communication Guidelines) is to ensure that the company does not experience bad press as a result of searching for a Turnaround Leader or informing the wrong people at the wrong time during the turnaround process. If stakeholders receive information about the company through third parties there is a danger that they will be misinformed.[1097]

In PS 1 (Creating the Turnaround Mandate) the person who raised the possibility of a turnaround should involve only those who have decision-making authority. The TAB should be informed and discuss whether the company should consider a turnaround. Involving stakeholders in this component may cause more trouble and slow down the evaluation. If it is a shareholder who suggests the turnaround, other stakeholders will have to be convinced to participate in the turnaround in order to pressure the TAB to proceed with PS 2 (Preparing Basic Information). However, involvement in this component should be limited to the major shareholders that are absolutely necessary.

The public announcement of a possible or proposed turnaround may have a negative effect. Although such an announcement may help increase pressure on an unwilling top management,

---

[1097] (Schellenberg, 2008)

the public admission that a turnaround is necessary makes it obvious to stakeholders that the company is heading for trouble. As a consequence, suppliers may want their money sooner or may raise their prices, customers may stop buying the company's products for fear of losing support for them, and banks may refuse credit, request more information about the company, or even assign investigating accountants before the company can handle these procedures themselves.

The people involved in the pre-turnaround should sign confidentiality agreements, especially stakeholders who want regular updates from the TMT.

Secrecy forms or confidentiality agreements should also be signed whenever an external analyst evaluates the company based on internal information, and by employees who are directly involved in the turnaround process and have access to sensitive data such as financial reports, restructuring plans, discussion protocols, and recordings.

Typical personnel who should sign confidentiality agreements are:

- Stakeholder representatives
- Top- and mid-level managers
- Members of the TMT
- Secretaries
- Directors

Output

- Signed confidentiality agreements

Responsibility

The TAB is responsible for this subcomponent.

CP 3 – Assigning a Communications Manager

Summary

In this subcomponent a Communications Manager is assigned.

Context

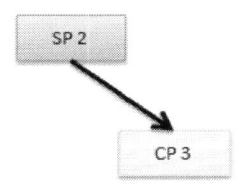

Description of the Subcomponent

The Communications Manager should be an experienced communications/public relations expert. From this subcomponent on, they will handle all outside communications with stakeholders and will advise the TMT on internal communications. One of their main duties is the creation and maintenance of the Communications Plan.

"The ideal communications manager has the ability to communicate concisely, when needed, on task, through all channels and all means of communication, and to steer the team toward fast, to-the-point communication that works both ways."[1098]

Communication in the Start-Up Stage

The start-up stage of a turnaround is important in gaining stakeholder support, which is why a Communications Manager should be appointed early in the process. Credibility and candor with vendors are needed to gain their support in the Crisis Stabilization Stage.[1099] This can be achieved by a Communications Manager who has experience of crisis situations.

[1098] (Roman, 2010, p. 70)
[1099] (Bibeault, 1981, p. 270)

Responsibility

The TAB or, if already available, the Turnaround Leader is responsible for this subcomponent.

CP 3 – Communicating with Lenders

Summary

Communication with banks and lenders is important from the beginning.

Context

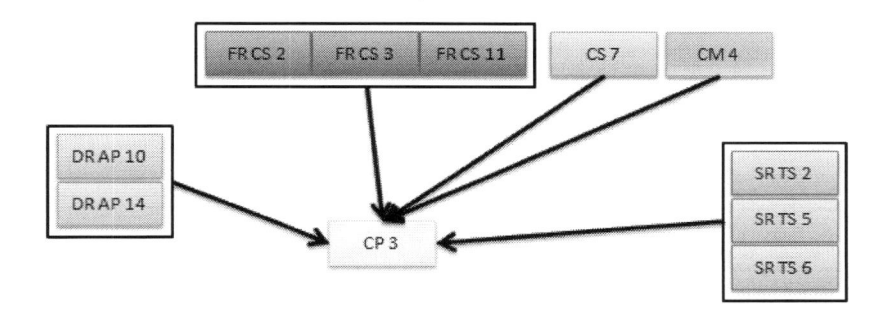

Description of the Subcomponent

Communicating the turnaround process properly is not easy, and the turnaround must be sold to key managers. The whole turnaround process also needs to be sold to the stakeholders. Marketing such a turnaround is not just a matter of formal presentations; it also often involves informal lobbying and influencing of key stakeholders.[1100]

Communication with major lenders such as banks is important from the outset in order to retain their trust. The success of the turnaround may depend on their support, so the bank must feel comfortable working with the TMT. The best way to gain their support is if the company lays everything out on the table, maintains honesty, and honors commitments made to the lender.[1101]

Although there should not be too much communication at the pre-start-up stage, the banks should know that a turnaround process is being considered. Later on in the turnaround process,

---

[1100] (Simonsen & Cassady, 2007, p. 17)
[1101] (Collard, 2002, p. 27)

lenders should always be the first to receive information from the Communications Manager as soon as the Turnaround Leader has cleared the information to be passed on.

Responsibility

The Communications Manager on the TMT is responsible for this subcomponent.

CP 4 – Establish Communications for the Diagnostic Review Stage

Summary

This subcomponent establishes communication procedures for the Diagnostic Review Stage.

Context

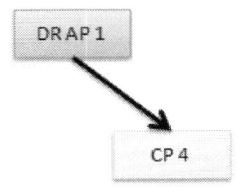

Description of the Subcomponent

This subcomponent establishes the communication procedures for the Diagnostic Review Stage. Confidentiality agreements are signed by all personnel involved with the turnaround in order to control the information flow. Hence the Turnaround Leader confirms the communication procedures set up in this subcomponent with the TAB.

The general policy is that no information about the turnaround process reaches the public during the Diagnostic Review Stage. The first to be informed of the outcome is the TAB, which is informed by the Turnaround Leader in the TID. All communication to the outside is approved by the TAB.

Output

- Communication procedures for the Diagnostic Review Stage.

Responsibility

The Communications Manager and the Turnaround Leader, who is acting on behalf of the TAB, are responsible for this subcomponent.

CP 5 – Communicating Emergency Procedures

Summary

Emergency Procedures should be communicated only to the people affected by them in order to avoid worrying others.

Context

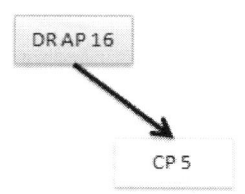

```
DR AP 16
   |
   v
 CP 5
```

Description of the Subcomponent

The reason for Emergency Procedures is usually known only to the TAB and the TMT. If unrelated parties find out about the procedures stories may circulate that will damage the company's reputation. The Emergency Procedures should be kept as quiet as possible while keeping the influential stakeholders as informed as necessary.

For example, if the company has to divest a business or a product and sell it to another company, the price that can be achieved may be lower if potential buyers know of the level of the seller's urgency. In order to protect the company's assets, communication should be limited to the people who must be involved. Special information-sharing contracts should be developed that require the stakeholders to keep confidential any information they receive during this stage.

The Crisis Stabilization Stage is used to rebuild the credibility of the company and build the trust of its stakeholders in the TMT and the Turnaround Plan.

Output

- Communication guidelines for Emergency Procedures

Responsibility

The Communications Manager on the TMT is responsible for this subcomponent.

CP 6 – Creating the Communications Plan

Summary

The Communications Plan is created in this subcomponent.

Context

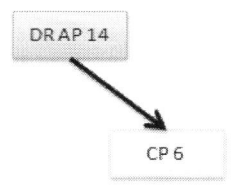

```
DRAP 14
   ↓
  CP 6
```

Description of the Subcomponent

It is important that the management establishes a system of consistent and credible communications to all stakeholder groups[1102] because companies in crisis situations usually don't have the best relationships with their stakeholders.[1103] The Communications Manager uses this subcomponent to identify all interested parties in the turnaround process, such as stakeholders, and to determine their need to receive information about the turnaround. It must also be established "which information the stakeholders want, recalling that what is not said is often more destructive than what is said".[1104] During this subcomponent a Communications Plan is drafted containing information about who is to inform whom, in what situation, and when.

Creating the Communications Log

A Communications Log is also created in this subcomponent. The Communications Log, which lists all information packages sent to each contact and when, is maintained by the Communications Manager.

[1102] compare (Davis & Sihler, 2002)
[1103] compare (Slatter, Lovett, & Barlow, 2006, p. 25)
[1104] (Collard, 2002, p. 29)

Developing a Communications Plan

The Communications Plan states who needs to be informed, at what time, and about what during the turnaround process. It states who has access to what information, who can provide what information, and how information should be transmitted. A good Communications Plan also identifies the audiences for information, the goals for each audience, and the information that will be needed from each audience.[1105] It should include "a timetable for reporting progress to external stakeholders and an internal communications program to roll out the business plan throughout the organization".[1106]

The Communications Plan identifies who receives what information at what time during the turnaround. The Communications Manager establishes the procedures required for the efficient and confidential distribution of information within the company and to external parties, and classifies recipients into vital stakeholders, other stakeholders, and interested parties.

The Communications Manager has the difficult task of evaluating what information should be passed along and what should be kept confidential.

Establishing liaisons between departments for the duration of the turnaround project will help to ensure that proper channels of communication are open both ways and that the intended process is followed for resource selection and allocation, workload management, and time management against a strict calendar of deliverables.[1107] This is also the job of the Communications Manager.

It is the ultimate goal of the Communications Plan that the stakeholders support the turnaround process and stay loyal to the company at a difficult time. Many researchers argue that there must be strong commitment to a company for true loyalty to exist.[1108] A study into customers' trust of retailers showed that trust—or confidence in the retailer's reliability and integrity—is

---

[1105] (Roman, 2010, p. 34)
[1106] (Slatter & Lovett, 2004, p. 195)
[1107] (Roman, 2010, p. 55)
[1108] (Zentes & Morschett, 2011, p. 235)

closely connected to commitment. It is important, then, that the Communications Plan works to retain trust and commitment.[1109]

Stakeholder Support

When a company is not doing as well as it once did, many business areas suffer. Communication with the company's stakeholders—such as staff, customers, suppliers, government regulators, and equity and debt providers—also suffers. A history of poor trading, inadequate communications, unfulfilled promises from management, and unpleasant surprises, coupled with the risk of failure, erodes stakeholders' confidence in the business.[1110] Even though stakeholders have different opinions, priorities, and objectives, it is helpful to get them in line and to rebuild their trust in the company and the management team during a turnaround. Since it may not always be possible to get the stakeholders to agree on the same agenda, it can be helpful to divide them into those that are very important for the mission and those that are less important.

A well-prepared Communications Plan can help to build stakeholder support by encouraging open communications, and rebuilding reliability and predictability by avoiding surprises. "Success depends upon getting the stakeholders to recognize and accept the reality of the company's position and to work cooperatively toward solutions to the business's problems."[1111] This can be achieved by giving selected shareholders a true picture of the company's financial position; it does not make sense to make the situation look better than it is since doing so may lead to disappointment and even more loss of trust. Stakeholders who are willing to support the turnaround process should be invited to participate in creating the Turnaround Plan, and their formal approval should be sought once the plan has been written. It may be necessary and helpful to reach a standstill agreement with suppliers during the negotiations to support the turnaround process. During this process, open and clear communication should be sustained by regular updates regarding the company's trading and cash positions. Where a good relationship has been established with the company's bankers, shared information can lead to banks supporting the company even when initiatives are delayed or ineffective.[1112]

[1109] (Hunt & Morgan, 1995)
[1110] (Slatter & Lovett, 2004, p. 82)
[1111] (Slatter & Lovett, 2004, p. 82)
[1112] (Slatter & Lovett, 2004, p. 132)

In an effort to gain the support of its employees early in the restructuring component, the management of United Airlines made the company's crisis sound worse than it was. Quite early on in the negotiation process, the management threatened to break up the airline and lay off thousands of employees if a consensual agreement could not be reached.[1113] To underscore this threat, a restructuring plan was created and presented to the employees.

Improve Company Communications

When a company slides into a crisis, it often happens that less information about its situation is communicated to the stakeholders. This erodes the trust of customers and suppliers and demoralizes the workforce, all of which contributes to the company's decline. The Turnaround Leader and their TMT must develop credibility quickly if they want to harness the company's resources. Therefore the TMT must establish a Communications Plan that lays out how to communicate information, what to communicate and what to hold back, and who gets the information. It is also important that TMT members and the senior management communicate the same message.

Cooperation with Banks

If the company does not have the necessary cash to finance the turnaround, its relationship with the banks becomes increasingly important. In this situation, the bank may choose to appoint an investigating accountant to determine the true value of the company, its true financial position, and its chances for survival from a financial point of view. The investigating accountant's responsibility to the bank includes determining whether the numbers that the company provides to the bank are accurate and whether full disclosure has been made. It is vital that the company cooperates fully with the banks and involves them in the turnaround process. If the banks appoint an investigating accountant it is usually not beneficial for the company. The troubled company should try to avoid such an appointment by providing all the materials the bank requires in the requested timeframe and keeping it informed at regular intervals. The Communications Manager should keep track of all information that is passed on to the banks and ensure the cooperation of the TMT and other company advisors. Financial restructuring is a costly business, and the firm can contain these expenses by giving the external

---

[1113] compare (Gilson, 2010, p. 7)

stakeholders access to its advisors.[1114] However, different rules apply for suppliers and customers, communication to whom is managed in the Communications Plan.

The willingness to disclose critical data may depend on who is in charge of the turnaround—whether a TMT, as suggested in this standard, or the company directors—especially if company directors see their own positions threatened if their mistakes are revealed in the financial statements. "In many cases, company directors are in denial mode or do not wish to make full disclosure." If there is more than one creditor, it is helpful for the turnaround process if one appointed representative of all creditors has some decision-making power. This is more difficult to achieve in moratorium negotiations than in banking situations, but even in that case the company should limit the number of advisors, consultants, and principal parties involved.[1115]

Output

- Communications Plan

Responsibility

The Communications Manager on the TMT is responsible for this subcomponent.

[1114] (Slatter & Lovett, 2004, p. 314)
[1115] (Slatter & Lovett, 2004, p. 314)

CP 7 – Review Communications Plan

Summary

The Communications Plan should be revised at regular intervals.

Context

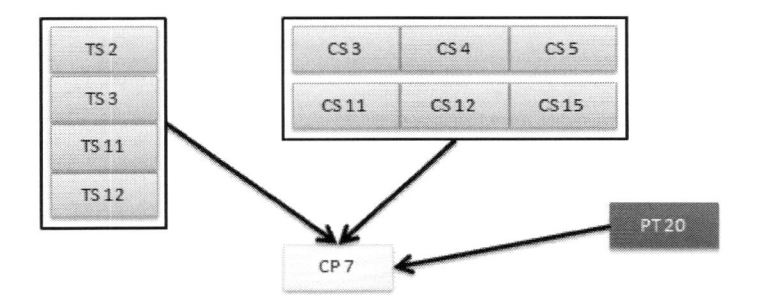

Description of the Subcomponent

The Communications Plan should be reviewed for changes in circumstances, changes in addresses, changes in the parties to be informed, and changes in the information that is to be sent to each party. The priorities may change with a change in equity in the company or when the stakeholder's support level for the company changes, but they may also change with time. The goal of the Communications Plan is to inform only those people who absolutely need the information and minimize its exposure to people who don't need the information right away.

Output

- Revised Communications Plan

Responsibility

The Communications Manager on the TMT is responsible for this subcomponent.

CP 8 – Workforce Kick-Off Meeting

Summary

The first meeting with the workforce is critical in gaining the employees' support for the turnaround process and their trust in the Turnaround Leader.

Context

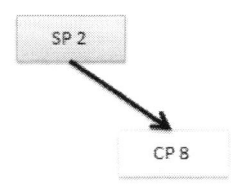

Description of the Subcomponent

The kick-off meeting with the workforce is an important meeting in which the Turnaround Leader will face many questions that must be answered. The employees may already be upset and worried, and everyone will be afraid that they will lose their jobs. It is important here to be as clear as possible, so if lay-offs are necessary that fact should be communicated.

What employees often hear is that "they are the firm's most valuable assets; what they know is that they're the most expendable assets".[1116] This kick-off meeting is therefore a good opportunity to build up the workforce's trust in the TMT. It should be made clear that all are pulling in the same direction and that everyone counts in making the turnaround possible. After all, winding up the business would not be good for jobs either.

Strikes can be avoided by using the right communications in this subcomponent. The Turnaround Leader must make clear that the damage done by strikes or other harmful acts will make the survival of the company less likely and harm everyone because time will be lost and deeper cuts will be necessary.

[1116] (Hamel & Prahalad, 1996, p. 11)

The employees have the most to lose and usually have little influence on the decisions that impact their lives so dramatically. It is quite challenging for the Turnaround Leader to create a new corporate reality that changes the way stakeholders perceive the company. The employees must be able to envision this reality and understand the new reality as something better and more impressive; thus they will support its creation and be able to imagine living the new reality and culture. Creating the new culture will not be possible without the employees being convinced of it.

There is a three-step method for creating a new corporate reality.[1117] First, the "why" and the "why now" of the transformation program must persuade them, and the benefits of success and penalties for failing to act must be equally obvious. Second, the company's new future—the "where to"—must be clear and compelling. Third, each employee must understand the personal benefits of the program; the leadership must have credible answers to that natural question, "What's in it for me?"

There might be resistance to the new reality/culture. "The Turnaround Leader should have the ability to gently push back on the territoriality and hostility of others and considerately persuade them to implement changes without engaging in unconstructive conflict and without carrying grudges."[1118] They must also have high levels of confidence in what they are saying and how, as the employees will recognize immediately if what is being said is not backed up with confidence. The Turnaround Leader should start by explaining how the corporation got into its current situation—how is has performed financially over the last few years, how the competition developed and the corporate advantages of the firm deteriorated, or whatever other reasons there might be for the crisis.

In short, the kick-off meeting should:

- Explain why the change is necessary
- Explain what will drive the turnaround process and the change
- Address concerns
- Set expectations openly
- Answer questions

[1117] compare (Day & Jung, 2000)
[1118] (Roman, 2010, p. 70)

- Explain what is at stake for everyone involved
- Explain the rewards that come with the change and how people can reach them

There must be time to address concerns—an element of change management. The employees need to be encouraged to talk freely about their concerns. The Turnaround Leader has nothing to lose at this point as they are not responsible for past mistakes made by another management team, therefore they should not take criticism personally but should allow employees to vent their frustration and address the issues. The Turnaround Leader must deal not only with employees' concerns but also with the underlying emotional issues.[1119]

The Turnaround Leader must also be able to deal with competing interests within the company. "[E]ven though one might expect the business and functional heads whose units are affected to take an enterprise-wide view, parochial considerations do exist."[1120]

Here is an example from John M. Collard.[1121] Asked about a time when the interviewee had to give the orders, the interviewee replied:

> *I was running a commercial printing company in central Pennsylvania. The salespeople were gone and we had just fired a couple of others that hadn't produced anything in ages. I walked into a room of 180 employees and three union reps and started talking about these cutbacks. They kept asking if I read their contract. I said, "Wait a minute, you have this goofed up. You need to understand that you just are not my top priority" ... After repeating it several times throughout the conversation, one guy sitting in the front row looked at me and said, "You've said we are not your priority. If that's the case, what is?" I thought, "Hallelujah, somebody in this place is thinking." I made it real simple for them. I explained to them that they'd lost the entire sales force, and revenue had been cut dramatically. If we didn't change this situation quickly and develop new business, half of them wouldn't be there next week. I told them that my job is to go out and convince some of the customers who have left to return, and to hire a new sales force*

[1119] compare (Müller, 1986, p. 17)
[1120] (Simonsen & Cassady, 2007)
[1121] (Collard, 2010)

that could bring in business. I asked if anyone disagreed with those priorities.

Change management requires great care to be taken in communicating with employees. Simply mentioning a proposed cost reduction in a certain department can make the department head defensive as they are likely to see the decision as a sign of their inefficiency and of the company assigning blame to them for the trouble the organization is in. This fear of change is more specifically dealt with in the change management component.

Responsibility

The Turnaround Leader is responsible for this subcomponent.

CP 9 – Communicating Draft Plans

Summary

This subcomponent is triggered if draft plans are to be communicated.

Context

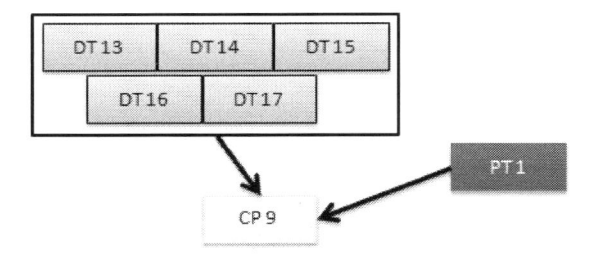

Description of the Subcomponent

Once the operational, financial, and strategic plan has been created and reviewed by the TAB it should be presented to the stakeholders as a draft plan, even though it should be as complete and thought through as the final plan. The presentation of a draft plan gives the stakeholders an opportunity to have their thoughts and comments included, makes them feel more involved in the turnaround process, and serves as another step toward gaining their commitment. Banks in particular need to feel involved in the planning of the turnaround to avoid the appointment of investigating accountants.

Once this review presentation to the stakeholders is completed and all concerns have been addressed, the plan is sent back to the TAB for final approval before being carried out by the TMT. If major changes or disagreements come up when the draft plan is presented, the plan is sent back to the TAB for re-evaluation.

Responsibility

The Communications Manager on the TMT is responsible for this subcomponent.

CP 10 – Communicating Plans

Summary

This subcomponent is triggered if new plans are to be communicated.

Context

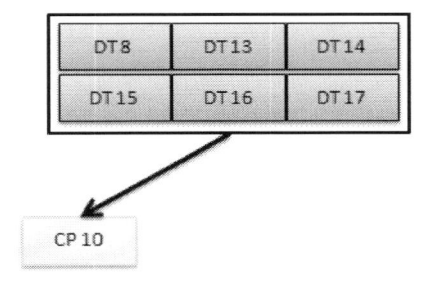

DT 8	DT 13	DT 14
DT 15	DT 16	DT 17

CP 10

Description of the Subcomponent

Selling a turnaround strategy to internal stakeholders is not easy. Once the operational, financial, and strategic plan has been produced the finished Turnaround Plan must be communicated to the stakeholders, but how to do this is determined in this subcomponent. Usually the plan is distributed to the whole company in sufficient detail that the departments can understand it without overloading them with information. It is vital "that the key strategies, the desired end-state, and the action plans be explained to middle and junior management as soon as possible so [...] implementation can begin".[1122] Even though it would be nice if everyone stood behind the proposed plans, not everyone will. It is not realistic to expect that everybody in the organization will support the turnaround strategies; therefore it is important how convincingly the Turnaround Plan is communicated.

Responsibility

The Communications Manager on the TMT is responsible for this subcomponent.

[1122] (Slatter & Lovett, 2004, p. 213)

CP 11 – Reporting Updates

Summary

This subcomponent is triggered if changes occur that should be communicated.

Context

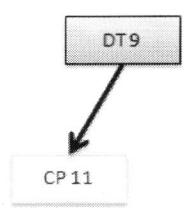

Description of the Subcomponent

During this subcomponent, updates from the stages are prepared to be passed on to the stakeholders and parties outlined in the Communications Plan.

As soon as the turnaround process starts it is vital that everybody in the organization is kept up to date on its progress. Not all employees are aware of how the organization is doing during the turnaround process; they may have a good understanding of the capabilities and contributions their team is making, but whether their efforts are doing any good for the organization can remain a mystery. Therefore, it is important to communicate the progress of the organization to every employee, broken down into divisions and departments if possible. Monthly review scorecards can be displayed. The updates communicated to the workforce should include what decisions have been made, why they were made, and the key milestones necessary to reach them.[1123]

The Communications Manager should not forget the stakeholders' fears, regardless of how well the turnaround process is going. The perception differs for each stakeholder, but the fear is always the same: they are afraid to lose their investment, be it money, time, energy, goodwill,

---

[1123] (Roman, 2010, p. 176)

job, or reputation.[1124] The IT department should be informed as well. IT, which reflects the whole organizational structure, optimizes communications and maintains security clearances. The Turnaround Leader should establish a communications process that informs IT of all changes, and assign a dedicated IT manager to become a part of the team and advise on the IT implications of each decision and action.[1125]

Responsibility

The Communications Manager on the TMT is responsible for this subcomponent.

[1124] (Collard, 2010)
[1125] (Roman, 2010, p. 55)

CP 12 – Communicating Lay-Offs

Summary

Whenever employees are laid off it must be communicated, triggering this subcomponent.

Context

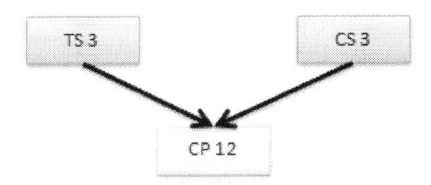

Description of the Subcomponent

Literature and case studies suggest that employees should be told early on if they are going to be laid off and that they should receive an explanation of exactly what is going on during the business transformation.[1126] However, there is some risk in doing this, which is discussed in RM 1 (Laying Off Employees). Whether employees are informed early or later on, communication with those that are being laid off is important. "[D]etailed planning should be [done] to ensure that all terminations are announced and executed at the same time so that uncertainty and anxiety among the remaining personnel are minimized as much as possible."[1127] Certain groups, such as government departments (if necessary) and trade unions, should be notified at the same time as the employees, depending on common practice in the applicable country. If possible, the TMT should appoint someone from the company's HR team to work with employment agencies in order to help laid-off personnel find new jobs.

People who are in key positions but who are incapable of performing or unwilling to perform what is required of them must be let go. While doing so creates a gap that must be filled quickly, it is also an opportunity to increase organizational capabilities.[1128]

[1126] compare (Bibeault, 1981, p. 297)
[1127] (Bibeault, 1981, p. 297)
[1128] compare (Bibeault, 1981, pp. 328-329)

The TMT must carefully manage the company's relationships with the remaining workforce and the press in order to motivate the remaining employees to work.[1129] If some long-standing members of a team are laid off the others may go into a kind of state of shock, which is not very motivating for them.

Responsibility

The Communications Manager on the TMT is responsible for this subcomponent.

[1129] compare (Simonsen & Cassady, 2007, p. 10)

CP 13 – Restrictive Communication on Issues

Summary

Information that can harm the company's reputation or endanger the turnaround process, such as issues that need to be escalated and components that are out of tolerance, is handled in this subcomponent.

Context

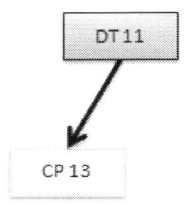

```
    DT 11
      |
      v
    CP 13
```

Description of the Subcomponent

This subcomponent is designed to communicate information about an issue to only those stakeholders who require it. Information passed on in this subcomponent can harm the turnaround process or the company's reputation, or even increase the threat to the company's existence. The information to be passed on is classified according to the Communications Plan laid out in CP 6 (Creating the Communications Plan). If further confidentiality agreements are necessary they are sought through CP 2 (Confidentiality Assurance).

Responsibility

The Communications Manager on the TMT is responsible for this subcomponent.

CP 14 – Communicating with the Sales Force

Summary

Communication with the sales force requires specific guidelines.

Context

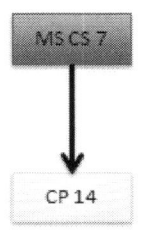

```
MS CS 7
   |
   v
 CP 14
```

Description of the Subcomponent

Communication with the sales force deserves a separate subcomponent because it differs from other communication procedures. The positive attitude of the sales force is very important in a turnaround situation in order to achieve the necessary changes. If possible, the Turnaround Leader should hold a meeting with the whole sales force to provide motivation and to encourage them to buy in to procedures that they may not appreciate in a normal situation. The TMT must give a clear indication to the sales force that they know what they are doing. Some tangible evidence of the benefits that the sales force can expect should be offered as well.[1130] They may be demotivated at the time of a crisis because they cannot sell the products anymore, because they have heard too many complaints from clients, or because they were not treated well by the past management. The purpose of this meeting is to overcome these difficulties and to gain their trust in and support for the TMT. Maintaining clear and open two-way communication with the sales force "will help with these situations and with discerning which of the objections are driven by insecurity and which come from a 'taboo' frame of mind".[1131] Addressing the objections raised will help the Turnaround Leader execute the Turnaround Plan more quickly.

[1130] (Slatter & Lovett, 2004, p. 275)
[1131] (Roman, 2010, p. 89)

Several subcomponents—such as MS CS 7 (Monitoring the Performance of the Sales Force), MS CS 6 (Sales Force Motivation), and MS CS 4 (Focusing the Sales Effort)—should only be triggered after this subcomponent.

Responsibility

The Turnaround Leader is responsible for this subcomponent.

CP 15 – Motivating the Workforce

Summary

The workforce should be motivated regularly throughout the turnaround process.

Context

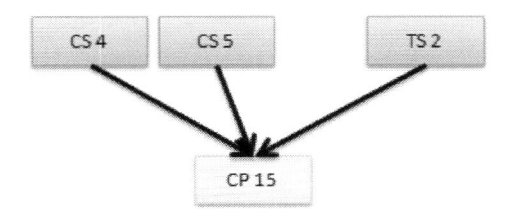

Description of the Subcomponent

The Turnaround Leader needs to explain to the workforce why the company needs to transform and what would happen if it did not. Every single person needs to understand that they are making a difference and that they are needed in the turnaround process. The Turnaround Leader needs to create a vision of the company that they want to create and be confident that the scenario created will come true. "Effectively framed, such a story can help people strengthen their convictions and start experiencing 'the new world' even before it arrives."[1132]

It is also important for the Turnaround Leader to motivate the sales force to stay on board. Every person who leaves the company and needs to be replaced costs the company money and time at a moment when both are scarce. The best employees leave the company first because they have little trouble finding jobs elsewhere, but motivation helps the company keep these people.

What is true for external stakeholders is true for the workforce as well: a little early success during the turnaround process is motivating. Delays caused by people not supporting a turnaround drain businesses of cash, time, and the morale of the remaining employees. Once

---

[1132] (Day & Jung, 2000)

people begin to see the early realities created by the transformation and believe that the scenario created by the Turnaround Leader can come true, they will often try to do what it takes to complete it on their own.[1133]

Regular updates about the progress of the turnaround and how many goals and milestones have been achieved can also motivate the workforce because each employee can see that they are getting closer to the scenario the Turnaround Leader described at the kick-off meeting.[1134]

Responsibility

The Turnaround Leader and the Communications Manager are responsible for this subcomponent.

[1133] (Day & Jung, 2000)
[1134] compare (Faulhaber & Landwehr, 2005, p. 255)

CP 16 – Communicating Standards and Culture

Summary

A new corporate culture, new standards, and new goals are communicated.

Context

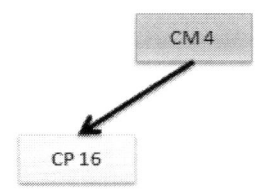

Description of the Subcomponent

This subcomponent starts once the Crisis Stabilization Stage is finished, the workforce has been reduced due to overstaffing, and any financially necessary reductions are completed. The emphasis here is on pushing higher standards down the organization and on implementing a new culture.

"[T]he first step is to establish meaningful standards of performance, and the second is to take direct action to ensure that the performance spotlight is put on every layer of the organization."[1135]

Setting Performance Standards

Setting performance standards is essential. Leaving profit center managers entirely to their own devices in achieving substantial improvements using the existing mix of people seldom works in a tightly scheduled turnaround effort.[1136] If people bring up good arguments against the new standard they should be listened to and considered; however, public resistance without valid arguments should not be tolerated.

[1135] (Bibeault, 1981, p. 328)
[1136] compare (Bibeault, 1981, p. 328)

Responsibility

The Communications Manager on the TMT is responsible for this subcomponent.

CP 17 – Keep Up Open Communication

Summary

Communication with stakeholders should run both ways. This subcomponent ensures that stakeholders' worries and ideas are recorded.

Context

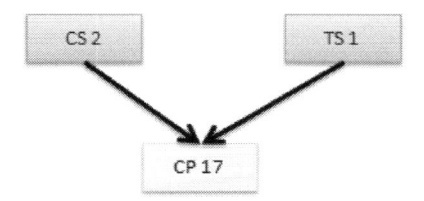

Description of the Subcomponent

Open, regular, and honest communication with the workforce and external stakeholders should be maintained, but the stakeholders must also feel that someone at the company is listening to and considering their concerns. The Turnaround Assurance Team can handle some of the complaints and ideas from the workforce, but a complaints and ideas database should be created to monitor the development of fears within the company.

To keep up the morale of his staff, Leonard, CEO of AirTran, encouraged open lines of communication and communicated appreciation for the grievances about the implications of his cost-cutting measures.[1137] Employees and unions should know that their concerns are heard and not ignored or pushed away.

Responsibility

The Communications Manager on the TMT is responsible for this subcomponent.

[1137] compare (Rajendar, 2007, p. 21)

CP 18 – Communicating the Closure of the Turnaround Process

Summary

This subcomponent publishes the public announcement of the formal closure of the turnaround process.

Context

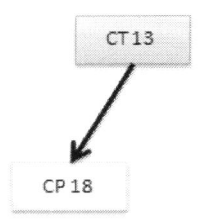

```
CT 13
  ↓
CP 18
```

Description of the Subcomponent

A note for all stakeholders and participants involved in the turnaround process should inform them of its outcome and that it is to be shut down. The major stakeholders should also get a copy of the Turnaround Leader's proposed follow-on actions. The workforce and external stakeholders need to know when the turnaround process is over, what the results are, and what reward is waiting for them. Possible rewards could be an extension of their job contracts, bonus payments, and so on. From that point on, employees will be more motivated and relieved.

"[I]t is well worth the investment to put together a communication ... that ... details the actions that have been completed: quality gains, efficiencies, cost-reduction and cost-avoidance success stories, and all improvement work—completed and in progress."[1138] This material can also include names of employees who have been central contributors to the turnaround success. Ideas that were used or considered should also be published so stakeholders find themselves in the announcement and are rewarded for their loyalty and success.

[1138] (Roman, 2010, p. 262)

Output

- Formal closure communication

Responsibility

The Communications Manager on the TMT is responsible for this subcomponent.

Closing the Turnaround Process (CT)

CT 1 – Starting Closure Procedures

Summary

The formal closure of the turnaround management component starts in this subcomponent.

Context

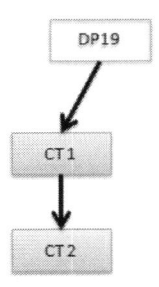

Description of the Subcomponent

Every turnaround process should have a defined end. It does not matter whether the turnaround process was successful in terms of its original goals or designated outcome, or whether these goals were changed during the component, but the Turnaround Leader should confirm when the last goals of the component have been reached. The formal closure of the turnaround process is also the formal start for further proceedings. The major stakeholders should agree on the closure of the process, after which resources that were used for the component can be decommissioned and people who provided support can be given notice of its closure. Records that were created during the component should be retained for use in later audits.

This subcomponent is triggered by assessing the progress of the stage and then handing the process to the TAB to approve the closure of the turnaround.

During this subcomponent, the TMT begins to hand the company over to either new management, the old management, or an interim management. The TMT determines whether the proposed outcome of the turnaround, based on the Turnaround Business Case and its goals, was successful. If not, the reasons for the failure should be added to the Lessons Learned Log.

The new CEO should confirm that the company can continue to operate in its environment, if this was the intention. All relevant information regarding the turnaround process should be completed and filed.

The Turnaround Leader prepares a recommendation for the TAB that includes:

- What resources can be dismissed
- What support services can be dismissed
- Clear documentation of the state of the company
- Whether the acceptance criteria, goals, or objectives have been met

A configuration audit should be performed to determine whether activities were carried out correctly and objectives have been reached.

Responsibility

The Turnaround Leader is responsible for this subcomponent.

CT 2 – Future Recommendations

Summary

This subcomponent prepares a Future Recommendations Report. To make a transition possible and easier, suggestions for company development are made in this subcomponent.

Context

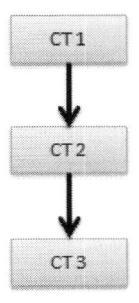

```
CT 1
 ↓
CT 2
 ↓
CT 3
```

Description of the Subcomponent

This subcomponent is triggered once the TAB has agreed to close down the turnaround process. The Turnaround Leader is responsible for preparing a list of recommendations regarding future operations and management of the business, and identifying and documenting any activities that are not yet closed or need further monitoring and maintenance. Many of these items will come from the Risk Log and the Issue Log. If a post-turnaround review is considered necessary the Turnaround Leader should propose a date for it. Many of the strategies, components, and activities that were implemented during the turnaround process should be re-evaluated after some time, so they need to be identified and documented. A copy of the follow-on actions should be sent to independent notaries and to the major stakeholders.

A post-turnaround review is not part of the turnaround process but it is planned at this stage. A review plan should define:

- What achievements can and should be evaluated
- How the evaluation can be done

- The scale for the evaluation; that is, the outcome to which it is to be compared
- What resources and skills are needed to carry out the post-turnaround review

Whether the firm can be systematically encouraged to pre-emptively restructure remains a question. One recommendation could be "to increase the firm's financial leverage so it has less of a cushion when the business begins to suffer or to increase senior managers' equity stake so they are directly rewarded for restructuring that enhances value".[1139] Such approaches are not widespread, however.[1140] There is also the risk of a backlash if it appears to the public that managers are profiting at the expense of the company.[1141] In any case, existing research suggests that companies do not undertake serious restructuring efforts unless they are in a crisis or threatened by a takeover.[1142]

Outcome

- Future Recommendations Report

Responsibility

The Turnaround Leader is responsible for preparing the Future Recommendations Report.

[1139] (Simonsen & Cassady, 2007, p. 8)
[1140] compare (Jenson, 1993), (Wruck, 1994)
[1141] compare (Dial & Murphey, 1995)
[1142] compare (Denis, Denis, & Sarin, 1997)

CT 3 – Preparation for Growth Strategies

Summary

This subcomponent develops or refines the long-term strategy of the business once the turnaround process is over. "[T]he new long-term strategy serves as the backbone for the company that got turned around, driving cohesion around a common growth vision, promoting stability and engaging employees."[1143]

Context

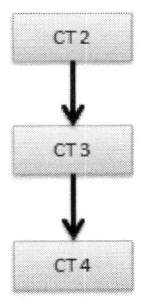

Description of the Subcomponent

An important part of a sustainable turnaround process is to redefine the long-term strategy. Once the survival of the firm has been assured, preparations for the growth stage begin. However, the growth stage is no longer part of this standard. In this subcomponent the TMT develops or refines the long-term strategy for the turned-around business.

Being a customer-centric organization requires systematic and continuous effort in the areas of technology, system and process optimization, and continuous innovation.[1144] Contracts must also be re-evaluated regularly. When the most critical part of the turnaround process is complete, the goals need to adjust to the changed circumstances and should reflect reasonable, ambitious, but also achievable standards that are in line with the long-term strategy. Targets

---

[1143] (Roman, 2010, p. 262)
[1144] (Roman, 2010, p. 180)

should also be set for employees to strive for achievable, stable, and profitable performance aimed toward continuous improvement.

Outcome

- Long-term growth strategy

Responsibility

The Turnaround Leader is responsible for this subcomponent.

CT 4 – Refocusing the Business on its Long-Term Strategy

Summary

This subcomponent begins the company's refocusing on its long-term strategy.

Context

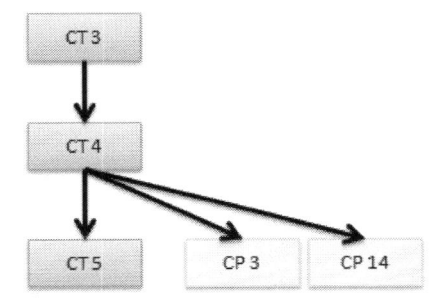

Description of the Subcomponent

This subcomponent prepares the business to focus on its long-term growth strategy. The turnaround strategy, which should be in line with the long-term strategy, is replaced with the long-term strategy that was formulated during the turnaround process. Any goals that must be set differently should be communicated to the management and the workforce.

Information Needs

- Long-term strategy

Responsibility

The Turnaround Leader is responsible for this subcomponent.

CT 5 – Re-evaluate Cost-Cutting Activities

Summary

The cost-cutting activities implemented in the Crisis Stabilization and Turnaround Stages may have pushed the company to the limit so it may be necessary to commit more resources to some components or activities.

Context

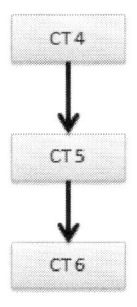

```
CT 4
 ↓
CT 5
 ↓
CT 6
```

Description of the Subcomponent

Cost-cutting activities should be re-evaluated in case costs were cut in places that may not be obvious because they are logged in different accounts. In many cases, some components, activities, and processes may have pushed the corporation to its limits, so documentation that was filed in the Turnaround Leader's Daily Log about the capabilities and limits of the company should be made available for reference. In the long term, some processes may not be sustainable if additional resources are not dedicated to them. Therefore, some elements of the cost-cutting may have to be reversed in order for the company to function properly. "[D]uring the turnaround process, some limits may have become obvious; by examining these limits along with ... documented levels of productivity and other metrics and the relationships between them ... the company can find the optimal ranges for many processes."[1145]

[1145] (Roman, 2010, p. 263)

Responsibility

The Operational Turnaround Manager is responsible for this subcomponent.

CT 6 – Appointing a Permanent Crisis-Monitoring Agent

Summary

This subcomponent is voluntary, but it is recommended for large and complex companies that can afford to pay someone to take this position.

Context

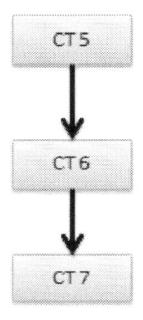

Description of the Subcomponent

The Crisis-Monitoring Agent's responsibility is to monitor the company's business in order to detect crisis symptoms at an early stage, to come up with possible solutions, and draw up scenarios of what would happen if the cause of a possible crisis were not addressed. If the business is not in a crisis situation, the Crisis-Monitoring Agent's power is limited to the role of a consultant to the TAB and top management. The person in this position should develop short-term controls, such as cash management, purchasing and capital expenditure controls, and communication plans that can be put in place quickly if the company is in a crisis. It is their responsibility to collect data that can be useful during the Diagnostic Review Stage of a turnaround, and they are one of the first points of contact for an external TMT.

Some CEOs turn a blind eye to the warning signs of an oncoming crisis until they become so obvious that they can no longer be ignored.[1146] The top management team's awareness of a

---

[1146] compare (Weitzel & Jonsson, 1989)

possible crisis situation depends on how well it monitors the internal and external environment, interprets signs,[1147] and gathers information.[1148]

Responsibilities:

- Product-market refocusing
- Component re-engineering

The person in this position must not only have a finance background but also understand strategic issues, marketing, the law, and human resources.

Responsibility

The Turnaround Leader is responsible for the subcomponent.

[1147] compare (Daft & Weik, 1984), (Milliken, 1990), (Clark & Gioia, 1993)
[1148] compare (Daft & Weik, 1984)

CT 7 – Re-evaluation of the Product-Market Mix

Summary

The re-evaluation of the product-market mix is central to determining whether products are positioned correctly and whether the company can be handed over in good faith.

Context

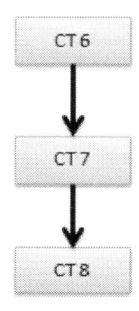

Description of the Subcomponent

Once the turnaround has been achieved and sustainable growth has been targeted, a re-evaluation of the product-market mix is necessary in order to determine whether the choice is still appropriate for the growth stage. The major growth strategies can be summarized as "a change in product-market focus as new product-development strategies (introducing new products to the firm's existing customer base), market-development strategies (introducing existing products to new customers), and diversification (entering totally new areas of business)".[1149] These strategies are not particularly useful in turnaround situations as they usually require considerable investment in marketing, research and development, and/or production facilities.

[1149] (Slatter & Lovett, 2004, p. 237)

Responsibility

The Turnaround Leader, supported by the marketing and sales expert on the TMT, is responsible for this subcomponent.

CT 8 – Realign Compensation

Summary

The compensation of the workforce was aligned during the turnaround to the goals of that process. Now, close to the end of the turnaround, compensation should be realigned to support the objectives of the long-term strategy.

Context

```
CT 7
  ↓
CT 8
  ↓
CT 9
```

Description of the Subcomponent

At the end of the turnaround process, the goal changes from crisis management to growth. The long-term strategy kicks in and compensation should be aligned to these goals. At the end of the turnaround the level of risk is lower than it once was so the level of reward should decline as well.

Variable compensation programs such as the ones introduced in prior stages are appropriate for a turnaround situation but rarely for a more normal growth stage. Retaining them would lead to low morale.[1150] The focus of the future compensation program should be on revenue growth with close attention to the margin. The short-term programs that were targeted at achieving the turnaround must be modified to include the wider workforce and to be in accordance with the long-term goals of the company. However, "the key to a successful bonus

---

[1150] compare (Bibeault, 1981, p. 360)

program remains: make it aggressive enough to make a difference with frequent payouts and clear, ambitious, yet achievable deliverables".[1151]

Information Needs

- Long-term strategy

Responsibility

The HR Turnaround Manager is responsible for this subcomponent.

[1151] (Roman, 2010), (r92; 232)

CT 9 – Decentralizing Power in Closing the Turnaround

Summary

This subcomponent concludes the process of decentralizing power.

Context

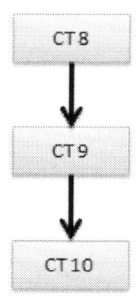

Description of the Subcomponent

When the turnaround is close to completion, the power that was centralized with the TMT in the start-up stage is handed back to business unit managers, department managers, profit center managers, or division heads. At the beginning of the turnaround, centralized control was useful and important as it allowed the TMT to act quickly. Even though the focusing of power and decision-making is appropriate for control purposes in the Crisis Stabilization and Turnaround Stages, it is not usually appropriate for growth strategies.[1152]

Responsibility

The Turnaround Leader is responsible for this subcomponent.

[1152] (Bibeault, 1981, p. 360)

CT 10 – Evaluating the Turnaround

Summary

In this subcomponent the turnaround process is evaluated.

Context

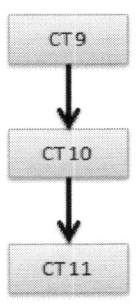

Description of the Subcomponent

The ITMS is based on many organizations' experiences, so it is important that the lessons learned throughout the turnaround process are documented in the Lessons Learned Log when they occur, and are filed in the Lessons Learned Report when the turnaround process is complete. The aim of this evaluation is not to judge the outcome but to evaluate to what degree the turnaround process was successful. The Lessons Learned Log is completed, filed as a Lessons Learned Report, and stored by the company and the TMT. It is also advisable to provide a copy of the Lessons Learned Report to the TMS, either anonymously or confidentially.

For publicly traded companies, the success of a restructuring is ultimately judged by how much it contributes to the company's market value.[1153] In that case, the evaluation also needs to include a section on the development of the market value. However, the market value should definitely be higher when the crisis situation is resolved.

[1153] (Simonsen & Cassady, 2007, p. 12)

Creating the Lessons Learned Report

The Lessons Learned Report outlines issues encountered, certain activities, risks and issues, how the management dealt with them, and how they were solved or turned into other issues. Contributions to the achievements of the turnaround, special techniques, processes, or methods involved should be mentioned along with their outcomes, positive or negative, for the turnaround process. The goal is to have a document that states what should be done differently next time or in other turnaround processes, and which procedures worked well.

The Lessons Learned Report should answer several questions:

- What were the major decisions made and what were they based on?
- Was it easy to achieve the goals and objectives, and how were they achieved?
- Which procedures to sustain quality worked well during the turnaround process and which did not?
- Which management procedures and components worked well and which caused problems?
- Were any weaknesses encountered during the quality components?
- How effective was the risk management?
- Were tolerances used or broken and, if so, where and why?
- Did the management encounter risks that were not foreseen?
- Were support tools employed and, if so, which ones, and how well did they work in the different components?
- How well did the training prepare the management or employees for the tasks encountered during the turnaround process?
- Were the employees' skills adequate? Which ones were available, which ones were used, and which were required?
- Were there deviations or problems with the TAB and, if so, of what nature, when did they occur, and how were they resolved?
- Did the TAB have concerns about accepting the turnaround's closure?

By documenting the positive and negative changes, combined with "red flag" values for parameters and action plans, the management can learn from past mistakes to avoid making them again.[1154]

Outcome

- Lessons Learned Report

Responsibility

The Turnaround Leader is responsible for the evaluation of the turnaround.

[1154] compare (Roman, 2010, p. 265)

CT 11 – Post-Turnaround Review

Summary

The Post-Turnaround Review is planned in this subcomponent.

Context

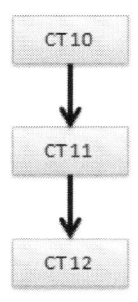

```
CT 10
  ↓
CT 11
  ↓
CT 12
```

Description of the Subcomponent

The Post-Turnaround Review is a review of the achievements and changes that took place during the turnaround process and how they affected the company after the turnaround. It also determines whether activities that were suggested in the Future Recommendations Report were carried out, and whether the incentive reward system has been revised so it can continue paying out for the right things for the long term.[1155] External auditors and due diligence experts should perform the Post-Turnaround Review.

In order to avoid falling back into the same crisis, controls that monitor the symptoms and causes of the crisis should be set up. If a Crisis-Monitoring Agent is appointed, they will monitor and implement these controls. The Post-Turnaround Review can then be completed more quickly because relevant data was monitored.

[1155] (Bibeault, 1981, p. 361)

The Post-Turnaround Review should be planned for a time well after the turnaround process; alternatively two reviews can be planned, for example, one six months after the turnaround process has ended and one eighteen months later.

The review does not focus on how good or bad the TMT was, but determines whether actions taken during the turnaround process affected the turnaround time and whether the business developed as planned. A Post-Turnaround Review Report should be sent to the TMS for evaluation.

Outcome:

- Post-Turnaround Review plan

Responsibility

The Turnaround Leader is responsible for planning the Post-Turnaround Review.

CT 12 – Handing Over

Summary

This subcomponent formally concludes the turnaround process for the TMT, although there is an introduction period for the new management.

Context

Description of the Subcomponent

During this subcomponent the company's management is handed over from the TMT to either new directors and managers or the old management team depending on what the TAB decides to do based on the TMT's recommendations from the Diagnostic Review Stage. In some cases, an interim manager is hired to take over until a competent management team is found.

If the turnaround process was carried out by the original management and no TMT was involved, this subcomponent formally concludes the turnaround management process as a project. The TMT is released and responsibilities are handed over to new management. The TMT should organize an introduction period for the new management.

Responsibility

The Turnaround Leader is responsible for this subcomponent.

CT 13 – Closing the Turnaround Process

Summary

The turnaround is formally closed.

Context

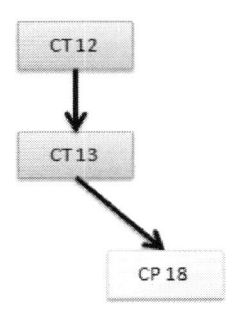

Description of the Subcomponent

During this subcomponent, which marks the formal end of the turnaround process, the following tasks are completed:

- The Turnaround Plan is updated for the last time and filed with the turnaround process files.
- The Turnaround End Report is created.
- The performance of the turnaround is compared against the TID.
- Achievements and non-achievements are assessed.
- An assessment of the turnaround's intended outcome and achieved outcome is performed.
- The Risk Log, Issue Log, and Quality Log are examined to determine the quality of the management in terms of how risks were prepared and avoided, how the management dealt with issues, and how well objectives were reached.

When the turnaround challenge is complete, new challenges to growth and profitability will take its place.[1156]

Creating the Turnaround End Report

The Turnaround End Report describes how well the TMT performed compared to the proposed plan, as well as changes and issues filed. It assesses how well objectives were achieved and if they were not achieved why not. The Turnaround End Report is approved by the TAB, after which it can be made available to interested parties.

Filing the Turnaround Process Files

All files that were collected and created during the turnaround process should be stored in a secure area for research and legal purposes in case legal proceedings should result.

Formal Closure of the Turnaround Process

The turnaround process should be formally closed whether the company is liquidated or sold, or the turnaround process was successful and the company is turned over to the growth component. The formal closure is an agreement between the Turnaround Leader and the stakeholders or the management of the company.

Responsibility

The TAB is responsible for this subcomponent.

[1156] (Bibeault, Corporate Turnaround: How Managers Turn Losers into Winners, 1981, p. 361)

Qualifications

Certified International Turnaround Manager
certified by the TMS Turnaround Management Society

To set a high standard for turnaround management professionals, the Turnaround Management Society has developed an education program for practitioners, academics and others interested in turnaround management. We currently offer one certification, the Certified International Turnaround Manager (CITM), with four different levels, A-D, depending on the theoretical knowledge demonstrated as well as practical experience.

Qualification Levels

CITM – Level A

To acquire Level A the candidate must demonstrate mastery of the International Turnaround Management Standard™ (ITMS) as well as general knowledge about crisis situations and classifications, early warning signs, and crisis prevention.

CITM – Level B

To acquire Level B of the CITM program, the candidate must have successfully achieved the Level A and also demonstrate that he or she has studied and solved different case scenarios in which the International Turnaround Management Standard™ can be applied.

CITM – Level C

To acquire Level C certification, the candidate must have passed all tests required for Levels A and B, plus have direct work experience of at least 3 years in the crisis management / turnaround management industry. During this time a mentor must provide expertise and advice to the candidate and observe whether the candidate follows and upholds the ethical guidelines. A candidate that has already 10 or more years work experience can apply for Level D.

CITM – Level D

A Level D Certified International Turnaround Manager, after meeting the requirements for levels A, B, and C, must demonstrate intense and expansive knowledge of the industry and have extensive recent work experience in the area of crisis management / turnaround management. Only a Level D CITM can serve as a mentor to Level C candidates.

Maintaining the Qualification

A qualification expires after 4 years if the qualified person does not work in the industry, does not keep up to date with industry developments, and does not participate in any qualification or training within the industry. This expiration provides customers with the assurance that the turnaround professional they are working with has maintained ties to the industry and has been involved in continuing education to keep a competitive edge and to stay up to date with the latest developments, cases and success strategies.

The Turnaround Management Society provides continuous training and education material for its members so their qualifications can stay valid:

- online training
- conferences
- the Turnaround Management Journal
- Updates to the International Turnaround Management Standard™ (ITMS)
- Newsletters
- Focus groups
- Case studies
- Assessment centers

Certification Holders

The Turnaround Management Society has certified individuals from over 300 different companies.
For pre 2010 certification holders please contact us directly. We started in 2010 with obtaining the permission to publish certification holders publically. The names of pre 2010 certification holders can be verified by writing us an email:

exams@turnaround-society.com

Following is a list of certification holders that obtained their qualification in 2013:

Hagen, Wiebke; Hahnemann, Eike; Klahn, Anja; Kropf, Dennis; Bauer, Rebekka; Bonhagen, Janine; Chomek, Janine; Gündüz, Melanie; Köhler, Sebastian; Miess, Samuel; Motl, Norman; Rieper, Lisa-Kathrin; Schneider, Maria; Bergmans, Melanie; Findeisen, Caroline; Gundlach, Kim; Hacker, Anna; Jacob, Sonja; Klein, Victoria; König, Katharina Johanna; Özbek, Ferhat; Poel, Helge; Samow, Jan; Tenhagen, Christine; Tiedemann, Martina; Ullosat, Katrin; Degenhard, Björn; Dennstedt, Anika; Harms, Kathleen; Haustein, Fabian; Hellrung, Axel; Hische, Anne; Przybylski, Maik; Steinberg, Jenny; Erichsen, Julia; Hoffmann, Ralf; Karner, Nikolai; Malchow, Thorsten; Scholz, Britta; Trost, Sebastian; Voß, Katharina; Xu, Zheng; Ahlfeld, Henning; Mäckelmann, Marike; Range, Mike; Rapke, Anne; Rüger, Britta; Weiß, Andreas; Ajducic, Allen; Gebhardt, Sarah; Wiens, Marc; Filipow, Mario; Friedrich, Saskia; Wechsler, Alexander; Bach, Martin; Kobs, Dana; Lattke, André; Rodenwald, Thies; Eichler, Sandra; Heyden, Claudia; Mandin, Marcel; Riemer, Heike; Rossow, Carmen; Schrickel, Mathias; Schubert, Maria; Utermark, Katharina; Gosch, Astrid; Heuer, Anna-Theresa; Kurzal, Kathrin; Mörig, Amelie; Prott, Thorsten; Puls, Torben; Schäper, Kerstin; Teuchert, Jan; Bovensiepen, Isabel; Franck, Jennifer; Mundorf, Philipp; Sonntag, Robert; Willenborg, Anja; Himmelsbach, Martin; Meklenburg, Claudia; Schmitz, Stefanie; Schwarz, Sarah; Wunderlich, Kai; Borkowsky, Guido; Kuhrt, Christopher; Spilker, Tobias; Wagner, Marc

Following is a list of certification holders that obtained their qualification in 2012:

Starck, Simone; Blohm, Henrike; Engler, Ines; Fahrenholz, Jasmin; Pannenborg, Ruben; Ratschat, Isabell; Sigart, Alexander; Ueberschär, Sonja; Dittrich, Kolja; Ginnow, Karin; Herbst,

Tobias; Jegorow, Alina; Muschter, Andrea; Schierle, Simone; Suck, Dennis; Barow, Maria; Fehlandt, Sören; Hindel, Ingo; Hoffmann, Nils; Lachmann, Bianca; von Ahnen, Kai; Abid, Antoine; Binsch, Gabriele; Danöhl, Claudia; Kruschinski, Bartosch; Pohle, Ina; Rehr, Birte; Wentland, Christine; Zorn, Christian; Blättry, Marc; Bohle, Andreas; Deditius, Nicole; Enders, Stefan; Falkenberg, Carmen; Garcia, Pilar; Jonas, Sandra; Keibel, Alexander; Langfeld, Michael; Mönkemeyer, Nadja; Peters, Kai; Sobotzki, Anja; Borchert-Kummutat, Katja; Dzadon, Lenka; Hamann, Jennifer; Martin, Alexander; Steingraf, Eve; Witthöft, Melanie; Sosnowski, Anke; Vogt, Karina; Wildfang, Ronni; Babst, André; Otto, Benjamin; Siekro, Koffi Leopold; Bandrabura, Olesja; Bahlburg, Kristin; Konzelmann, Jan; Martoni, Nina; Volpert, Benny; Saborosch, Sven; Gröschl, Daniela; Möhl, Jan-Peter; Tamm, Markus; Hoppe, Ellen; Techel, Annekatrin; Yilmaz, Ali Ekber; Heucke, Sarah; Reimer, Beke; Röbschläger, Anke; Scherping, Janet; Koppenberger, Janina; Szczyglinski, Olaf; Langkamp, Tobias; Grebe, Timo; Meyer, Jessica; Scharnberg, Anja; Stobbe, Michel; Freund, Johannes; Lüthje, Sven; Prüter, Nicolle; Dück, Kristina; Wilbourne-Davies, Michilda; Heiden, Monik; Aubrecht, Nadja Kristina; Baumann, Thomas; Flindt, Janine; Brunkhorst, Sven; Wangler, Thomas; Mahnke, Tina; Ivanov, Marina

Following is a list of certification holders that obtained their qualification in 2011:

Surname, Name: Ahrens Laura, Ahrens Sandra, Alves Vidal Nicole, Appel Alexander, Arnholdt Konrad, Arning Janina Silvien, Bazyar Karim, Becker Robert, Benett Sara-Bettina, Berg Nadine, Borchers Nadine, Bouchir Meriam, Bründel Tom, Cabrelles Angelika, Carlson Ingmar, Christoph Susanne, Claus Constanze, Czaplewski Ivonne, Czaplewski Roland, Dahlke Michaela, Diedrich Ivonne, Dietze Stephanie, Falk Saskia, Fix Marlene, Freith Peter, Freudenberg Janina, Frömelt Annett, Gehrke Claudia, Glinka Michael, Gosebrink Johanna, Gremliza Petra, Grothe Antje, Gruhl Heike, Hahn Diana, Hass Aneta, Hedemann Daniela, Heinatz Sebastian, Henke Stefanie, Heyen Thomas, Hieke Claudia, Hoffmeister Daniel, Holzhaus Arno, Huettche Stefanie, Jahn Viktorija, Jessen Kolja, Kabajew Murat, Kadur Jana, Kempke Anja, Kilian Torsten, Kinter Björn, Klevenow Jan, Klitsch Christian, Knüppel Peter, Komar Julian, Korch Mandy, Kreienhop Christopher, Krooß Petra, Kuhn Thorben-Christian, Kühl Katharina, Lehmann Ralph, Lehmann Reyko, Lohse Yvonne, Lüdecke Axel, Maltsev Anastasia, Marchlewski Anne, Mehlhose-Loeffler Ann-Claire, Meyer Karoline, Michel Frederik, Mucha Natalie, Muths Saskia, Möller Katja, Nadolny Stefanie, Otto Kerstin, Pagel Unja, Pahl Nicola, Panknin Sandra, Patzelt Annika, Pauksztat Michele, Paulenz Konrad, Penning Michael, Person Nicole, Pinnecke Michael, Plönnigs Frank, Prljaca Sanela, Rathje Melanie, Redemann Wiebke, Richter Christoph, Romhi

Bohackova Petra, Ropers Svenja, Rundshagen Jessica, Rust Peter, Rückert Nadine, Schlicht Faye-Electra, Schmidt Florian, Schmitz-Bettels Marcella, Schmutte Frank, Scholz Sara, Schulz Hendrik, Schulz Susanne, Schäfer Lars, Schäfer Michael, Siemens Miriam, Stahl Mandy, Stawicki Monika, Steinkühler Jens-Uwe, Stumpenhagen Timo, Süßenberger Natalia, Tischmeyer Rebecca, Tonder Svenja-Kristin, Trochim Sindy, von Harten Malte, Watermann Wolfgang, Wende Sandra, Witt Hans-Hendrik, Wohlberg Annamaria, Wojciechowski Andre, Wolff-Bigge Felix Sebastian, Wrobel Daniel, Collard John M.

Following is a list of certification holders that obtained their qualification in 2010:

Surname, Name: Bach, Bino Bellin, Katja Blunck, Mario Brandt, Ines Burow, Janine Crasemann, Isa Czinczel, Frank Czuba, Katrin Dolezyk, Tobias Drühl, Remo Eggert, Johanne Fischmann, Gordon Floeter, Jennifer Frahm-Illhardt, Manuela Friedrich, Christian Funcke, Birte Hettinger, Magdalena Husmann, Iris Jans, Marco Jeske, Marc Kaynak, Derya Koch, Patricia Lambrecht, Tahir Lange, Sandra Langmann, Sven Lay, Ilona Lock, Harald Mergard, Nancy Merkel, Anja Meyer, Kathrin Möller, Annika Mutlu, Fatih Paulich, Simone Putzke, Claudia Richter, Jan Richter, Jan-Peter Rostami Goran, Silke Sänger, Antje Schack, Monique Scheper, Dominic Schmidt, Nadine Schulze, Anja-Karolin Schulze, Jan-Frederik Schuster, Caroline Sibrins, Anne Sliwinski, Bartosz Springborn, Ilka Stammberger, Denise Stein, Pascale-Christine Stiller, Kirsten Suckow, Sebastian Thiemann, Stephan Ungefug, Thomas Velten, Bettina Voigtsberger, Larysa Westphal, Rainer Zimmermann, Ursula Adermann, Nicole Andabak, Ante Angres, Patrick Baetcke, Ricarda Bayer, Susi Bergmann, Nils Henrik Bilandzija, Renato Boddin, Dennis Bokelmann, Melanie Braunger, Andrea Breite, Claudia Brück, Benjamin Böhme, Annett Büttner, Sabrina Daniel, Lukasz Dubberke, Ronny Freudenhammer, Peter Grabic, Jasmin Graw, Melanie Grothge, Patrick Gädke, Daniel Göttsch, Patricia Hackemesser, Siri Hallmann, Carmen Heitmann, Dennis Hempel, Martin Herndorf, Mike Kathmann, Simone Kirchner, Jürgen Krause, Katharine Kurzhauer, Michael Kämmerer, Matthias Lange, Claudia Leschnik, Fabian Martens, Stephan Matthiesen, Anne Meyer, Daniela Mischke, Susanne Morgenstern, René Nguyen, Anh Tu Oehme, Manja Pahl, Marius Rauch, Bettina Rethage, Florian Rienecker, Katrin Schallert, Sabrina Schröder, Ronny Sperzel, Tim Staben, Tamara Stoll, Alexander Voss, Jan-Henning Warnsholz, Kirsten Westphal, Daria Zabel, Jennifer

References

Aaker, D. A. (1993). *Brand equity & advertising: Advertising's role in building strong brands.* Hillsdale, NJ: Erlbaum.

Altman, E. (1968). Financial ratios, discriminant analysis and the prediction of corporate bankruptcy. *Journal of Finance*(23), pp. 588-609.

Altman, E. (1983). *Corporate Financial Distress: A Complete Guide to Predicting, Avoiding, and Dealing with Bankruptcy.* New York: Wiley.

Altman, E. I. (1976). Capitalization of leases and teh predictability of financial rations: A comment. *The Accounting Review*, p. 408.

Argenti, J. (1976). *Corporate Collapse: The Causes and Symptoms.* New York, NY: Wiley.

Argyle, M., Furnham, A., & Graham, J. A. (1981). *Social Situations.* Cambridge, UK: Cambridge University Press.

Arogyaswamy, K., Barker, V. L., & Yasai-Ardekani, M. (1995). Firm turnarounds: An integrative two-stage model. *Journal of Management Studies*(32), pp. 493-525.

asdf, d. d. (324). *adsff.* adsf: zutz.

Baden-Fuller, C., & Stopford, J. M. (1994). *Rejuvenating the mature business: The competitive challenge.* Boston, MA: Harvard Business School Press.

Baker, J. (1998). *Activity-based costing and activity-based management for health care.* Gaithersburg, MD: Aspen.

Baker, M. J., & Hart, S. J. (2008). *The marketing book* (6 ed.). Oxford, Boston: Butterworth-Heinemann.

Balgobin, R., & Pandit, N. (2001). Stages in the turnaround process: The case of IBM UK. *European Management Journal*(19), pp. 301-316.

Barker III, L. V., & Mone, M. A. (1994). Retrenchment: Cause of turnaround or consequence of decline? *Strategic Management Journal*(18), pp. 395-405.

Barker III, V. L., & Mone, M. A. (1998). The Mechanistic structure shift and strategic reorientation in declining firms attempting turnarounds. *Human Relations*(51), pp. 1227-1258.

Barker III, V., & Patterson Jr., P. (1996). Top management team tenur and top manager causal attributions in declining firms attempting turnaround. *Group and Organization Management*(21), pp. 304-336.

Barker III, V., Patterson Jr., P., & Mueller, G. (2001). Organizational causes and strategic consequences of the extent of top management team replacement during turnaround attempts. *Journal of Management Studies*(38), pp. 238-269.

Barker, & Duhaime. (1997). Strategic change in the turnaround process: theory and empirical evidence. *Strategic Management Journal*(18), pp. 13-38.

Barney, J. (1991). Firm resources and sustained competitive advantage. *Journal of Management*(17), pp. 99-120.

Baus, J. (1999). *Bilanzpolitik: Internationale Standards : Analyse.* Berlin: Cornelsen Girardet.

Beer, M., & Nohria, N. (2001). Cracking the code of change. In *Harvard Business Review on Turnarounds.* Boston, MA: Harward Business Schhool Press.

Belz, C., Müllner, M., & Zupancic, D. (2010). *Excellence in key account management: The St. Gallen KAM concept.* München.

Berends, W. R. (2004). *Price & Prift: The essential guide to product & service pricing and profit forecasting.* Berends & Associates.

Bertok, J. (2004). *Public sector transparency and accountability: Making it happen.* Organization for Economic Cooperation and Development, OECD Publishing .

Bertram, P., & Gottwald, P. (2006). Insolvenzrechts-Handbuch. In Drukarczyk, & Kippes. München.

Bethel, J., & Liebeskind, J. (1993). The effects of ownership structure on corporate restructuring. *Strategic Management Journal*(14), pp. 15-31.

Bhatia, R. S. (2002). *Encyclopaedia of Corporate Management.* Anmol Publications Pvt Ltd.

Bhimani, A., Horngren, C. T., Datar, S. M., & Foster, G. (2008). *Management and cost accounting* (4 ed.). Harlow: Financial Times Prentice Hall.

Bibeault, D. B. (1981). *Corporate Turnaround: How Managers Turn Losers into Winners.* NY, USA: McGraw-Hill.

Bibeault, D. B. (1981). *Corporate Turnaround: How Managers Turn Losers into Winners.* NY, USA: McGraw-Hill.

Bickhoff, N. (2004). *Die Unternehmenskrise als Chance: Innovative Ansätze zur Sanierung und Restrukturierung.* Berlin, Heidelberg: Springer.

Blayney, M. (2005). *Turning a business around: How to spot the warning sings and ensure a business stays healthy* (2 ed.). Oxford, UK: Howtobooks.

Blöse, J. (2006). In Klein, *Unternehmenskrisen: Ursachen - Sanierungskonzepte - Krisenvorsorge - Steuern.* Berlin: Schmidt Verlag.

Blythe, J. (2005). *Sales and key account management.* London: Thomson Learning.

Böckenförde, B. (1996). *Unternehmenssanierung.* Stuttgart: Schäffer-Poeschel.

Boles, J. S., Donthu, N., & Lothia, R. (1995). Salesperson evaluation using relative performance efficiency: the application of data envelop analysis. *Journal of Personal Selling and Sales Management*(3), pp. 31-49.

Booth, A., & Jefferys, K. (1996). *British economic development since 1945*. Manchester: Manchester University Press.

Bourgeois, L. (1981). On the measurement of organizational slack. *Academy of Management Review*(6), pp. 29-39.

Bourgeois, L. J. (1980, 1). Strategy and environment: a conceptual integration. *Academy of Management Review*(5), pp. 25-41.

Bradford, K. D., & Weitz, B. A. (1999). Personal selling and sales management: A relationship marketing perspective. *Journal of the Academy of Marketing Science*(27), pp. 241-254.

Branch, B., & Hugh, R. (1992). *Bankruptcy Investing: How to profit from distressed companies.* Dearborn Financial Publishing, Inc. .

Brigham, E. F., & Ehrhardt, M. C. (2008). *Financial management: Theory and practice* (12 ed.). Mason, OH: Thomson South-Western.

Brühl, V., & Göpfert, B. (2004). *Unternehmensrestrukturierung: Strategien und Konzepte.* Stuttgart: Schäffer-Poeschel.

Bruton, D. G., Ahlstrom, D., & Wan, J. C. (2003). Turnaround in East Asian firms: Evidence from ethnic overseas Chinese communities. *Strategic Management Journal*(24), pp. 519-540.

Bruton, G. D., & Rubanik, Y. T. (1997). Turnaround of high technology firms in Russia: The case of micron. *The Academy of Management Journal*(11), pp. 68-79.

Burghardt, M. (2002). *Projektmanagement - Leitfaden für die Plannung, Überwachung und Steuerung von Entwicklungsprojekten* (8 ed.). Publicis Publishing.

Buschmann, H. (2006). *Erfolgreiches Turnaround-Management.* Germany: DUV Gabler Edition Wissenschaft.

BusinessWeek. (2003, 11 24). *Cisco's Comeback*. Retrieved 03 04, 2010, from http://www.businessweek.com

Buth, A. (2004). *Restrukturierung, Sanierung und Insolvenz* (2 ed.). München: C.H. Beck.

Cameron, K. S., Whetten, D. A., & Kim, M. (1987). Organizational dysfunctions of decline. *Academy of Management Journal*(30), pp. 126-139.

Cameron, K., Kim, H., & Whetton, D. (1987). Organisational effects of decline and turbulance. *Administrative Science Quarterly*(32), pp. 222-240.

Cannon, J. P., Gundlach, G. T., & Narayandas, N. (1997). The nature of trust and its impact on relationship management activities. *NAMA Leadership Conference.* NAMA.

Castanias, R., & Helfat, C. (2001). The managerial rents model. *Journal of Management*(17), pp. 155-172.

Castrogiovanni, G. C., & Bruton, G. D. (2000). Business turnaround processes following acquisitions: Reconsidering the role of retrenchement. *Journal of Business Research*(48), pp. 25-34.

Chakravarthy, B. (1986). Measuring strategic performance. *Strategic Management Journal*(7), pp. 437-458.

Chakravarthy, B., & Lorange, P. (2008). *Profit or growth? Why you don't have to choose.* Upper Saddle River, N.J: Wharton School Publishing.

Challenger, Gray & Christmas. (2006). *challengergray.ca.* Retrieved 10 10, 2010, from www.challengergray.ca/Pressreleases/2006HolidaySurvey.doc

Chen, M.-J., Farh, J.-L., & MacMillan, I. (1993). An exploration of the expertness of outside informants. *Academy of Management Journal*(36), pp. 1614-1632.

Chowdhury, S. D., & Lang, J. R. (1996). Turnaround in small firms: An assessment of efficiency strategies. *Journal of Business Research*(36), pp. 169-178.

Christensen, C. M., Alton, R., Rising, C., & Waldeck, A. (2011, 03). The new M&A playbook. (89), pp. 48–57.

Cichelli, D. J. (2010). *Compensating the sales force: A practical guide to designing winning sales reward programs* (2 ed.). New York: McGraw-Hill.

Clark, T. J., & Gioia, D. (1993). Strategic sensemaking and organisational performance: linkages among scanning, interpretation, action, and outcomes. *Academy of Management Journal*(33), pp. 239-270.

Clasen, J. P. (1992). *Turnaround Management für mittelständische Unternehmen.* Wiesbaden: Gabler.

Cohen, S., & Roussel, J. (2006). *Strategisches Supply Chain Management.* Berlin Heidelberg: Springer-Verlag.

Cokins, G. (2006). *Activity-based cost management in government* (2 ed.). Vienna, VA: John Wiley and Sons.

Collard, J. M. (2002). Stearing clear of the brink. Early warning signs pinpoint business troubles - changing leadership style to accomplish a turnaround. *Journal of Equity.*

Collard, J. M. (2010, 03 16). (O. Wolak, Interviewer) interimceo.com.

Concentro Management AG. (2009). *Concentro Turnaround Investment Guide.* Kölln: Concentro Management.

Cotts, D. G., & Rondeau, E. P. (2004). *The facility manager's guide to finance and budgeting.* New York: AMACOM, American Management Association.

Coyle, B. (2000). *Cash flow forecasting and liquidity.* Chicago, New York: Lessons Professional Publishing.

Crone, A., & Werner, H. (2007). *Handbuch modernes Sanierungsmanagement.* München, Germany: Vahlen.

Cyert, R., & March, J. (1963). *A Behavioral Theory of the Firm.* Engelewood Cliffs, New York: Prentice Hall.

Daft, R., & Weik, K. (1984). Toward a model of organizations as interpretative systems. *Academy of Management Review*(9), pp. 284-295.

Dam Jespersen, B., & Skjøtt-Larsen, T. (2008). *Supply chain management - in theory and practice.* Copenhagen: Copenhagen Business School Press.

D'Aveni, R. (1989). The aftermath of organizational decline: a longitudial study of the strategic and managerial characeristics of declining organizations. *Academy of Management Journal*(32), pp. 577-605.

D'Aveni, R. A. (1989). Dependability and Organiszational Bankruptcy: An Application of Agency and Prospect Theory. (35), pp. 1120-1138.

Davenport, T. H. (1997). *Process innovation: reengineering work through information technology.* Boston, MA: Harvard Business Press.

Davenport, T. H. (1997). *Reengineering work through information technology.* Boston, MA: Harvard Business School Prss.

Davis, H. A., & Sihler, W. W. (2002). *Financial turnarounds: Preserving enterprise value.* Upper Saddle River, NJ: Financial Times Prentice Hall.

Day, J. D., & Jung, M. (2000). Corporate transformation without a crisis. *McKinsey Quarterly*(4), pp. 117-127.

Deakin, E. B. (1972). A discriminant analysis of predicators of business failure. *Journal of accounting research*(10), pp. 167–179.

Denis, D., Denis, D., & Sarin, A. (1997). Agency problems, equity ownership, and corporate diversification. *Journal of Finance*(52), pp. 135-160.

Denis, D., Denis, D., & Sarin, A. (1997). Agency Problems, Equity Ownership, and Corporate Diversification. *Journal of Finance*(52), pp. 135-160.

DeWitt, R., Harrigan, K. R., & Newmann, W. (1998). Downsizing Strategically. In D. J. Ketchen (Ed.), *Turnaround Research: Fast Accomplishments and Future Challenges* (pp. 21-37). Stanford, CN.

Dial, J., & Murphey, K. (1995). Incentives, Downsizing, and Value Creation at General Dynamic. *Journal of Financial Economics*(37), pp. 261-314.

Dibb, S., Simkin, L., & Bradley, J. (1996). *The marketing planning workbook: Effective marketing for marketing managers.* London: Routledge.

Doelling, R. (2003). *Turnaround bei schweren Unternehmenskrisen* (1st Edition ed.). Norderstedt, Germany: GRIN Verlag.

Dollinger, M. (1984). Environmental boundary spanning and information processing effects on organizational performance. *Academy of Management Journal*(27), pp. 351-368.

Donaldson, G. (1994). *Corporate restructuring: Managing the change process from within.* Boston, MA: Harvard Business School Press.

Droms, W. G., & Wright, J. O. (2010). *Finance and Accounting for Nonfinancial Managers: All the Basics You Need to Know (Finance & Accounting for Nonfinancial Managers)* (6 ed.). Basic Books.

Drummond, G., & Ensor, J. (2005). *Introduction to marketing concepts.* Oxford : Elsevier Butterworth-Heinemann.

Drury, C. (2011). *Cost and management accounting.* Cengage Learning Emea.

Duke, S. (2008, 11 26). Retrieved 8 13, 2010, from http://www.dailymail.co.uk/money/article-1089496/Investors-snub-RBS-15billion-emergency-rights-issue.html

Eskew, L. G. (1999). Cooperative strategies for forest science management and leadership in an increasingly complex and globalized world. *IUFRO Group 6.06.00 workshop.* Fort Collins, CO: Rocky Mountain Research Station.

Fandel, G., Fey, A., Heuft, B., & Pitz, T. (2008). *Kostenrechnung* (3 ed.). Berlin, Heidelberg: Springer.

Faulhaber, P., & Landwehr, N. (2005). *Turnaround Management in der Praxis.* Frankfurt/Main: Campus.

Ferrier, F. W., Smith, C., & Grimm, C. (2002). The impact of performance distress on aggressive competititve behavior: a reconsiliation of conflicting views. *Managerial and Decisions Economics*(23), pp. 85-106.

Ferrier, W., Fhionnlaoich, C., Smith, K., & Grimm, C. (2002). The impact of performance distress on aggressive competitive behavior: a reconsiliations of conflicting views. (23), pp. 301-316.

Financial Times Deutschland. (2008, 10 24). *Unternehmen*. (FTD Online) Retrieved 10 27, 2008, from FTD: http://www.ftd.de/unternehmen/finanzdienstleister/:Niederlage-f%FCr-CSU-BayernLB-Chef-Kemmer-bleibt-im-Amt/430076.html

Finkelstein, S. (1992). Power in top management team: dimensions, measurement, and validation. *Academy of Management Journal*(31), pp. 85-106.

Fischer, G., Lee, J., & Johns, L. (2004). An exploratory study of company turnaround in Australia and Singapore following the aisa crisis. *Asia Pacific Journal of Management*(21), pp. 149-170.

Fleege-Althoff. (1930). *Die notleidende Unternehmung*. Deutschland.

Forbes.com. (2010). *Forbes.com*. Retrieved 06 20, 2010, from Robert C. Wilson: http://people.forbes.com/profile/robert-c-wilson/36928

Fox, H. (1973, 11/12). A framework for functional coordination. *Atlanta Economic Review*, pp. 10-11.

Fredenberger, W., Lipp, A., & Watson, H. (1997). Information requirements of turnaround managers at the beginning of engagements. *Journal of Management Information Systems*(13), pp. 167-192.

Fuller, T., & Telma, B. (2007). Relationship strategies; Explaining idiosyncrasies in entrepreneurs' internationalisatio;. *Frontiers of Entrepreneurship Research*(27).

Fulmer, R. M., & Rue, L. W. (1973). *The practice and profitability of long-range planning*. Oxford, OH: Planning Executives Institute.

Gattorna, J. (2003). *Gower handbook of supply chain management* (5 ed.). Aldershot, Hants, England; Burlington, VT, USA: Gover.

Gilson, S. C. (2010). *Creating Value Through Corporate Restructuring: Case Studies in Bankruptcies, Buyouts, and Breakups* (2 ed.). Wiley.

Gladstone, D., & Gladstone, L. (2002). *Venture capital handbook: An entrepreneur's guide to raising venture capital*. Upper Saddle River, NJ: Prentice Hall.

Gless, S. E. (1996). *Unternehmenssanierung: Grundlagen - Strategien - Maßnahmen*. Wiesbaden: Gabler.

Gluck, F., Kaufman, S., & Walleck, A. S. (1982). The four phases of strategic management. *Journal of Business Strategy*(2), pp. 9-22.

Gordon, D. (1994). *Corporate restructuring: Managing the change process front within*. Boston, MA: Harvard Business School Press.

Gottfredson, M., Schaubert, S., & Saenz, H. (2008). *Der Weg zum Erfolg: Wie Sie die Performance Improvement-Diagnose in Ihrem Unternehmen durchführen.* Bain & Company, Inc.

Graham, K., & Richards, M. (1978). Relative performance deterioration, management, and strategic change in rail-based holding companies. *Proceedings of the 39th meeting of the Academy of Management*, (pp. 118-121).

Grant, R. M. (2010). *Contemporary Strategy Analysis* (7 ed.). John Wiley & Sons Inc.

Grinyer, P. H., Mayes, D., & McKiernan, P. (1990). The Sharpbenders: Managerial Recipes for Strategic Improvement in Performance. *Long Range Planning*(23), pp. 116-125.

Groß, H. (1998). Beiträge zur Restrukturierung/Sanierung: Personalwesen. In A. K. Buth, & M. Hermanns (Ed.), *Restrukturierung, Sanierung und Insolvenz* (pp. 185-199). München: Beck.

Halebian, J., & Finkelstein, S. (1992). Top management team size, CEO dominance, and firm performance. *Academy of Management Journal*(36), pp. 844-863.

Hambrick, D. C., & Schecter, S. (1983). Turnaround strategies for mature industrial product business units. *Academy of Management Journal*(26), pp. 231-248.

Hambrick, D., & D'Aveni, R. (1988). Large corporate failures as downward spirals. *Administrative Science Quarterly*(33), pp. 1-23.

Hambrick, D., & D'Aveni, R. (1992). Top management deterioration as part of the downward spiral of large corporate bankruptcies. *Management Sience*(38), pp. 1445-1466.

Hambrick, D., & Schecter, S. (1983). Turnaround strategies for mature industrial-product business units. *Academy of Management Journal*(26), pp. 231-248.

Hambrick, D., Cho, T., & Chen, M. J. (1996). The influence of top management team heterogeneity of firms' competivtive moves. *Administrative Science Quarterly*(41), pp. 659-684.

Hamel, G. (1990, May - June). The core competence of the corporation. *Harvard Business Review*(68).

Hamel, G., & Prahalad, C. K. (1996). *Competing for the future.* Boston, MA: Harvard Business School Press.

Hamlin, R. E., & Lyons, T. S. (1996). *Economy without walls: Managing local development in a restructuring world.* Westport, CO: Praeger.

Hämmerlein, M. (2009). *Marketing 2.0: Neue Strategien, Chancen und Risiken der digitalen Mundpropaganda.* Diplomica Verlag.

Hansen, G., & Wernerfelt, B. (1989). Determinants of firm performance. *Strategic Management Journal*(10), pp. 399-411.

Hardy, C. (1987). Investing in retrenchment: Avoiding the hidden costs. *California Management Review*(29), pp. 111-125.

Harker, M. (1996). Managing the company turnaround process: A case study of the Australien heavy engineering industry. *Journal of Engineering and Technology Management*(13), pp. 245-261.

Harrington, J. H., Conner, D. R., & Horney, N. L. (2000). *Project change management: Applying change management to improvement projects.* New York, NY: McGraw-Hill.

Harvard Business Press. (2009). *Harvard business review on sales and selling.* Harvard Business Press.

Harvey, O. J. (1996). System structure, flexibility and creativity. In O. J. Harvey, *Exerience, Structure, and Adaptability.* New York: Springer.

Harz, M., Hub, H. G., & Schlarb, E. (2006). *Sanierungs-Management: Unternehmen aus der Krise führen* (3 ed.). Düsseldorf: Verl. Wirtschaft und Finanzen.

Hatten, K., Schendel, D., & Cooper, A. (1978). A Strategie model of fthe U.S. brewing industry: 1952-1971. *Academy of Management Journal*(21), pp. 592-610.

Hauschildt, J. (1983). Aus Schaden klug. *Manager Magazin*(10), pp. 142-152.

Hauschildt, J. (1996). *Erfolgs-, Finanz- und Bilanzanalyse: Analyse der Vermögens-, Finanz- und Ertragslage von Kapital- und Personengesellschaften* (3 ed.). Köln: Schmidt Verlag.

Hauschildt, J., & Leker, J. (2000). *Krisendiagnose durch Bilanzanalyse* (2 ed.). Köln: Schmidt.

Have, S., Have, W., Stevens, F., & Van Der Elst, M. (2010). *Handbuch Management-Modelle: Die Klassiker: Balanced Scorecard, Crm, Die Boston-Strategiematrix, Porters Wettbewerbsstrategie Und Viele Mehr .* Wiley-VCH Verlag GmbH.

Haveman, H. (1992). Between a rock and a hard place: organizational change and performance under conditions of fundamental environmental transformation. *Administrative Science Quarterly*(37), pp. 48-75.

Hedburg, B., Nystrom, P., & Starbuck, W. (1976). Camping on seesaws: prescriptions for self-designing organization. *Administrative Science Quarterly*(21), pp. 41-65.

Helms, B., & Grace, L. (2004). *Microfinance product costing tool* (2 ed.). Washington, DC: Consultative group to assist the poor (CGAP).

Hendrick, H. (190). Perceptual accuracy of self and others and leadership status as functions of cognitive complexity. In K. Clark, & M. Clark, *Measures of Leadership.* West Orange, NJ: Leadership Library of America.

Hertlein, A. (1956). *Die Statistik im Dienste der Bankorganisation* (2 ed.). München: Uni-Dr.

Hertlein, A., & Meisner, K. (1956). *Abschluss und Prüfung der Unternehmungen einschliesslich Steuerprüfung* (4 ed.). Wiesbaden: Gabler.

Hess, H., Fechner, D., & Freund, K. (2004). *Sanierungshandbuch.* Luchterhand (Hermann).

Hess, R. (2007). *Private Equity: Finanzierungsalternative für den Mittelstand.* Berlin: Bwv - Berliner Wissenschafts-Verlag.

Hill, B. (2011, 01 06). *How to Develop a Corporate Strategy*. Retrieved 02 05, 2011, from eHow: http://www.ehow.com/how_7741813_develop-corporate-strategy.html

Hitt, M. A., Ireland, R. D., & Palia, K. A. (1982). 'Industrial firms' grand strategy and functional importance: moderating effects of technologlogy and uncertainty. *Academy of Management Journal*(25), pp. 265-298.

Hofer, C. W. (1980). Turnaround strategies. *Journal of Business Strategy*(1), pp. 19-31.

Hofer, C. W., & Schendel, D. (1978). *Strategy Formulation: Analytical Concepts.* St. Paul, Minnesota: West Publishing Co.

Hoffman, L., & Maier, N. (1961). Quality and acceptance of problem soluctions by members of homogeneous and heterogeneous groups. *Journal of Abnormal and Social Psychology*(62), pp. 401-407.

Hogan, J. (2008, 08 20). Retrieved 12 30, 2009, from http://business.theage.com.au/business/equity-injection-possible-for-pbl-20080819-3y9g.html

Höhn, R. (1974). *Das Unternehmen in der Krise: Krisenmanagement und Krisenstab.* Bad Harzburg.

Homburg, C., Krohmer, H., & Wokman Jr, J. (1999). Strategic consensus and performance: the role of strategy type and maket-related dynamism. *Strategic Management Journal*(20), pp. 339-357.

Hoskisson, R. E., Hitt, M. A., Ireland, R. D., & Harrison, J. S. (2007). *Competing for Advantage* (2 ed.). South-Western College Publications.

Hunt, S. D., & Morgan, R. M. (1995). Relationship marketing in the area of network. *Marketing Management*(3).

InfoWorld. (1991). *Semiconductor book-to-bill ratio down for August.* InfoWorld Media Group Inc.

International Directory of Company Histories. (2001). *Laura Ashley Holdings plc* (27 ed.). St. James Press. Retrieved from http://www.funduniverse.com/company-histories/Laura-Ashley-Holdings-plc-Company-History.html

ISU Institut für die Standartisierung von Unternehmenssanierungen . (2008). *Mindestanforderungen an Sanierungskonzepte (MaS)*. Heidelberg: Finanz Colloquium Heidelberg.

Jankulik, E. (2009). *Praxisbuch Prozessoptimierung: Management- und Kennzahlensysteme als Basis für den Geschäftserfolg.* Erlangen: Publicis Publ.

Jensen, O. (2004). *Key-Account-Management.* Deutscher Universitätsverlag.

Jenson, M. (1993). The modern industrial revolution and the challenge to internal control systems. *Journal of Finance*(48), pp. 831-880.

Jobsky, T. (1998). Mergers & Acquisitions bei Restrukturierung/Sanierung. In A. Buth, & M. Hermanns (Ed.), *Restrukturierung, Sanierung und Insolvenz* (pp. 329-349). München.

Johnson, G., Scholes, K., & Whittington, R. (2005). *Exploring Corporate Strategy.* Edinburgh Gate: Pearson Education .

Johnson, L. (2005, 4 11). *Computer History Museum.* Retrieved 10 12, 2010, from http://corphist.computerhistory.org/corphist/view.php?s=select&cid=9&PHPSESSID= ccd241

Kall, F. (1999). *Controlling im Turnaround-Prozess.* Frankfurt am Main: P. Lang.

Kamerer, H. (n.d.). *Developing Leadership Within Your Enterprise.* Kamerer Consulting.

Kapferer, J.-N. (2001). *The new strategic brand management: Creating and sustaining brand equity long term* (4 ed.). London: Kogan Page.

Kaufmann, D., Kraay, A., & Zoido-Lobatón, P. (2002). *Governance matters II: Updated indicators for 2000-01.* Washington, D.C: World Bank, Development Research Group, and World Bank Institute, Governance, Regulation, and Finance Division.

Keiser, H. (1966). *Betriebswirtschaftliche Insolvenzen bei mittelständischen Einzelhandlungen.* Köln.

Kempeners, M. A., & van der Hart, H. W. (1999). Designing account management organizations. *Journal of Business & Industrial Marketing*(14), pp. 310-335.

Khandwalla, P. N. (2001). *Response Books.* New Dehli: Response Books.

Kieser, A. (2002). Schwächung der Wettbewerbsposition durch wertorientierte Verschlankung. In K. Macharzina, & H.-J. Neubürge, *Unternehmensführung: Strategien - Controlhng - Strukturen* (pp. 141-168). Stuttgart.

Kliege, H. (1962). *Outsourcing der Internen Revision?*

Klinger, M. (2008). *The Surety's Indemnity Agreement: Law and Practice.* American Bar Association.

Kochhar, R., & David, P. (1996). Institutional Investors and firm innovation: a test of cometing hypotheses. *Strategic Management Journal*(17), pp. 73-84.

Kottier, P., & Bliemel, F. (2001). *Marketing Management: Analyse, Planung und Verwirklichung* (10 ed.). Suttgart.

Kramer, M. (1999). *Small business turnaround.* Holbrook, MA: Adams Media Corporation.

Krieger, K. (2005). *Customer-Relationship-Management und Innovationserfolg.* Wiesbaden: Deutscher Universitäts Verlag.

Krystek, U. (1987). *Unternehmungskrisen: Beschreibung, Vermeidung und Bewältigung überlebenskritischer Prozesse in Unternehmungen.* Wiesbaden: Gabler.

Kühn, C. (2006). *Capital Structure Decisions in Insitutional Buyouts.* DUV.

Laasholdt, N. (2005). *Business economics: An introductory casebook for the commercial upper-secondary course .* Systime.

Lafrenz, K. (2004). *Shareholder-value-orientierte Sanierung.* Wiesbaden, Germany: Deutscher Universitäts-Verlag.

Lagae, W. (2005). *Sports sponsorship and marketing communications: A European perspective.* Harlow, England, New York: Financial Times Prentice Hall.

Le Coutre, W. (1926). *Praxis der Bilanzkritik.* Berlin: Späth u. Linde.

Ledgerwood, J., & White, V. (2006). *Transforming microfinance institutions: Providing full financial services to the poor* (2 ed.). Washington DC: World Bank.

Leist, E. (1905). *Die Sanierung von Aktiengesellschaften.* Berlin: Siemenroth.

Lewis, R., & Pendrill, D. (2003). *Advanced Financial Accounting* (7 ed.). Financial Times Management.

Lohrke, F. T., Bedeian, A. G., & Palmer, T. B. (2004, 6). The role of top management teams in formulating and implementing turnaround strategies: a review and research agenda. *International Journal of Management Reviews, 5/6*, pp. 63-90.

Lohrke, F. T., Bedeian, A. G., & Palmer, T. B. (2004, 6). The role of top management teams in formulating and implementing turnaround strategies: a review and research agenda. *International Journal of Management Reviews*(5/6), pp. 63-90.

Lohrke, F., & Bedeian, A. (1996). *The performance effects of strategy, top-management characteristics, and environment: an integrative study of decline and turnaround.* Unpublished doctoral dissertation, Louisiana State Universtiy.

Lohrke, F., & Bedeian, F. (1998). Managerial responses to declining performance: turnaround investment strategies and cruicial contingencies. *Advances in Applied Business Strategy*(5), pp. 3-30.

Lymbersky, C. (2008). *Market Entry Strategies.* Hamburg: Management Laboratory Press.

Lymbersky, C. (2011, 9). Defining Turnaround Management. (T. M. Society, Ed.) *Turnaround Management Journal*, pp. 10-16.

Lyons, T. S., & Hamlin, R. E. (2001). *Creating an economic development action plan: A guide for development professionals.* Westport, CO: Praeger.

Lysons, K., & Farrington, B. (2006). *Purchasing and supply chain management* (7 ed.). London, New York: Financial Times/Prentice Hall.

Malano, H. M., & Dr. Burton, M. (n.d.). *, International Program for Technology Research in Irrigation and Drainage. Guidelines for benchmarking performance in the irrigation and drainage sector.* Food & Agriculture Organisation.

Matthews, J. R. (2009). *The customer-focused library: Re-inventing the library from the outside-in.* Santa Barbara, Calif: Libraries Unlimited.

Melin, L. (1985). Strategies for managing turnaround. *Long Range Planning*(18(1)), pp. 80-86.

Mentzer, J. T., & Moon, M. A. (2005). *Sales forecasting management: A demand management approach* (2 ed.). Thousand Oaks, CA: Sage Publications.

Meyer-Piening, Arnulf, A. (1998). *Zero Base Planning als analytische Personalplanungsmethode im Gemeinkostenbereich. Einsatzbedingungen und Grenzen der Methodenanwendung.* Schäffer-Poeschel Verlag.

Miller, D. (1991). Stale in the saddle: CEO tenure and the match between organizations and environment. *Management Science*(37), pp. 34-52.

Milliken, F. (1990). Perceiving and interpreting environmental change: An examination of college administrators' interpretations of changing demopraphics. *Academy of Management Journal*(33), pp. 42-63.

Moral, F. (1924). *Revision und Reorganisation industrieller Betriebe.* Berlin: Springer.

Muller, M. (2011). *Essentials of Inventory Management.* AMACOM.

Müller, R. (1986). *Krisenmanagement in der Unternehmung* (2 ed.). Frankfurt/Main.

Müller, R., & Turner, R. (2010). *Project-Oriented Leadership.* Gower Publishing Ltd.

Mütze, M., Möller, J. C., & Senff, T. (2007). *Real Estate Investments in Germany: Real estate investments in Germany.* Berlin Heidelberg: Springer-Verlag GmbH.

N.A. (2009, 4). *Harvard Business Manager.*

Newby, C. (1998). *Sales strategies: Negotiating and winning corporate deals.* London : Kogan Page.

Nicholson, J. L., & Rohrbach, J. F. (1919). *Cost accounting.* New York, NY: Ronald Press Co.

Nieschlag, R., Dichtl, E., & Hörschgen, H. (2002). Berlin: Duncker & Humblot.

Noble, C. (1999). The eclectic roots of strategy implementation research. *Journal of Business Research*(45), pp. 119-134.

O'Callaghan, S. (2010). *Turnaround leadership: Making descisions, rebuilding trust and delivering results after a crisis.* London: Kogan Page.

OGC Office of Government Commerce. (2005). *Managing successful projects with PRINCE2.* Norwich, UK: TSO.

O'Neill, H. (1986). Turnaround and recovery: what strategy do you need? *Long Range Planning*(19(1)), pp. 80-88.

O'Neill, H. M. (1986, 3). An analysis of the turnaround strategy in commercial banking. *Journal of Management Studies*(23:2).

Ott, W., & Göpfert, B. (2005). *Unternhemenskauf aus der Insolvenz.* Wiesbaden: Gabler.

Pandit, N. R. (2000). Some recommendations for improved research on corporate turanround. *Management*(3), pp. 31-56.

Park, R. J. (1999). *Value engineering: A plan for invention.* Boca Raton, FL: St. Lucie.

Payne, S. (2002, 09 01). *allbusiness.com.* Retrieved 06 03, 2010, from http://www.allbusiness.com/management/272074-1.html

Pearce , J., & Robbins, D. (1993). Toward improved theory and research in business turnarounds. *Journal of Management*(19), pp. 613-636.

Pfeffer, J. (1999). *Managing with power: Politics and influence in organizations.* Boston, MA: Harvard Business School Press.

Pfeffer, J., & Salancik, G. R. (2009). *The external control of organizations: A resource dependence perspective.* Stanford, CA: Stanford Business Books.

Plewa, F. J., & Friedlob, G. T. (1995). *Understanding Cash Flow.* New York, NY: John Wiley & Sons.

Pomerleano, M., & Shaw, W. (2005). *Corporate restructuring: Lessons from experienced.* Washington, D.C.: The World Bank.

Porter, M. (1989). *Competitive strategy: Techniques for analyzing industries and competitors ; with a new introduction.* New York, NY : Free Press.

Porter, M. E. (1979). The structure within Industries and companies' performance. *Review of Economics and Statistics*(61), pp. 214-227.

Porter, M. E. (1999). *On competition.* Harvard Business Press.

Power, H. (2008, 04 03). Retrieved 12 30, 2009, from http://www.telegraph.co.uk/finance/newsbysector/banksandfinance/2787438/Imperial-resorts-to-emergency-rights-issue.html

Preß, B., Rieker, S., Weiber, R., Plinke, W., & Kleinaltenkamp, M. (1996). *Geschäftsbeziehungsmanagement*. Springer.

Pring, M. J. (2002). *Technical analysis explained: The successful investor's guide to spotting investment trends and turning points* (4 ed.). New York, NY: McGraw-Hill.

Proud, J. F. (2007). *Master scheduling: A practical guide to competitive manufacturing* (3 ed.). Hoboken, N.J: John Wiley & Sons.

Putzmann, U. (2003). *Die Ausgestaltung der Entgeltsysteme für Key-Account-Manager: Theoretische Grundlagen und empirische Überprüfung*. Diplomarbeiten Agentur.

Quinn, J. B. (n.d.). *The Strategy Component*. Prentice Hall.

Rajendar, S. R. (2007). *Case Studies on Corporate Turnarounds* (Vol. 1). Punjagutta, Hyderabad: ICFAI Books.

Ramanujam, V. (1984). Environmental context, organizational context, strategy, and corporate turnaorund: an empirical investigation. *Unpublished doctoral dissertation*. University of Pittsburgh.

Reichheld, F. F. (2005). *The ultimate question: For simplicity, speed, and success - up and down the supply chain*. T.F. Wallace & Company.

Rembor, E. (2004). *Geschäftlich erfolgreich in den USA: Doing Business with Americans*. Beltz.

Reske, W., Brandenburg, A., & Mortsiefer, H. J. (1978). *Insolvenzursachen mittelständischer Betriebe* (2 ed.). Göttingen: Schwartz.

Richard, L. D., & Dorothy, M. (2010). *Understanding Management*.

Robbins, D., & Pearce, J. (1992). Turnaround: retrenchement and recovery. *Strategic Management Journal*(13), pp. 287-309.

Robbins, K., & Pearce II, A. J. (1992). Turnaround: Recovery and retrenchment. *Strategic Management Journal*, pp. 287-309.

Roman, I. (2010). *Turnaround Strategies for Customer Centric Operations: Turn by Turn Directions on the Path to Recovery*. Toronto Canada: Italics Publishing Inc.

Rommel, G. (1995). *Simplicity wins: How Germany's mid-sized industrial companies succeed*. Boston, MA: Harvard Business School Press.

Ross, J. E., & Kami, M. J. (1973). *Corporate Management in Crisis: Why the Mighty Fall*. Englewood Cliffs, NY: Prentice-Hall.

Rumelt, R. (1974). *Strategy, Structure and Economic Performance*. Graduate School of Business Administration, Harvard University, Boston, MA.

Sato, Y., & Kaufman, J. J. (2005). *Value analysis tear-down: A new process for product development and innovation.* New York, NY: Industrial Press; Society of Manufacturing Engineers.

Schell, E. H. (1957). *Technique of executive control.* New York, NY: McGraw-Hill.

Schellenberg, B. (2008). *Sanierungsmangement: Sofortmaßnahmen in der Unternehmenskrise.* Berlin: ESV.

Schendel, D., & Patton, G. R. (1976). Corporate stagnation and turnaround. *Journal of Economics and Business*(28), pp. 236-241.

Schendel, D., Patton, G. R., & Riggs, J. (1976). Corporate turnaround strategies: a study of profit decline and recovery. *Journal of General Management*(3), pp. 3-11.

Schmalholz, C. G. (2009, 11). Lichtgestallten. *Manager Magazin*, pp. 69-70.

Seefelder, G. (2003). *Unternehmenssanierung: Zerschlagung vermeiden, Ursachen analysieren, Konzepte finden, Chancen erkennen.* Stuttgart: Schäffer-Poeschel.

Seefelder, G. (2007). *Unternehmenssanierung.* Stuttgart: Schäffer-Poeschel Verlag.

Shein, J. B. (2011). *Reversing the slide: A strategic guide to turnarounds and corporate renewal.* San Francisco, CA: Jossey Bass.

Shepherd, W. (1970). *Market Power and Economic Welfare.* New York: Random House.

Shim, J. K., & Siegel, J. G. (2008). *Financial Management* (3 ed.). Barron's Educational Series.

Simons, T., Pelled, L., & Smith, K. (1999). Making use of difference: diversity, debate, and decision comprehensivness in top management teams. *Academy of Management Journal*(42), pp. 652-673.

Simonsen, E. A., & Cassady, B. (2007). 'Off-the-Rails' to 'Back-on-Track: The Collapse and Rescue of Jarvis PLC. *The Journal of Private Equity; Special Turnaround Management Issue*(10), pp. 113-127.

Singh, J. (1986). Performance, slack, and risk taking in organizational decision making. *Academy of Management Journal*(29), pp. 562-585.

Skinner, R. (1975). *Pricing strategies to cope with inflation.* London: Industrial Market Research Ltd.

Slatter, S. (1984). *Corporate recovery: Successful turnaround strategies and their implementation.* New York: Penguin Books.

Slatter, S., & Lovett, S. (2004). *Corporate Recovery: Managing companies in distress.* Washington, D.C.: Beard Books.

Slatter, S., Lovett, D., & Barlow, L. (2006). *Leading corporate turnaround: How leaders fix troubled companies.* San Francisco, CA: Jossey-Bass.

Sloma, R. S. (1985). *The turnaround manager's handbook.* New York, London: Free Press.

Smith, R., & Winakor, A. (1935). *Changes in the financial structure of unsuccessful industrial corporations.* Urbana.

Smith, S. G. (2002). *Managerial accounting for libraries and other not-for-profit organizations* (2 ed.). Chicago, Ill: American Library Association.

Sneyd, P. (1994). *Principles of accounting and finance.* London : Routledge.

Sousa deVasconcellos e Sa, J., & Hambrick, D. (1989). Key success factors: test of a general theory in mature industrial-product sector. *Strategic Management Journal*(10), pp. 367-382.

Stalk (Jr.), G., & Hout, T. M. (1990). *Competing against time: How time-based competition is reshaping global markets* (1 ed.). Free Press.

Stanwick, P. (1992). *CEO Characeristics, strategy, and performance: an empirical study of declining organizations.* Unpublished doctoral dissertation, Florida State University.

Statistisches Bundesamt. (2008). *Statistisches Jahrbuch 2008.*

Staw, B. M., Sandelands, L. E., & Dutton, J. E. (1982). *Threat-rigidity effects in organizational behavior: A multilevel analysis.* Berkeley, CA: Institute of Industrial Relations, University of California.

Stickney, C. P., & Weil, R. L. (2000). *An introduction to concepts, methods, and uses* (9 ed.). Fort Worth: Dryden Press.

Sundaramurthy, C., & Mahoney, J. (1997). Board structure, antitakeover provisions, and stackholder wealth. *Strategic Management Journal*(18), pp. 231-245.

Sutton, R. I. (1990). Organizational decline process: A social psychology perspective. In L. L. Cummings, & B. M. Straw, *Research in organisational behavior* (pp. 205-253). Greenwich: JAI Press.

Thomas, J. G. (n.d.). *Reference for BusinessEncyclopedia of Business* (2nd ed.). 2012.

Timmons, J. A., Spinelli, S., & Zacharakis, A. (2004). *How to raise capital: Techniques and strategies for financing and valuing your small business.* New York, NY: McGraw-Hill.

Tracy, J. A. (2009). *How to read a financial report: Wringing vital signs out of the numbers* (7 ed.). Hoboken, N.J: John Wiley & Sons.

Tuckerman, B. (1964). Personality structure, groups composition and group functioning. *Sociometry*(27), pp. 469-487.

Turner, R. (2008). *Gower handbook of project management* (4 ed.). Gower Publishing Ltd.

Turner, R., & Bredillet, C. (2010). *Perpsectives on Projects.* Routledge Chapman & Hall.

Umbriet, W. T. (1996, 8). Fairmont hotels' turnaround strategy. *Cornell Hotel and Restaurant Administration Quarterly*, pp. 50-57.

van Weele, A. J. (2005). *Purchasing & supply chain management: Analysis, strategy, planning and practice* (4 ed.). London, UK: Thomson Learning.

Vance, D. (2009). *Corporate Restructuring: From cause analysis to execution.* Berlin, Heidelberg: Springer Verlag.

Vaz, P. (1996). The turnaround in BT's payphone business. *Long Range Planning*(29), pp. 24-29.

Venkatraman, N., & Ramanujam, V. (1986). Measurement of business performance in strategy research: a comparison approaches. *Academy of Management Review*(11), pp. 801-814.

Vignola, L. (1974). *Strategic divestment.* New York: AMACOM.

Vinturella, J. B., & Erickson, S. M. (2004). *Raising entrepreneurial capital.* Oxford, UK: Elsevier.

Wallace, T. F., & Stahl, R. A. (2002). *Sales forecasting: A new approach* . Cincinnati, OH: T.F. Wallace & Co.

Wallace, T. F., & Stahl, R. A. (2005). *Master scheduling in the 21st century.* T.F. Wallace & Company.

Walsh, J., & Elwood, J. (1991). Mergers, acquisitions, and the prunning of managerial deadwood. *Strategic Management Journal*(12), pp. 201-217.

Warren, C. S., Reeve, J. M., & Duchac, J. E. (2009). *Financial & managerial accounting* (10 ed.). Mason, OH: South-Western Cengage Learning.

Waters, D. C. (2002). *Operations management: Producing goods and services.* Harlow: Financial Times Prentice Hall.

Wayne , T. M. (2008). *The sales manager's success manual.* New York, NY: AMACOM.

Webb, M., & Gorman, T. (2006). *Sales and Marketing the Six Sigma Way.* Kaplan.

Weitzel, W., & Jonsson, E. (1989). Decline in organisations: a literature integration and extension. *Administrative Science Quarterly*(34), pp. 91-109.

Wengler, S. (2006). *Key account management in business-to-business markets: An assessment of its economic value.* Wiesbaden: Deutscher Universitats-Verlag.

Whitney, J. O. (1992). *Taking charge.* New York, NY: Warner Books.

Wickham, P. A. (2000). *Financial times corporate strategy casebook.* London: Financial Times Management.

Wiersema, M., & Bantel, K. (1993). Top management team turnover as an adaption mechanism: the role of the environment. *Strategic Management Journal*(14), pp. 485-504.

Witte, E. (1981). Der Praktische Nutzen empirischer Forschung: Empirische Theorie der Unternehmung. *14*.

Woodburn, D., & McDonald, M. (2011). *Key account management: The definitive guide* (3 ed.). Wiley.

Wruck, K. (1994). Financial policy, internal control, and performance: Sealed air corporation's leveraged special dividend. *Journal of Financial Economics*(36), pp. 157-192.

Younker, D. L. (2003). *Value engineering: Analysis and methodology.* New York, NY: Marcel Dekker.

Zentes, J., & Morschett, D. (2011). *Strategic retail management: Text and international cases* (2 ed.). Wiesbaden: Gabler.

Zimmermann, F. (1989). Managing a successful turnaround. *Long Range Planning*(22), pp. 105-124.

Zimmermann, F. M. (1989). Managing a successful turnaround. *Long Range Planning*(22), pp. 105-124.

Zimmermann, F. (n.d.). Turnaround: a painful learning process. *Long Range Planning*(19(4)), pp. 104-114.

Zoltners, A. A., Sinha, P., & Zoltners, G. A. (2001). *The complete guide to accelerating sales force performance.* New York, NY: AMACOM.

Because together we can reach more.

TMS — Turnaround Management Society

We are turnaround professionals, distressed dept investors and academics joined together in the Turnaround Management Society.

The TMS is a non profit organisation founded to support the Turnaround Management profession and serve its members to achieve their goals by providing them with contacts, research and education.

- Research - Publications - Certifications - Networking - Seminars -

Apply for your membership today!
www.Turnaround-Management.com

Room for your Notes:

Room for your Notes:

Room for your Notes:

Printed in Great Britain
by Amazon